George Brubaker Kulp

Families of the Wyoming Valley

Biographical, genealogical and historical. Sketches of the bench and bar of Luzerne

County, Pennsylvania

George Brubaker Kulp

Families of the Wyoming Valley
Biographical, genealogical and historical. Sketches of the bench and bar of Luzerne County, Pennsylvania

ISBN/EAN: 9783337388447

Printed in Europe, USA, Canada, Australia, Japan

Cover: Foto ©ninafisch / pixelio.de

More available books at **www.hansebooks.com**

FAMILIES

OF THE

WYOMING VALLEY

BIOGRAPHICAL, GENEALOGICAL, AND HISTORICAL.

SKETCHES OF THE BENCH AND BAR

OF LUZERNE COUNTY, PENNSYLVANIA.

BY

GEO. B. KULP.

HISTORIOGRAPHER OF THE WYOMING HISTORICAL AND GEOLOGICAL SOCIETY.

"There be of them that have left a name behind them, that their praises might be reported. And some there be which have no memorial; who are perished as though they had never been; and are become as though they had never been born; and their children after them."—*Ecclesiasticus* (*Apocrypha*) *XLIV: 8-9.*

IN THREE VOLUMES.

VOL. III.

WILKES-BARRE, PENNSYLVANIA.

1890.

TO MY ESTEEMED FATHER-IN-LAW
JOHN STEWART,
AND HIS WIFE
ELIZABETH ANN WILLIAMS,
A GRAND-DAUGHTER OF THAT HERO OF WYOMING,

SERGEANT THOMAS WILLIAMS,

THIS VOLUME IS RESPECTFULLY DEDICATED BY

THE AUTHOR.

PREFACE.

The volumes of which this is the third and last, are records of the lives of the resident members of the Luzerne county bar, of its law judges and the associate or lay judges who have sat upon the Luzerne bench. In fact, they not only warrant, but in common justice demand, the title that has been given them—"Families of the Wyoming Valley." In collating faithfully the incidents of moment in the careers of those who have practiced the profession of the law in Luzerne county, and of the judges of its courts, and in giving such attention as was possible and proper to the genealogies in each case, the author has, of necessity, had to deal with practically every family of note in the Wyoming valley, and has brought into review almost every prominent fact in their history and in the history of the valley itself. He has in this way been enabled to cover many matters not heretofore reduced to print, and to throw fresh light upon others many times and much discussed. He believes and contends, in brief, that no study of the history of the valley can be esteemed to even approach completeness that does not include a careful reading of these books, an insistance that will be found to be fully justified by the merest reference to the exhaustive analytical index appended to this volume.

As to the gentlemen of the bar, reviewing the list from the date of the organization of the Luzerne county courts, May 27, 1787, shows that from then on to the date of the last admission herein recorded, there has been a total of four hundred and eighty-seven members, of whom one hundred and sixty-five are deceased, one hundred and sixty-three are non-residents and one hundred and fifty-nine are still with us, a rather remarkably equal division, by the way.

Of the ten president judges, eight are dead and two living. Of the six additional law judges, one only is dead and five are living. The only separate Orphans' Court judge we have had is still in service. Of the thirty-five associate or lay judges, but two survive, thirty-three having been called to that Higher Court from whose decrees there is no appeal. The larger proportion of deaths among these latter has no special significance, as might at first glance appear to be the case, since it was generally the fact that the men were already well advanced in years when chosen to the position. The last associate judge for the county was elected in 1871, the practice of having lay judges on the bench in counties constituting separate judicial districts having ceased with the passage of the first judicial apportionment under the new constitution.

The total of judges and lawyers dead and living, resident and non-resident, is five hundred and thirty-nine; and as giving some idea how busy death has been in the ranks of the number, it may be stated that fifty have departed this life since the work of compiling these volumes was begun in 1881.

Since compiling our list of lawyers at the end of this volume two members of the bar have deceased—Caleb E. Wright, December 2, 1889, and William J. Hughes, December 30, 1889. One attorney has been admittd—E. F. McHugh, November 23, 1889.

Nine Luzerne lawyers have abandoned the profession to take places in the pulpit. Of these, four became Protestant Episcopal ministers, one finally rising to the dignity of a bishopric, three preached in the Methodist Episcopal church, one in the Presbyterian and one in the Baptist. Popular prejudice will stand surprised to learn that a calling, the practices of which are so persistently ascribed to satanic influences, has contributed thus liberally to the grand army marshalled for the overthrow of its alleged patron.

To the armies of the country the Luzerne bar has given more than her quota. She had two soldiers in the revolution, two in the war of 1812, and ten in the Mexican war. To the forces whose energies won in the civil war of 1861-65, she contributed five generals, three colonels, one lieutenant colonel, three majors, twelve captains, ten lieutenants and twenty-three privates, while three others served in the navy.

In high civic offices she has had one United States senator, sixteen congressmen, two governors, two attorneys general, one minister in the diplomatic service, four judges of the Supreme

Court, two judges of United States Courts and eleven judges of Common Pleas Courts in other counties or states, in addition to ten law judges she has furnished our own bench.

While this volume also deals with a few of our lawyers whose careers at the bar have, in effect, only just begun, it takes on a special interest in the fact that its pages record:

First. An outline history of the Connecticut-Pennsylvania controversy as to the possession of the territory of which what is now Luzerne county, once formed a part, and of the final official organization of the county and the leading details thereof, as also a complete list of the officials during the years that it remained under the jurisdiction of Connecticut as the town of Westmoreland, in the county of Litchfield, and afterwards as Westmoreland county, of that state.

Second. Biographical sketches, so far as they were obtainable, of the deceased justices and judges of the courts who were not members of the Luzerne bar previous to their becoming justices or judges, or if members, were not treated in the first or second volumes in the order of their admission to practice; of deceased associate judges or judges unlearned in the law, and of deceased lawyers. In this category are many notable men, among them Burnside, Bidlack, Catlin, Collins, Conyngham, Gibson, Griffin, Jessup, Jones, Ketcham, Mallery, Wilmot, Woodward, Wright and others, whose names and deeds became widely known and whose characters and abilities exerted marked influence upon the affairs amid which they lived, and who are still remembered and revered.

Third. A carefully compiled series of pages, twelve in all, covering additions to, and alterations and corrections of the several biographies in the three volumes, rendered necessary, either by events occuring subsequently to the original writings, or mistakes discovered or further information secured after they were put to press.

Fourth. A list of deceased president judges, additional law judges, associate judges, non-resident members of the bar, living judges and resident lawyers of Luzerne county, with the place and date of birth, date of admission or commission, the date of death of those deceased and the present location of those non-resident. This detailed information is given in all save a comparatively few instances, where the most careful search and diligent inquiry failed to secure it.

Fifth. An analytical index to the entire three volumes of all the names mentioned in each of the biographies and all the notable facts and incidents therein recorded. Much labor and pains were expended in preparing this latter compilation and its usefulness for reference purposes will be apparent at a glance.

The biographer feels that the volume thus constituted brings the accomplishment of his purpose to a state as near completeness as, with the materials at hand, was possible of attainment. The three books represent the fruits of many months' of hard work, including a correspondence that has reached to every corner of the country and even into foreign countries; a tedious and sometimes exasperating scrutiny of musty records, and persistent application to and patient waiting upon many men who, while being the only attainable sources of necessary information, were, from pressure of their own personal matters, indifference to this one or other cause, vexatiously slow in coming to the responsive mood. To many of these, however, he is under great obligations, since but for their aid, no matter how tardily accorded, much interesting and important data now set down in these fourteen hundred pages could not have been secured. But wearisome as the task has sometimes been; and slender as must be the money reward for the time and labor bestowed, there has been no small satisfaction in the doing of it, and there is more in the reflection that it is now finished. The pride of authorship is something. Much as most of those who write books may affect to be above that sort of pride, it may safely be set down as the principal impelling force in a majority of cases, and unfortunately, in a very larger number, it is about the only recompense. There is reward, also, of no mean proportion in the knowledge that a duty when once undertaken has been performed with righteous earnestness and to the exhaustion of every source from which assistance could be secured. But in this instance, that upon which the writer chiefly congratulates himself is the fact that he knows he has saved and set down in fair order many facts and circumstances essential to a proper rounding out of the recorded history of a famous valley and a great county that, save for his efforts, might forever have been lost, and that he has paid merited though often feebly worded tribute to many good men whose deserving might not otherwise have been properly made known to the generations that are to come. To some extent these books must have a value as part of the general history of the state and country. To the descendants and friends of those whose lives are sketched in them, they should, and in most cases probably will be, regarded as possessing a special value. If time shall even measurably justify these beliefs and expectations, the biographer will feel that he has been amply compensated.

In glancing over the pages of the three volumes we discover a few serious typographical and grammatical errors. We hope our readers will kindly overlook them.

For valuable assistance rendered in connection with our labors, we are indebted to Rev. Horace Edwin Hayden (who wrote the sketches under the head of Charles Miner Conyngham, William LaFayette Raeder and Paul Ross Weitzell), Sheldon Reynolds, Hon. Steuben Jenkins, C. Ben Johnson, W. H. Egle, M. D., Eugene T. Giering and Harry R. Deitrick.

Wilkes-Barre, Pa., February, 1890.

FAMILIES
OF THE
WYOMING VALLEY.

By an Act of the General Assembly of the Commonwealth of Pennsylvania passed September 25, 1786, the county of Luzerne was formed, and embraced the greater portion of the lands settled by the New England emigrants. Prior to that time it was a portion of Northumberland county, Pa. While under the jurisdiction of Connecticut it was a portion of the town of Westmoreland, attached to the county of Litchfield, Conn., subsequently the county of Westmoreland, Conn. As claimed by Connecticut, Westmoreland was sixty by one hundred and twenty miles square, embracing over seven thousand square miles. This territory included the principal parts of the counties of Bradford, Clearfield, Columbia, Elk, Lackawanna, Luzerne, McKean, Montour and Wyoming; smaller portions of Centre, Northumberland, Susquehanna and Union, and the whole of Cameron, Lycoming, Potter, Sullivan and Tioga. It has a present population of one million souls. This is a goodly domain, and would have made a state larger in area and with a greater population than the present state of Connecticut. Three companies of troops were raised here for the continental establishment, and were part of the Twenty-fourth Regiment of the Connecticut line. This territory was claimed by both the states of Pennsylvania and Connecticut. The governor of Connecticut issued his proclamation forbidding any settlement in Westmoreland except under authority*from Connecticut. About the same time the governor of Pennsylvania issued his proclamation, prohibiting all persons from settling on the disputed lands except under the authority of the proprietaries. In 1774 Zebulon Butler and Nathan Denison were commissioned under Connecticut as justices of the peace of the county of Litchfield, with authority to organize the town. In March, 1774, the whole people of Westmoreland, being legally warned, met and organized the town, and chose selectmen, a treasurer, constables, collector of taxes, surveyor of highways, fence viewers, listers, leather sealers, grand jurors, tything men, sealer of weights and measures and key keepers. Eight town meetings were held in the year 1774. The conflict in title gave rise to numerous contests, in many instances leading to fatal results, and is known in history as the Pennamite and Yankee war. Promptly on the appearance of peace, after the surrender of Cornwallis at Yorktown, Pennsylvania, by petition of her president and executive council, prayed congress to appoint commissioners "to constitute a court for hearing and determining the matter in question agreeably to the ninth article of the confederation." Commissioners were appointed and met at Trenton, N. J., November 19, 1782. On December 30, 1782, they pronounced the following judgment: "We are unanimously of opinion that the state of Connecticut has no right to the land in controversy. We are also unanimously of opinion that the jurisdiction and preëmption of all the territory lying within the charter boundary of Pennsylvania and now claimed by the state of Connecticut do of right belong to the state of Pennsylvania." The Trenton decree settled the legal right as to the jurisdiction of Pennsylvania. Clear, comprehensive and explicit, Pennsylvania was satisfied, and Connecticut submitted without breathing a sigh for the loss of so noble a domain, the right to which she had so strenuously maintained, or a murmur at a decision which seemed to the surrounding world so extraordinary. With the close of the year 1782, and the Trenton decree, the jurisdiction of Connecticut ceased, and the cheerful and salutary town meetings were no longer holden. While Luzerne county, or more properly Westmoreland, was under the jurisdiction of Connecticut, she sent the following persons as representatives to the Connecticut legislature, which met at Hartford and New Haven:

1774. Zebulon Butler, Timothy Smith, Christopher Avery, John Jenkins.

1775. Captain Zebulon Butler, Joseph Sluman, Major Ezekial Pierce.

1776. John Jenkins, Captain Solomon Strong, Colonel Zebulon Butler, Colonel Nathan Denison.

1777. John Jenkins, Isaac Tripp.

1778. Nathan Denison, Anderson Dana, Lieutenant Asahel Buck.

1779. Nathan Denison, Deacon John Hurlbut.

1780. John Hurlbut, Jonathan Fitch, Nathan Denison.

1781. John Hurlbut, Jonathan Fitch, Obadiah Gore, Captain John Franklin.

1782. Obadiah Gore, Jonathan Fitch.

From 1772 to 1775 the following persons were justices of the peace of Litchfield county: John Smith, Thomas Moffitt, Isaac Baldwin, John Jenkins, Zebulon Butler, Nathan Denison, Silas Parks, Bushnall Bostick, Joseph Sluman, Increase Moseley, John Sherman, Uriah Chapman. Joseph Sluman and John Sherman were judges of probate, as was Nathan Denison, of Westmoreland county.

In 1776 Jonathan Fitch was commissioned sheriff of Westmoreland county. The same year John Jenkins was appointed judge of the county court in and for the county of Westmoreland. On June 1, 1778, Governor Jonathan Trumbull appointed the following named persons justices of the peace for the county of Westmoreland: Nathan Denison, Christopher Avery, Obadiah Gore, Zera Beach, Zebulon Butler, William McKarrican, Asaph Whittlesey, Uriah Chapman, Anderson Dana, Ebenezer Marcy, Stephen Harding, John Franklin, 2d, Joseph Hambleton, and William Judd. Of the foregoing, Nathan Denison, Christopher Avery, Obadiah Gore and Zera Beach were appointed to assist the judges of Westmoreland. Other justices of the peace were appointed as follows: Caleb Bates, Zebulon Marcy, John Hurlbut, Nathaniel Landon, Abel Pierce, Hugh Fordsman, John Franklin, John Vincent, John Jenkins. In 1781 Nathan Denison was judge of Westmoreland county. The above contains the names of the officers of Litchfield and Westmoreland counties. There were probably others, but we are unable to ascertain who they were. The only lawyers in Westmoreland were Anderson Dana and —— Bullock. As they were both killed in the battle and massacre of Wyoming, Lieutenant John Jenkins was appointed by the court state's attorney. The fourth section of the act incorporating Luzerne county provided: "That Courts of Common Pleas and General Quarter Sessions of the Peace to be holden in and for the said county of Luzerne shall be opened and held on the Tuesday succeeding the Tuesday on which the court of Northumberland is held in each and every term hereafter; and that the Court of Quarter Sessions shall sit three days at each sessions and no longer, and shall be held at the house of Zebulon Butler, in the town of *Wilkesburg*, in the said county of Luzerne, until a court house shall be built, as hereafter directed, in the said county, which said courts shall then be holden and kept at the said court house on the days and times before mentioned." Section ninth of said act provided "That Zebulon Butler, Nathaniel Landen, Jonah Rogers, John Philips and Simon Spawlding are hereby appointed trustees for the said county of Luzerne, and they, or any three of them, shall take assurances of and for a piece of land situated in some convenient place in or near *Wilkesburg*, within the said county of Luzerne, for the seat of a court house and of a county gaol or prison for the said county, in the name of the commonwealth, in trust and for the use and benefit of the said county of Luzerne, and thereupon to erect a court house and prison sufficient to accommodate the public service of the said county. On May 27, 1787, William Hooker Smith, Benjamin Carpenter and James Nesbitt, Esqs., justices of the county Court of Common Pleas for Luzerne county, convened at the dwelling house of Zebulon Butler, in Wilkes-Barre (corner of River and Northampton streets, on the site of the residence of Hon. Stanley Woodward), in the said county, when and where the following proceedings were had:

Proclamation having been made by the sheriff of said county commanding all persons to keep silence, there were read:

I. The commissions issued by the supreme executive council of Pennsylvania to the said William Hooker Smith, Benjamin Carpenter and James Nesbit, and also to Timothy Pickering, Obadiah Gore, Nathan Kingsley and Matthias Hollenback, constituting them justices of the county Court of Common Pleas for the said county.

II. The *dedimus potestatum* to Timothy Pickering and Nathan Denison, Esqs., issued by the supreme executive council, empowering them to administer the oaths to persons who were or should be commissioned in said county.

III. Then William Hooker Smith, Benjamin Carpenter and James Nesbit, Esqs., took the oaths of allegiance and of office, and justices of the peace and of the county Court of Common Pleas for said county (as required by the constitution of Pennsylvania), before Timothy Pickering, Esq., impowered as aforesaid to administer them.

IV. The Court of Common Pleas was then opened and Joseph Sprague appointed crier.

V. Then were read the other commissions granted to Timothy Pickering, Esq., by the supreme executive council, constituting him prothonotary of said Court of Common Pleas, clerk of the peace, clerk of the Orphans' Court, register for the probate of wills and granting letters of administration, and recorder of deeds for said county.

VI. The court, upon application to them made, admitted and appointed Ebenezer Bowman, Putnam Catlin, Rosewell Welles and William Nichols (the latter being a non-resident) to be attorneys of the same court, who were accordingly sworn.

VII. Then appeared Lord Butler, Esq., sheriff of the same county, and petitioned the court to take some order relative to the erection of a jail within the said county, whereupon it is ordered that he immediately apply to the trustees for that purpose appointed, and request them to execute the powers granted them by the law of the state so far as respects the erection of a county jail.

The next regular term of court was held September 5, 1787, and was presided over by Justices Obadiah Gore, Matthias Hollenback, William Hooker Smith, Benjamin Carpenter, James Nesbit and Nathan Kingsley. Courts were continued to be held by the justices until the changes wrought by the constitution of 1790 and subsequent legislation.

TIMOTHY PICKERING.

Timothy Pickering, who was appointed a justice of the Court of Common Pleas of Luzerne county, Pa., October 12, 1786, was the great-great-grandson of John Pickering, who came from England and settled in Salem, Mass., in 1642. Timothy Pickering was born in Salem July 17, 1745. He was graduated at Harvard College in 1763, and soon afterward became a clerk to John Higginson, register of deeds for the county of Essex, Mass. In 1768 he was admitted to the bar. From 1770 to 1777 he served at different times in most of the municipal offices in Salem, and on the committees of correspondence, inspection and safety. In August, 1774, he, with other members of the committee of correspondence, was arrested at the instance of Governor Gage for calling a town meeting on public grievances, but in September the magistrate who had issued the warrant for the arrest recalled it, being alarmed by the unpopularity of his act. In 1775 Mr. Pickering was appointed one of the judges of the Court of Common Pleas for the county of Essex, and sole judge of the prize court for the middle district, composed of Suffolk, Essex and Middlesex. In the autumn of 1776, the army under General Washington being greatly reduced in numbers, a large reenforcement of militia was called for and Mr. Pickering, who then held a commission as colonel, took the command of the regiment of seven hundred men, furnished from the county of Essex. On this tour of duty, which terminated in March, 1777, at Boundbrook, N. J., he had interviews with General Washington, and in May he was invited by him to take the office of adjutant general, which he at first declined, but afterward accepted. In this capacity he was with Washington in the battles of Brandywine and Germantown. In November congress elected him a member of the continental board of war, in which office he served until August 5, 1780, when congress by a unanimous vote elected him quartermaster-general as successor to General Greene. He continued in this station until July 25, 1785, when the office was abolished. He was present during the siege of Yorktown in

1781, and at the surrender of Cornwallis. On the return of peace he engaged in business in Philadelphia as a commission merchant. In 1786, having been invited to assist in composing the controversy between the state of Pennsylvania and certain emigrants from Connecticut, who had settled an extensive tract of land in the valley of Wyoming, and at the same time to organize the new county of Luzerne, embracing a great part of the territory in dispute, he removed to Wilkes-Barre with the understanding that he was authorized to give assurances that the legislature would quiet in their possessions a certain class of the Connecticut settlers. An act was passed accordingly, and his efforts as a peacemaker promised a successful result, but the legislature proved inconstant, and by first suspending and then repealing the act, increased the acrimony and strength of the discontented settlers. Their leader, John Franklin, having been arrested for high treason, some of his adherents, with the hope of obtaining his release, retaliated on Colonel Pickering on June 26, 1788, by entering his house at night and carrying him into the woods, where they detained him for nineteen days. On October 12, 1786, he was appointed prothonotary, clerk of the Orphans' Court, Quarter Sessions and Oyer and Terminer, register of wills and recorder of deeds of Luzerne county, and on May 24, 1787, one of the commissioners to examine the Connecticut claims. In 1787 he was the delegate from Luzerne county to the Pennsylvania convention for acting upon the proposed constitution of the United States, and was earnestly in favor of its adoption. In 1789 he was the delegate from this county to the convention for revising the constitution of Pennsylvania. Under appointments from President Washington he made satisfactory treaties with the Six nations collectively, and with some of them severally, in 1790, '91 and '94, and in 1793 he was joined with General Lincoln and Beverly Randolph in a commission to negotiate with the hostile Indians north-west of the Ohio, but the manœuvres of Simcoe, governor of Canada, prevented a meeting with those tribes. In 1792 he returned with his family to Philadelphia, having in August of the preceding year been appointed postmaster-general. On January 2, 1795, he was transferred to the office of secretary of war, and on December 12 to that of secretary of state. This position he held during the remainder of Washington's administration, and for more than three years under President Adams, who removed him from office May 12, 1800. He now retired to his wild lands in Harmony township, Luzerne (now Susquehanna) county, with the intention of bringing a portion of them into cultivation, but his friends in Massachusetts joined in the purchase of a large proportion of his lands in order to enable and induce him to return to his native state. In 1801 he removed to Massachusetts and subsequently purchased a farm in Wenham, near Salem. In 1802 he was appointed chief justice of the Court of Common Pleas for the county of Essex. In 1803 he was elected a senator in congress for the residue of the term of Dwight Foster, who had resigned, and in 1805 he was re-elected for the term of six years. After the commencement of hostilities against Great Brittain in 1812, he was appointed a member of the Massachusetts board of war. From 1813 to 1817 he was a member of the United States house of representatives. In politics he was a federalist, and ardently opposed to some of the leading measures of the administrations of Jefferson and Madison. In religion he was a Unitarian. He married, April 8, 1776, Rebecca White, who was born in Bristol, England, July 18, 1754. For the main facts connected with the life of Colonel Pickering we are indebted to Appleton's American Cyclopedia. Colonel Pickering died in Salem January 29, 1829.

MATTHIAS HOLLENBACK.

Matthias Hollenback was appointed a justice of the Court of Common Pleas of Luzerne county, Pa., May 11, 1787. He was also appointed, August 17, 1791, one of the judges of the Court of Common Pleas under the constitution of 1790. For a sketch of his life see article headed Harrison Wright.

WILLIAM HOOKER SMITH.

William Hooker Smith was appointed a justice of the Court of Common Pleas of Luzerne county, Pa., May 11, 1787. (See page 219).

BENJAMIN CARPENTER.

Benjamin Carpenter was appointed a justice of the Court of Common Pleas of Luzerne county, Pa., May 11, 1787. He represented Luzerne county in the legislature of the state in 1794. One of his daughters became the first wife of Jacob Bedford, and another was the wife of Lazarus Denison. He came to Wyoming from Orange county, N. Y., and subsequently removed to Sunbury, Delaware county, Ohio, where he became an associate judge.

JAMES NESBITT

James Nesbitt was appointed a justice of the Court of Common Pleas of Luzerne county, Pa., May 11, 1787. For a sketch of his life see page 507.

OBADIAH GORE.

Obadiah Gore was appointed a justice of the Court of Common Pleas of Luzerne county, Pa., May 11, 1787. He was also appointed, August 17, 1791, one of the judges of the Court of Common Pleas under the constitution of 1790. For a sketch of his life see page 435.

NATHAN KINGSLEY.

Nathan Kingsley, who was appointed one of the justices of the Court of Common Pleas of Luzerne county, Pa., May 11, 1787, was the oldest son of Salmon Kingsley. He was born in Scotland, Windham county, Conn., January 23, 1743. He came to Wyoming about 1772 or 1773, and was one of the original proprietors of Springfield, Luzerne (now Bradford) county, Pa. On August 8, 1776, he was appointed one of the committee of inspection of the county of Westmoreland. About the latter part of the year 1777 he was captured by the Indians and remained a prisoner nearly a year. While in captivity he secured the friendship and confidence of the Indians by his skill in doctoring their horses. He was in consequence allowed considerable liberty, and permitted to go into the woods to gather herbs and roots for his medicines. Seizing a favorable opportunity he made his escape and reached Wyoming in safety. During his captivity his family found a home with Jonathan Slocum, of Wilkes-Barre. Here his son, Nathan, was killed and another son carried into captivity by the Indians. Mr. Miner gives the account as follows: "A respectable neighbor, Nathan Kingsley, had been made prisoner, and taken into the Indian country, leaving his wife and two sons to the charity of the neighbors. Taking them home, Mr. Slocum bade them welcome until Mr. Kingsley should be liberated or some other mode of subsistence present. On November 2, 1778, the two boys being engaged in grinding a knife, a rifle shot and cry of distress brought Mrs. Slocum to the door, where she beheld an Indian scalping Nathan, the eldest lad, with the knife he had been sharpening. Waving her back with his hand he entered the house and took up Ebenezer Slocum, a little boy. The mother stepped up to the savage, and reaching for the child, said: 'He can do you no good; see, he is lame.'" As a matter of fact, Ebenezer Slocum may have been lame at that time, but never afterwards. He settled in what is now Scranton, and from him and his brother, Benjamin Slocum, the place took its name of Slocum Hollow. "With a grim smile the Indian gave up the boy and took Francis, her daughter, aged about five years, gently in his arms, and seizing the younger Kingsley by the hand, hurried away to the mountains, two savages who were with him taking a black girl, seventeen years old. This was within one hundred rods of Wilkes-Barre fort. An alarm was instantly given, but the Indians eluded pursuit and no trace of their retreat could be found." (See page 340). At the close of the war Mr. Kingsley returned to his old home in Wyalusing. His wife and one son, Wareham, had survived the perils of the war, and now he enjoyed a few years of quiet and comfort. He resigned his justiceship in a letter dated January 14, 1790, addressed to the president of the supreme executive council, as follows:

"Nathan Kingsley, of the county of Luzerne, commissioned one of the judges of the Court of Quarter Sessions and Common Pleas, for the county aforesaid, finding it impracticable many times by reason of high water to attend courts and living sixty miles from the county town, joined to the smallness of the fees allowed him in this behalf, is obliged, from necessity, to inform council that he cannot, in future, serve in his aforementioned capacity. Were his abode nearer than what it is at present to the county town, he would not think of resigning his office, but would continue in it with pleasure and satisfaction. The fall and spring sessions happen at a time when the waters are high, and of consequence, make his travelling not only expensive but very difficult and dangerous. The time of attending, coming to and returning from courts takes up so considerable a part of the seasons of summer and fall that he is obliged to neglect his agricultural pursuits to the singular injury of this interest. From these considerations he desires council to accept his resignation and take such other order in directing the choice of another judge in his district as to them shall seem meet."

NATHAN KINGSLEY.

His resignation was accepted February 1, 1790. Mr. Kingsley is described as a large, tall man, of more than ordinary intelligence, deeply interested in the prosperity of the community and the development of the country. He died in the state of Ohio in 1822. Prof. James L. Kingsley, of Yale College, was his nephew.

ROSEWELL WELLES.

Rosewell Welles, who was admitted to the bar of Luzerne county, Pa., May 27, 1787, was the son of Captain Jonathan Welles, of Glastonbury, Conn., who was of the fifth generation from Governor Thomas Welles, of Connecticut. The wife of Captain Jonathan Welles was Catharine, daughter of Captain Roswell Saltonstall, of Bradford, Conn., the eldest son of Governor Saltonstall, of Connecticut. Rosewell Welles was born at Glastonbury, August 20, 1761. It is said that he graduated from Yale College in 1784. He emigrated to Wilkes-Barre in 1786. On April 26, 1793, he was appointed one of the judges of Luzerne county. About 1800 he commanded a regiment of Pennsylvania militia. From 1807 to 1810 he was one of the trustees of the Wilkes-Barre Academy. On December 14, 1820, he was appointed by Governor Findlay a justice of the peace for the borough and township of Wilkes-Barre, and part of the township of Covington. His wife was Hannah, eldest daughter of Colonel Zebulon Butler. Mr. Welles died in Wilkes-Barre March 19, 1830. For further facts concerning the history and ancestry of Rosewell Welles see pages 119 and 660.

EBENEZER BOWMAN.

Ebenezer Bowman is the first name on the list of lawyers admitted at the first session of the courts of Luzerne county, Pa., May 27, 1787. He was a descendant of Nathaniel Bowman, who is on the earliest list of proprietors (February, 1636-7) "then inhabiting" Watertown, Massachusetts. He moved from there to Cambridge Farms, Lexington, where he died January 26, 1681. Francis Bowman, son of Ebenezer Bowman, was admitted a freeman in 1652, and on September 26, 1661, married Martha Sherman, a daughter of Captain John Sherman, who was born in Dedham, county of Essex, England, in 1613, came to America in 1634, admitted freeman May 17, 1637, a land surveyor, selectman very many times from 1637 to 1680, town clerk 1648, and afterwards representative 1651, 1653, 1663. He was chosen ensign 1654, and was steward of Harvard College 1662. Captain Joseph Bowman, son of Francis Bowman, was a justice of the peace of Lexington. He died April 8, 1762, aged eighty-eight years. Captain Thaddeus Bowman, son of Captain Joseph Bowman, was born September 2, 1712, at Lexington. He married, February 8, 1753, his second wife, Sybil Woolson, then of Lexington, widow of Isaac Woolson, of Weston. Her maiden name was Rooper, and it is probable that she was a daughter of Ephraim and Sybil Rooper, or Roper, of Sudbury. He died in New Braintree May 26, 1806. Ebenezer Bowman, tenth child of Captain Thaddeus Bowman, was born July 3, 1757. He graduated at Harvard College in 1782. He was in the battles of Lexington and Bunker Hill. He studied law with Samuel Sitgreaves, at Easton, Pa., and settled in Wilkes-Barre about 1789. He married, in New York, November 10, 1796, Esther Ann Watson, who was born in Ireland. He died March 1, 1829, and his widow died July 21, 1848. Ebenezer Bowman was one of the trustees of the Wilkes-Barre Academy from 1807 until his death, and for five years was president of the board. He represented Luzerne county in the legislature of the state in 1793.

PUTNAM CATLIN.

Putnam Catlin, who was admitted to the bar of Luzerne county, Pa., May 27, 1787, was a descendant of Thomas Catlin, a native of Wales, who was a resident of Hartford, Conn., as early as 1644. He had a son John Catlin, who had a son Samuel Catlin, who had a son John Catlin. Eli Catlin, son of John Catlin, was the father of Putnam Catlin. Eli Catlin enlisted in the revolutionary war as lieutenant in the Second Connecticut Regiment in January, 1777, coming out as captain. Captain Catlin came to Pennsylvania from Connecticut probably in 1789. He died at

Hopbottom, Susquehanna county, Pa., March 13, 1820. His wife, Elizabeth Catlin (*nee* Way), mother of Putnam Catlin, died April 4, 1796, and is buried at Litchfield, Conn. Putnam Catlin was born at Litchfield April 5, 1764. At the time his father, Eli Catlin, entered the service of the colonies, Putnam Catlin enlisted with him in the same company and regiment. He served until June 9, 1783. He was fife major of his regiment, and received a "badge of merit." He read law with Uriah Tracy, at Litchfield, in the years from 1783 to 1786, and was admitted to the bar the latter year. He removed to Pennsylvania in the spring of 1787, settling in Wilkes-Barre, and in 1789 he married Polly Sutton, daughter of James and Sarah Sutton. (See page 213.) In consequence of failing health, a result of arduous services at the bar, Mr. Catlin removed with his family from Wilkes-Barre, in 1797, to a farm in Ona-qua-gua valley, now Windsor, Broome county, N. Y., about fifty miles from this city. Here he lived until 1808, when he sold his farm and bought one at Hopbottom. In 1813 the Hopbottom post office was established, with Putnam Catlin as postmaster. Here he remained until 1818, when he removed to Montrose, Pa. After residing until 1821 at Montrose, he removed to a farm at Great Bend, Pa., where he died in 1842. Mrs. Catlin died at Delta, Oneida county, N. Y., July 15, 1844.

ABRAHAM BRADLEY.

Abraham Bradley, who was admitted to the bar of Luzerne county, Pa., September 2, 1788, was a descendent of Stephen Bradley, who emigrated from England about 1660, and settled in Guilford, Conn., where he died, June 20, 1702, aged about sixty years. Abraham Bradley, son of Stephen Bradley, was born in Guilford May 13, 1675, and died April 20, 1721. His wife was Jane Leaming. Abraham Bradley, son of Abraham Bradley, was born July 26, 1702, graduated at Yale College, and died in 1771. His wife was Reliance Stone. Abraham Bradley, son of

Abraham Bradley, was born in Guilford December 11, 1731. In 1763 he married Hannah Baldwin, of Litchfield, Conn., where he settled and resided for upwards of thirty years. In 1796 he removed to Hanover township, in this county, and in his latter years went to reside with his son, Phineas Bradley, near Washington, D. C. He was successively master of a vessel, surveyor of lands, selectman, town treasurer, representative to the legislature, justice of the peace, captain in the militia and in the revolutionary war, judge, town clerk, &c. While a resident of this place Mr. Bradley wrote a work entitled, "A Philosophical Retrospect on the General Outline of Creation and Providence, wherein is considered the Origin of Matter and Works of Creation, and also the Immutable and Systematic Dispositions of Divine Providence, in consequence whereof the World was at some ancient epoch Destroyed by an Exundation of the Sea, subsequent to which the Creation of all Terrestrial Animals took place. Comprising also, a general view of the Origin of Nations, and of the general characteristics of the several Varieties of Mankind." It was a book of one hundred and ninety-four pages and was printed and published by Asher and Charles Miner, and gave great alarm to many ladies, among others, to Mr. Bradley's good wife. The work was thought to be infidel in its character, advancing doctrines not in conformity with the teachings of Holy Writ. These orthodox ladies and others were active in its destruction, committing the book to the flames whenever a copy fell into their hands. This circumstance accounts for the present scarcity of the work. Mrs. Bradley died in Wilkes-Barre September 18, 1804, aged sixty-seven years, and her husband died in Oneida county, N. Y., about 1825. Abraham Bradley, son of Abraham Bradley, was born in Litchfield February 21, 1767. He was educated in his native town and read law with Judge Tapping Reeve, of Litchfield. He practiced here from 1788 to 1791. In a letter written by Timothy Pickering to Governor Mifflin, dated August 16, 1791, he thus speaks of Mr. Bradley: "Permit me now, sir, to mention a gentleman there, who can well execute, and who well deserves all these offices (register, recorder, clerk of all the courts, and prothonotary), I mean Abraham Bradley, Esq., whose prudence, steadiness and sobriety are exemplary—whose integrity is unblemished—whose industry has no rival—and whose judgment and law knowledge have there, no superior. I think I shall speak more accurately if I were to say, no equal. In pleadings, and the necessary forms, he is decidedly superior to all. But he came later into practice than the other three attorneys—was younger—somewhat diffident, and has not formed a habit of speaking. He has, therefore, had few causes to manage, and his fees have been trifling. He studied law and wrote in the office of Tapping Reeve, Esq., an eminent lawyer at Litchfield, in Connecticut. He writes a fair, strong, legible hand, perfectly adapted to records. During frequent absences in the last two years he has done the business in the court and in my office with great propriety. 'Tis a business in which he takes pleasure. His law knowledge renders him peculiarly fit to hold all the offices before mentioned, and will give great facility in the execution. And his law knowledge will not be stationary—it will advance. For he has an inquisitive mind, and a taste for literature in general. This, sir, is not the language of hyperbole; I speak the words of truth and soberness from an intimate personal acquaintance with Mr. Bradley." Mr. Bradley did not get "the offices," but the governor on the next day, August 17, 1791, appointed him one of the judges of Luzerne county. He soon after left Wilkes-Barre and removed to Washington, D. C., and from 1791 to 1799 he was confidential clerk to Colonel Pickering, in the post office and other departments, and from 1799 to 1829 he was assistant postmaster-general of the United States. He was secretary of the Franklin Insurance Company, of Washington for two years before his death, which occurred at Washington, May 7, 1838. His wife was Hannah Smith, of Pittston, daughter of Thomas Smith. (See page 869.)

NOAH MURRAY.

Noah Murray, who was appointed one of the justices of the Court of Common Pleas of Luzerne county, Pa., November 28, 1788, was a native of Litchfield county, Conn. He served in the revolutionary war, after which he settled in the Wyoming valley. He removed to Athens, Luzerne (now Bradford) county, about

1791. He was a clergyman, first of the Baptist church and afterwards of the Universalist; for some years he was pastor of the Universalist church in Philadelphia. He was one of the proprietors of the old academy at Athens, and chairman of the board of trustees. He died May 11, 1811, leaving two sons and several daughters. On a marble monument standing in a cemetery at Springfield, Bradford county, Pa., is this inscription: "Sacred to the memory of Rev. Noah Murray, the first preacher of Universalism in Bradford county, who died May 11, 1811, in the seventy-fifth year of his age. Erected as a token of grateful remembrance by the North Branch Association of Universalists, September, 1867."

JOSEPH KINNEY.

"Joseph Kinney," says Timothy Pickering, in a letter to Governor Mifflin, dated August 16, 1791, "was pretty early appointed a judge of the Common Pleas, but fully expecting to remove to the state of New York, he sent to the court a letter of resignation, but I do not know that his resignation was ever declared to the executive council. I believe it was not. He lived near Tioga, where Esquire Hollenback was sometimes present, and to which neighborhood Esquire Murray moved up from Shawnee. Mr. Kinney was disappointed in respect to the lands in York state to which he meant to go, and has remained in Luzerne." His commission is not on record in the recorder's office, and the first time that he sat as judge was June 2, 1789. Joseph Kinney was born in Plainfield, Conn., about the year, 1755. He was a revolutionary soldier, and his first engagement was at Dorchester Heights, about March 2, 1776, which resulted disastrously to the British troops. He was wounded in the leg on Long Island, captured and was a prisoner three months in the old Jersey prison ship, and suffered all its horrors. He limped home on foot, and was at the battle of Saratoga, October 17, 1777, where Burgoyne surrendered, when he returned to Plainfield and remained until about 1778, when he settled at Wyoming. There he married Sarah, the eldest daughter of Captain (afterwards General) Simon Spalding, and with that gentleman and others removed to Sheshequin, Luzerne (now Bradford) county, in 1783, which thereafter became his permanent home. Mr. Miner has the following in his History of Wyoming: "On Sunday, June 18, 1781, Joseph Kinney and Sarah Spalding were called off, that is, the bans were published, and on Thursday, the 22d, were married. It was an occasion of unusual festivity and joy. The bride was the eldest daughter of Captain Simon Spalding, the gallant commander of the Connecticut Independent Company." He was a school teacher in Wyoming, but changed his occupation to that of a farmer in his new home, a calling in which he prided himself, executing his work in an exceedingly tidy and in some respects peculiar manner. He was not only a great reader, but was also a close and logical reasoner, and analyzed thoroughly everything offered before he stored it away in his memory as knowledge. He was particularly apt in theological themes, and had many a gusty bout with the preachers of the day, and when sent to oppose and confound Mr. Murray in his first seed sowing of the doctrines of universal salvation, at Athens, "went wool gathering and came home shorn," after a three days' protracted effort. Mr. Kinney's house was the home of all the itinerants of the gospel in his day. He was emphatically domestic in his tastes, and hence disliked and refused political positions generally. On September 1, 1791, he was appointed a justice of the peace for the district of Tioga, which comprised at that time what is now the larger part of Bradford county. He was also one of the first commissioners of Bradford county, but resolutely declined all further preferment. He died in 1841. Mr. and Mrs. Kinney had a family of thirteen children. Their son Simon was the first white child born in the present town of Sheshequin. His descendants are distinguished in the various walks of life.

CHRISTOPHER HURLBUT.

Christopher Hurlbut was appointed a justice of the Court of Common Pleas of Luzerne county, Pa., August 5, 1789. For a sketch of the Hurlbut family see page 628.

LAWRENCE MYERS.

Lawrence Myers was appointed a justice of the Court of Common Pleas of Luzerne county, Pa., July 7, 1790. For a sketch of the Myers family see page 629.

NATHAN DENISON.

Nathan Denison was appointed a judge of Luzerne county, Pa., August 17, 1791. For a sketch of his life see article headed George Denison. His son, George Denison, and grandsons, Charles Denison and Lazarus Denison Shoemaker, members of the Luzerne bar, represented Luzerne county in the congress of the United States.

By the constitution of 1790 the judicial power of the commonwealth was vested in a Supreme Court, in Courts of Oyer and Terminer and general jail delivery, in a Court of Common Pleas, Orphans' Court, Register's court, and a Court of Quarter Sessions of the peace for each county, in justices of the peace, and in such other courts as the legislature should from time to time establish. Section 2 of Article V provided that the judges of the Supreme Court and Courts of Common Pleas hold office during good behavior. Section 3 provided that the jurisdiction of the Supreme Court extend over the state, and the judges thereof were by virtue of their office justices of Oyer and Terminer, &c., in the several counties. Section 4 provided that the Courts of Common Pleas were to be established as follows: The governor shall appoint in each county not fewer than three nor more than four judges, until it shall be otherwise directed by law, who shall reside in such county. The state shall be divided into circuits, none of which should contain more than six nor fewer than three counties. A president of each circuit was to be appointed. The president and judges, any two of whom shall be a quorum, were to compose the respective Courts of Common Pleas. Section 5 provided that two of the judges, the president being one, could hold a Court of Oyer and Terminer. Section 7 provided that two of the judges constituted a quorum to hold a Court of Quarter Sessions and Orphans' Court. At the first session of the legislature following the adoption of the constitution an act was passed (April 13, 1791,) to carry into effect its provisions respecting the courts, &c., and by section second of the act the state was divided into five districts or circuits. Luzerne, together with Berks, Northampton and Northumberland counties, constituted the third district or circuit. Section third of the act directed the governor to commission "a person of knowledge and integrity and skilled in the law" in each district as "president and judge," and "a number of other proper persons, not fewer than three nor more than four," as judges in each county. Their jurisdiction, &c., was to commence after the next 31st August.

JACOB RUSH.

Jacob Rush, who was appointed, August 17, 1791, president of the Court of Common Pleas of the circuit consisting of the counties of Berks, Luzerne, Northampton and Northumberland, was a native of Byberry township, Philadelphia county, Pa., where he was born in 1746. His ancestor, John Rush, who was captain of horse in Cromwell's army, emigrated to this county in 1683 and left a large number of descendants. His father died in 1751. Jacob Rush graduated from Princeton (N. J.) College in 1765, and was admitted to the bar of Philadelphia county February 7, 1769. After his admission he practiced his profession in Philadelphia, and also in the counties of Bucks, Chester and York. In January, 1775, he was a member of the provincial convention assembled in Philadelphia to consider the proper measures of self defense against the oppressions of our mother England. In 1779 and 1780 he was a member of our state legislature. He was appointed a judge of the Supreme Court of Pennsylvania February 15, 1784, in place of John Evans, deceased, and as such was a member of the high Court of Errors and Appeals before the adoption of the constitution of 1790. Judge Rush presided here until 1806, when he was succeeded by Thomas Cooper. From 1806 to 1820 Judge Rush was president judge of the Court of Common Pleas of Philadelphia, where he died January 5, 1820. Princeton gave him the degree of LL. D., in 1804. While a judge of our circuit he resided in Reading, Pa. He was a brother of the celebrated Dr. Benjamin Rush, signer of the declaration of independence. David Paul Brown says of him: "He was a man of great ability, and great firmness and decision of character. He was also an eloquent man. Perhaps there are few specimens of judicial eloquence more impressive than those charges which he delivered during his occupation of the bench. An accurate idea of his style may be readily formed from an extract from his charge to a grand jury in 1808, and his sentence pronounced upon Richard Smith for the murder of Carson in 1816. We refer as much to the moral tone of his productions as to their literary and intellectual power. Some of his early literary essays were ascribed to Dr. Franklin, and for their terseness and clearness were worthy of him. Judge Rush's charges to the jury, and decisions generally, were marked by soundness of principle and closeness of reasoning. Having been a judge of the Supreme Court and of the high Court of Errors and Appeals he never appeared to be satisfied in his position in the Court of Common Pleas, yet his uprightness of conduct and unquestionable ability always secured to him the respect and confidence, if not the attachment of his associates, the members of the bar, and the entire community. He was one of the gentlemen of the old school, plain in his attire and unobtrusive in his deportment; but while observant of his duties towards others, he was never forgetful of the respect to which he was himself justly entitled." He was the author of "Charges on Moral and Religious Subjects," published in 1803; "The Character of Christ," 1806, and "Christian Baptism," 1819. There were some ceremonies connected with the courts now entirely abrogated, and which, in fact, would be annoying in the present day, which are worthy of being noted in the records of the past. At the opening of every term the sheriff, with his staff of office, attended by the crier of the court, and frequently by several constables, waited upon the judges at their lodgings, and then conducted them in formal prosession to the court house. It is certainly more agreeable in this day for a judge to regulate his own time and enter the court house without any such idle parade. Judges McKean, Smith, Yeates, and others, of the Supreme Court, always wore swords when they attended court in Wilkes-Barre,—some bearing rapiers, others, heavier weapons. The first court house was erected on the public square and was constructed of hewn logs, and consisted of two stories, the lower one being used for the purposes of a jail and as a dwelling place for the jailor; the upper story for court purposes, and also as a place where the people of the vicinity met for religious services and duties. In this secluded spot the weeks of court, years since, attracted more of interest in the inhabitants than is found at present. They were decidedly, as tradition remembers and brings down to us, gala days and periods of frolic and of fun. The lawyers were assembled from various parts of the state, and, while business was not so burdensome and pressing as it is now, much time was afforded for amusements.

NATHAN PALMER.

Nathan Palmer, a lineal descendant of Myles Standish, was admitted to the Luzerne county, Pa., bar in 1794. He was a native of Plainfield, Conn., and removed in early manhood to Pennsylvania. On January 8, 1800, he was appointed by Governor McKean prothonotary, and clerk of the Courts of Quarter Sessions, Oyer and Terminer and Orphans' Court, for the term of three years. From 1808 to 1810 he represented Luzerne and Northumberland counties in the senate of Pennsylvania. In 1813 he was treasurer of Luzerne county. In 1814 he was appointed one of the trustees of the Wilkes-Barre Academy, and served for five years in that position. Judge Strange N. Palmer, of Pottsville, was his son, and Hon. Robert M. Palmer, of the same place, his grandson.

NOAH WADHAMS.

Noah Wadhams was admitted to the bar of Luzerne county, Pa., in 1794. In the minutes of the sessions of the court for the last named year it is stated that the only attorneys in Luzerne county are Ebenezer Bowman and Putnam Catlin (Rosewell Welles had been appointed judge and A. Bradley had removed); that E. Bowman had declined practice and P. Catlin was about to decline; that Nathan Palmer and Noah Wadhams, jr., having been admitted in the Supreme Court of Connecticut, be, "under the circumstances," admitted, &c. (the two years residence and study within the state being dispensed with). For further information regarding Mr. Wadhams see pages 109 and 755.

JESSE FELL.

Jesse Fell was appointed a judge of Luzerne county, Pa., February 5, 1798. For a sketch of his life see page 344.

THOMAS GRAHAM.

Thomas Graham was admitted to the bar of Luzerne county, Pa., in 1798. In 1805 he was appointed to the offices of register and recorder, and in 1807 he was appointed prothonotary and clerk of the Courts of Quarter Sessions, Oyer and Terminer and Orphans' Court. In 1809, 1810 and 1811 he represented Luzerne county in the legislature of the state. From 1807 to April 26, 1814 (the date of his death), he was one of the trustees of the Wilkes-Barre Academy.

WILLIAM PRENTICE.

William Prentice was admitted to the bar of Luzerne county, Pa., in 1799. He was then thirty-four years of age, and was the first full-fledged attorney in that part of Luzerne county which is now Bradford county. He was a descendant of Captain Thomas Prentice, born in England, 1620, who had a son, Thomas, born in 1649, who had a son, Samuel, born in 1680, who had a son, Samuel, born November 25, 1702, who had a son, Amos Prentice, M. D., born April 24, 1748. The latter removed with his family from New London, Conn., to Athens township, Luzerne (now Bradford) county, and was among the early physicians of the county. He was one of the sufferers in New London at the time the city was burned by Arnold, in 1781, where he practiced his profession for several years. His wife was the daughter of Rev.——Owen, of Groton, Conn., a friend and contemporary of President Edwards. William Prentice was the son of Amos Prentice, M. D., and died suddenly at the home of his father in Milltown, Luzerne (now Bradford) county, October 6, 1806. He had studied law and had been admitted to the bar in New London previous to his coming to this county. After the dismemberment of the county he practiced in Lycoming county until his death. The history of this dismemberment is as follows: Colonel John Franklin was a resident of Athens, after the troubles at Wyoming were settled and the organization of Luzerne county completed. In the years 1795 and 1796 he represented Luzerne county in the assembly of Pennsylvania. From 1799 to 1803 he was also a member of the legislature. An attempt was made in the session of 1802-3 to expel him from the assembly on account of his indictment under the intrusion law, but on account of political reasons, many in the land-holders' interest were induced to vote against his expulsion. Determined, however, to get rid of him, the legislature in 1804 passed an act dividing the county of Luzerne, and setting off that part which contained the residence of Colonel Franklin to Lycoming county. It is said that the first draft of the bill included that part of Luzerne west of the Susquehanna and north of the Towanda creek. When the bill was read Colonel Franklin arose in his seat and remarked, "he wished to inform the gentlemen that he lived east of the river." The boundaries were accordingly changed, so as to include him in the dismembered portion. In 1805, however, much to the chagrin of his enemies, he was elected by the people of Lycoming, and appeared in triumph at Lancaster, and took his seat. Subsequently, a portion of the dismembered portion was recovered to Luzerne county. Hon. William Ellwell, of Bloomsburg, is a nephew of William Prentice, his mother being Nancy Prentice, who was the wife of Daniel Elwell, the father of the judge.

GEORGE GRIFFIN.

George Griffin was admitted to the bar of Luzerne county, Pa., in 1800. He was a descendant of Jasper Griffin, who was born in Wales in the earlier half of the seventeenth century. He came to America before 1670. The first notice of him is in that year, in Essex county, Mass. In 1674 he was at Marblehead, Mass. In 1675 he and his wife Hannah settled at Southold, Long Island. She was born at Manchester, New England, and died at Southold April 20, 1699, aged forty-six years, eight months, and "was the mother of fourteen children." Mr. Griffin was commissioned major of militia, and had charge of two guns, which were mounted near his house, and fired on public days. He died at Southold April 17, 1738, aged eighty years. Jasper Griffin, son of Jasper Griffin, and eldest of his fourteen children, was born at Southold in 1675. After his father's death he removed to Lyme, Conn., where he had married, April 29, 1696, Ruth Peck, born August 19, 1676, daughter of Joseph Peck, of New Haven, Conn., and Sarah, his wife. Joseph Peck was the third son of William Peck, one of the original proprietors of New Haven, and was the progenitor of all the Pecks in New England. Mr. and Mrs. Griffin had five children. He was over ninety years of age at the time of his death. Lemuel Griffin, second son of Jasper Griffin, was born at Lyme in 1704. He married Phœbe Comstock. She "was of literary and artistic tastes." They had two sons—George Griffin, eldest son of Lemuel Griffin, was born at East Haddam, Conn., July 10, 1734. He married, March 9, 1762, Eve Dorr, born March 4, 1733, daughter of Edmund Dorr and Mary Griswold. Edmund Dorr was born at Roxbury, Mass., October 16, 1692; married, September 4, 1719, Mary Griswold, daughter of Matthew Griswold and Phœbe Hyde, daughter of Samuel and Jane (Lee) Hyde, of Norwich, Conn. Edmund Dorr was sixth son of Edward and Elizabeth (Hawley) Dorr. Edward Dorr, born in the west of England, 1648, is supposed to be the progenitor of all the Dorrs of New England. Samuel Hyde was the eldest son of William Hyde; both were of the thirty-five original proprietors of Norwich. Matthew Griswold was the eldest son of Matthew Griswold and Anna Wolcott, of Lyme. Matthew, the first, was an assistant of the colony, and a man of mark in the community. Mary (Griswold) Dorr was the aunt of Governor Matthew Griswold. "George Griffin was a man of strong mental ability, of rare judgment and decided character. He endeavored to develop the mental powers of his children."—*Sprague's Memoirs of Rev. E. D. Griffin.* Eve (Dorr) Griffin died April 3, 1804. George Griffin died August 6, 1804. They had three sons and five daughters. The daughters married into the families of Jewett, Beckwith, Lord, Welles and Austin, well known names in Connecticut. The eldest son, Colonel Josiah Griffin, born June 7, 1765, was also judge of the county court, and for several years a legislator of his native state. He "was a man of commanding presence, dignified mien and strong intellect, of rare judgment and taste for mental culture, a man of prominence in the community. It is said of him that he was scarcely less gifted than his more distinguished brothers." His descendants live at East Haddam. The second son, Rev. Dr. Edward Dorr Griffin, born January 6, 1770, graduated at Yale College in 1790. He married, May 17, 1796, Frances Huntington, niece and adopted daughter of Governor Samuel Huntington, of Norwich, and sister of Governor Samuel Huntington, of Ohio. Dr. Griffin was one of the most eloquent and effective preachers of the day, was professor of pulpit eloquence at Andover, pastor of the Old South church, Boston, and for fifteen years president of Williams College. Dr. Griffin died November 8, 1837. He had no sons, but two daughters—Frances Louisa, a poetess, married Dr. Lyndon A. Smith, of Newark, N. J., and left descendants. Ellen married the Rev. Dr. Crawford, and also left descendants. The third son, and youngest child of George Griffin and Eve (Dorr) Griffin, was George Griffin, born at East Haddam, Conn., January 14, 1778. He graduated from Yale College in 1797, studied law with Noah B. Benedict, at Woodbury, Conn., for six months, and then entered Judge Reeve's law school at Litchfield, Conn., where he was admitted to the bar in December, 1799. He removed to this city in the summer of 1800, and practiced here until 1806. He married, July 3, 1801, Lydia, daughter of Colonel Zebulon Butler. (See page 326). The immediate cause of Mr. Griffin's leaving Wilkes-Barre was the perpetration of a practical joke upon him by electing him high constable at the first election under the borough charter of Wilkes-Barre. He removed from here to the city of New York, where he became a very eminent lawyer. It is related of him, that after he was settled in that city he was engaged for the plaintiff in the trial of a slander suit growing out of an altercation over a game of cards. Not very much had been said by the defendant, but Mr. Griffin opened his argument to the jury with the proverb, "the constant falling of the water drop will wear away the hardest stone," and from this he proceeded to argue that, though the words spoken did not at first blush seem injurious, yet the frequent repetition of what the defendant was responsible for setting in motion, was calculated to undermine the fairest reputation in any community. The verdict was for $5000, which the plaintiff gave Mr. Griffin as his fee, and from that time forward his reputation was made. The trial of Goodwin, for killing James Staughton, was one of the occasions in which Mr. Griffin's forensic eloquence shone forth with peculiar splendor. The case was tried at New York in 1820. It was one of all absorbing interest in the city, occupying an entire week. Mr. Griffin's address to the jury was, without doubt, one of the great legal speeches which have rendered the New

York city bar so distinguished before the nation. He closed his speech in the following language: "The siren voice of pity has been sounded in your ears in behalf of the prisoner's youth, and you have been invoked, as you value your own salvation, to temper justice with mercy. Mercy is indeed a heavenly attribute—it is the very attribute of the Godhead to which erring mortals will cling in that day of retribution, when we must all appear before the judgment seat, not as judges, or jurors, or counsel, but to await our final sentence. Nor is this favorite of the skies a stranger to our jurisprudence. Our constitution has provided a place for it to dwell, even the mercy seat of the executive. But jurors may not, must not tamper with it; an oath enjoins them to forbear. It is chiefly because the law knows that jurors have compassionate and erring hearts, that it fortifies them by an oath compelling them to lay their hands upon the word of life and to call upon God to help them as they decide according to the law and evidence. Awful alternative, cleaving unto or renouncing the *help of God*. And yet, gentlemen, this oath, with all its sanctions, rests upon your souls."

He was in full practice in New York for fifty-two years. He received the degree of LL. D. from Columbia College in 1837. He was "a profound scholar in every department of literature and science, but he was above all things a lawyer." He died at his residence, 15 West Twentieth street, New York, May 6, 1860. His wife died May 1, 1864. They are buried in the "Marble cemetery," between First and Second streets and First and Second avenues, New York. He died of a softening of the brain, ending in paralysis, and superinduced, thought the celebrated Dr. Delafield, by a complete cessation from all mental labor. He stopped the machine too quickly. Just before retiring from active practice he published two religious works—"The Gospel Its Own Advocate," (New York, Harpers, 1850), and "The Sufferings of Christ," (New York, Harpers, 1852). He was seventy-four years old when the former book issued from the press. All the courts of New York city and the Supreme Court adjourned out of respect to his memory, and he was eulogized by famous lawyers. Judge Hoffman, of the Supreme Court, said: "He was, both in professional and private life, a gentleman of the highest and purest character." Justice Woodruff, of the same court, made similar remarks. In seconding the motion for an adjournment of the Supreme Court, Mr. David Dudley Field termed him "the Nestor of our bar; eloquent, learned and painstaking." Others, in newspaper editorials and sketches, said: "Removing to New York in 1806, he rose at once to a distinguished position in the profession, and divided forensic honors with such men as Colden, Emmett, Ogden, Hoffman and Wells. Possessed of a well-stored and highly-cultivated mind, great powers of analysis, untiring energy of purpose and industry, a gift of eloquence excelled by few, a tall, commanding figure and polished manner—he won the respect of opponents and the admiration of friends. In his successful career he acquired a handsome competency, and always dispensed his charities with a liberal hand. Few men have ever succeeded in using more conscientiously the gifts of intellect." (New York *Herald*, May 7, 1860.) James W. Gerard, who studied in his office, wrote the obituary which appeared in the *Journal of Commerce;* Henry Alexander that in the *Post.* Some of his speeches have been published in books, from which school boys get speeches. The "National Orator" contains his celebrated speech for the plaintiff in the slander case of Livingston vs. Cheetham. He wrote (but by the law of courts martial the defendant himself spoke it) the defense of Captain (afterwards Commodore) A. S. Mackenzie, tried at the Brooklyn navy yard in 1843 for the hanging of Midshipman Spencer, and others, for the celebrated mutiny on board the United States brig "Somers." George Griffin was six feet two and a half inches in height—*almost* as tall as either of his two brothers, each of whom exceeded six feet three inches, and well proportioned. His head was of rare intellectual beauty. George and Lydia (Butler) Griffin had children, viz:

1. Francis, born November 26, 1802, at Wilkes-Barre.
2. Edmund Dorr, born September 10, 1804, at Wilkes Barre.
3. Ellen, born February 15, 1807; died December 9, 1823, at New York, unmarried.
4. Caroline Ann, born May 7, 1809; died April 23, 1810, at New York, unmarried.
5. George, born February 25, 1811, at New York.
6. Charles Alexander, born November 8, 1814, at New York.

7. Caroline Lydia, born March 1, 1820; died May 10, 1861, at New York, unmarried.

8. Ellen Ann, born February 6, 1826; died November 30, 1831, at New York.

I. Francis Griffin graduated at Yale College 1820, studied law with his father and was admitted to practice at New York in 1823. He married, November 29, 1829, Mary I. Sands, born April 17, 1804, daughter of Joseph and Theresa Sands, of Sand's Point, N. Y. He became a prominent and very popular lawyer. At his death eulogies were pronounced by William Kent, F. B. Cutting, John Van Buren, J. W. Gerard, J. J. Roosevelt, and others. He was "of honorable standing, unsullied integrity, and distinguished attainments, endeared to us by his manly deportment, generous nature and kindly sympathies." He died at New York January 12, 1852. Mary (Sands) Griffin died at Dresden, Saxony, March 9, 1888. She had printed, for private distribution, several volumes of novels and tales, at Dresden. She endowed liberally an orphan asylum in that city. They had children:

1. Theresa, born at New York July 27, 1832; married, June 3, 1850, Egbert L. Vielé, born at Waterford, N. Y., June 17, 1825, and educated at West Point. He was brigadier general of United States volunteers during the civil war, 1861-5. They have several children. She lives at Paris. Her son Francis, educated there, is a rising member of the Parisian bar. Another son, Herman, is a civil engineer in New York city. Mrs. Vielé published "Following the Drum" in 1858. It is a sketch of her garrison life in Texas.

2. Edmund Dorr, born in New York May 27, 1833; educated at Bonn and Heidelberg, Germany; became a lawyer in New York; married, April 3, 1853, Lillie Hicks, of Flushing, L. I. He died April 22, 1864, at New Rochelle, N. Y. They have children living in New York, one son a lawyer and one a physician. Edmund Dorr left poems of merit in manuscript.

3. Emily Seaton, born at New York October 2, 1836; married, February 27, 1857, at Dresden, Saxony, Karl Emil von Lengwicke, an officer of the Saxon army. He distinguished himself in the Prusso-Austrian and Franco-Prussian wars. They had several children; all died in childhood.

4. Charles Ferdinand, born at New York April 25, 1838; educated at Bonn and Carlsruhe, Germany; became a civil engineer in New York city. His health failing, he went again to Europe, and died, unmarried, October 26, 1864, at Vienna, Austria, where he is buried.

II. Edmund Dorr Griffin graduated with the highest honors of his class, at Columbia College in 1821, aged seventeen; graduated at the Theological Seminary of New York in 1825; became an Episcopal clergyman; travelled extensively in Europe; was a poet, and at the time of his early death, at New York, September 1, 1830, was professor of belles lettres at Columbia College. He was a very brilliant man, and was called the handsomest man in New York. His head resembled that of Byron in intellectual beauty, but he was six feet in height and exceedingly well made. His literary "Remains" were published by his brother Francis (two volumes, 8vo, New York, Carvill, 1831).

V. George Griffin graduated at Williams College 1834; entered no profession, and lived at Kaatskill, N. Y.; married, first, April 2, 1834, Anne Augusta, daughter of James Neilson and Malvina (Forman) Neilson, of New Brunswick, N. J. She died at Kaatskill March 20, 1841. He then married, May 20, 1845, Mary Augusta, daughter of Judge Apollos Cooke, of Kaatskill. She died there August 19, 1848. He then married, October 14, 1851, Elizabeth Frances, daughter of Abraham Benson, of Fairfield, Conn. He died at Kaatskill in 1880. She is living (1889) at Elizabeth, N. J. He had children by all three wives. The sons now living are lawyers, physicians and merchants in New York city.

VI. Charles Alexander Griffin graduated at Williams College in 1833, and at the Yale Law School in 1835; married, October 26, 1836, Pastora Jacoba DeForest, third daughter of David Curtis DeForest and Julia (Wooster) DeForest, of New Haven, Conn. Pastora J. (DeForest) Griffin was born December 25, 1815, at Buenos Ayres, South America. Julia Wooster was born at Huntington, Conn., and was of the same family as Admiral Wooster and General Wooster. David C. DeForest was a descendant of an ancient French Walloon family of Hainault. Early in the seventeenth century Jesse DeForest, of Leyden, had been the originator of a scheme of colonization in America. He died ——. Henry and Isaac DeForest, his sons, and Dr. Jaen La Montague, his son-in-law, were the leaders of the first Walloon colony at New Amsterdam, in 1636. Henry and Isaac DeForest were founders of Harlem, now part of New York city. Isaac DeForest married, at New Amsterdam, 1641, Sarah, daughter of Phillippe de Trieux (Truax) and Susanne de Cheney. David C. DeForest, fifth in descent from Isaac, was born 1774. In early life he went to Buenos Ayres, South America; became a prominent and successful merchant; returned to New Haven and built what was then the finest house there; was consul-general of Buenos Ayres in this country; established the "DeForest fund" and the prize known as the "DeForest medal" at Yale College; died February 22, 1822.

Charles Alexander Griffin lived in New York and at New Brighton, N. Y., and practiced law in New York city. He cared more for literature than for law, and though he published very little, left a mass of manuscript, consisting of poems, and the results of historical research. Charles Alexander Griffin died at New Brighton, N. Y., October 6, 1859. Pastora J. (DeForest) Griffin is living (1889) at New Haven, Conn. They had children:

1. George Butler Griffin, born at New York September 8, 1840.

2. Ellen Anne Griffin, born at New York September 19, 1842, living (1889), unmarried.

3. Caroline Lydia Griffin, her twin sister, died December 7, 1844.

4. Charles DeForest Griffin, born at New York September 17, 1844; died at Clifton Springs, N. Y., July 8, 1863, unmarried.

All these were born at 74 Leonard street, New York city.

1. George Butler Griffin graduated at Columbia College 1857; became a civil engineer; in 1857–8 went in the United States expedition for a ship-canal survey at the south end of the Isthmus of Darien, under the late Captain T. A. M. Craven, U. S. N. In 1858–59 was assistant engineer on the Tehuantepec railway surveys. After his father's death he studied law at Yale Law School and the University of Albany; was admitted at May (13th) term of the Supreme Court of New York, at Albany, 1861; married, No-

vember 26, 1861, Sara (born March 11, 1841) daughter of Judge James Edwards and Susan (Tabor) Edwards, of Albany; practiced at Davenport, Iowa; returned to Albany. Had two children— Llewellyn Edwards Griffin, born at Davenport, September 5, 1862, and Edmund Dorr Griffin, born at Albany, in 1864. Her health failing, he removed to St. Paul, Minn. She died there March 19, 1866, and the youngest child soon afterwards. Llewellyn E. had died in Albany in 1864. He remained in Minnesota a year, hunting and fishing; had not practiced law since leaving Davenport. In 1865–6 became chief of field-work of the United States survey of the Illinois river for a ship canal. In 1867 he went to the republic of Colombia, South America; became chief of engineers (lieutenant colonel) in their service; resigned, and in 1869 became chief engineer of Buenaventura and Cali railroad, and soon after chief engineer of state of Antioquia; resigned in 1874 and made a visit to the United States; returned to Colombia and became a planter at Palmira, in the Cauca valley; took part in a revolution in 1876, and was exiled and his property seized; went to San Francisco January 27, 1877, and became an assistant to Mr. H. H. Bancroft in the preparation of historical works for the press. In 1880 he visited Europe. In the autumn of that year he accompanied the late Mr. J. B. Eads to Mexico as his chief of staff, and aided in obtaining the concession for the Tehuantepec ship-railway. In 1881 he located the Atlantic and Pacific railway across the Mojave desert, in California. In 1882 he was admitted to the bar of California at Los Angeles, where he now resides. He gives his exclusive attention to land titles. October 26, 1870, he married, at Buga, United States of Colombia (*by proxy*), Eva Guadalupe, born at Palmira, in that republic, December 12, 1850, third daughter of Manuel Maria Garcia de la Plaza, doctor of civil law, and Maria Engracia Gil de Tejada, his wife. His children are:

1. Eva Rosa, born at Medellin, state of Antioquia, United States of Colombia, June 19, 1872.

2. Pastora Engracia, born at same place, May 29, 1874.

3. Helena Maria, born at Palmira, state of Cauca, United States of Colombia, May 19, 1876.

4. Georgina Lydia, born at San Francisco, California, April 23, 1878.

5. Francisca Julia, born at San Francisco, California, April 30, 1880; died at Los Angeles, Cal., November 26, 1881.
6. Jasper, born at Los Angeles, Cal., June 26, 1883.
7. Clementina Ruth, born at Los Angeles, Cal., September 7, 1886.
8. Carolina Alma DeForest, born at Los Angeles, Cal., February 25, 1889.

THOMAS DYER.

Thomas Dyer, who was admitted to the bar of Luzerne county, Pa., in 1802, was a descendant of Thomas Dyer, a native of Weymouth, Massachusetts, who settled in Windham, Conn., about 1715. He married Lydia, a daughter of John Backus, gathered a good estate, was a deputy to the general assembly in several sessions, and major of a Windham county regiment. His only son, Eliphalet Dyer, grandfather of the subject of our sketch, born in Windham, September 14, 1721, was sent to Yale College and graduated in 1740, studied law and began practice in his native town. On May 9, 1745, he married Huldah Bowen, a daughter of Colonel Jabez Bowen, of Providence, R. I. He was chosen deputy to the general assembly in 1747, and again in 1752, but his real entry to public life was through his connection with the project of establishing a Connecticut colony in the valley of the Susquehanna. Mr. Dyer was an active and influential promoter of this enterprise; an original member of the Susquehanna Company, formed in 1753, one of the committee to purchase the Indian title to the land selected for the proposed colony at Wyoming, and one of the company's agents to petition the general assembly in 1755 for permission to settle on these lands, which were then believed to be within the chartered limits of Connecticut. The operations of the Susquehanna Company were interrupted by the war with France. In 1755 Mr. Dyer was appointed lieutenant colonel of one of the regiments sent by Connecticut to assist in the reduction of Crown Point, and in 1758 he was made colonel of a regiment in the expedition against Canada. In 1759 and 1760 he was a member of the general assembly, and in 1762 was elected an Assistant (or member of the Upper House), and was continued in that office by annual reëlection until 1784. In 1763 Colonel Dyer went to England as the agent of the Susquehanna Company to solicit from the crown a confirmation of their title to the tract purchased of the Indians at Wyoming, and permission to settle a colony there. The application was resisted by Pennsylvania and was still pending when war broke out between Great Britain and her American colonies. In 1765 he was appointed one (the first named) of the delegates from Connecticut to the "Stamp Act Congress" at New York—"the first great step toward Independence." Through the ten years' struggle against the exactions of Great Britain to the actual outbreak of the revolution, Colonel Dyer never wavered in his devotion to the popular cause. When the Connecticut Committee of Correspondence met at New London, July 13, 1774, authorized by the general assembly to appoint delegates to the congress at Philadelphia, their first choice fell upon Colonel Dyer, and he unhesitatingly accepted the appointment. He was present at the opening of the congress, September 5, and was a member of the committee on the rights of the colonies, appointed on September 7. He was reëlected to the congress of 1775, and to each succeeding congress till 1783, except those of 1776 and 1779. In the spring of 1775 he was named one of the "Council of Safety," to assist the governor in the management of all public affairs when the general assembly was not in session, and the journals of this body show that he was continually employed in arduous duties and in the discharge of important trusts. He had been appointed a judge of the superior court in 1766, and retained his seat on the bench until 1793, becoming chief judge in 1789. In 1787 Yale College conferred on him the honorary degree of doctor of laws. He appeared as one of the agents for Connecticut before the court of commissioners appointed by congress to finally determine the controversy with Pennsylvania respecting the Susquehanna lands, at the hearing at Trenton, in November, 1782. After his resignation of the office of chief judge he retired from public life. He died at Windham May 13,

1807, aged 86 years. Yale gave him the degree of D. D. in 1777. John Adams said of him: "Dyer is long winded and roundabout, obscure and cloudy, very talkative and very tedious, yet an honest, worthy man; means and judges well." Major Thomas Dyer, an officer of the revolutionary war, was the son of Eliphalet Dyer, who was the father of Thomas Dyer, of the Luzerne bar, who was born at Windham, Conn., in 1771, and died at Wilkes-Barre September 21, 1861. He was appointed a justice of the peace in 1806, and held the office over forty-five years. He was one of the trustees of the Wilkes-Barre Academy from 1807 to 1838, and for seven years was its president. In 1811 he was treasurer of the county of Luzerne. He first visited this valley in 1797, remaining only a short time, but again he returned and located himself permanently in Wilkes-Barre in 1800. At that time he was nearly twenty years of age, and commenced his active duties in this place by taking charge of the academy, pursuing the study of the law at the same time. Familiarly known among lawyers as the chief justice, he was often, from his great experience, consulted by his brother justices and even by judges on the bench, for his practice under and construction of the act of 1810 and its supplements. There were in those days no Binn's or McKinney's justice to appeal to, and the *ipse dixit* of Squire Dyer upon such questions was regarded as safe and reliable authority. His duties as a justice prevented his giving much attention to the *practice* of the law, yet he was a sound and thoroughly read lawyer. Abstruse questions in legal science delighted him much, and no one could give him greater pleasure than the suggestion of *questio vexata* or a disputed point which would require investigation and search in the books. Fearne, on Contingent Remainders, was more interesting to him than the newest novel or the light production of some celebrated writer is to an ordinary reader. He had no taste for works of mere imagination, and as to fiction, we doubt if he ever thought of it, except in connection with the legal inventions and forms connected with common recoveries or feigned issues. He was rather a terror to the young law student under examination who, with forwardness or want of becoming modesty, threw down the gauntlet for his opposition; but to modest and diffident worth, which showed an honest inquiry after knowledge, the kindness of his heart opened with great satisfaction the gathered stores of his own acquirements. The polemic or theologian too who in the days of his prime rashly attacked him on doctrinal or disputed questions found him a ready combatant, an able disputant, and one from whom in such a contest he would not often escape unscathed. Bred in the school of the Puritans, he was ever a reader of the book of books —the Holy Bible ; familiar with every part of it, its moral lessons and its holy truths were always weapons of his argument. Sometimes when citizens came to consult him on questions of man's law of perhaps doubtful morality, he did not hesitate to answer by another significant question—" What says the law of God ?" Mr. Dyer had no children. He married late in life the widow of the late Silas Jackson of this city, who preceded him into the land of spirits about twelve years. He departed from among us full of years, and has left behind him the name of an honest, worthy, and excellent citizen.

JOHN EVANS.

John Evans was admitted to the Luzerne county, Pa., bar as early as 1804. He resided here and probably practiced his profession until about 1816. He purchased, May 3, 1810, of James Thompson, "two certain quarries or beds of stone coal" in Pittston township, under one hundred and twenty-six acres of land, for the sum of eight hundred dollars. This shows that he was far ahead of his day in estimating the value of coal. We have been unable to ascertain anything of his family.

By the act of February 24, 1806, entitled "An Act to alter the judiciary system of the Commonwealth," the state was redistricted and several new districts were created. Among these was the eighth, composed of the counties of Luzerne, Lycoming and Northumberland. The governor was directed to appoint a president in each of the new districts created by the act. Section 15 of the same act provided "That if a vacancy shall hereafter happen in any county at present organized, by the death, resignation or removal of any associate judge or otherwise, the governor shall not supply the same unless the number of associates shall be thereby reduced to less than two, in which case, or in any case of any county hereafter organized, he shall commission so many as will complete that number in each county and no more." The first court held in Luzerne after the passage of the foregoing act was April term, 1806, and was presided over by Thomas Cooper as president judge.

THOMAS COOPER.

Thomas Cooper was admitted to the Luzerne county, Pa., bar in 1796, and appointed president judge of the eighth judicial district March 1, 1806. He was born in London, England, October 22, 1759. He was early sent to Oxford, where he thoroughly studied the classics, though the bent of his mind was toward the natural sciences. While studying law he extended his researches into anatomy and medicine. He was admitted to the bar and travelled a circuit for a few years; but entering into the political agitations of the period, he was sent, in company with Mr. Watt, the inventor of the steam engine, by the democratic clubs of England to the affiliated clubs in France. In this latter country he took part with the Girondists, but perceiving their inevitable downfall, escaped to England. For this journey he and his friend Mr. Watt were called to account by Mr. Burke in the house of commons, which led to a violent pamphlet from Mr. Cooper. His publisher, proposing to put it in a cheaper form for general circulation, received a note from Sir John Scott, attorney general, informing him that, although there was no exception to be taken to his pamphlet when in the hands of the upper class, yet the government would not allow it to appear in a shape to insure its circulation among the people. While in France he had learned the secret of making chlorine from common salt, and he now became a bleacher and calico printer in Manchester, but his business was unsuccessful. He came to America in 1793, whither his friend Priestley had already emigrated, and established himself at Northumberland, Pa., as a lawyer. But the politics of this country was also attractive to him, and uniting with the democrats, he opposed with vivacity the administration of John Adams. For a violent attack on Adams in a Pennsylvania newspaper in 1799 he was tried for a libel under the sedition act of 1800, and sentenced to six months' imprisonment and a fine of $400. The democratic party coming into power, he transacted in 1806 the business of a land commissioner on the part of the state with such energy as to triumph over difficulties with the Connecticut claimants in this county which had broken down two previous commissioners; but, being appointed to the office of judge of this judicial district, was exceedingly stern and severe; became obnoxious to the members of his own party, and was removed on the following, among other charges of arbitrary conduct: The first charge against him was fining persons and immuring them in prison for whispering in court. Cooper's reply was: "One Hollister, a constable, was merely given in custody of the sheriff one hour, until the disposal of a case, and then fined two dollars." This was in Wilkes-Barre in 1807. The next week Mr. Hollister published a communication in the *Federalist* in which he denounced Judge Cooper as an English tyrant, and called on the people to unite against him to secure his removal and the appointment of an American judge. The third charge against him was: "After sentencing a felon, calling him from prison and pronouncing a second sentence, increasing the penalty." This referred to the case of young Gough, a horse thief, convicted at Wilkes-Barre. The court sentenced him to twelve months, he having plead guilty. The next morning Judges Hollenback and Fell informed Judge Cooper they had understood he was an old offender. "I gave it as my opinion," says Judge Cooper, "that during the sessions the judgments were in the power of the court and subject to revisal. He was re-sentenced to three years." The committee to investigate the charges met March 7, 1811. John B. Gibson, subsequently Judge Gibson, was one of the committee. After the examination of many witnesses the committee reported that the judge's "conduct had been arbitrary, unjust and precipitate," and in favor of an address to the governor for his removal. More than two-thirds of the legislature voted for his removal, and he was accordingly superseded by the governor on April 2, 1811. Judge Wilson, of Northumberland county, said that "the court was very disorderly before Judge Cooper's time. I have seen Judge Rush leave the bench. It is now very orderly." The late George W. Woodward used to relate that when Judge Burnside held his first court in Clearfield county the people crowded in among the lawyers and in front of the bench. An indictment was brought in against one Pennington. The judge called out, "Is Pennington in court?" A stalwart man standing in front of the crowd said: "Jedge, you better call out the whole damn grist of the Penningtons." The judge put on a severe look and commenced a lecture to the man for disturbing the court. After he proceeded for awhile the man said: "Hush up, jedge, you are making a damned sight more disturbance than I did." Subsequently Judge Cooper successively occupied the chair of chemistry in Dickinson College, in the University of Pennsylvania, and in Columbia College, South Carolina, of which last institution he became president in 1820, and in which he discharged also the duties of professor of chemistry and of political economy. On his retirement in 1834, the revision of the statutes of the state was confided to him, and he died in the performance of this duty, May 11, 1840, at Columbia, S. C. Mr. Cooper was alike eminent for the versatility of his talent and the extent of his knowledge. He published, in 1794, in London, a volume of "Information Concerning America;" in 1800, a collection of "Political Essays," reprinted from a Pennsylvania newspaper; in 1812, in Philadelphia, a translation of the "Institutes of Justinian;" in 1819, a work on "Medical Jurisprudence;" in 1812–14, two of the five volumes entitled the "Emporium of Arts and Sciences," which were published in Philadelphia; and in 1826, at Charleston, South Carolina, his academic "Lectures on the Elements of Political Economy." He was a vigorous pamphleteer in various political contests, and an admirable conversationalist. In philosophy he was a materialist, and in religion a Unitarian.

WASHINGTON LEE.

Washington Lee, who was admitted to the bar of Luzerne county, Pa., April 25, 1806, was born in Harrisburg, Pa., June 18, 1786. His father, Andrew Lee, captain of dragoons in the army of the revolution, and one of the band celebrated in Pennsylvania history as the "Paxtang Boys," had served his country with some distinction under General Sullivan, and had even been permitted to see the interior of one of the British prison hulks in New York harbor, famous then, as now, as "floating hells." The captain survived the horrors which were fatal to so many of his comrades, and being finally exchanged, hastened home to Paxtang, Pa., to recruit his shattered health. Before the close of the year, however, Cornwallis had surrendered. Great Britain saw the futility of her efforts to retain these colonies and finally, September 3, 1783, signed with her late rebellious subjects a definitive treaty of peace. With this conclusion Captain Lee found his occupation gone, and taking unto himself a wife in the person of Mrs. Priscilla Stewart (*nee* Espy), the widow of James Stewart, he moved to Harrisburg, purchased a well known inn there, and prepared to entertain the travelling public. In this house was born Washington Lee and his brother James S. Lee. James S. in after years moved to Hanover township, in this county. Washington Lee, after attending school at Harrisburg, entered the law office of George Fisher, a prominent practitioner of that place, and on March 3, 1806, was duly admitted to practice law in the courts of Dauphin county. He had determined, however, that a military career would be more to his tastes, and he early sought the influence of his friends to aid him in gaining a position in the army. A staunch friend of his father, Hon. John Joseph Henry, was then presiding on the bench of Dauphin county, and from him he readily secured a commendatory letter to Henry Dearborn, the secretary of war. By the same influence he also enlisted Hon. Andrew Gregg, United States senator from Pennsylvania, in his service, and May 3, 1808, he rejoiced in the receipt of his commission as second lieutenant in the army of the United States, and a letter from the war department ordering him to report at the rendezvous at Lancaster. In compliance with this order he hastened to his post and immediately entered upon the performance of his duties. From this date until that of his retirement from the service, eight years later, his career was one unbroken series of successes. He was commissioned first lieutenant of the fifth regiment of infantry April 1, 1811. He had already served as judge advocate of the southern army, under General Wade Hampton, since February 19, 1810, and continued so to act until appointed assistant adjutant general, June 24, 1812. On July 23 following, he was commissioned captain, and March 3, 1813, received his majority. In June of this year he was appointed deputy postmaster general of the United States forces, and he received his commission as lieutenant colonel of the eleventh infantry January 1, 1815. On May 3, 1816, Colonel Lee withdrew from the military service, and on June 16, 1817, he married Elizabeth Campbell, the daughter of an episcopal minister, residing in Carlisle, Pa. The young couple immediately removed to Nanticoke, Pa., where Colonel Lee had purchased a farm of about one thousand acres. This land he afterwards sold for one million two hundred thousand dollars. Here in a comfortable mansion erected on the east bank of the Susquehanna river, at the very foot of the valley of Wyoming, they began, passed and ended a half century of wedded life. In December, 1867, just fifty years from the date of her first acquaintance with the old homestead, Mrs. Lee died childless. Her husband, full of years and feeble in health, bore with his loneliness until May, 1869, when, at the urgent solicitation of his friends, he removed to Wilkes-Barre. Here two years later, September 10, 1871, ready and willing, he peacefully breathed his last. In person Colonel Lee was tall and of dignified presence. His gentle manners and courtly bearing greatly endeared him to all who possessed his acquaintance. His habits were of the strictest simplicity. His mind had always been of a studious character, and in the later years of his life he found refuge from his isolation in his acquaintance with the philosophy and classics of the ancients. He was the impersonation of integrity and rectitude. He possessed his faculties to the very end, and with the utmost composure saw the approach of that messenger from whose coming old and young alike shrink with dread.

FRANCIS McSHANE.

Francis McShane, who was admitted to the Philadelphia bar March 1, 1802, was admitted to the Luzerne county bar, Pa., August 8, 1810. He was a native of Philadelphia, where he was born in 1779, and was a son of Barnabas McShane, of Philadelphia. In 1811 he erected a small cut-nail manufactory in Wilkes-Barre, and used anthracite coal in smelting the iron. He conducted a successful business for two or three years, selling nails by wholesale or retail, to suit purchasers. On January 18, 1813, he was appointed a justice of the peace for the townships of Hanover, Newport and Wilkes-Barre. His wife was Frances Bulkeley, daughter of Eliphalet Bulkeley, a native of Colchester, Conn. (For further particulars regarding the Bulkeley family see page 287.) Mr. McShane died in 1815, and his widow subsequently married Colonel Henry F. Lamb. Mr. McShane left no children. Hon. Robert McShane, who died at Pointe Coupee, La., October 18, 1811, was judge of that parish. He was a brother of Francis McShane, and was born in Philadelphia in 1780. He was admitted to the bar there December 26, 1803.

Judge Cooper was succeeded by Seth Chapman, who took his seat, and first held court in Luzerne at August term, 1811. He continued to preside in the county until 1813. The last term of court at which he presided in Luzerne was April term, 1813.

SETH CHAPMAN.

Seth Chapman, the third president judge of Luzerne county, Pa., held his first court in Wilkes-Barre at the August term, 1811. His letter of acceptance is as follows:

NEWTOWN, July 16th, 1811.
SIR: I this day received yours of the 11th inst., inclosing a commission from the Governor of President Judge of the Court

of Common Pleas of the Eighth district of Pennsylvania, and in answer beg you will please to inform his Excellency, the Governor, that I sincerely thank him for the good opinion he has been pleased to entertain of me, and that I accept the commission with great diffidence, fearing that my abilities are not competent for the performance of the duties of so delicate and important an office upon my part. Integrity, industry and impartiality shall not be wanting, but that I shall sometimes err in the decision of law questions must be expected, as it has been the lot of all human Judges.

I am respectfully your obedient servant,
James Trimble, Esq.   S. CHAPMAN.

His district embraced the counties of Luzerne, Lycoming and Northumberland, and subsequently Union county. He was the son of John Chapman, M. D., and was born in Wrightstown, Bucks county, Pa., January 23, 1771. He was a lineal descendant of the "first settler," John Chapman, who came from the town of Stannah, in Yorkshire, England, and took up his residence in the woods of Wrightstown, Pa. Being a staunch Friend, and having suffered numerous persecutions for opinion's sake, including loss of property, he resolved to find a new home in the wilds of Pennsylvania. Leaving home June 21, 1684, he sailed from Aberdeen, Scotland, and reached Wrightstown sometime toward the close of December. Until he was able to build a log house, he and his family lived in a cave, where twin sons were born February 12, 1685. Game from the woods supplied them with food until crops were grown, and often the Indians, between whom and the Chapmans there was the most cordial friendship, were the only reliance. A stone erected at his grave bore the following inscription:

> Behold John Chapman, that Christian man, who first began
>   To settle in this town;
> From worldly cares and doubtful fears, and Satan's snares,
>   Is here laid down;
> His soul doth rise above the skies in Paradise,
>   There to wear a lasting crown.

Judge Chapman received his early education at a school in Upper Makefield township, in his native county. At an early age he removed to Norristown, Pa., and was there admitted to the bar at September term, 1791. After his appointment as judge by

Governor Snyder, he removed to the town of Northumberland, where he continued to reside until 1833, when he resigned his seat on the bench. An effort was made to impeach him for misdemeanor in office in 1826, but he was acquitted by the senate, twenty-six senators voting not guilty, five voting guilty. At the time Judge Chapman took his seat Judge Cooper caused to be served on him a notice that if he should presume to exercise the duties of president judge he (Cooper) would make application to the Supreme Court for a writ of *quo warranto*. Accompanying this notice was an elaborate argument contending that the whole proceedings of the legislature and governor in removing him were unconstitutional, and as a consequence the commission of Judge Chapman was absolutely void and of no validity. There is little in the term of service of Judge Chapman worth noting. The members of the bar, as well as suitors and the public, soon made the discovery that Judge Cooper was not on the bench. He could not be reckoned a talented man, and was a judge of inferior abilities, lacking courage and firmness, besides being indolent. The people of Luzerne soon found that they had made a losing bargain by the exchange of Cooper for Chapman. Judge Chapman presided in this county until 1813, and was succeeded by John Bannister Gibson.

GARRICK MALLERY.

Garrick Mallery, who was admitted to the bar of Luzerne county, Pa., August 8, 1811, was born in Middlebury, Conn., April 17, 1784, and died in Philadelphia, Pa., July 6, 1866. He was of unmixed descent from the early English settlers of New England, being in direct line from Peter Mallery, who arrived in Boston in 1638 and went to New Haven settlements with Rev. Theophilus Eaton's company in 1644. Through his mother, Hannah Minor, he was in direct descent from Thomas Minor, who was a member of John Winthrop's company in 1630. Several of his ancestors were military officers in the colonial service and in the revolutionary war. He graduated at Yale College in 1808, and after a term at Litchfield Law School read law in Wilkes-Barre, Pa., with Judge Welles. He was elected from Luzerne county to the legislature of Pennsylvania in the years 1826, 1827, 1828, and 1829, being distinguished for promoting the internal improvement and establishing the prison discipline systems of this state. From 1811 to 1832 he was one of the trustees of the Wilkes-Barre Academy. In 1831 he was appointed by Governor Wolf president judge of the third judicial district, composed of the counties of Berks, Northampton, and Lehigh, but resigned in 1836 and removed to Philadelphia, where he practiced law and for several years immediately before his death held the office of master in chancery of the Supreme Court of Pennsylvania. In 1840 Judge Mallery received the degree of LL. D. from Lafayette College. He was thrice married; first, in June 1811, at Wilkes-Barre, Pa., to Sylvina Pierce, daughter of Colonel Lord Butler, born March 5, 1874, died —— 1824, by whom he had five children, born in Wilkes-Barre, viz: Pierce Butler, born 1812, died 1838; Amelia, died in childhood; Priscilla Lee, born October 6, 1816, died April 8, 1844; Charles Bronson, born 1820, died May 6, 1848; Edward Garrick, born 1824, died May 27, 1852; all of whom died without issue except Priscilla, who at Reading, Pa., November 28, 1836, married William Strong, justice of the Supreme Court of the United States, and left two daughters, Emily Elizabeth, born February 5, 1838, who, October 14, 1874, married James M. Flanagan, of Philadelphia; and Amelia Mallery, born July 31, 1840, who in 1880 married Frank Slade, of New York city. Second, he was married June 30, 1830, at Harrisburg, Pa., to Catherine Julia, daughter of Dr. Henry Hall, born August 14, 1804, died July 17, 1832, at Reading, Pa., by whom he had one son, Garrick, born April 23, 1831, in Wilkes-Barre, now captain and brevet lieutenant colonel United States army, and ethnologist in the bureau of ethnology, living at Washington, D. C., who, April 14, 1870, at Richmond, Va., was married to Helen Marian, daughter of Rev. A. V. Wyckoff, of New Brunswick, N. J., born February 12, 1849, at Prattsville, N. Y. Third, he was married June 27, 1838, at Philadelphia, to Jeannette, daughter of Dr. John C. Otto, by whom he had four children, born in

Philadelphia, viz: Eliza, born September 23, 1839, died July 18, 1872; John Conrad, born October 21, 1843; James Dundas, born September 1, 1845, died November 24, 1869; and Isabel Augusta, born December 6, 1847, died August 7, 1855, who have all died unmarried except John C., now captain of the corps of engineers United States army, who was married at Cincinnati, Ohio, June 27, 1873, to Anna L., daughter of A. S. Winslow.

Garrick, son of Garrick, soldier and ethnologist, was born in Wilkes-Barre, Pa., April 23, 1831. Through his mother, Catharine J. Hall, he was descended from John Harris, founder of Harrisburg, Pa., and William Maclay, first United States senator from Pennsylvania. He was graduated at Yale College in 1850, in 1853 received the degree of LL. B. from the University of Pennsylvania, and the same year was admitted to the bar of Philadelphia, where he practiced law and engaged in editorial work until the first call for troops in the civil war, when he entered the volunteer service, his first commission, that of first lieutenant, dating from April 15, 1861. By subsequent promotions he rose to the rank of lieutenant colonel and brevet colonel, and at the reorganization of the regular army in 1870 was appointed captain of the First United States infantry. He was twice severely wounded and received three promotions by brevet for gallantry in action. In the reconstruction period in 1869 and 1870, being on military duty in Virginia as judge advocate on the staff of the successive generals commanding, he was appointed to both the offices of secretary of state and adjutant general of the state of Virginia, with the rank of brigadier general. In August, 1870, he was the first officer detailed by the secretary of war for duty with the chief signal officer of the army at Washington to carry into effect the then recent legislation initiating the meteorological duties of the signal service. His rank being next to that of General Myer, he was for long periods in charge of the bureau, and was its executive officer during the remainder of the time, until August, 1876, when he was ordered to the command of Fort Rice in Dakota Territory, and there made investigations into the pictographs and mythologies of the North American Indians, which led to his order on June 13, 1877, by the secretary of war, at the request of the secretary of the interior, to report to Major J. W.

Powell, then in charge of the geological survey of the Rocky
Mountain region, for duty in connection with the ethnology of
the North American Indians. In this work he has continued,
being on July 1, 1879, retired from active service on account of
wounds received in action, and thus left at liberty to accept the
appointment of ethnologist of the bureau of ethnology on its
organization at Washington in that year, which office he still
holds. General Mallery is an honorary or active member of several
scientific and literary societies in Europe, as well as in the United
States, and was a founder and president of the anthropological
society and of the Cosmos club, both of Washington. He has
contributed largely to periodical literature, but his most important
works, some of which have been translated, are the following:
"A Calendar of the Dakota Nation" (Washington, 1877); "The
Former and Present Number of our Indians" (Salem, 1878);
"Introduction to the Study of Sign Language Among the North
American Indians as Illustrating the Gesture Speech of Mankind"
(Washington, 1880); "A Collection of Gesture-Signs and Signals
of the North American Indians, with some Comparisons" (1880);
"Sign Language among North American Indians, Compared with
that Among Other Peoples and Deaf Mutes" (1881); "Pictographs of the North American Indians" (1886).

ALPHONSO C. STEWART.

Alphonso C. Stewart, who was admitted to the bar of Luzerne
county, Pa., August 8, 1812, was previously admitted to the bar
of Berks county, Pa. After his admission here he removed to
that part of Luzerne now embraced in the county of Bradford,
and at the opening of the courts of the last named county, in
January, 1813, he was present. The end of Stewart was a tragic
one. About 1817 he removed to Belleville, Ill., where for some
reason one Bennett proposed to him to fight a sham duel. The
guns were loaded by individuals who put no balls in either
weapon, but before reaching the ground selected for the duel to

take place Bennett stepped to one side and put a ball into his rifle and Stewart fell mortally wounded. Bennett made his escape but was apprehended about a year after, tried, convicted, and executed.

GEORGE DENISON.

George Denison, who was admitted to the bar of Luzerne county, Pa., April 7, 1813, was a descendant of William Denison, who was born in England about 1586, came to America in 1631 and settled in Roxbury, Mass., having with him his wife, Margaret, his three sons, Daniel, Edward and George, and John Eliot, who seems to have been a tutor in his family. Mr. Eliot became pastor of the church in Roxbury and did missionary work among the Indians. Mr. Denison was a deacon of the Roxbury church. He had been liberally educated and his sons were also carefully educated. He died in Roxbury January 25, 1653. George Denison, son of William Denison, was born in 1618, was married first in 1640 to Bridget Thompson, daughter of John Thompson, *gent*, of Preston, Northamptonshire, England, whose widow, Alice, had come to America and settled in Roxbury. The wife, Bridget, died in 1643. George Denison then went to England, served under Cromwell in the army of the Parliament, won distinction, was wounded at Naseby, was nursed at the house of John Borodell, Cork, Ireland, by his daughter Ann, was married to Ann, returned to Roxbury, and finally settled at Stonington, Conn. George Denison died in Hartford October 23, 1694, while there on some special business. His wife, Ann Borodell, died September 26, 1712, aged ninety-seven years. They were both remarkable for magnificent personal appearance and for force of mind and character. They held a foremost place in Stonington. At the time of their marriage, in 1645, she was thirty years old and he twenty-seven. He has been described as "the Myles Standish of the settlement," but he was a greater and more brilliant soldier than Standish. He had no equal in any of the colonies for conducting a war against the Indians excepting, perhaps, Captian John Mason. Miss Calkins, in her history of New London, says of him: "Our early history presents no character of bolder and more active spirit than Captain George Denison; he reminds us of the bordermen of Scotland." In emergencies he was always in demand, and he was almost constantly placed in important public positions. George Denison, son of George Denison and Ann, his wife, was born in 1653. He married Mercy Gorham, daughter of Captain John Gorham, whose wife was Desire Howland, daughter of John Howland, of the May Flower. They lived in Westerly, R. I. Joseph Denison, son of George Denison, was baptized November 14, 1683, was married February 17, 1707, to Prudence Minor, daughter of Dr. Joseph Minor. He lived and died in Stonington, Conn. Nathan Denison, son of Joseph Denison, was born February 20, 1716, was married to Ann Carey, daughter of Eleazer Carey, of Windham, Conn., where he settled. He married second, March 15, 1778, Hannah Fuller, and about the year 1800 he went to Kingston, Pa., where he died March 10, 1803. His children were all by his first wife. Colonel Nathan Denison, son of Nathan Denison, was born January 25, 1741. He emigrated to Pennsylvania in 1769, and April 1 of that year, was married to Elizabeth Sill, eldest daughter of Jabez Sill. The knot was tied in a log cabin which stood on the corner of River and South streets in this city, where the residence of Reuben J. Flick now stands, and was the first white marriage in Wyoming. Colonel Denison commanded the left wing of the patriot forces in the battle and massacre of Wyoming, July 3, 1778. The terms of capitulation were signed by him and the articles are in the following language:

WESTMORELAND, July 4th, 1778.

Capitulation made and completed between Major John Butler, on behalf of his Majesty, King George the Third, and Colonel Nathan Denniston, of the United States of America.

ART. 1. That the inhabitants of the settlement lay down their arms, and the garrisons be demolished.

2d. That the inhabitants are to occupy their farms peaceably, and the lives of the inhabitants preserved intire and unhurt.

3d. That the continental stores be delivered up.

4th. That Major Butler will use his utmost influence that the private property of the inhabitants shall be preserved intire to them.

5th. That the prisoners in Forty Fort be delivered up, and that Samuel Finch, now in Major Butler's possession, be delivered up also.

6th. That the property taken from the people called Tories, up the river, be made good, and they to remain in peaceable possession of their farms, unmolested, in a free trade in and throughout this state as far as lies in my power.

7th. That the inhabitants that Colonel Denniston now capitulates for, together with himself, do not take up arms during the present contest.

       NATHAN DENISON,
       JOHN BUTLER.

ZURAH BEECH,
SAMUEL GUSTIN,
JOHN JOHNSON,
WILLIAM CALDWELL.

Colonel Denison was a man of strong ability and character, and stood among the foremost in the region where he lived. In 1774 he was appointed a justice of the peace for the township of Westmoreland, in the colony of Connecticut, and on June 1, 1778, he was appointed one of the judges for the county of Westmoreland, in the state of Connecticut. In 1776, 1778, 1779 and 1780 he was one of the members from Westmoreland to the Connecticut assembly. He was also a member of the council or member of the Pennsylvania assembly from Luzerne county for the years 1787, 1788 and 1789; and was also appointed, August 17, 1791, one of the associate judges of Luzerne county. He died at Kingston January 25, 1809. Lazarus Denison Shoemaker, of this city, is a grandson of Colonel Nathan Denison, through his eldest daughter Elizabeth S., who married Elijah Shoemaker, jr. Judge Denison was one of the most prominent men of his day. Doctor Peck in his "History of Early Methodism," says: "Colonel Denison and his lady and three daughters became members of the Methodist church. He was a man of great influence in the county, of which sufficient proof was given by the responsible positions which he was called by his fellow citizens to fill. He was a kind hearted and ardently pious man. His house was open to the weary itinerants, and too much could scarcely be done by the family for their comfort. All the preachers made it a place of rest and refreshment, while several at different times were quartered there as a regular boarding place. The colonel died in great peace. His excellent lady survived him several years, and then followed him to the abodes of the blessed. The venerable Asbury was there several times entertained, as we learn from his journal." George Denison, third son of Colonel Nathan Denison, was born in Kingston, Pa., February 22, 1790. He was educated at the Wilkes-Barre Academy, then under the charge of Garrick Mallery. In his minority he served as the deputy of his brother, Colonel Lazarus Denison, the register and recorder of Luzerne county, and on April 30, 1812, he was himself appointed to these offices for a term of three years. From 1811 to 1814 he was clerk of the Wilkes-Barre borough council, and was for many years a member of the council, serving as its president in 1823 and 1824. In 1818 he was elected a member of the board of trustees of the Wilkes-Barre Academy, and served until his death. In 1815 he was elected to the legislature of Pennsylvania and reëlected in 1816, 1827, 1828, 1829 and 1830. He was a member of congress from 1818 to 1822. In 1824 he was appointed deputy attorney general of Pennsylvania. In 1828 he was one of the presidential electors on the Adams ticket. From May, 1829, to May, 1830, he was burgess of the borough of Wilkes-Barre. On May 30, 1816, he married Caroline Bowman, daughter of Ebenezer Bowman. (See page 1050) They had three children. His youngest son, Rev. Henry Mandevile Bowman, married Alice, daughter of President John Tyler. Mr. Denison died August 20, 1832. His wife died July 1, 1833. It is believed that all their children are now deceased.

By the act of March 24, 1812, the eleventh judicial district was formed and originally included the counties of Bradford, Susquehanna, Tioga and Wayne. The governor was directed to appoint a president of the district and two judges for each county, their jurisdiction and authority to begin after the second Tuesday in the following October. By the act of March 12, 1813, Luzerne was attached to and made part of the eleventh district; the president of said district and the associate judges of the county to hold the several courts. Under this change the first term of court was held in July 1813 and was presided over by Judge Bannister Gibson. He continued to be president judge until June, 1816, when he was commissioned one of the justices of the Supreme Court. The last term of court held by him in Luzerne as president was April term 1816.

JOHN BANNISTER GIBSON.

John Bannister Gibson, the fourth president judge of Luzerne county, Pa., was the son of Lieutenant Colonel George Gibson, a native of Lancaster, Pa., where he was born October 10, 1747. He received an academic education, entered a mercantile house in Philadelphia, and made several voyages as supercargo to the West Indies. When the revolution began he raised a company and was appointed captain in a state regiment. His soldiers were distinguished for good conduct and bravery, and were known in the army as "Gibson's Lambs." In order to obtain a supply of gunpowder he descended the Mississippi with twenty-five picked men, and after a hazardous journey succeeded in accomplishing his mission. On his return he was appointed to a command in a Virginia regiment, joined General Washington before the evacuation of New York, and was engaged in all the principal battles of the campaign of 1778. He retired to his farm in Cumberland county, Pa., after the war, and was county lieutenant until 1791, when he took command of a regiment in the St. Clair expedition against the Ohio Indians. At the battle of Miami, November 4, 1791, he received a mortal wound, and died in Fort Jefferson, Ohio, December 14, 1791.

John Bannister Gibson, who held his first court here at July term, 1813, was commissioned as president judge of the eleventh judicial district October 16, 1812. He was a native of Shearman's Valley, now in Perry county, Pa., where he was born November 8, 1780. He was educated at Dickinson College, Carlisle, Pa., read law under Thomas Duncan, afterwards judge of the Supreme Court of this state, was admitted to the bar of Cumberland county in 1803, practiced successively in Carlisle and Beaver, Pa., and in Hagerstown, Maryland; returning to Carlisle, was elected by the then republican party in 1810 and again in 1811 to the state legislature, in which he filled a prominent station, giving a zealous support to the administrations of Governor Snyder and President Madison. He was appointed president judge by Governor Snyder, and resided here until June, 1816, when he was made an associate judge of the Supreme Court of this state. On the death of Chief Justice Tilghman, in 1827, he became chief justice, and held that position until 1851. So distinguished was his ability, learning and impartiality, that, after the adoption of the amended constitution of 1838, in times of the highest and bitterest party excitement, Governor Ritner, forgetting his personal and party feelings, and looking only to the qualifications necessary for that high office, reappointed him chief justice of this commonwealth. He sat on the supreme bench with twenty-six different associates, of whom eighteen preceded him to the grave. During the long period of his judicial labors he discussed and decided innumerable questions. His opinions are found in no less than seventy volumes of reports, from 2 Sergeant & Rawle to 7 Harris. At the time of his death he had been longer in office than any contemporary judge in the world, and in some points of character he had not his equal on the earth. Such vigor, clearness and precision of thought were never before united with the same felicity of diction. Brougham has sketched Lord Stowell justly enough as the greatest judicial writer that England could boast of for force and beauty of style. He selects a sentence and calls on the reader to admire the remarkable elegance of its structure. We believe that Judge Gibson never wrote an opinion in his life from which a passage might not be taken stronger, as well as more graceful in its tone of expression, than this which is selected with so much care by a most zealous friend from all of Lord Stowell's. His written language was a transcript of his mind. It gave the world the very form and presence of his thoughts. It was accurate because he knew the exact boundaries of the principles he discussed. His style was rich, but he never turned out of his way for figures of speech. He never sacrificed sense to sound, or preferred ornament to substance. His words were always precisely adapted to the subject. He said neither more nor less than just the thing he ought. When a legal principle passed through his hands he sent it forth clothed in a dress which fitted it so exactly that nobody ever presumed to give it any other. Almost universally the syllabus of his opinion is a sentence from itself; and the most heedless student, in looking over Wharton's Digest, can select the cases in which Gibson delivered the judgment as readily as he could pick out gold coins from among coppers. For this reason it is that, though he was the least voluminous writer of the court, the citations from him at the bar are more numerous than from all the rest put together. An opinion of his was an unbroken chain of logic from beginning to end. His argumentation was always characterized by great power, and sometimes it rose into irresistible energy, dashing opposition to pieces with force like that of a battering ram. He was inflexibly honest. The judicial ermine was as unspotted when he laid it aside for the habiliments of the grave as it was when he first assumed it. Next after his wonderful intellectual endowments, the benevolence of his heart was the most marked feature of his character. His was a most genial spirit; affectionate and kind to his friends, and magnanimous to his enemies. Benefits received by him were engraved on his memory as on a tablet of brass; injuries were written in sand. He never let the sun go down upon his wrath. He lacked the quality which Dr. Johnson admired. He was *not* a good hater. His accomplishments were very extraordinary. He was a born musician, and the natural talent was highly cultivated. He was a *connoisseur* in painting and sculpture. The whole round of English literature was familiar to him. He was at home among the ancient classics. He had a perfectly clear perception of all the great truths of natural science. He had studied medicine carefully in his youth, and understood it well. His mind absorbed all kinds of knowledge with scarcely an effort.

Judge Gibson was well appreciated by his fellow citizens; not so highly as he deserved, for that was scarcely possible. But admiration of his talents and respect for his honesty were universal sentiments. This was strikingly manifested when he was elected, in 1851, with no emphatic political standing, and without manners, habits or associations calculated to make him popular beyond the circle that knew him intimately. With all these disadvantages, it is said, he narrowly escaped what might have been a dangerous distinction—a nomination on both of the opposing tickets—and was the only one of the former incumbents who was nominated by the democratic party, remaining on the bench as an associate justice until his death.

His residence in Wilkes-Barre was on Northampton street, between Franklin and Main, now occupied by Mrs. Hugh Murray, and next door to the residence of Agib Ricketts, Esq. In the hours of relaxation from the exercise of official duties and his law and literary reading, he seemed to take especial pleasure, in company with his scientific friend, the late Jacob Cist, Esq., to visit different portions of the valley, note its geological structure, particularly the extent and position of the anthracite coal deposits, then, from the praiseworthy experiments of Judge Fell and their fortunate results, just beginning to merge into importance, and also with more than common curiosity and delight to visit the remains of the ancient Indian fortifications. In one of their excursions to examine the large fortification on the farm late of James Hancock, in Plains township, they found a medal bearing on one side the impress of King George I., dated 1714, the year in which he began his reign, and on the other side the likeness of an Indian chief. He was one of the trustees of the Wilkes-Barre Academy from 1814 to 1817, two years of which time he was president.

When called to the supreme bench his departure from Wilkes-Barre was regarded with emotions of mingled pleasure and regret. All were glad at the occurrence of an event so propitious to him personally, and promising increased utility to that elevated tribunal, yet all were sorry to part with him either as a judge or citizen.

He married, in 1810, Sarah W. Galbraith, of East Pennsboro

township, Cumberland county, Pa. She was the great-granddaughter of James Galbraith (son of John Galbraith), of Scotch parentage, who was born in 1666, in the north of Ireland, from whence he emigrated in 1718, settling in Conestoga (afterwards Donegal) township, then Chester county, province of Pennsylvania. He was one of the founders of old Derry church, a man of prominence, and the head of a remarkable family. His wife was Rebecca Chambers. He died August 23, 1744. James Galbraith, son of James Galbraith, was born in 1703, in the north of Ireland. He took up a tract of land in now Derry township, Dauphin county, Pa., on Spring creek, in 1737. He became a man of note on the frontiers, and the early provincial records of Pennsylvania contain frequent reference to him; was elected sheriff of the county in 1742; for many years was one of the justices for the county of Lancaster, and served as an officer during the Indian wars, 1755–1763; towards the revolutionary period removed to Cumberland county. He married, April 6, 1734, Elizabeth Bertram, daughter of Rev. William Bertram. He died June 11, 1786, in East Pennsboro township, Cumberland county, Pa. Andrew Galbraith, son of James Galbraith, was born about 1750, in Derry township, and died about 1806, in East Pennsboro township. His wife was Barbara Kyle, daughter of John Kyle, of Donegal township, Lancaster county, Pa. These were the parents of Mrs. Gibson. Mr. and Mrs. Judge Gibson left a family of five children, two sons and three daughters. Judge Gibson died in Philadelphia May 3, 1853.

THOMAS BLEASDALE OVERTON.

Thomas Bleasdale Overton, who was admitted to the bar of Luzerne county, Pa., December 31, 1813, was a native of Manchester, England, where he was born May 21, 1791. He practiced law in this city and died at Mobile, Alabama, about 1819. He was a brother of Edward Overton, of the Luzerne bar. He married, in 1813, in this city, Anna Maria Hodkinson, a native of Honduras, who came to this country in 1791 at the age of eight years to be educated, but never returned home. Mr. and Mrs. Overton had two daughters, both of whom are now deceased. The eldest, a maiden lady, died at Towanda April 21, 1886, and the youngest, Ann Heartly, became the wife of Matthias Hollenback Laning. She died in Towanda, October 30, 1877.

CHARLES CATLIN.

Charles Catlin, the eldest son of Putman Catlin, was admitted to the bar of Luzerne county, Pa., March 28, 1814. He was born in this city March 15, 1790. In 1819 he removed to Montrose, Pa., and resided there until his death. (See page 1051.)

HENRY KING.

Henry King, whose ancestor, John King, came from Suffolk county, England, to this country about 1718, was admitted to the Luzerne county bar April 3, 1815. He was a native of Palmer, Hampden county, Massachusetts, where he was born July 6, 1790. In 1812 he moved to this city and prepared for the bar in the office of Garrick Mallery. Shortly after his admission he removed to Allentown, Pa., where he was for some time the only lawyer. In 1825 he was elected to the state senate for the term of four years, upon the expiration of which he was again elected. In 1830, before his second term expired, he was chosen a representative in congress, which position he filled from 1831 to 1835. He died at Allentown July 13, 1861. Hon. Thomas Butler King, of Georgia, was a brother of Henry King.

THOMAS MEREDITH.

Thomas Meredith, who was admitted to the bar of Luzerne county, Pa., August 3, 1816, was born in Philadelphia September 4, 1779. He was a descendent of Reese Meredith, of Philadelphia, whose wife, Martha, was a daughter of John Carpenter, of Philadelphia, and granddaughter of Samuel Carpenter, provincial treasurer and an early councillor. Samuel Meredith, son of Reese Meredith, was born in Philadelphia in 1741, and was educated at Dr. Allison's academy. He married Margaret Cadwalader, a daughter of Thomas Cadwalader, the councillor. He was a partner in business with his father and his brother-in-law, George Clymer. He enlisted as major in the third battalion of Associators in 1775. In December, 1776, he was made lieutenant colonel and afterwards participated in the battle of Princeton. As brigadier general of the Pennsylvania militia he served at Brandywine and Germantown. He resigned in 1778 and was subsequently a member of the assembly for several years, and a member of the continental congress from 1786 to 1788. At the organization of the federal government Washington appointed him treasurer of the United States. He held the office more than twelve years. The first money ever paid into the treasury was twenty thousand dollars loaned by him to the government. He subsequently loaned one hundred and forty thousand dollars. He retired after 1801 to his seat called "Belmont," near Mount Pleasant, Wayne county, Pa. He owned seventy-five thousand acres of land in Wayne county, and sixty-seven thousand acres in Luzerne, Lackawanna, and Wyoming counties, and George Clymer and himself owned altogether nearly a million of acres in Pennsylvania, New York, West Virginia, and Kentucky. He died at Belmont in 1817. Thomas Meredith was the only son of Samuel and Margaret Meredith. He studied law with John Read and was admitted to the Philadelphia bar in 1803, but in 1805 removed to his father's residence, Belmont. He was a major of Pennsylvania militia in the war of 1812. He also filled the offices of prothonotary, register of wills, and recorder of deeds for Wayne county from 1821 to 1823. He afterwards lived at Meredith cottage, in Carbondale township, in Luzerne (now Lackawanna) county. He died at Trenton, New Jersey, April 22, 1855. He married September 19, 1823, Sarah, daughter of William Gibson.

THOMAS BURNSIDE.

Thomas Burnside, the fourth president judge of Luzerne county, Pa., succeeded Judge Gibson as president of the eleventh judicial district. At a court held July 29, 1816, his commission dated June 28, 1816, was read and he took the oath. He continued to preside at the regular terms of court from August term, 1816, until April term, 1818. He resigned July 6, 1818. Thomas Burnside was born at Newton Stewart, Ireland, July 28, 1782. M. Auge in his "Lives of the Eminent Dead and Biographical Notices of Prominent Citizens of Montgomery county, Pa.," states that "Some years ago the author interviewed several of our older inhabitants to learn what might linger in their memory as to the olden time. One of them stated that before the commencement of the present century, there resided a short time on Main street, near Stony Creek (Norristown), a Scotsman named William Burnside, who adhered to the old continental costume of looped-up hat, straight coat, buckskin breeches, with long stockings and large silver shoe buckles. He had recently arrived from the old country and stayed here a short time only, before locating, as he afterwards did, near Fairview, in Lower Providence township. Here he had several sons born to him. When quite a young man Thomas Burnside, son of William Burnside, was thrown from a horse and had a limb broken. The tedious hours of his confinement were therefore spent in reading, and shortly after he entered upon the study of the law, which was soon mastered, and he was admitted to the bar February 13, 1804. He did not long remain here, but went to Centre county." His parents emigrated to the United States in 1792, and settled in the county of Montgomery, in this state. Thomas was apprenticed to a trade, but this not suiting his inclination or ambition, he managed to lay by money sufficient to pay for one year's schooling in the city of Philadelphia, and immediately after commenced reading law with Hon. Robert Porter, from whose office he was admitted to the bar of Philadelphia in 1804. In March of that year he went west and settled permanently at Bellefonte, Centre county, Pa., then on the frontier, and which he always regarded as his home, though his occupation in after life on the bench in different parts of the state called him away. He at once commenced a lucrative practice, and in this laid the foundation of that eminent position to which he attained in subsequent years as a land lawyer. No man in Pennsylvania better understood the land laws of his state than he. It is doubtful if he had his equal. His name is intimately blended in the settlement of titles to real estate in Pennsylvania. Warrants and surveys, Indian purchases, tax titles and Yankee claims were familiar matters with Thomas Burnside, and he was always regarded as authority on these questions. Possessing that peculiar fervid temperament which seems to belong eminently to the Scotch character he entered into the profession with great zeal, and at the same time took an active part in the politics of the country, which was then running at fever heat. He was of the Jefferson, McKean and Snyder school in politics, and a leader. He represented his district in the state senate in 1811, his first public honor. Three years later he was sent to congress. At the close of the session of 1816 he returned home, and in the summer of that year he was appointed judge, as before stated. Hon. David Scott succeeded him as president judge of this judicial district. During his residence in Wilkes-Barre he was a great favorite with the citizens from his social, genial habits. His duties on the bench were discharged with signal ability, and he was as popular with the bar as he was with the people of the town. It was here that he formed that life-long intimacy with the late George M. Hollenback, Esq. No two men were ever more closely united in personal intimacy. It was, indeed, remarkable, the friendship that existed between them. In 1817 he was elected a member of the borough council of Wilkes-Barre, and was president of the council. Garrick Mallery, Samuel Maffit and Andrew Beaumont were also members of the council that year.

Judge Burnside returned to Bellefonte in 1818 and resumed his profession at the bar. In 1823, or thereabouts, he was again elected to the senate of the state. During this term he was speaker of that body. In 1826, while a member of the senate, he was appointed president judge of the fourth district, which included Centre county. Here he remained continuously on the bench for fifteen years, discharging with great tact and signal ability the delicate duties of his place. In 1841 he was appointed, on the death of Judge Fox, president judge of the Bucks and Montgomery district. In 1845 he was commissioned by Governor Shunk as one of the justices of the supreme bench of the state, where he remained till his death, which occurred on March 25, 1851, at the ripe age of three score and ten years. As an advocate, Judge Burnside ranked in the profession more as a substantial lawyer and profound jurist than what we understand as an orator. He was strong before the jury. No man had a better knowledge of human nature. In his intercourse in the different positions of life he had acquired that important element of success in all occupations, of knowing the character, and weighing them too, of the masses. That crowning feature of the human intellect, which Pope has defined as the greatest acquisition, the knowledge of man, was the predominating element in the well balanced mind of Thomas Burnside. As a judge, he ever aimed at the all important point of administering fair and impartial justice. He had a contempt for legal technicalities when they crossed the beaten track of equity. His whole mind seemed occupied with the noble desire of rendering equal and exact justice, and in carrying it out, to disregard the cobweb meshes which sometimes intervene between right and wrong. His opinions were short and terse, always to the point, and not clouded by a multiplicity of verbiage. He was a man of strong impulses, and maintained his opinions most strenuously. This one can afford to do when in the right. Judge Burnside was a most agreeable man in his social relations. He enjoyed a joke, and in turn he could give one. Some of his anecdotes are still fresh in the minds of those who survive him in this city, though over half a century has intervened since he left the bench of this county. This biographical notice may be summed up in saying: That Judge Burnside was a genuine and acknowledged example of the men who in the early history of the country gave the stamp and impression upon their age, as one marked by stern necessity, simple manners, generous in hospitality, and whose professional labors far exceeded the compensation awarded to them; the type of a race of men, if not extinct, at least adulterated by the customs and manners and practices of the age succeeding them; a character, resulting from the close economy and limited means of their day and generation; their descendants have acquired lessons of ease and prodigality unknown to their ancestors. A judge now receives four times the salary of one in the days of Burnside, and very probably does not do half the labor of a judge of that time. Of the lawyers and judges of the forepart of the nineteenth century, Thomas Burnside may be justly compared with the best of them in ability, learning and honesty of purpose. In these particulars he was an ornament to the legal profession, and his ermine as a judge maintained its purity to the close of his eventful life. He left to survive him ten children. His wife was Miss Mary Fleming, of Bellefonte.

JOSIAH H. MINER.

Josiah H. Miner was admitted to the bar of Luzerne county, Pa., October 31, 1816. He was principal of the Wilkes-Barre Academy for a short period, and in 1816 served as one of the trustees of the same. He died of consumption March 14, 1818.

DAVID SCOTT.

By the act of February 25, 1818, the counties of Bradford, Susquehanna, and Tioga were taken from the eleventh judicial district and formed into a separate district—the thirteenth. By the act of March 26, 1814, the county of Pike had been erected out of a part of Wayne and was attached to the eleventh district. Hence, after the creation of the thirteenth district the eleventh consisted of the counties of Luzerne, Pike, and Wayne. The county of Monroe was erected in 1836 and attached to the eleventh district. David Scott, commissioned July 7, 1818, succeeded Judge Burnside as president of the eleventh district as constituted in 1818. As such he presided in the courts of Luzerne from August term, 1818, to January term, 1838. He resigned March 17, 1838, on account of deafness. Judge Scott was succeeded by William Jessup, who was commissioned April 7, 1838. (For a sketch of Judge Scott's life see page 392).

EDWARD OVERTON.

Edward Overton, who was admitted to the bar of Luzerne county, Pa., August 5, 1818, was a native of Clithers, Lancashire, England, where he was born December 30, 1795. His father was Thomas Overton, from Wales, and his mother Mary Bleasdale, of Lancashire, England. Mr. Overton was educated at Kirkby, Lonsdale, Westmoreland, England, and read law with his uncle, Giles Bleasdale, barrister, London, England. He practiced law in this city, at Athens and Towanda, in Bradford county, Pa. He married in this city, May 13, 1818, Eliza Clymer, a daughter of Henry Clymer, son of George Clymer, who was born in Philadelphia in 1739—a signer of the declaration of independence, one of the framers of the constitution of the United States, first president of the bank of Philadelphia, and first president of the academy of fine arts, first continental treasurer; served four years in congress. He also filled other responsible positions in connection with the government. He died at Morrisville, Pa., January 23, 1813. The mother of Mrs. Overton was Mary Willing, a daughter of Thomas Willing, a partner of Robert Morris, mayor of Philadelphia, president of the first chartered bank of America, and president of the first bank of the United States. Edward Overton died at Towanda October 17, 1878.

GEORGE CATLIN.

George Catlin was admitted to the bar of Luzerne county, Pa., January 4, 1819. He was the fifth child of Putnam Catlin. (See page 1051). He was born in this city July 26, 1796. During the first fifteen years of his boyhood he lived much with nature, and became an accomplished hunter and sportsman. He says: "In my early youth I was influenced by two predominant and inveterate propensities, viz., for hunting and fishing. My father and mother had great difficulty in turning my attention from these to books." His only education was that usual for the sons of persons of means in the colonies, but it was supervised by the counsel of his judicious father, and added to by the constant care of his mother, from whom, unquestionably, he received his artistic taste and love of nature. Of the story of his boyhood days nothing is preserved save a few notes in his own publications, but in the surroundings of his youth we see the beginning of the germ that developed into the future Indian enthusiast. His early life in New York and in the valley of Wyoming was filled with legends and traditions of the red men. Long winter nights were spent by the fireside with sturdy pioneers, whose conversation was of midnight raids and assaults by day. Hospitality was the watchword of his father, and the traveling stranger was welcomed with open hands to the family table. Revolutionary soldiers, Indian fighters, trappers, hunters and explorers were constant guests, and young George, with hungering mind, eagerly caught up the stories and preserved traditions. Coupled with this were days spent in the harvest fields, where the noonday rest was the time for stories of the early settlement, which will account for the sturdy desire for Indian adventure which later years satisfied. His description of his boyhood home from his tenth to his twentieth year best expresses one reason for the acquirement of his desire for romantic life and research amongst the Indians: "My father's plantation (farm), in the picturesque little valley of the Ouaquaga, on the banks of the Susquehanna river, hemmed in with huge mountains on either side, * * * though not the place of my nativity, was the tapis on which my boyish days were spent, and rife with legends of Indian lore." Here he received additional impressions from his surroundings and the incidents he heard related, which gave him his love for the Indians. Though the Indians had long since disappeared, legends and stories of them were constantly told and kept before his boyish mind the heroism and life of the red man, even then being pushed toward the far west. His youthful fancy was thus fed by traditions, and his sight by objects which constantly fed his increasing love of Indians and Indian romance. His father sold the New York farm in 1808 and removed to one at Hopbottom. He taught school for a while at Brooklyn, Susquehanna county, Pa. In 1817 he went to the law school of Reeves & Gould, at Litchfield, Conn., where he remained until 1818. While there he became noted as an amateur artist. While at law school in 1818 Mr. Catlin painted a portrait of Judge Tapping Reeves. In 1819 he returned to Pennsylvania, where he entered upon the study and then the practice of the law in the courts of Luzerne and adjoining counties. All the time, however, his taste for art was growing, and his dislike for the irksome exactions of the law increasing. Of this in 1861 he writes: "During this time (while practicing law from 1820 to 1823) another and stronger passion was getting the advantage of me, that for painting, to which all my love of pleading soon gave way; and after having covered nearly every inch of the lawyers' tables (and even encroached upon the judge's bench), with penknife, pen and ink and pencil sketches of judges, jurors and culprits, I very deliberately resolved to convert my law library into paint pots and brushes, and to pursue painting as my future and apparently more agreeable profession." In 1871 Mr. Catlin related an incident to Prof. Joseph Henry in connection with his attempt to practice law at Wilkes-Barre: "My first case was the defense of an Irishman who was arraigned for stealing a hand saw and broad axe. The prisoner acknowledged to me that he stole the articles, but notwithstanding this, by making the worse appear the better cause, I succeeded in convincing the jury that he was not guilty. The man afterwards asked me whether or not I had informed the jury that he had stolen the articles. 'No,' was the answer; to which the client replied: 'How then did they acquit me? Did you not say that to get me clear I must tell you the truth?'" His sensible father and mother did not interfere, and he went to Philadelphia to reside and practice the calling of an artist. He settled in that city in 1823, and was at once admitted to the fellowship of the fraternity of artists in that city. Thomas Sully, John Nagle, Charles Wilson and Rembrandt Peale became his friends. He was entirely self taught as an artist. In the pursuit of his calling he visited Washington, 1824 to 1829, painting some public men and many of the first people of that city, notably Mrs. Dolly Madison, in a turban, a picture which has been reproduced many times. At Richmond in 1829-30 he painted the famous constitutional convention of 1829 (one hundred and fifteen figures) in session, with a key, a most comprehensive and exact work, and invaluable, as it contains portraits of the distinguished gentlemen who composed the convention. The portraits in it are good, and the persons easily recognized. In Philadelphia he was very popular as a miniature and portrait painter. He visited Albany in 1828, and painted many of the members of the legislature and other prominent men. He painted at that time a portrait of Governor DeWitt Clinton, which now hangs in the governors' room in the city hall, New York. In the practice of his art he was in New York, Buffalo, Norfolk, and other cities, and for a long time before and after these duties was in the path of all Indian delegations on the way to and returning from Washington. In the early days, when the Indian tribes were recognized as separate nations, a frequent pilgrimage to the seat of government under national auspices was an almost indispensable element of control of the Indians. When the congress of the confederation was in Philadelphia, and often while Washington was president, delegations of Indians were constantly coming and going. Red Jacket, Black Hawk, Keokuk, and other famous Indians were familiar faces to its citizens. Mr. Catlin, in his earlier years, was very ambitious in his art. He was constantly searching for a special field in which he could become distinguished. In 1861, writing of this, he says: "I there (at Philadelphia) closely applied my hand to the labors of the art (painting) for several years, during which time my mind was continually reaching for some branch or enterprise of the art on which to devote a whole lifetime of enthusiasm, when a delegation of some ten or fifteen noble and dignified looking Indians from the wilds of the far west suddenly arrived in the city, arrayed and equipped in all their classic beauty, with shield and helmet, with tunic and manteau, tinted and tasseled off exactly for the painter's pallette." This sight turned his thoughts toward his Indian gallery. Reflection upon the possibilities of Indian art confirmed his impressions, and he determined to execute his idea of "Catlin's North American Indian Gallery." Of this, in 1861, he writes: "In the midst of success (as a painter) I again resolved to use my art and so much of the labors of my future life as might be required in rescuing from oblivion the looks and customs of the vanishing races of native men in America, to which I plainly saw they were hastening before the approach and certain progress of civilization." It was a high and noble ambition, worthily conceived and most faithfully executed. Mr. Catlin became an enthusiast in his work, and necessarily so, for no one but an enthusiast could have executed so difficult a task and so thoroughly. He hoped and believed that his work would survive him, and throughout his writings can be found the frequently occurring statement that he was painting for the future. From 1829 to 1871, a period of forty-two years, he entirely followed his life work. In all lands and in all climes, in North and South America and in Europe, his name was a familiar one from 1830 to 1871. In that time he saw the dreams of his early manhood realized, and knew that the world felt the influence of his work. Steadiness of character and firmness of opinion were his aids; with these and indomitable courage he succeeded. His friends were many and faithful; his enemies few, and they from motives of self-interest. He was never even comfortably off in money matters, relying for his livelihood upon his brush or his pen. He lived poor and died the same. He received no pecuniary aid, governmental or individual, in the prosecution of his work. He was a gentleman by instinct and culture, and in all stations of life, whether on the plains with the Indians, or in a palace with a king, he was at home. He received many earthly distinctions and honors in his lifetime, but none above his merit. The larger portion of his

Indian Gallery is in the United States National Museum (Smithsonian Institution) at Washington, D. C. He was the author of several works on Indian customs and manners and on general subjects. He married, May 10, 1828, Clara B. Gregory, of Albany, N. Y. Mr. Catlin died at Jersey City, N. J., December 23, 1872. Mrs. Catlin died in Paris July 28, 1845. Three children survived the death of Mr. Catlin—Elizabeth Wing Catlin, Clara Gregory Catlin, of New York, and Mrs. Louise Victoria Kinney, of Washington, D. C.

ORISTUS COLLINS.

Oristus Collins, who was admitted to the bar of Luzerne county, Pa., April 8, 1819, was born in Marlboro, Connecticut, September 22, 1792. His lineage on the father's side is distinctly traceable to one John Collins, of Boston, Massachusetts, the date of whose crossing the Atlantic and settlement in this country has never been satisfactorily determined. The stock is supposed to be English, but some things dispose to a doubt. The usual stature, complexion, vigor, and length of life, in one and all, indicate Irish blood. This doubt hardly had its origin in an amusing anecdote, familiar to the judge's friends: An Irishman was tried before him at Lancaster, Pa., and when he received his sentence, a lighter penalty was imposed than the convicted man expected. So great was his surprise, he complimented the judge by the remark, that "he knew the O'Collinses in Ireland, and they were among the most respectable." The judge seldom, if ever, signed his name in full—Oristus. With no little humor, he was pleased to descant upon the names of his more immediate or remote relatives: his brothers, Alonzo, Decius, Lucius, Lorenzo, Abner, Theron, Aretas, or running further back—Cyprian, Ambrose, Triphena, Homer, Cicero, Plato, and Virgil, Ruhamah, Hephsibah, Sibyl, Asenath, even Tyrannus.

The first John, of Boston, is supposed to have been a merchant, and this form of business appears to have marked the next two generations. But in the third following appeared a clergyman, one Timothy, graduated from Yale College, class 1718, a native of Guilford, Connecticut, born 1699. He was the first pastor of the Litchfield Congregational church, served 31 years, and then retiring, for twenty years practiced medicine within the bounds of his former charge, serving also acceptably as justice of the peace in the same town. At the attack upon Crown Point, 1755, Timothy was appointed surgeon of a Connecticut regiment. His wife, Ann Leete, daughter of William Leete, was at this time noted for her knowledge of one branch of surgery, midwifery; and it is recorded that in an extreme case she was drawn upon a hand-sled four and one-half miles to relieve suffering. It is perhaps worthy of remark that the home of the Leetes was distinguished as a place of retreat for Whalley and Goffe, the regicides of Charles. So, also, that this William Leete, afterwards Governor Leete, was bred to the law in England, and for a considerable time served as clerk in the Bishop's Court, in Cambridge. Here, observing the oppression and cruelties practiced on the Puritans, he was led to examine the subject, and giving up his office he became a Puritan. Thus early did the religious element appear in this family, in connection with independent thinking.

The law of heredity might lead us to expect, what we find in the next generation, a physician in the son Charles, of whom, however, we have little more than date of birth, marriage, etc.,—his marriage into the distinguished family of Huntington; the birth of ten children—one of whom became the mother of the American poet, John Pierrepont, and Lewis, the eldest son, father of Oristus. Lewis was born October 29, 1753. A physician of ability and repute, he married, for a second wife, into the family of Huntington, and with a family of seven children set out from New England for Pennsylvania, a colony of Connecticut. A desire to withdraw his sons from the temptations of a seafaring life disposed him to seek a home far from the Atlantic coast, and in 1804 he settled permanently at Cherry Ridge, Wayne county, Pennsylvania. There, amid no little responsibility on the farm, turning a hand to various employments, fruit growing, sugar making, and bee culture, the boy Oristus ripened into manhood, except in so far as he was afforded occasional educational opportunities at Owego, New York, or at Litchfield, Connecticut. It is narrated that, at a visit from a clergyman, the father, Dr. Collins, was seen in the field making hay, having five sons following him with scythes, and five raking and binding.

Oristus' mother, Louisa Huntington, a daughter of Hon. Oliver Huntington, of Lebanon, Connecticut, brings into view a line noted in the history of this country, and easily traceable to the *hunting* grounds of Saxon, Dane, and Norman—that tract of England lying between Cambridge on the east and Northampton and Bedfordshire, on the west, filled with all kinds of English game. This hunting ground gave a name to families of greatest eminence and most distinguished culture, on both eastern and western continents. Thence they have radiated, until they are reckoned by thousands bearing, through marriage, names Bingham, Backus, Carew, Chauncey, Clark, Crane, Fitch, Forbes, Goodrich, Hyde, Lathrop, Lincoln, Leffingwell, Tracey, Wales, Walworth, Wheelock, Wright. Says one biographer: "In five of our states we have furnished members for political conventions, in which state constitutions were made, or ratified, or amended. In Connecticut we were represented by three of the name, in the convention of 1788, for ratifying the constitution of the United States. In the convention of 1818, we had another. New York had two at work upon hers. Ohio, her second Governor upon hers. New Hampshire, upon hers. As representatives or senators, and they are about equally divided, we have furnished not less than thirty for state legislatures, and a solid half dozen for our national congress. Of judges of county courts, superior judges, and federal and chief justices, we can count at least fifteen. Nearly one hundred on our list have taken collegiate honors, a number which, for its ratio to the entire list, is probably unequaled by any other New England family. Our ministers have exceeded one-third of our college list, and our lawyers and doctors have nearly equaled one third each."

"In days when to cling to our country's cause was treason, patriotism was our family trait. No threats of governmental vengeance and no seductions of governmental favor could, for a moment, weaken or repress. It was no mean compliment that General Washington, all through the war, made Jedediah a counselor and confidant. As regards the religious element of the family, note such names in the church as Lyman, Strong, Griffin, Perkins, Smith, and Baldwin, or of noble women, Winslow, Hutchins, and Perry, whose names have a holy savor on heathen soil." Whether the subject of this sketch had any connection with the English poet, Collins, can not be determined. But there is no question as regards his relation to Lydia M. Sigourney and John Pierrepont. To justify so full a reference to the maternal side, it may be well to quote. "Our sons and daughters, their character and influence, made what it is more by maternal influence—these are the natural testimonials of the character and worth of our *mothers*." Of the boyhood of Oristus little is known, as indicating his promise, unless it be the fact that as a student at school it became quite habitual for him to pass from school to school, having in each exhausted the stock of learning possessed by the teacher to whom he was sent. Such unusual rapidity of acquisition is confirmed by the appearance of his Latin grammar, which shows no signs of being thumbed, but is as clean as on the day of its purchase. In six weeks from commencing Latin, he had read Virgil. It was with an eye twinkling with conscious ability or caustic criticism, he was wont to remark to the youths in his family that "he was graduated at the foot of sign posts and grave stones." His hand writing had much of the elegance of engraving, and even in his old age remained distinct and legible. His style of composition was concise and clear; careful, but easy and graceful; free from all attempts at adornment; severe in its logic, showing self discipline and a due sense of responsibility to his own keen criticism. Indeed, he was wont to remark that he did not see that there was any reason, but laziness or incompetency, which should render criticism by another necessary to the improvement of one's style. He was early conversant with the wide field of English literature; had read all the British poets and essayists. With metaphysics, as such, he had little patience, but in early youth he had studied "Watts on the Mind," and later had mastered "Locke on the Human Understanding." He was a careful reader of the best works by the British bar, and Grattan, Curran, Emmett, and Burke were familiar studies. All that he read seemed to dispose him the more to look to the power of his own mind, for whatever success he might hope to gain. He was no servile imitator of any man, never could have thought of calling any man master—*nullius addictus jurare in verba magistri.*

In 1817, after an unsatisfactory effort to please his father by the study of medicine, having little relish for that profession, he entered the office of Hon. Garrick Mallery, at Wilkes-Barre, as a student of law. In this village was a family by the name of Jewett, recently come from New London, Connecticut, seeking a better fortune and a suitable home. With five daughters and three sons, the widow of David H. Jewett, M. D., afforded the subject of this sketch a home, and eventually he found in it a wife, winning the affections of the youngest daughter, Nancy, whom he married July 17, 1823. Dr. David H. Jewett was a well known surgeon and warm personal friend of General Washington. He was a son of Rev. David Jewett, D. D., a missionary to the Mohican Indians, afterwards a chaplain in the French and Indian war, and later in the American revolution. Rev. Dr. Jewett read the burial service over Uncas, "the last of the Mohicans." David Jewett, a brother of Nancy, was commodore of the Brazilian navy, under Dom Pedro I. (See page 782.)

In all his domestic life Judge Collins was a devoted student of the bible. All the theological systems, of which he was a careful reader, he brought to the bar of the revealed word of God. Members of his family coming home at their vacation, fresh from the discussions of professors of theology, were glad to listen to his words of wisdom, and he was never found unwilling to discuss any of the questions which had engaged councils and drawn out able and world-renowned debate. He was wont to remark that every faithful student of the English bible would show the effects of its pure Saxon in fashioning his style, and that a careful reader of it could not seriously err in idiom, or be faulty in grammar. It was a notable fact in his religious life that in his old age he repeated his excursions through the penitential Psalms again and again, until at that one point he wore out Bible after bible. Decent disposal of the Holy Book could be found only in the fires of the furnace. He never failed to commend the close examination of the book to younger members of the bar, and a simple but earnest and unyielding advocacy of its claims marked his life. Illustration in point is afforded by Hon. Stanley Woodward, at the meeting of the bar on the morning of Judge Collins' burial. He referred to the pleasant surprise which the aged counselor gave the bar by once remarking that "he had just visited the law library, and had painfully observed the absence of a volume which was the fountain of legal principles," whereupon, he drew from its concealment a copy of the bible, and begged the court's acceptance of it from him as a gift to the library which they were forming. To no small degree he inherited a temperament marked by coolness and fearlessness; but added to this was a firmness, which came from the depth of his convictions—convictions of the claims of truth and righteousness—his deep and hearty assurance that there was at the helm of the universe, and, how much more, of the church, a power whose supervision was rendered unquestioned and immutable by promises which declared Him a God of truth and holiness, ever watchful over the weakest disposed to serve him. It was this that emboldened him to break up a horse-race on Main street, Wilkes-Barre, and, amid the gathered multitude, to seize the horse and lead him away as forfeited by law. It was this that gave him confidence on the grounds of an adverse political gathering in Lancaster, Pennsylvania, during his judgeship, to which he was appointed by Governor Ritner, August 8, 1836. He was taking notes upon a speech by Hon. James Buchanan, when roughs threatened him and sought to drive him from the grounds. Coolly putting his hand beneath his coat, where might have been firearms—which he never carried—he kept the bullies at respectful distance, while he deliberately withdrew to a place of safety. He was not easily alarmed, as was once proven in the court room at Wilkes-Barre, when an inconsiderate lawyer threatened to "pitch him over the bar." Rising from his seat, he unflinchingly approached the braggadocio and assured him that the best moment for the attempt was the one at hand. History fails to record any conflict. His unassuming manner may have been mistaken for a want of spirit. At his first entering the office of Hon. Garrick Mallery as a student of law some young lawyers induced a young woman to disguise herself, and, entering the office, to threaten a personal assault. Seeing their numbers, and determined to make less of the first assailant, he would have made the experiment a pitiful joke, had not the party begged for the release of their foolish victim, and in disgrace beaten a retreat.

In church, no less than in state, his deep sense of the right and the true kept him loyal and prompt in action. He had a tender regard for the dignity of the pulpit; was its ever ready defender, saying to his pastor, "They may remove you, but cannot disturb me," as he often assumed the responsibility of delicate cases. He was a true churchman. In his youth a Congregationalist, as all his fathers were, he turned his attention to questions of church government, and accepted the claims of Presbyterianism as having a broader basis than those of Congregationalism. He thereupon urged a change in the organization of the church, which is now the "First Presbyterian" of Wilkes-Barre, effected his purpose, and, becoming one of its first bench of elders, served in that capacity for more than fifty years. As was remarked by Hon. Henry W. Palmer, at the meeting of the bar, on the day of the judge's burial, "Had he lived in the troublous days of the revolution, he would have stood with Cromwell, Hampden, and Sir Henry Vane, in defence of the people's rights, against kingly prerogative or priestly assumption."

He was the friend of the poor, and not once or twice was their testimony rendered to his praise. Here is an instance, reported in later years by the man himself: "I bought a horse of the judge and gave him my note. The horse not long after died. I reported the loss and my inability to pay." 'It matters not,' replied the judge, '*When the horse died, the note died.*' It hardly need be said that he was the friend of the oppressed African, and an ardent supporter of the administration, during the late war. Long before that, he was, on every principle of humanity, the black man's friend; and, while more prudent than abolitionists generally, he was no less determined in his opposition to slavery. As a Presbyterian, he for some time accepted the philosophy that slavery was not wrong *per se*. He was a colonizationist of the Henry Clay school, and had the south not proved so aggressive, he would have approved measures looking to the indulgence of slavery, till colonization might have wiped it out.

He was an earnest advocate of temperance, and a plea made by him was the first published temperance document in this portion of the state. It is worthy of mention, but sad to relate, that while he, according to the customs of the times, was in the habit of taking his morning "dram," as was supposed beneficial to the health, he was induced to yield this custom and brought to maintain the cause of temperance by one who afterwards sank into a drunkard's grave. Upon the transition of the judgeship in Pennsylvania from the life tenure to periodic election, he returned from Lancaster to Wilkes-Barre, and resumed the practice of the law. In this he continued till 1874, when, owing to diminished acuteness of hearing, being then eighty-two years of age, he retired from the courts. In the same year when his only son and heir, Rev. Charles Jewett Collins, born in this city, June 25, 1825, withdrew from the superintendence of the public schools of the city of Wilkes-Barre to take charge of the preparatory school of the college of New Jersey, the judge accompanied him. But he never would withdraw his citizenship from Pennsylvania. In 1881, he followed his son to Rye, N. Y., where he peacefully passed away, as was remarked by the attendant physician, "without disease," at the age of ninety-two. His unassuming monument stands in Hollenback Cemetery.

JOHN NESBIT CONYNGHAM.

John Nesbit Conyngham, was admitted to the bar of Luzerne county, Pa., April 3, 1820. He was a native of Philadelphia, Pa., where he was born December 17, 1798. In that city he received his education, graduating with high honors at the University of Pennsylvania in 1817. Selecting the law for his profession, he was entered as a student in the office of Joseph R. Ingersoll, and in due time was admitted to the bar and at once began the active practice of his profession. In 1820 he left his native city and decided to establish himself at Wilkes-Barre, where, after a few years' practice, he was elevated to the bench and became president judge of the courts of the county. While traveling to this city he came in contact with two persons, one of whom, Samuel Bowman, was a young law student, who, after his admission to the bar of this county, abandoned legal pursuits for the ministry and ultimately became the assistant bishop of the Protestant Episcopal church of Pennsylvania. The other was a granddaughter of the old revolutionary patriot and hero, Colonel Zebulon Butler, and who a few years later became his wife. Among Judge Conyngham's ancestry and connections were several prominent divines and prelates of the Church of England and Ireland. His grandfather, Redmond Conyngham, was connected with old Christ church in Philadelphia. Subsequently he was elected vestryman and warden by the same church, and in 1758 was one of the foremost to assist in the erection of St. Peter's church at Third and Pine streets, Philadelphia. This church was first opened for divine service in 1761, and he was a member of the vestry of the united parishes of both this and Christ church until his decease. The father of John N. Conyngham was David Hayfield Conyngham, who was also connected with the last named church, and was ever prompt to serve its interests with pecuniary assistance or able counsel. In that parish the child was baptized and watched over in his days of infancy and boyhood. While residing in Wilkes-Barre he interested himself greatly in the welfare of St. Stephen's church, and in 1821 was elected a vestryman. In 1826 a special convention, held in St. Peter's church, Philadelphia, was called by Bishop White to take into consideration the expediency of electing an assistant bishop of the diocese, and it was upon this occasion that he first took his seat in the diocesan convention as a member of that honorable body. In 1844 he was nominated and elected by the convention to the position of deputy to the general convention. In the following October, in company with his lay colleagues, George M. Wharton, Judge Stroud, and Herman Cope, he took his seat with that body at Cincinnati. Subsequently, with but a single exception, he was returned to the general convention at every session. In the diocesan convention he was one of the most prominent and influential members, was placed on many important committees, and was highly respected for his earnestness and sterling talents. In the general convention, a body composed of four clergymen and four laymen from each diocese, and meeting every third year in order to legislate on matters involving the interests of the whole church in the United States, Judge Conyngham early attained an active and prominent position. In 1862 he was placed on the most important of all committees, of the house of clerical and law deputies, that known as the committee on canons. On this occasion his lay colleagues were Murray Hoffman, of New York; Judge Chambers, of Maryland; and Robert C. Winthrop, of Massachusetts. As a deputy he was never absent from his post, ever punctual to every appointment, and always ready to sacrifice all personal considerations to his onerous duties. Calm, logical, and withal liberal in his views, he strongly deprecated extreme views and actions and was never willing to compromise by any unwise alliance the polity or the ritual of his church. In 1868 he was elected president of the American church missionary society. This is one of the most important organizations in the Protestant Episcopal church, having its central office in New York, and embracing in its officers and members clergymen and laymen from nearly every diocese. "In this office," say the minutes adopted by that society and prepared by the Rev. Dr. Tyng, "his presence has brought commanding dignity to the fulfillment of his duties, his eminent christian character has added veneration and respect to his position, and his decided evangelical judgments and expressions have enhanced the confidence with which its operations have been regarded." In every public work or movement designed to benefit his brethren or his country he was always an energetic actor, and in all the questions which have agitated the commonwealth or the nation in general during the last fifty years he never failed to take a decided stand upon what he conscientiously believed to be the rightful and truthful side. In early life he was warmly interested in state and national politics, and, though invariably decided and inflexible in his attitude, was respected and admired even by his opponents. In 1849 he represented Luzerne county in the legislature of the state. In all matters of social advancement and public improvement, and for the developing of the resources of Pennsylvania in the wise utilization of its vast mineral wealth, he was an able and enterprising mover. From 1824 to 1838 he was one of the trustees of the Wilkes-Barre Academy. As a judge he was the recipient of countless encomiums, and when he resigned his president judgeship the whole bar of Luzerne county testified to his rare abilities, while sixteen judges gave in writing their deliberate judgments concerning his character and talents. For thirty years he was president judge of Luzerne county, for fifty years a vestryman in St. Stephen's church in this city, and was, since 1826, the representative of that church in the diocesan convention of Pennsylvania. At the time of his death he was president of the Wilkes-Barre Tract Society, of the Luzerne County Bible Society, and of the American Church Missionary Society of New York. He was also vice president of the American Sunday School Union, and of the institution for the deaf and dumb of Philadelphia. His death resulted from an accident. While on his way to Texas to bring home Colonel J. B. Conyngham, an invalid son, he fell on the railroad track at Magnolia, Mississippi, and the wheels of a passenger car passing over both of his legs they were so terribly crushed and mutilated that he died within two hours from the time of the accident. This occurred on the evening of February 23, 1871. The township of Conyngham in this county and the Conyngham public school on St. Clement street, in this city, were named after Judge Conyngham. From May, 1827, to May, 1828, and from May, 1834, to May, 1837, Judge Conyngham was burgess of the borough of Wilkes-Barre, and in 1849 and 1850 he was president of the borough council. He was a member of the first board of directors of the Wyoming (national) bank, organized in November, 1829. Hon. H. B. Wright, at our request, a few years ago, wrote an article on Judge Conyngham for the *Luzerne Legal Register*. We here reproduce the greater part of that article.

"When Judge Conyngham was admitted to the bar of Luzerne county, it had a reputation for learning and talent that it has probably not had in the last twenty years. While it is not our purpose to make an unfavorable comparison with the Luzerne bar of 1820 and any subsequent period, it will be frankly admitted that there was at that time a professional array of unusual talent. Roswell Welles, Ebenezer Bowman, Garrick Mallery,

and George Denison were all men of a high order of legal ability
who resided here. And then there were other gentlemen of high
professional attainments who were in the habit of attending the
courts here. Among these were Judge Duncan, afterwards
placed on the supreme bench of the state; David Watts, of Carlisle; John Ross, of Easton; Alem Marr, of Danville; and
William Cox Ellis, of Lycoming. These men, from the adjoining
counties, with the home talent, fully their equal, made an array
of legal ability that had position equal to that in any part of the
state, not excepting Philadelphia, which claimed the ascendancy
in legal lore and learning over any other bar in the United States.
David Scott, a man honored and respected, then held the commission of judge of the Common Pleas—a man of stern integrity
and iron will; upright in the administration of justice, and fearless in the discharge of his official duties; determined and positive, but just in his decisions, and merciful in his sentences.
Such was the bench and such was the bar of the county of
Luzerne when Judge Conyngham came to this town to make
his permanent abode, and enter the conflict, with this array of
talent occupying the arena. Under ordinary circumstances this
would seem to have been a hopeless adventure. But he had
untiring industry and perseverance, temperate habits, extraordinary ambition to master his profession, and this, with a fine commanding personal appearance, and a remarkably gentle and
agreable manner, with a high order of intellect, enabled him to
enter the tournament with every prospect of success. I have it
from his own mouth, that in the first two years of his residence
here, his prospects were exceedingly doubtful as to success.
'But,' said he, 'I landed here, and burned my boats; there was
no return, and I made up my mind to work hard, early and late;
to ride the circuit with or without a brief, and to use every effort
to obtain position; and, amidst toil and energy, I achieved my
purpose. And it was during these early years of incessant reading, and attending the courts during the entire session, practice
or no practice, that I learned the science of the law, and the
mode of conducting a cause. For never had pupil more intelligent masters, and I profited by it all. I made my point, and
established my reputation.' As early as the fourth year after he
commenced practice, he may be said to have had as good a position at the bar as any one, save Garrick Mallery. While Judge
Mallery was at the bar, during the years I am speaking of, he
was the acknowledged head. No one questioned this. Not far
from this date (say 1824), the branch bank established in this
town by the old Philadelphia bank suspended business here. The
business of the people in this valley did not require a bank, and

so the agency was closed. A large amount of money (that is, for those times) had been loaned out, and the endorsers, mostly composed of the farmers of the county, had become liable, and there was much commotion, and great fears were apprehended. To have closed up these surety matters suddenly would have ruined the best men of the county. Many of the men who had obtained discounts on the strength of their endorsements had failed, and the load came home to the guarantors. John P. Arndt, a merchant, residing and doing business where E. P. Darling's house stands, on River street, and Henry Buckingham, of Kingston, were among the noted failures of that time. There was a general feeling of despondency throughout the entire valley. Many of these endorsers were soldiers of the revolution, and several of them had survived the terrible massacre of Wyoming. These old veterans being thus threatened with impending ruin, the whole community was in sympathy with them. These facts were represented to the bank in Philadelphia, and John N. Conyngham was deputed agent and attorney for the bank, with discretionary power to do what he should think best, under the circumstances. It was in his capacity as agent of the bank that he made that fame and reputation for benevolence and kind-heartedness that established his reputation in the county. He gave these old veterans time, indulged them in their misfortunes, and saved most of them from total and absolute ruin. And they remembered these acts of generosity, and their children after them did also. And he acted in good faith to the bank, which, in addition to his fees, presented him a set of silver as a token of the satisfactory manner in which he had discharged the trust confided to him. The just and merited influence thus acquired in the bank agency, his habits of industry, his acknowledged ability and gentlemanly deportment, all combining, placed him at the head of his profession, though not yet thirty years of age. But what was of more account, his high position as a man of integrity, and possessing all the amiable qualities which decorate the individual character, and which he had fully exhibited in closing the bank affairs, gave him a firm and unquestioned stand, high up among his fellow men. Another reason for his success at the bar arose from the fact that most of the gentlemen in the adjoining counties gradually relinquished their practice, and the field was left open to a comparatively few members. In 1828, when the writer of this notice entered the office of Judge Conyngham as a student, with the late Ovid F. Johnson, afterwards attorney general of the state, the legal business of the county was almost exclusively in the hands of Garrick Mallery, George Denison, John N. Conyngham, Oristus Collins, and James McClintock.

The late Chief Justice Woodward was a student at that time in Judge Mallery's office. During the ensuing five years George Denison died, and Mr. Mallery was commissioned by Governor Wolf president judge of the Northampton district. These occurrences gave Judge Conyngham the choice of selecting which side he chose of every cause upon the list. He was the absolute and acknowledged head of the bar. And yet, with all these advantages, I doubt if he realized two thousand dollars a year in fees. The counsel fees then, compared with the practice now, were probably not an eighth of what they are now. And to see the energy and zeal that these lawyers manifested in the preparation and trial of causes is almost marvelous. The amount in controversy mattered not. As much hard labor would be bestowed in the trial of an issue involving fifty dollars, on an appeal from a justice of the peace, as is expended at the present time on a trial involving a million. In the former case the fee might have been ten dollars, in the latter ten thousand. The pioneers of the law made the practice of the law their business. They knew nothing about outside speculations. They worked for a moderate subsistence, and with that they were satisfied. I have known Judge Conyngham, when in the height of his practice, to devote a half day or more to the preparation of an elaborate opinion, and accept a fee of five dollars! I have oftener seen him charge three dollars than five. During all the time I was a student in his office, the price of preparing and writing a deed for the conveyance of land was always *one dollar and a quarter*, and this included the examination of the docket as to liens. I always wondered why the extra quarter of a dollar was added! Judge Conyngham was a man of remarkable industry. He was always at his post. He would annually devote a week or ten days to visit his father in Philadelphia. This was the extent of his pastime. He labored incessantly. He was a great reader (of law, I mean); he had every decision at his tongue's end. He prided himself on this; and he told me time and again that he attributed all his success to his industry. He was too modest a man to admit that he had enough of natural ability to reach the position he knew he enjoyed as a lawyer. His power at the bar was with the jury. No man had more weight and influence than he had over the twelve. He was more verbose than most successful advocates. It was repetition, however, which sprang from a desire to leave no doubt upon the minds of the jury. He had a very fine flow of language. At times, it reached a high order of eloquence. He spoke fluently and he spoke well. Added to his remarkably fine person —standing six feet, erect, and graceful in all his motions—his verdict was always sure, if the evidence warranted it, and somtimes the verdict came in his favor when it should not. The modulation of his voice was excellent. It was always a pleasure to listen to him. His plea was solid argument; he did not have the gift of satire or repartee. He had more force with the jury than the court. I do not mean by this that he had less force with the court than his most talented colleagues, but that he had a greater influence than they with the jury. This commanding position at the bar Judge Conyngham maintained to about the year 1837. I think it was in that year in which the celebrated trial of the Commonwealth v. the Gilligans and others occurred. The prisoners were indicted for the murder of McComb, a short distance below White Haven, at the time of the construction of the Lehigh slack water navigation. The prisoners were defended by Judge Conyngham, the late Judge Kidder, and the writer of this notice. The evidence was circumstantial, and a strong effort was made to convict. This elicited a corresponding effort on the part of the defence. Two of them were convicted of murder in the first degree, the other three of the lower grades of homicide. The two convicted of murder in the first degree were awarded a new trial on the ground of the admission of irrelevant testimony. On the second trial they were acquitted—wrongfully, I fear. The sentiment in Luzerne at that time was against capital punishment. It was hard to convict; but trials for homicide were rare. In conducting the defence in the Gilligan trial—that is, the first one; in the second he was unable to participate—Judge Conyngham broke down. He made in it the best speech of his life. He overdid the matter. At the close of the trial his violent effort brought on a bronchial affection of the throat, from which he never entirely recovered. He was confined with this attack for more than a year. He recovered so far as to be able to discharge thirty years' service on the bench. But he never appeared in court as an advocate after the Gilligan trial. He may have been there occasionally, but he had made his last great effort with the jury. And the counsel whose voice had echoed in the courts for nearly twenty years had now ceased; and, in that capacity, forever. This state of his health was, of course, matter of deep regret to the bench, the bar, and the people. All remedies failed to restore him, and the common voice was, that he must go upon the bench, and there he went, with a reputation for ability, legal learning, and honesty of purpose, all of which he most faithfully sustained. And thus much of the man, as a member of the bar. We may say, in conclusion, in this particular, that as a practitioner he was an example of integrity of purpose. True in every sense to his client; just to his opponents; open and candid to the court; truthful at all times;

a model as a practitioner; and with a name unblemished. We now come to speak of him as a judge. In this capacity, for some thirty long years, he presided in our courts; and his name is a synonym with all that is good which pertains to that high office. He was commissioned a judge of the Court of Common Pleas in 1839, in the Bradford and Susquehanna district. In 1841, by an exchange between him and Judge Jessup, under sanction of law, Judge Conyngham came upon the Luzerne bench, and Judge Jessup took the place of Judge Conyngham in the Bradford and Susquehanna district. And from the April term, 1841, up to his resignation in 1870, with the exception of the years of 1850 and 1851, he remained upon the Luzerne bench. During this long time, almost a third of a century, he maintained a high position as a man of much legal learning, and a purity of character that was not surpassed by any of his cotemporaries. I may not do better in the delineation of his judicial life than by a reference to the opinions of some of the best legal minds of the state. Upon the occasion of his resignation, in 1870, many learned men in the law were invited to participate at the banquet given him. In their responses, I refer to some of the opinions of some of them. Mr. Justice Sharswood, of the Supreme Court of this state, says: 'It would afford me the sincerest pleasure to unite in doing honor to one who has done so much honor to the bench and the profession. To unsuspected purity of purpose, he has joined the greatest fidelity and the most eminent legal learning and ability. It will be a blessing to the bar and people of Luzerne if this mantle should fall on his successor.' Mr. Chief Justice Thompson writes: 'To a faithful and able judge, such as yours has been, the tribute of respect you propose on his retirement is graceful and proper; and in this instance will sincerely mark the respect the bar must feel towards one on whom devotion to duty and justice in discharging it, was to all most distinctly apparent.' The late Chief Justice Woodward says: 'No tribute to a public servant was ever better deserved than that which you propose to tender to Judge Conyngham. He has executed for a long time and with great fidelity one of the most difficult and responsible offices in the government; the office upon which, more than upon all others, depend the safety and the happiness of the great and rapidly growing community of Luzerne county. And to official fidelity, Judge Conyngham has added the sanction of a good life. In morals and manners he has been in all times a good man.' Chief Justice Agnew remarks: 'I cannot forbear adding my testimony to that of others, of the high character Judge Conyngham has always borne as a man and as a jurist.' My limits forbid giving any further extracts from the learned men of the state on the bench and in the profession, who wrote complimentary letters in response to the committee, upon the occasion of the banquet. But of the great number received, they are all in the same tone and character with those from which I have made the foregoing extracts. It is the compliment of the living to the living. Unstrained because these evidences confer a just and proper tribute. They all come from the heart, and they are the frank and unbiassed opinions of his cotemporaries; they are modestly and truthfully written. The praises of these persons, judges and lawyers, are in keeping with the opinions of the whole population of this county. It is not the learned judge and able lawyer that is portrayed; but, along with it, comes those other conceded qualifications which constitute the moral and upright man, as well as the learned judge. And without this there is much wanting in establishing the status of the 'model' man. He who has held in his hands the balances of justice for nearly a third of a century, and escaped the tongue of malice and scandal, must needs be a most notable man. It is one case in a thousand. We are not aware of an unfavorable criticism or a charge of biassed judgment made against this man in his long occupation of the bench. That he was pure, and just, and upright, during all this time, is, in our judgment, the unanimous opinion of all our people. It may be, that as a judge, he put more faith in the opinions of others than in his own; but who shall say that this is a fault? Lord Bacon, in his celebrated picture of a good judge, says that 'The judge is a man of ability, drawing his learning out of his books, and not out of his brain.' But then he says further: 'He has right understanding of justice, depending *not so much* on reading other men's writings, as upon the goodness of his own natural reason and meditation.' He well remarks, however: 'He is a man of integrity, of well regulated passions, beyond the influence, either of anger, by which he may be incapable of judging; or of hope, either of money or worldly advancement, by which he may decide unjustly; or of fear, either of the censure of others, which is cowardice; or of giving pain, when it ought to be given, which is improper compassion. He is just both in private and public, quick in apprehension, slow in anger. He is cautious in his judgment, not forming a hasty opinion; not tenacious in retaining an opinion, when formed; and never ashamed of being wiser to-day than yesterday. He hears what is spoken, not who speaks, whether it be the president or a pauper, a friend or a foe.' How admirably do these definitions of the judicial character apply to the gentleman of whom we are writing. We give but a part of that world-renowned description of Lord Bacon, in describing the judge, but enough for our purpose. The crowning feature of Judge Conyngham was the confidence the profession placed in his ruling. They were aware that his decisions were not the result of an inconsiderate conclusion. They knew that the rule of law adopted was the conclusion deduced from authority, or from close consideration, most generally the former. For his industry was wonderful; and the moment the legal questions were raised in a cause he was incessant in his labors in finding out the established principle that should govern the case. During an adjournment of court he would frequently go without his meal, spending the whole time in his library, that he might be ready at the assembling of the court to meet the questions that the case presented. Labor seemed to be a pleasure to him. He was proud of his reputation as a judge. He disliked to be reversed; and his great desire was that he should be sustained by the court of review, and it was very seldom that he was reversed. Therefore, no labor was too much for him to perform. When he was in the midst of a trial he was lost to everything else; his mind was on that, and that alone. Hurrying, with his head down, absorbed in his own reflections, in passing from his own office to the court, he would scarcely notice any one. He had the law in his head, and this he was nursing, to the exclusion of everything else. Never was man more devoted to his occupation, and never did man have a more earnest desire to administer the law correctly and in all its purity. Thus, with his research and his well balanced mind, and his scrupulous desire to administer justice, he could not be otherwise than a most excellent judge, and such he was. Of the long list of distinguished jurists of Pennsylvania, I do not think that among them all was there an instance where any one performed more labor, or had a greater desire to do even and exact justice, than Judge Conyngham. There have been, undoubtedly, among them men of greater legal capacity and breadth of intellect than he possessed, but he was the peer of any of them in integrity of purpose, and a desire to do what was right. When he retired from the bench he left it with an unsoiled reputation. The ermine was as spotless when he laid it aside as when it was placed upon his shoulders. And the wish and prayer of those who survive him should be, that his example as lawyer, judge, citizen, and christian may be the theme of imitation."

(For further particulars concerning the Conyngham family, see page 203.) He married December 17, 1823, Ruth Ann Butler, the daughter of General Lord Butler (See page 335). His family numbered seven children of which six grew to manhood—Colonel John Butler Conyngham, William Lord Conyngham, Thomas Conyngham, Major Charles Miner Conyngham, Mary, who married Charles Parrish, of this city, and Anna, who married Right Rev. William Bacon Stevens, D. D., LL. D., Bishop of Pennsylvania. The University of Pennsylvania in 1869, conferred the degree of LL. D. on Judge Conyngham. Redmond Conyngham, a brother of Judge Conyngham, was a native of Philadelphia and a graduate of the College of New Jersey, at Princeton. He inherited from his paternal grandfather an estate of two thousand pounds per annum in the county of Donegal, Ireland, where he spent several years of his early life. Whilst in Ireland he was the companion of Curran, Grattan, and other bright intellects of Hibernian soil. Amongst the most brilliant of these was his cousin, William Conyngham Plunkett, afterwards lord chancellor of Ireland, and who was named after Mr. Conyngham's ancester. Mr. Conyngham lived many years in this county, and in 1815 represented Luzerne county in the state legislature. In 1820 he was elected a state senator. His district was composed of the counties of Columbia, Luzerne, Northumberland, Union, and Susquehanna. In the same year he laid out the village named by him Dundaff, in Susquehanna county, in honor of his friend, Lord Dundaff, of Scotland. The village of Conyngham, in Sugarloaf township, in this county, was named in honor of Mr. Conyngham, where he resided for many years. He subsequently removed to Lancaster, Pa., where he spent the balance of his days. He married Elizabeth, a daughter of Judge Yeates, of the Supreme Court of Pennsylvania, and died June 16, 1846, aged 65 years.

BENJAMIN DRAKE WRIGHT.

Benjamin Drake Wright was admitted to the bar of Luzerne county, Pa., April 7, 1820. He was born in this city January 23, 1799. He was the second son of William Wright, who probably emigrated from Ireland with his brother, Thomas Wright, about 1663. He served through the revolutionary war, and when peace was declared he removed to Wrightsville, in this county, now the borough of Miners Mills, where his brother Thomas resided. He was a schoolmaster, and at one time lived at the corner of Union and North Main streets, in this city, where his relative, Thomas Wright Miner, M. D., resided, and where he died. The wife of William Wright was Sarah Ann Osborne, a Quakeress. They had four sons—Major Thomas Wright, U. S. A.; J. J. B. Wright, a surgeon in the United States army, who died at Carlisle, Pa.; William Wright, who resided at Prairie du Chien, Wisconsin; and Benjamin Drake Wright. One daughter married Benjamin Drake, and another, Job Barton, the father of the late Samuel M. Barton, postmaster of this city. In his early manhood Benjamin Drake Wright removed to Florida. He was an alderman of Pensacola, Fla., subsequently mayor of the city, and also collector of the port. He was United States district attorney of Florida, under the territorial government, judge of the United States court of Florida, and chief justice of the Supreme Court of the state of Florida. He married, February 23, 1826, Josephine de la Rua, daughter of John de la Rua, granddaughter of Francisco de la Rua, a native of Madrid, Spain. The latter's wife was Josefa de la Rua, a native of Canary Islands. Mr. and Mrs. Wright had a family of eight children, six sons and two daughters, of whom three survive, Laura—wife of A. T. Yniestra; George Wright and Henry T. Wright. Benjamin D. Wright died April 28, 1875.

CHESTER BUTLER.

Chester Butler, who was admitted to the bar of Luzerne county, Pa., August 8, 1820, was a native of this city, where he was born March 21, 1798. He was the son of General Lord Butler and the brother of the late Lord Butler and John L. Butler, of this city. (See page 335). He represented Luzerne county in the legislature of the state in 1832, 1838, 1839 and 1843, and from 1845 to 1850 was in the congress of the United States. In 1832 he was on the anti-masonic electoral ticket of Pennsylvania. He was elected in 1818 one of the trustees of the Wilkes-Barre Academy, and served for twenty years, three years of which he was secretary of the board. He was a teacher and also a student in the old academy. From 1821 to 1824 he was register and recorder of Luzerne county. He was a graduate of Princeton (N. J.) College in the class of 1817, and read law at the Litchfield, Conn., law school. His wife was Sarah Hollenback, widow of Jacob Cist, deceased. One son, George H. Butler, was the only issue of their marriage. Chester Butler died in Philadelphia October 5, 1850. His son, George H. Butler, died unmarried in the same city March 16, 1863. The latter read law with Andrew T. McClintock, in this city, but we can find no record of his admission to the bar. He was also a graduate of Princeton College.

JAMES WATSON BOWMAN.

James Watson Bowman was admitted to the bar of Luzerne county, Pa., August 8, 1820. He was the second child of Ebenezer Bowman, and studied law with his father. (See page 1050.) He married, in 1825, Harriet Drake, of Wilkes-Barre, and died in 1834, leaving two children—George Drake Bowman and Amelia Watson Bowman, who married George Painter, of Muncy, Pa.

SAMUEL BOWMAN.

Samuel Bowman was admitted to the bar of Luzerne county, Pa., August 8, 1821. He was born in Wilkes-Barre May 21, 1800, and was the sixth child of Captain Samuel Bowman, a son of Captain Thaddeus Bowman. At the outbreak of the revolution Captain Samuel Bowman enlisted and became a captain in the continental army, and served until the close of the war. It is said that he was with Major Andre the night before his execution, and commanded the guard that led him to the gallows. He married, in Philadelphia, November 3, 1784, Eleanor Ledlie, of Easton, Pa., whose parents were from Ireland. About 1789 he moved to Wilkes-Barre, where his wife had a large landed estate, to which he devoted his time. He died June 25, 1818, being gored to death by a bull. He was one of the trustees of the Wilkes-Barre Academy from 1807 until his death. In 1794 he was captain of a company, and led the Luzerne volunteers to help quell the whiskey insurrection, and to Newburg in 1799. Ebenezer Bowman, of the Luzerne bar, was the uncle of Samuel Bowman. (See page 1050.) Samuel Bowman was educated at the Wilkes-Barre Academy. The law had been chosen as his profession, but he soon became a student of divinity, having been brought under deep religious conviction by the sudden death of his father, as before stated. He was ordained in Philadelphia, August 25, 1823, and entered upon his ministerial duty in Lancaster county, Pa., the same year, preaching his first sermons in Leacock and Salisbury townships, where he remained about two years. In 1825 he was stationed at Easton, but in the following year he returned to his former charge in Lancaster county. In 1827 he accepted a call to the rectorship of St. James' church in Lancaster, Pa., one of the oldest Episcopal parishes in the state. His attachment to his parish and to the community was so deep that he would never accept any position which involved the necessity of abandoning Lancaster as his home. In 1845 he was, against his own inclination, voted for as the candidate of those in convention who opposed Rev. Dr. Tyng for bishop, and was several times elected by the clergy, but the laity refused to concur. The contest was long and exciting, and Bishop Potter was finally elected as a compromise candidate, much to Dr. Bowman's gratification, who would have accepted the office with much reluctance, if at all, for the reason above stated. In 1848 he was elected bishop of the diocese of Indiana, which he declined, again reiterating his desire to remain with the flock between whom and himself there was such a strong attachment. With regard to the two parties which unfortunately exist in the Episcopal church, Bishop Bowman was a conservative, even to the extent of ignoring the existence of what are called "High and Low Church."

His last discourse was based upon the words of St. Paul: "For I am determined not to know anything among you save Jesus Christ and Him crucified." And this was the spirit in which he accepted the office of assistant bishop three years before. The convention failing to make a choice between Dr. Vinton and himself, Dr. Bowman offered a resolution for a committee to report to the convention a candidate, which he advocated with great earnestness and ability, solemnly and emphatically withdrawing his name from the nomination before the convention. He said God brought men together by ways unknown to them. His name had been placed there without any feeling of ambition on his part. His great and only desire was that he might pass the remainder of his days in the humble yet honorable station of the ministry to which he was so sincerely attached. He expressed the hope that the carrying out of this resolution would prove the breaking down of the partition that existed between some portions of the church, in which church all should be of "one Lord, one faith, and one baptism. Let the only strife be," he continued, "as to who shall expend most labor in the cause of God. Let us no longer array ourselves under party leaders. Let our only motto be, '*Pro Deo, pro ecclesia, et hominum salute.*'" After the election of Dr. Bowman he was introduced to the convention by a committee as the assistant bishop. He closed a feeling address with the "fervent hope that the work which the convention had accomplished that day would redound to the unity and advancement of the church through Jesus Christ our Lord." The death of Bishop Bowman occurred in this wise: He had left home on a tour of western visitation in his official capacity, and had taken the 6 A. M. train on the Allegheny Valley railroad, *en route* for Butler, where he had an appointment to administer the rite of confirmation on the following Sabbath. At Freeport, twenty-four miles from Pittsburg, he proposed taking the stage to Butler. After proceeding about nineteen miles the train was halted in consequence of a bridge which had been injured by a late freshet and a land slide nearly two miles beyond. Arrangements had been made to convey the passengers over this part of the road in a hand car, a locomotive and a passenger car being in readiness on the other side to carry them on. Several gentlemen preferred walking, and among them Bishop Bowman. The workmen having charge of the hand car, when returning to the bridge, found the bishop lying by the road side, having fallen upon his face as if seized with apoplexy. His face was buried in his hat, in which was his pocket handkerchief that he had saturated with water in a small stream a few paces back, doubtless as a preventive of sunstroke. Genesee College conferred the degree of doctor of divinity on Bishop Bowman. He married Susan Sitgreaves, daughter of Samuel Sitgreaves, of Easton. She died in 1830, and he married, in 1836, Harriet Clarkson, of Lancaster. Bishop Bowman died August 3, 1861.

AMZI FULLER.

Amzi Fuller was admitted to the bar of Luzerne county, Pa., January 11, 1822. (See page 580 for further particulars concerning Mr. Fuller.) He spent the greater part of his life in Wayne county, Pa. A few years before his death he purchased the property on River street now occupied by the widow of his son, Henry M. Fuller, and Henry A. Fuller, his grandson, of Hon. Charles D. Shoemaker, and removed here, where he spent the latter years of his life.

JOEL JONES.

Joel Jones, who was admitted to the bar of Luzerne county, Pa., January 14, 1823, was a native of Coventry, Conn. He was a descendant of Colonel John Jones, who was born at Fregarion, in the Isle of Anglesey, North Wales, in 1580. He was married in 1623 to Henrietta, second sister of Oliver Cromwell, lord protector of England, was one of the judges of Charles I in 1648, and of Cromwell's house of lords in 1653, and lord lieutenant of Ireland from 1650 to 1659. He was beheaded by Charles II October 17, 1660.

William Jones, son of Colonel John Jones, was born in London in 1624, was a lawyer at Westminster for a number of years, was a resident of the Fields of St. Martin, Middlesex, and was married to Hannah Eaton, of the parish of St. Andrew's, Holborn, London, spinster, by the Rev. John Rowe, sr., Independent minister of the church, in July, 1659. She was the youngest daughter of Hon. Theophilus Eaton, the first governor of New Haven colony, and was born in London in 1633. Hon. William Jones was for several years deputy governor of the colonies of New Haven and Connecticut, retired from office in 1698, and died in New Haven October, 1706, aged eighty-two years. His wife died May 4, 1707, aged seventy-four years. They were buried under the monumental stone of Governor Eaton, and the following inscription was placed upon it, after giving their names and the date of their deaths:

> To attend you, sir, under these famed stones,
> Are come your honored son and daughter Jones,
> On each hand to repose their weary bones.
> The memory of the just is blest.

Isaac Jones, son of William and Hannah Jones, was born June 21, 1671, in New Haven, and was married to Deborah Clarke, daughter of James Clarke, of Stratford, Conn., by Hon. William Jones, deputy governor of Connecticut, November 25, 1692. He died in New Haven in 1741. His wife died in the same place May 28, 1735. Joel Jones, son of Isaac and Deborah Jones, lived and died in North Bolton, Conn. His eldest brother was Isaac Jones, of Saybrook, Conn. Joel Jones married a Miss Hale. He was born in 1695 and died in 1775. He left ten sons and five daughters living at the time of his death. Amassa Jones, son of Joel Jones, lived in Coventry, and removed to Wilkes-Barre, Pa., about 1818, where he died in 1843. His body and that of his wife were removed by his youngest son, Matthew Hale Jones, to Easton, Pa. The wife of Amassa Jones was Elizabeth Huntington, a daughter of Rev. Joseph Huntington, D. D., of Coventry, Conn. He was a descendant of Simon Huntington, of Norwich, Conn., and a brother of Samuel Huntington, a signer of the declaration of independence, governor of Connecticut, chief justice of the same state, and at one time president of the American congress. Huntington township, in this county, took its name from him.

JOEL JONES.

Joel Jones, eldest son of Amassa and Elizabeth Jones, was born October 26, 1795, and removed to Wilkes-Barre with his father's family. He was educated at Yale College, from which he graduated in 1817, and the Litchfield law school, and studied law with Judge Bristol, of New Haven, Conn., where he was first admitted to the bar. He practiced law at Wilkes-Barre, Easton, Pa., and Philadelphia. He was a man of large legal knowledge. When appointed with W. Rawle, who was upwards of eighty years of age when appointed, and T. I. Wharton to revise the civil code of the state, those gentlemen expressed to their friends surprise that a man of so little prominence should have made such acquisitions in the law, little knowing how many wearisome years he had spent in his small office on the northwestern corner of Independence square in studying the principles of jurisprudence. He did good service to the state as one of the revisers, and some of the reports of the commissioners which made the most important suggestions were written by him. Some parts of the new system were remodeled and re-written exclusively by him, as, for example, the disposition of estates of intestates, which passed the legislature without the change of a word, and they have scarcely been touched down to the present day. Some of the other matters for legislation which were acted upon by the commissioners were an act relating to registers and registers' courts, the Orphans' Court, relating to last wills and testaments, relating to executors and administratrators, relating to counties and townships and county and township officers, to weights and measures, to the organization of the courts of justice, to roads, highways and bridges, to inns, taverns and retailers of vinous and spiritous liquors, to the support and employment of the poor, to county rates and levies and township rates and levies, to the militia, to elections by the citizens of the commonwealth, to the inspection of articles of trade and commerce—most of which were passsed by the legislature as reported. Mr. Jones was subsequently appointed an associate judge and the president judge of the district court of Philadelphia. These offices he held from 1835 to 1847. Girard College never did a better thing than when it made Judge Jones its first president, and the career of usefulness on which that institution entered is largely due to the wise manner in which he interpreted the will of Mr. Girard and the legal provisions enacted concerning it. He filled this position during most of the years 1847 and 1848. He then returned to his favorite pursuit of studying and practicing law. Immediately thereupon he was nominated as a candidate for mayor of the city of Philadelphia, and was elected by a large popular vote. On retiring from the office in 1849 he returned again to the law, and the force of his speech and his pen was frequently felt in the courts. He also wrote for the magazines of the day on literary, philosophic and religious subjects. The volume published after his death, which he had modestly entitled "Notes on Scripture," will long attest the thought which he gave to the profoundest themes with which the human mind can become conversant. Judge Jones was a most exemplary christian and an active and useful member of the Presbyterian church. He died February 3, 1860. Anson Jones, an American physician, and president of the republic of Texas at the time of its annexation to the United States, was a kinsman of Judge Jones. He settled in Brazoria, Texas, in 1833, and took a prominent part in the political and military movements which resulted in the independence of that republic. He was minister to the United States in 1838, and afterwards for three years secretary of state under President Houston. In 1844 he succeeded Houston as president. He died by his own hands in 1858. In that year he was the rival of Louis T. Wigfall for a seat in the United States senate, and when defeated, invited all the leaders of the party and Wigfall himself to a public dinner, and after entertaining them blew his brains out at the dinner table, with the remark that as Texas did not need him any more he would emigrate. Judge Joel Jones married, in 1833, Elizabeth Sparhawk, a daughter of John Sparhawk, one of the non-importing merchants of Philadelphia in 1774, a grandson of Sir William Pepperill, of Kittery Point, Maine (then Massachusetts), who captured Louisburg during the old French war. The wife of John Sparhawk was Elizabeth Perkins, a native of Barbadoes. Judge Jones had six children, only two of whom survive—S. Huntington Jones, a Philadelphia lawyer, and Rev. John Sparhawk Jones, D. D., a Presbyterian clergyman. In his young days Judge Jones was principal of the Wilkes-Barre Academy. The late

Judge Sharswood said of Judge Jones: "As a judge he was remarkable for great courtesy, immovable patience, and unwearied attention. He was, therefore, a safe, though, it must be confessed, a slow judge. When he had once formed an opinion at *nisi prius*, which was after great deliberation, he was hardly ever known to change it. His law learning was very considerable, but it lay more among the ancients than the modern books, and it was with much difficulty that he could turn the current of his ideas upon legal subjects into new channels. Kind in his disposition, yielding in his temper, affable in his manner, unbending in his integrity, and pure in his life, his memory is that of the just—is blessed. He was an excellent Hebrew and Greek scholar, and an earnest student of the bible in the original tongues. He published a volume entitled 'The Patriarchal Age; or, The Story of Joseph,' in which much critical acuteness, as well as extensive Oriental erudition, was exhibited."

BENJAMIN ALDEN BIDLACK.

Benjamin Alden Bidlack was admitted to the bar of Luzerne county, Pa., January 5, 1825. He was a descendant of Christopher Bidlack, who came from England to Windham, Connecticut, in 1722. Captain James Bidlack, a descendant of Christopher Bidlack, came with his family to the Wyoming valley in 1777. A son of his, Captain James Bidlack, jr., fell at the head of his company in the battle and massacre of Wyoming, only eight of the whole number surviving that fearful tragedy. Another son was made a prisoner on Long Island, and "was starved to death by the British." Benjamin Bidlack, another son, came with his father to the valley of Wyoming. The history of the Bidlack family is identified with the romantic period of the history of this far-famed valley. The father, when quite advanced in years, was captain of a company of old men organized for the defense of their homes while their sons entered the regular service and were called away to other points of danger. He was surprised by a company of Indians and suffered a distressing captivity, which only terminated with the end of the war. He returned to the Wyoming valley and lived to see his country rise into almost unhoped for prosperity—the fruit of the services of the patriots of the revolution. Benjamin Bidlack was seven years in the service as a soldier. He was at Boston when Washington assembled his forces to oppose Gage, at Trenton at the taking of the Hessians, at Yorktown at the surrender of Cornwallis, and in the camp at Newburg when the army was disbanded. When peace with the mother country was concluded he returned to the lovely valley of Wyoming, as he hoped to live in quiet and to give succor to his aged sire in the decline of life. But alas! He came to this spot, rendered so beautiful and lovely by the hand of nature's God, to see further exhibitions of the malignity of the human heart—"The Pennamite and Yankee war," a fierce and bloody conflict between the Connecticut and Pennsylvania settlers — for the title of the soil was then renewed. Young Bidlack was what the Pennsylvanians called a "wild Yankee." He was not disposed to engage in the fray, for although he was as good a soldier as ever breathed, he had a kind heart, and of course, hated this unnatural war. He engaged in business and made a trip down the Susquehanna to Sunbury about the distance of fifty miles. Here he was seized by the Pennsylvania party and put in jail. He was a jovial fellow and manifested so much good nature and was so fine a singer that a company from the neighborhood frequently assembled in the evening to hear him sing. On one occasion he told them that he had a favorite song they had never heard. It was "The Old Swaggering Man," but he could not sing it without more room, and he must have a staff in his hand, as the effect depended much on the action. Nothing suspicious, they gave him a cudgel and allowed him liberty to make his sallies into the hall. All at once as he commenced his chorus, "Here goes the old swaggering man," he darted out of the door, and in a trice was out of their reach, outdistancing the fleetest of them. The next day he was safe at home and was never more disturbed. Bidlack having a most splendid voice, and being full of fun and frolic, was not unfrequently the center and life of sporting and drinking parties. Still he had religious notions and religious feelings, and wild and wicked as he was, he would go to the Methodist meetings and lead the singing, sometimes, indeed, when he was scarcely in a condition to do it with becoming gravity. The Methodist preachers who planted the gospel standard in the interior of this state were the pioneers of the country, and many of them officers or soldiers of the revolution. They were consequently men of nerve and capable of great endurance. At length Mr. Bidlack was awakened and converted to God, and henceforth he "sowed" no more "wild oats." He soon began to exhort his neighbors to "flee from the wrath to come," and to sing the songs of Zion with a heart and a power that moved the feelings, while it charmed the ear. " Ben Bidlack has become a Methodist preacher," rang through the country and stirred up a mighty commotion. His first circuit embraced his own neighborhood and even the jail from which but a few years before he had escaped, shouting, " Here goes the old swaggering man." The appointment at least shows the state of the public mind in relation to him where he was best known, and is very much to his credit. Mr. Bidlack was married and had three children when he commenced travelling. During his effective relation to the conference he had sixteen appointments, standing in the following order: Wyoming, Seneca, Delaware, Ulster, Herkimer, Mohawk, Otsego, Chenango, Pompey, Seneca, Lyons, Shamokin, Northumberland and Lycoming. Look at his removes. One year he goes from Wyoming to the Seneca Lake, and the next from that to the Delaware. This was itinerancy in deed and in truth. Any one who can recollect what was the condition of the roads sixty-five or seventy years ago in the regions in which he travelled and through which he removed his family can, in some measure, appreciate the labors which he performed. Mr. Bidlack was removed every year during his itinerancy, with the exception of three. His first wife was Lydia, a daughter of Prince Alden, of Newport township. He was the son of Andrew, who was the son of Captain Jonathan, who was the son of Hon. John Alden. (See page 305.) After the death of his first wife he married the widow of Lieutenant Lawrence Myers, of Kingston. Mr. Bidlack stood something over six feet, erect, with a full, prominent chest, broad shoulders and powerful limbs. His black hair sprinkled with gray hung upon his shoulders, and his large, open features bore an expression of gravity and benignity, mingled with cheerfulness, which at once prepossessed one in his favor. His voice was powerful and harmonious. Naturally, his voice was the very soul of music, and much of its melody remained until he was far advanced in life. He was an effective preacher, though not a profound thinker. His sermons were fine specimens of native eloquence, and were often attended with great power. One of his favorite discourses—at least it was a favorite with his hearers—was upon the words: "They that turn the world upside down have come hither also." In laying out his discourse on this text, he proceeded: First, I shall show that the world was made *right side up.* Secondly, That it has been turned *wrong side up.* And thirdly, That it is now to be turned *upside* down; then it will be *right side up again.* Here he had the main doctrines of every old-fashioned Methodist sermon directly in his way. First, man was created holy; secondly, he has fallen, and thirdly, he is redeemed by Christ, and must be regenerated by the Holy Ghost. The neame the *exhortation* to sinners to "repent and be converted." The sermons of Mr. Bidlack were plain expositions of scripture, and manifested a thorough knowledge of the bible, and considerable acquaintance with the writings of Wesley and Fletcher. He died November 27, 1845, in the eighty-seventh year of his age.

Benjamin Alden Bidlack, only son of Rev. Benjamin Bidlack and Lydia, his wife, was born in Paris, Oneida county, N. Y., September 8, 1804. He completed his education at the academy in this city, then under the charge of Joel and Samuel Jones, and read law with Garrick Mallery. Shortly after his admission he was appointed deputy attorney general for this county. In 1834 he was treasurer of Luzerne county. In 1835 and 1836 he represented this county in the legislature of the state. He was a representative in congress from this county from 1841 to 1845. Immediately after the expiration of his term in congress he was appointed minister to New Granada (now the United States of Colombia), and died in Bogota, February 6, 1849. The American residents of that city erected a very handsome monument to his memory. He established and edited *The Northern Eagle*, the first paper ever published in Pike county, Pa. In 1833 he, in connection with a Mr. Atherholt, purchased the *Republican Farmer*, and they in turn sold the newspaper to Samuel P. Collings in 1835. While in New Granada Mr. Bidlack wrote a work on the manners and customs of the natives and the resources of the country, fragments of which he sent home. He intended to publish the same, but his untimely death and the loss of his manuscript prevented its publication. He also negotiated a very important treaty between this country and New Granada, which received great commendation from the president and other men in high places. Mr. Bidlack was twice married. His first wife was Fanny Stewart, a daughter of James Stewart. (See page 836.) Mr. Bidlack married his second wife September 8, 1829. She was Margaret M. Wallace, daughter of James Wallace, and granddaughter of William Wallace. The wife of William Wallace was Elizabeth d'Aertz, a daughter of Francis Josephus d'Aertz, who came from France with General Lafayette, and who married the daughter of Colonel John Broadhead. Mr. and Mrs. Bidlack had the following children—William Wallace Bidlack, who, during the late civil war, served in the field and hospital as surgeon; Mary E. Bidlack, who married Edward James Reed, of Philadelphia; Benjamin Alden Bidlack; James B. W. Bidlack, who served as a soldier in the late civil war, and has been for the past year medical director of the American Exposition in London; Frances B. Bidlack; Helen Bidlack, and Blanche d'Aertz Bidlack. The widow of Benjamin Alden Bidlack married for her second husband the late Thomas W. Miner, M. D., of this city, and is still living.

HENRY PETTEBONE.

Henry Pettebone, who was admitted to the bar of Luzerne county, Pa., August 3, 1825, was the son of Oliver Pettebone, and grandson of Noah Pettebone, of Simsbury, Conn. (See page 460.) Henry Pettebone was born in Kingston, Pa., October 5, 1802. He was educated at the Kingston Academy, and read law with George Denison. On February 17, 1830, he was appointed prothonotary and clerk of the Orphans' Court, Quarter Sessions and Oyer and Terminer for a term of three years, and on January 21, 1833, he was re-appointed to the same offices for an additional term of three years. On March 6, 1845, he was appointed an associate judge of Luzerne county for a term of five years. He was also a merchant and a contractor on the North Branch Canal. In 1828 Mr. Pettebone, in connection with Henry Held, established *The Republican Farmer* in this city. In 1831 Mr. Pettebone sold his interest to J. J. Adam. The wife of Henry Pettebone was Elizabeth, daughter of John Sharps, a native of Greenwich township, Warren county, N. J. The Sharp family were very prominent in Greenwich at an early day. The name was originally Sharpensteins, and the family were of Dutch origin. Four brothers, John, Stuffle, Jacob and Peter each owned extensive farms, which they improved and upon which they resided. Jacob Sharps at a later day removed to Kingston, Pa. He was the father of John Sharps, the father of Mrs. Pettebone. The wife of John Sharps was Martha Welch. Mr. and Mrs. Pettebone left two children to survive them—William Pettebone and Martha, who married William Streater, son of Dr. Streater, of this city. Judge Pettebone was at one time clerk of the senate of Pennsylvania, and was at the time of his death, May 5, 1851, secretary and general ticket agent of the Lackawanna & Bloomsburg Railroad Company.

BENJAMIN PARKE.

Benjamin Parke read law in this city, and was admitted to the bar of Luzerne county, Pa., in 1825. He was the grandson of Captain Benjamin Parke, who was slain at the battle of Bunker Hill, June 17, 1775. Thomas Parke, son of Benjamin Parke, was brought up under the care of his grandfather, a clergyman, and received a good education. He removed from Charleston, R. I., in 1796, and was one of the first settlers of Dimock, Luzerne (now Susquehanna) county. In 1800 he married Eunice Champlin, of Newport, R. I. He was a fine mathematician, a good practical surveyor, and was an occasional contributor to the newspapers of the day. He had filled several minor offices in his native state, invested his patrimony and means in the purchase of the Connecticut title to lands in Pennsylvania, and came here the legal owner, as he supposed, of some ten thousand acres—nearly half the township of Bidwell—lying on the waters of the Meshoppen, and covering parts of what is now Dimock and Springville. He fixed his residence in the former (Parkvale), where he lived till his death in 1842. When he came to look up his lands he found only two settlers west of "Nine Partners," and they were near what is now Brooklyn Centre. West of that to the Wyalusing creek was a belt of twenty-five miles, north and south, an unbroken forest. With the aid of his compass he explored and marked a path to the forks of the Wyalusing, the nearest place where any breadstuffs could be obtained, from whence they were to be brought on his back until the next season, when a small green crop was raised. In the winter of 1797 he walked home to Charleston, and walked back the next spring. By the Trenton decree he lost all the wordly estate he possessed, and was afterwards obliged to purchase upon credit from his successful opponents, paying by surveying about six hundred acres, including the farm upon which he lived and died. He was for three years one of the commissioners of Luzerne county, and also in 1811 one of the three trustees appointed by the governor to run the lines, lay off and organize Susquehanna county.

Benjamin Parke, eldest son of Thomas Parke, practiced his profession in this city a few years after his admission, and then removed to Harrisburg, Pa. While there he, in company with William F. Packer (afterwards governor), edited and published the *Keystone*, then the central and leading organ of the democratic party in Pennsylvania. After disposing of that paper he for a time edited the Harrisburg *Argus*, and commenced the publication of the *Pennsylvania Farmer and Common School Intelligencer*. In 1834 he was appointed by Governor Wolf to be the prothonotary of the middle district of the Supreme Court, consisting of sixteen counties. He also held the office of commissioner in bankruptcy, and was the principal compiler of Parke and Johnson's "Digest of the laws of Pennsylvania," published in 1837. He returned to Susquehanna county in 1860.

JAMES McCLINTOCK.

James McClintock, who was admitted to the bar of Luzerne county, Pa., January 23, 1826, was a native of Jersey Shore, Pa. He was the son of Thomas McClintock, and grandson of James McClintock, both of whom were natives of Raphoe, county of Donegal, Ireland. He read law with his uncle, Ethan Baldwin, and was for some years one of the most prominent lawyers at the Luzerne bar. He was a great orator, and whenever he spoke the court room was certain to be crowded. In 1832 he was a candidate for congress against Thomas W. Miner and Andrew Beaumont, but was defeated by the latter. Soon after this he lost his wife (who was Miss Johnson, of Germantown, Pa.) and child. He then had a severe attack of brain fever, and became hopelessly insane. He survived his insanity over fifty years.

GEORGE C. DRAKE.

George C. Drake was admitted to the bar of Luzerne county, Pa., August 8, 1827. He was the son of Benjamin Drake, who was born April 22, 1778, in Mendham, Morris county, N. J. The latter was a merchant in this city for some years, and was also a blacksmith. His first wife, whom he married January 23, 1799, was Susanna Wright, a daughter of William Wright, an old resident of this city. (See page 1125.) His second wife, whom he married March 2, 1817, was Nancy S. Ely, a native of Abington, Montgomery county, Pa., where she was born February 10, 1788. The only living descendant of this second marriage is William Drake Loomis, of this city. George C. Drake was born in Wilkes-Barre, May 25, 1806. He practiced his profession in this city for a few years, was district attorney of the county, and in 1833 became a Protestant Episcopal minister. He officiated as such at Bloomsburg, Pa., Danville, Pa., Muncy, Pa., and other places. He was married three times. His first wife was Abigail Haines, a daughter of George Haines, of this city. There were two children by this marriage—Abigail and Elizabeth—both deceased. His second wife was Margaret Shoemaker, a daughter of Jacob Shoemaker and his wife, Sophia Robb, daughter of Robert Robb, of Muncy, Pa. By this marriage Mr. Drake left five surviving children—Margaret, wife of Dr. J. J. Whitney; Charles; Harriet, wife of F. C. Peterman; Benjamin and Anna Drake. His third wife was Sophia Robb, a daughter of William Robb and his wife Mary, daughter of Henry Shoemaker, of Muncy, Pa. Mr. Drake left two surviving children by this marriage—Susan, wife of Milo W. Ward, and John Drake. George C. Drake died at Muncy, Pa., June 27, 1878.

SYLVESTER DANA.

Sylvester Dana, who was admitted to the bar of Luzerne county, Pa., November 7, 1828, was a native of Wilkes-Barre, Pa., where he was born May 28, 1806. He was the son of Anderson Dana, a native of Connecticut, who was born August 11, 1765, who was the son of Anderson Dana, born in 1733, and his wife, Susanna (Huntington) Dana, who was the son of Jacob Dana, born in 1698, who was the son of Jacob Dana, born in 1664, who was the son of Richard Dana, who was born in France, April 15, 1612, and died in Cambridge, Mass., April 2, 1690. Sylvester Dana was educated at the Wilkes-Barre Academy, then under the charge of Rev. Joseph H. Jones, D. D., and at Yale College, from which he graduated in 1826. He read law with Garrick Mallery, and practiced in this city and Circleville, Ohio. Owing to failing health and trouble with his voice, which prevented public speaking, he returned to Wilkes-Barre from Ohio, and in 1835 became the principal of the Wilkes-Barre Academy, which position he held until 1839, when he established Dana's Academy. A few years since he gave up his school and removed to Lower Makefield, Bucks county, Pa., where he died June 19,

1882. Mr. Dana married, March 26, 1832, Elizabeth Brown, a daughter of Moses and Elizabeth (Frisbie) Brown, of Connecticut. Five children were the result of this union—Eunice A. Dana, Elizabeth Dana, Louisa A. Dana, Ellen Dana, and Robert S. Dana, whose wife is Fanny Pawlings, who have one son, Sylvester Dana.

WILLIAM STERLING ROSS.

William Sterling Ross was commissioned an associate judge of Luzerne county, Pa., May 6, 1829, as the successor of Jesse Fell, which position he held until 1839—the time of the adoption of the amended constitution of the state. His wife died June 23, 1882. They left no children. For a sketch of Judge Ross see page 296.

THOMAS EDWARD PAINE.

Thomas Edward Paine, who was admitted to the bar of Luzerne county, Pa., April 7, 1830, was a descendant of Thomas Paine, of Eastham, Cape Cod, Mass., who, at various periods from 1767 to 1782, was a member of the Massachusetts legislature, and in the list of deputies to the Old Colony court the names of his father and grandfather often occur as far back as 1671, the family having resided at Eastham from about the first settlement of the Cape. The name of Thomas Paine appears in the history of Eastham upon various committees appointed for carrying out the principles of freedom in resistance to British tyranny during the revolution. His mother, Alice Mayo, was a descendant of Governor Thomas Prince, and Robert Treat Paine, a signer of the declaration of independence, was his cousin, as was also William Payne, the father of John Howard Payne, author of "Home, Sweet Home." Having lost most of his property by the reverses of the war, and his wife dying, he removed from Cape Cod to Boston, and subsequently to Maine. He was a man of intelligence and piety. The family being thus broken up, the sons were thrown upon their own resources and widely scattered, though keeping up by correspondence the bond of family union. One of the elder brothers was an early volunteer in the continental army, and another was twice taken prisoner on board a privateer. Clement Paine, the son of Thomas Paine, was born August 11, 1769, at Eastham, and at the age of fourteen years went to Portland (then Falmouth), Maine, to learn the printing business. He was subsequently engaged in various publishing offices in Boston and New York, and in 1791 formed the project, in connection with his brother Seth, of establishing a press and journal at "Kaatskill on the Hudson." But the type and other material ordered by them from London was lost at sea in the brig "Betsy," and the enterprise was abandoned, although we find that the publication of the *Catskill Packet* was commenced a year or two later by Croswell & Co., with good success. In 1791 and 1792 Clement Paine was engaged in the office of Claypoole's *Daily Advertiser* at Philadelphia, then the seat of the general government under Washington's administration. It was there he frequently saw the first president, and a strong sentiment of respect and admiration then formed for the personal character of Washington remained with him through life. In September, 1792, Clement Paine, in connection with his brother, David Paine, erected a store and potash factory at Rensselaerville, N. Y. The business, however, did not prove a success. In March, 1794, David writes from "Owago on the Susquehanna" to Clement, who remained to wind up the concern, and soon after from Tioga Point, where the former had become connected with William Bingham in the purchase and sale of lands under the Connecticut title. Clement came to Tioga Point in December, 1794, and the brothers were there connected in trade and land operations. During the winter and spring of 1796 Clement had charge of the business of his brother Seth at Charleston, S. C., who was publishing the *City Gazette*, the first daily paper ever printed there. His partner was Peter Freneau, secretary of the state, and the brother of Philip Freneau, well known as a poet and journalist. In 1796 David and Clement Paine erected the house which was in after years and for a long period the family residence of the latter. It was in part built by the father of Judge Elwell. The conflicting land titles of Connecticut and Pennsylvania began to interfere much with both public and private property throughout the region, and in 1797 Clement Paine writes: "Many people are of opinion that violent measures will be resorted to before the dispute is finally settled, but I can hardly persuade myself that this State will attempt a thing so amazingly absurd as it would be, under the present circumstances, to send on troops to dispossess the settlers here, who, by estimation, now amount to from twelve to fifteen thousand people. We shall continue regularly to prosecute our business, notwithstanding the hostile attitude of our enemies, and such is the general intention of the people." Later in the same year he writes: "A great stagnation of mercantile and speculative business is the universal complaint throughout this northern country. The sale of new land in any situation seems entirely suspended, and it is difficult to obtain money for any kind of property." The brothers were associated with Colonel Franklin and others in vindicating the rights of the settlers, and in behalf of the common cause David made repeated journeys to Philadelphia and New England. During the uncertainty and depression of the times Clement began the study of law, and again spent a winter or two in Philadelphia. In March, 1801, on a passage from that city to New England, his vessel was wrecked on the south coast of Long Island, and he, with other passengers, barely escaped with their lives. In 1801 his esteemed brother, Seth Paine, whose publishing house had grown into an extensive business, died of yellow fever at Charleston, and at that city, for a part of several subsequent years, Clement Paine was engaged in the collection of claims and the settlement of the estate, in which he succeeded beyond expectation. For quite a long period after its first settlement Tioga Point, or Athens, as it is now called, was the centre of trade for a considerable part of the country. During the earlier years of his business there Clement Paine purchased his stocks of goods principally from Orrin Day and Dr. Croswell, at Catskill, from whence (as for more than twenty years afterwards from New York and Philadelphia) he had them transported in wagons to Athens.

Sometimes, however, they came up the river on "Durham boats," which were propelled with poles. In July, 1806, he was married to Anne Woodbridge, a native of Glastenbury, Conn., the daughter of Major Theodore Woodbridge, an officer of the revolutionary army, who removed to Wayne county, Pa., about 1800. She died in October, 1834, at the age of fifty years. In 1812 Clement Paine was a presidential elector, casting the vote of his district for James Madison and Elbridge Gerry. During the war of 1812 he was active in procuring volunteers for the army, together with arms and supplies for their use. In 1844 he removed to Troy, Pa., where he died at the residence of his son, in March, 1849.

Thomas E. Paine, son of Clement Paine, practiced his profession in this city for several years. He became a Protestant Episcopal minister, and was ordained deacon by Bishop Kemper July 23, 1837. He was rector of St. Paul's church, Palmyra, Mo., in 1841. He died at Woodville, Miss., in 1843.

GEORGE WASHINGTON WOODWARD.

George Washington Woodward was admitted to the bar of Luzerne county, Pa., August 3, 1830, and died in Rome, Italy, May 10, 1875. He sailed for Europe from Philadelphia on October 22, 1874, to join his daughter, Lydia C., accompanied by Mrs. Woodward and her niece. After visiting many parts of England they sojourned for awhile in Paris, and thence went to Italy, stopping at various places and cities of that country, and finally settled in Rome for the remainder of the winter. Colonel Forney, in several of his letters to the *Press* from Italy, mentioned the pleasure he had in meeting Judge Woodward and his family, and particularly remarked upon the Judge's great interest in the ruins of Pompeii, among which he spent many hours. Rome, always a residence exposing foreigners to the danger of typhoid and malarial fevers, had been particularly unpleasant and unhealthy during that winter. Letters received from Rome, not only those which had appeared in public papers, but also those written to family friends at home, had all mentioned the long continuance of cold weather and unusual rains, which brought as their concomitants fever and other forms of disease. It was but a few days before his death that a letter was received from Judge Woodward designating the following August as the time of his return home. At its date he was in good health; in fact, he had never complained of any ailment during his absence.

George W. Woodward was born March 26, 1809, and was consequently in the sixty-seventh year of his age at the time of his death. His birthplace was Bethany, then the seat of justice of Wayne county, Pa. His father, at the time of his birth, was sheriff of the county, and subsequently became an associate judge, an office which he held up to the date of his death in 1829. The family had settled in Pennsylvania before the revolution. The two grandfathers of Judge Woodward formed part of a colony from Connecticut which, cotemporaneously with the emigration to Wyoming, had occupied, in the year 1774, the valley of the Wallenpaupack, which forms the present boundary between the counties of Wayne and Pike. After the battle and massacre of Wyoming the colonists were driven from their homes by the tories and Indians. The women and children were enabled to find shelter and food in the counties of Orange and Dutchess, in the state of New York, while most of the men of the colony enlisted in the revolutionary army, and generally in different regiments of the Connecticut line. Jacob Kimble, the maternal grandfather of Judge Woodward, commanded a company as captain in the Connecticut line throughout the war. After the war of the revolution, in 1783, the survivors of the settlers returned to the valley of the Wallenpaupack, and commenced that career of toil and hardship which in that age was always, for at least one generation, incident to frontier life. The colony was remote and obscure; the early improvements, in consequence of their enforced abandonment for a series of years, had become valueless, and the means of the settlers had been exhausted by the necessity for their support during their absence. The winter following their return is still traditional throughout the countryside as the severest one of the century. The nearest settlement at which supplies could be obtained was Milford, on the Delaware, and every mouthful of the food of the colonists in all that dreary winter was carried upon the backs of men who traversed upon snow-shoes the thirty miles between Milford and their homes. The colony soon became prosperous, and, like all such communities, soon began to send out into the world large numbers of hardy, vigorous, and unflinching men. From the rugged character of the country in which they were reared, and from the habits of self-reliance which their isolation induced, the colonists of the Wallenpaupack have always been distinguished for a peculiar physical and mental energy. Imbued with the blood of the Wallenpaupack, Judge Woodward had inherited with it the unbending courage, the resolute will, the clear, concentrated power, and the outspoken and open contempt for baseness and base men, which always characterized the pioneers from whom he was descended.

The early education of Judge Woodward was such as the circumstances of the country and the period permitted. The county of Wayne was upon the frontier, and the schools were designed for only the necessary wants of a community of struggling and straitened settlers. It has been said, however, that he had the advantage of a training by an elder brother, who died early, but who for the time was an accomplished mathematician, and who gave to his pupil the foundation for a thorough mathematical education. As soon as he attained a suitable age his father placed him at the Geneva Seminary—now Hobart College—at Geneva, New York, where for some years he was the classmate of several young men who have since been distinguised in public life, including the Hon. Henry S. Randall, formerly secretary of state, and the Hon. Horatio Seymour, ex-governor of New York and the democratic candidate for the presidency in 1868. From there he was transferred to the Wilkes-Barre Academy, then in charge of Dr. M. P. Orton. In every respect this change was most fortunate. The school itself was one of the last of a class of institutions which, prior to the advent of the common school system, afforded to students the means of thoroughly mastering the groundwork of classical, mathematical, and scientific knowledge. While the course of study was not greatly extended, it was thorough as far as it went. And certainly no equivalent for the old system of academical education is now in existence, except in the few schools of a polytechnic character, where a scholar can be trained in and for a specialty and nothing else. Dr. Orton himself entertained adequate conceptions of the value of his own position and a conscientious sense of his responsibility to his pupils. The academy under his charge was successful for a long period of years, and in 1828 young Woodward left it with an education which, in thoroughness, clearness, and finish, he could not have elsewhere readily acquired.

Leaving school, Judge Woodward first entered the office of the late Thomas Fuller, of Wayne county, and then of the Hon. Garrick Mallery, at Wilkes-Barre, as a student at law. Mr. Mallery had long been the leading lawyer in northern Pennsylvania, and was at that time a member of the state legislature. In April, 1831, he was appointed by Governor Wolf president judge of the Berks judicial district, and Judge Woodward, who had been admitted to the bar in August, 1830, became the occupant of his office and succeeded to his business. His success at the bar was very rapid and very great. His intellect was one of those which mature early. He had great capacity for labor, and both physical and moral courage. He was an eloquent and impressive speaker, and his weight of character, as well as his abilities, soon gave him the influence which character always secures both with courts and juries. He was in full practice in Luzerne, Wayne, Pike, Monroe and Susquehanna counties, and in the Supreme Court of the state, within a very short time after the transfer of Mr. Mallery to the bench. He was a thoroughly bred lawyer, laboring every question and every cause with unfailing energy, and his success in practice was in proportion to the expenditure he bestowed upon it. He was a man of commanding personal appearance, being over six feet high and built in proportion. On the bench he was the very personification of noble dignity, and with him no lawyer or any other person dared to trifle. Nevertheless, he was a courteous judge, always regardful of the rights and privileges of all with whom he came in contact. He was deeply versed in all legal lore, was eminently a just and an upright judge, and an earnest and sincere christian gentleman. He was an honor to the bench and a citizen and statesman to whom our country will always point with honest pride, as being among the ablest and noblest men of his epoch.

His political connections, as well from his own instinct as from inherited influences, had always been with the democratic party. From the foundation of the government his family had also been democrats. Belonging to the yeomanry of the state, whigs during the revolution and soldiers in the continental army, they had no sympathy with, and nothing to hope from, the class of men who formed the federal party of that day. His father had been elected sheriff by the democracy of Wayne county and commissioned by Governor McKean, and his commission as judge had been given him by Governor Snyder, one of that staunch race of German governors who impressed sound views of public questions upon the people of Pennsylvania in a way that art, sophistry, falsehood, violence and terrorism have in vain sought to disturb. His brothers were also democrats, and were prominent in the politics of the northern part of the state. One of them died in 1825, holding the offices of register, recorder, prothonotary, and clerk of the courts in Wayne; and another of them subsequently represented the Northampton district, to which the county was then attached, in the legislature. Devoted as he was to his profession, he always exhibited a warm and abiding interest in the political issues then pending. The struggle between the administration of General Jackson and the United States Bank was going on with all its virulence, and the position of Judge Woodward in support of the administration was taken promptly and firmly and maintained with unyielding courage and vigor. In 1835, in the unfortunate division of the party between two rival candidates, which resulted in the disaster of the election of Governor Ritner, he took strong ground in favor of Mr. Muhlenburg and against Governor Wolf. The influence of Mr. Ritner's administration upon all the interests of Pennsylvania was evil in an inexpressible degree. It also brought into power for the first time a class of dangerous men. It led to the introduction into the government of the state maxims and practices previously unknown, which, fostered by one party and tampered with by the other, have tended to subvert all safe theories, to demoralize large numbers of the people of the state, and to destroy in many politicians all sense of personal honor and public virtue. The chartering by the state legislature of the United States Bank in 1836; the avowed and shameless profligacy in the management of public improvements; the encouragement given to corporations, and cognate questions, preparing as they did, in an insidious way, the public mind for that tendency to centralized despotism in the national government which is so lamentably manifest now, were all fruits of this original misfortune. From that time to the present there has been no single hour when the public interests have not required at the hands of every Pennsylvania patriot the most patient and vigilant watchfulness and the most energetic and unrelaxing effort to defeat the selfish schemes of speculators and jobbers, and to arrest the tendency which has been uniform and constant toward the subversion of all democratic institutions. In this duty, it is but justice to Judge Woodward to say, that he was always ready to make the sacrifices and to assume the burdens which patriotism required of him. Acting steadily with the democratic party, watching anxiously the course of public events, and always ready with his pen, his voice, and his vote to vindicate safe principles, he shrunk from none of the occasional odium and none of the local inconveniences which all men who keep unflinchingly in the path of duty must at some period encounter.

In 1836 Judge Woodward was elected a delegate to the convention called by the legislature to reform the constitution of the state. Associated with him from Luzerne county were Andrew Bedford, M. D., William Swetland and E. W. Sturdevant, Esqs. In May, 1837, the convention met. It embraced the most experienced and able men of the commonwealth. Its numbers included lawyers in the leading ranks of the bar, judges who had been long upon the bench, and gentlemen who had held high positions in the state and national governments. When it assembled there was a small majority opposed to any reform whatever, and that majority included almost every member of established reputation. As a leading member upon the judiciary committee, although only twenty-eight years of age, he at once took rank with such men as John Sergeant, James M. Porter, Thaddeus Stevens, Daniel Agnew, Tobias Sellers, William Findlay, and William M. Meredith. As a pungent, polished, erudite debater he found few equals and no superior, and soon took high rank. He believed in all that was expressed in the old democratic motto, "This world is governed too much," and "the best government is that which governs least." Judge Woodward was then an obscure and unknown lawyer from the north and one of the youngest men in the convention; and with defined and strong views in favor of reform, the prospect of success seemed disheartening and unpromising enough. But the feelings of the people of the state were distinct and soon came to be distinctly announced. One step after another was gained, and in the end every object which had been sought by the call of the convention was gained. These debates covered in their range all the leading and vital questions involved in the theories and practices of representative government. Under the old constitution the judges of the state had been appointed by the governor for life. A leading struggle in the convention was to limit this tenure, and it resulted in a provision for the appointment of judges of the Supreme Court for fifteen years and of the judges of original jurisdiction for ten years. Inferior magistrates had been appointed for life also. It was provided that they, as well as the executive officers of the different counties, should be elected by the people. The power of corporations to appropriate the private property of the citizen under legislative grant was restricted, and in all cases of such appropriation security to the citizen was required. In order to settle a question, which had even then become a source of anxious and angry controversy, by constitutional enactment, the right of suffrage was limited to the *white* inhabitants of Pennsylvania. In the earlier constitutions of the state no necessity had occurred to their framers for the insertion of this limitation. No man had dreamed that the rights of political citizenship would be ever claimed for negroes. The argument of Judge Woodward upon this question in the convention was the clearest, ablest, and most convincing vindication of the proposed amendment which the debates contain. In all that has been written and spoken upon the subject since there has been no such satisfactory discussion of the peculiar *status* of the negro in this country. It was proved that his race was a *caste*, and that for their benefit, as well as the benefit of the white population, his position of political and social inferiority must be recognized. It was shown that any attempt to inculcate practically the theory of the equality of the races would involve the inevitable necessity of leveling not the negro up, but the white man down. It was demonstrated that in all the history of the world, the order of Providence had been that in the struggle of races the weakest should depend on the strongest; that the development and civilization of mankind had been thus always promoted; and that all efforts founded on the morbid, uneasy, impatient, and restless conscientiousness of extreme men must end in incalculable injury to the superior race, and in the almost certain annihilation of the inferior and dependent caste. It is gravely to be regretted that principles so sound and salutary have come to be abandoned and derided by our present rulers.

At the close of the reform convention Mr. Woodward returned to Wilkes-Barre and resumed the practice of his profession. In the autumn of 1838, after a vigorous contest, David R. Porter, the democratic candidate for governor, was elected. He was supported by Mr. Woodward most ably and efficiently. In April, 1841, a vacancy having occurred in the office of president judge of the fourth judicial district, composed of the counties of Mifflin, Huntingdon, Centre, Clearfield, and Clinton, he was appointed to that office. His splendid career in that distinguished position is yet well remembered. Before him were then practicing in Bellefonte, where Judge Woodward resided, such men as James Macmanus, H. N. M'Allister, James T. Hale (afterwards on the bench), Colonel (afterwards judge) James Burnside, Andrew G. Curtin, (since governor and minister to Russia), Samuel Linn (since judge), D. C. Boal, and other distinguished lawyers. Shortly after his appointment a division of the district was made, leaving the counties of Centre, Clinton, and Clearfield to compose the fourth district, in which he remained until the expiration of his term, in April, 1851. He discharged the duties of the office acceptably to the people of the district and with great ability and great energy.

From the time of his appointment to the bench, in 1841, Judge Woodward was debarred, by the public opinion prevalent in his party, from active personal participation in political contests.

His interest in public events, however, was maintained, and he watched their progress with an observant eye, ever ready to counsel and advise those who were charged with the responsibility of the government. He supported Mr. Polk for president, and Francis R. Shunk for governor, in 1844, and after the election, as soon as it was ascertained that Mr. Buchanan was to become a member of the cabinet of Mr. Polk, the minds of the leading members of the party throughout the state were turned to Judge Woodward as the candidate for United States senator, to be selected in order to supply the vacancy thus created. He received the nomination of the caucus of the democratic members of the legislature, and by every rule regulating the action of political parties in the state was entitled to an election, which the majority of the democrats in the legislature was large enough fully to ensure. Influences, however, were brought to bear upon several members of the majority, whose votes secured his defeat and the election of Simon Cameron, the candidate of the whigs, and of a faction representing for the first time in the politics of the state a native American party. In the case of every democrat who voted against Judge Woodward, his motives, and the manner in which he was controlled, were well known, and, in most instances, fully disclosed at the time; but the pretext by which they attempted to justify their conduct was common to them all.

But although bad men thus gained a temporary triumph over Judge Woodward, by a base and slanderous representation of his feeling towards foreigners, our adopted citizens themselves well understood his position in relation to them. They knew that he had been more truly and earnestly their friend than any of the demagogues who have successively courted, abused, and spurned them. Whenever they have been the victims of popular prejudice—in 1844, when the native American party was first founded; in 1854, when the know-nothing organization swept the northern states with the pervading ruthlessness of an Egyptian plague—he was foremost in denunciation of the efforts of bad men to trample on their rights. And the support which he received from foreigners when a candidate for judge of the Supreme Court in 1852, proves that they recognized and realized the falsity of the charges which bad men, from time to time, made pretexts for defamation. Mr. Polk was inaugurated in March, 1845, and congress met on the first of the following December. In the interval, the Hon. Henry Baldwin, a justice of the Supreme Court of the United States for the circuit composed of the states of Pennsylvania and New Jersey, had died. On December 23 Mr. Polk appointed Judge Woodward to fill the vacancy. This was done without consultation or communication with him. In conferring the appointment, undoubtedly Mr. Polk was influenced by the result of the senatorial election, and by the purpose to rebuke the unprincipled and unscrupulous intrigue by which that result had been attained. Unfortunately for the success of Mr. Polk's object, the appointment had been made without consultation with Mr. Buchanan, the secretary of state, and his opposition to the confirmation, in connection with the hostility of General Cameron, led to the defeat of Judge Woodward in the senate. But although General Cameron succeeded in seducing some three or four democrats to unite with him, Judge Woodward had the proud satisfaction of receiving an immense majority of the democratic vote, including all the most illustrious senators of his party.

Judge Woodward thenceforth devoted himself to the discharge of the duties of his office during the remainder of his term, which expired in April, 1851. He then resumed the practice of law in his former office in Wilkes-Barre, and was thus employed until May, 1852, when Governor Bigler appointed him a judge of the Supreme Court, to fill a vacancy caused by the death of the Hon. Richard Coulter. By a constitutional amendment adopted in the year 1850, this office had become elective, and the appointment, therefore, extended only to the first of December, 1852. He was nominated as the democratic candidate by the convention of the party by acclamation, and thus for the first time was able to submit his merits and his claims to the decision and discrimination of the people of the state. He was a candidate in the year of the presidential election, and that was at that time dependent upon the result of the general election in October. It was found in his case, as has been often proved in other cases, that the man who is apparently the last choice of the political managers may well be the first choice of the mass of the voters. In the county of Luzerne, where he had spent the greater part of his life, and in several adjacent counties where he was intimately known, he received a larger vote than had ever been polled for a candidate in a contested election; and he succeeded by a majority in the state that vindicated most amply his professional fitness, his political position, and the integrity of his character.

Judge Woodward discharged the duties of this responsible and laborious office until 1867, and throughout the whole period his reputation as a judge had been deservedly high. With unusual powers of concentration and great capacity for labor, his style of discussing legal questions was singularly forcible, distinct, and clear. Avoiding all affectation of fine writing on the one hand, and all tendency to epigram on the other, he says of a case just that which it is necessary to say in English, that is always simple, elegant, and racy. There are no opinions in the Pennsylvania reports more intelligible to plain and unlearned men, and there are none more thorough, able, and exhaustive. The judgment of the Supreme Court upon the question of the constitutional right of soldiers to vote was prepared and entered by him. It was decided that this right did not exist, and the plain letter of the constitution was a sufficient warrant for the judgment.

The political position of Judge Woodward was perfectly familiar and perfectly intelligible to the people of Pennsylvania. Resolute in his opposition to any dismemberment of the union—ready to sustain the national government in every legitimate and constitutional effort—with two sons connected with the northern army in the east—with two nephews from the outbreak of the war in the armies of the west, and with multitudes of relatives in the military service of the nation everywhere, he insisted upon the maintenance of the institutions of the government in their spirit and integrity—upon the supremacy of the law—upon the preservation of the liberty of the citizen—upon freedom, within clear, legal limits of action, and thought, and speech. He insisted upon the maintenance of the constitutional immunities of the states. He was hostile to the whole theory of centralization. Upon this subject, in a letter written on the first day of July, 1852, he said: "The great lesson taught us is, that the Union itself, the product of the states, is to be preserved only by maintaining the just rights of the states. This truth, as old as our constitution, is too often forgotten. That the states were preexistant to the Union, as sovereignties absolutely free and independent, accountable to no power on earth for their domestic institutions and internal economy; that they exist still in all the plenitude of their original sovereignty, save in the few particulars and to the precise extent of their voluntary surrender of it in a written constitution, are first principles, to which we do well often to recur." He was opposed to the exercise of every form of arbitrary, discretionary, and despotic power, and was always prepared to resist it. That the existence of a war justifies a president in governing peaceable communities by martial law; that a temperate discussion of political questions, involving even criticism of the policy of the administration, may be punished at the mere whim of a subordinate military officer; that for such offense punishments may be *invented* which are unheard of in our jurisprudence; and that the life, liberty, and property of the citizen of a state containing no armed enemy may be invaded upon a government official's theory of "military necessity," are heresies to which Judge Woodward never assented in any position which the accidents of life called upon him to fill.

In 1863 Judge Woodward became the democratic candidate for governor of the state against Governor Andrew G. Curtin, but he was defeated by a majority of over 15,000, although Luzerne gave a majority of 2,786 in his favor.

For four years prior to the expiration of his term of office on the supreme bench, he acted as chief justice by virtue of seniority of commission, and he gave notice a year before his retirement that he should decline a re-election. Hon. George Sharswood succeeded him.

In June, 1867, he went to Europe, and the death of Hon. Charles Denison, who had been elected to represent the twelfth district of Pennsylvania in the fortieth congress, occurring, Judge Woodward was nominated and elected during his absence to fill the vacancy, his majority in Luzerne county being 1,881 over his opponent, Hon. Winthrop W. Ketcham. He was re-elected to a full term in 1868, his majority in Luzerne county being 3,074; his opponent was Hon. Theodore Strong, of Pittston, brother of Justice Strong, of the Supreme Court of the United States.

In 1870 he was unanimously nominated by the democratic party for the office of president judge of the eleventh judicial district, but owing to local dissentions in the party he was defeated along with the major part of the ticket, Hon. Garrick M. Harding being his opponent.

After the expiration of his congressional term Judge Woodward resumed the practice of the law at Wilkes-Barre, but having been retained in a number of important cases requiring his presence in Philadelphia, he removed in the fall of 1870 to that city. Here he opened an office on Walnut street, and entered at once upon his professional duties. Owing to his extensive acquaintance throughout the state, as well with the people as with the lawyers of the different counties, business came to him from all quarters, and his name will be found associated with many of the great causes of the five years previous to his death. Upon the very morning, and almost at the exact moment, that the telegram announcing his death arrived, the Supreme Court, at Harrisburg, was pronouncing its opinion in the case of Cox v. Deringer, in which he had originally brought suit, and in the trial of which he had participated as principal counsel. As a further coincidence it may be mentioned that the opinion of the court was read by Hon. Warren J. Woodward, a nephew and former student of the deceased, who had been elected to the supreme bench at the previous fall election.

While practicing law in Philadelphia Judge Woodward was elected as a delegate at large in the last constitutional convention on the democratic ticket. In that body he was chairman of the committee on "private corporations, foreign and domestic, other than railroads, canals, and religious and charitable corporations and societies," and a member of the committee on "judiciary." His long experience on the bench and wonderful forensic ability made his services very valuable to these committees. In July, 1873, he resigned his seat in the convention, but his resignation was not accepted, and he resumed his position when the convention re-opened the ensuing fall.

Hon. William M. Meredith was president of the convention, and, like Judge Woodward, was also a member of the constitutional convention of 1837, but died on August 17, 1873, before the convention had concluded its labors. Judge Woodward, in speaking of his death, said:

"Somebody has said that a great man has departed. A great man, indeed, sir! We did not appreciate him. It is the habit of the American mind not to appreciate their great men. The American people seem not to discover the good qualities of a man until he is dead. The old Romans treated their public men differently. If a general achieved a victory for the Roman arms, a triumphal arch was erected, he was welcomed home with wreaths and banners and music, and orations were pronounced upon him, and he was permitted to know what his fellow-countrymen thought of him. And so were men of genius, whether orators or poets, honored with public ovations. But in our day the case is very different. The living man is continually belittled. He is regarded as in the way of somebody; he is slighted; he is neglected; and yet, when we look at his works, when we listen to his thoughts, after death has set its great seal upon him, we all discover that our fellow-citizen was, indeed, a great and good man. We withhold the meed of praise during his life, but we hasten to bestrew his grave with flowers, now that he is gone.

"Mr. President, in that inimitable form of prayer that is used at the grave, prescribed by the church of England, we are directed to "render hearty thanks for the good examples of all those who, having finished their course in faith, do now rest from their labors." Hearty thanks, sir! "Hearty thanks" are due only for great blessings; and is it not a great blessing that we have such an example, the example of such a life as Mr. Meredith's; his learning, his acquisitions of knowledge, his use of that knowledge in illustrating his profession, his high-toned honor that never knew a stain, though he would have felt a stain worse than a wound? Yes, sir, let us be thankful for the good example of this man, especially now that his work is finished. There is no more danger to him. There is no mis-step that he can take. His labor is done; his work is finished; his record is made up forever. And, sir, allow me to add in conclusion that he died as he had lived, in the faith of Christ, because without touch of fanaticism about him, with no ostentation in his religion, Mr. Meredith was an humble and faithful believer in Christ, and a member of Christ church in this city, and for many years an honored representative in the diocesan conventions, as we all know."

When Judge Woodward was called to the Supreme Court bench the other judges were Black, Gibson, Lewis, and Lowrie, all able and eminent jurists, but with whom the new comer at once stood fairly equal. His opinions are exceedingly well written, clear and forcible, and on all constitutional questions, or questions in which personal rights were involved, they give forth no uncertain sound. His opinions are reported in thirty-six volumes of the Pennsylvania state reports, commencing with Deal v. Bogue, 8 Harris, and ending with Oakland Railway Company v. Keenan, 6 P. F. Smith.

Judge Woodward married, September 10, 1832, Sarah Elizabeth, only daughter of George W. Trott, M. D. Her mother was Lydia Chapman, daughter of Captain Joseph Chapman, formerly of Norwich, Connecticut, and subsequently of Brooklyn, Susquehanna county, Pennsylvania. Hon. Charles Miner, in 1849, writes: "On the 12th of February, 1799, in company with Captain Peleg Tracy, his brother Leonard, and Miss Lydia Chapman, in one sleigh, Mr. John Chase, of Newburyport, and myself in another, set out from Norwich, Connecticut, and arrived at Hopbottom the 28th. The snow left us the first night, when we were only twelve miles on our way, and we were obliged to place our sleighs on trundle wheels. Our cheerful, undaunted female friend, through the patience-trying journey of sixteen days (never a tear, a murmur, or a sigh), lived to see her grandchildren, the children of an eminent judge of the Supreme Court." And again he writes: "Miss Lydia Chapman, a lady of high intelligence and great merit, became an inhabitant of Wilkes-Barre and an instructress of a school. Married with Dr. G. W. Trott, their accomplished daughter intermarried with the Hon. George W. Woodward." The children of Judge and Mrs. Woodward were Hon. Stanley Woodward, of this city; Colonel George A. Woodward, of Washington, D. C.; Charles Francis Woodward, of Philadelphia; Ellen May Woodward, deceased; Lydia C. Hancock, deceased, wife of E. A. Hancock; Elizabeth, wife of E. Greenough Scott, of this city; William Wilberforce Woodward, deceased; John K. Woodward, deceased; Mary H. Williamson, deceased, wife of J. Pryor Williamson, deceased. Mrs. Woodward died June 21, 1869. In 1871 Judge Woodward married the widow of Edward Macalester, a man of note and large wealth, in Lexington, Kentucky, and a brother of the late Charles

Macalester, of Philadelphia. They had no children. She survives him and resides in Lexington.

The distinguished deceased was a man of the highest integrity and fidelity. No one, whether he agreed with him in sentiment or not, ever doubted his honesty of purpose, or the sincerity of his opinions. He was a man in whom could be placed universal and absolute trust; and no man ever did his duty to his country, his God and truth more earnestly and constantly than he. He was marked for his force of character. He was an earnest man in everything—a pretender in nothing. He was an able legislative debater, and had large views on constitutional law, and was an able judicial writer on questions of a broad and comprehensive character. He was noted also as a good *nisi prius* judge, his charge to the jury having always great weight, there being something about his presence which impressed those who first came in contact with him. His personal appearance contributed largely to this influence over the jury, as he was a man cast in a remarkably large mould, and of massive form and strength. He understood the science and the true principles of government, and knowing them, dared to maintain them with unflinching courage in the face of calumny, detraction, and even personal peril. To his brother members of the bar, and to the bar whilst on the bench, as well as in general society, he was most urbane and courteous. He was a sincere and exemplary christian, and had strong religious tendencies, being a consistent member of the Protestant Episcopal church, and took great interest in all church matters. In his family he was remarkably affectionate, and possessed and deserved the love and veneration of his family and kindred, and the warm regard of numerous friends who were bound to him with "hooks of steel." He was strongly affected by the death of his brother ex-chief justice, Judge Thompson, when that distinguished jurist fell, literally with the harness on, while arguing an important case before the Supreme Court, Judge Woodward being on the other side. The following is from the latter's speech at the bar meeting of Judge Thompson in which Judge Woodward is describing his deceased brother: "An acute critic has said, 'Perhaps the perfection of the judicial character consists in the exhibition of pure intellect divested of human sympathy.' And yet who would choose for his judge such a monster of perfection. He is the fortunate judge who can so conduct himself on the seat of justice, and clothe his decisions in such language, that both he who wins and he who loses his cause can unite in paying a deserved tribute to his wisdom and integrity. 'Then,' 'Now,' were his last words. And how significant! *Then* he was addressing to your honors the words of wisdom his mature years, his active life, his large reading had stored away in his well furnished mind. *Now*, he lies a pallid corpse in your honors' presence. And this little interval, only a few minutes long, spans the space between life and death, between the active duties of a well spent life and the dread realities of eternity. When have your honors witnessed a more impressive scene—one that tells us more solemnly how near we are to death even in the heat and stir of life? 'In the midst of life we are in death.' "

The death of such a man as Judge Woodward is a national calamity. His great ability, his profound legal knowledge, his personal and official integrity, his enlarged and statesmanlike views, his christian character, his undoubted patriotism, made him one of the noblest men in the union, and in all sections, north, south, east and west, his demise was deeply lamented. His life was one of spotless purity, and of him it may be truly said that his was

> "One of the few, the immortal names
> That were not born to die."

The Supreme Court met at Harrisburg May 11, 1875, and was occupied in hearing the argument of McLellan's Appeal, an important case from Chambersburg. Hon. A. K. McClure concluded the argument, and when he closed he announced the death of the late Chief Justice Woodward as follows:

"And now, may it please the court, turning from the perishable things of time which so strangely concerns us, I am charged with a painful duty. George W. Woodward is dead! From a far-off land the swift message has come unseen, like the summons of the inexorable messenger whose solemn decree it records, and a voice once most familiar in this learned court is hushed forever. In the presence of his associates and successors, mine is not the task of eulogy. His stainless judicial record, that has long been as a text for the profession, would make even the most eloquent praise feeble. It is well to take pause over the death of such a judge. Only a man like his fellows—mortal, fallible, and sharing the infirmities, which are a common inheritance, and living and acting during a period when demoralization and distrust have been widespread in both authority and people, his adornment of public station by the highest measure of intellectual power, and a purity of purpose that is confessed by friend and foe, must leave his memory green among us wherever ability and integrity are honored. His life was replete with uncommon vicissitudes. Honored in the outset of his career by his native state beyond any other citizen of his years, it was but natural that he should not be exempt from the disappointments of ambition. They are the price of bright promise in the highway to distinction, and are the thorns which remain to wound the hopeful grasp as the beauty and fragrance of the flower perish. From the withered field of political preferment to which he had been called by other efforts than his own, he ever came back to himself—to his one great calling and his grandest possible triumphs; and as judge and chief justice for two-thirds of a generation, he has written an imperishable record. And now, in the fulness of his days, ripe in years, and wearing the chaplet of honors that even malice would not dare to stain, he has passed away. The fitful clouds and angry tempests of prejudice and passion, which at times obscure the attributes of greatness, have long since vanished like the mists of the morning, and in the calm, bright evening-time, he that has so justly judged between man and man appears before the Great Judge of all the living. But his blameless life, his pure example, his reverenced judgments remain, and like the beautiful dream of the departed sun, that throws its halo over the countless jewels which soften the deep lines of darkness, so will his lessons of wisdom and honesty illumine the path of public and private duty for generations to come. In respect to his memory, I move that the court do now adjourn."

Chief Justice Agnew responded to Mr. McClure's address as follows:

"We have listened to the announcement of the death of Hon. George W. Woodward, a former chief justice of this court, with feelings of unusual sadness. The suddenness of the melancholy event adds greatly to our sorrow. Chief Justice Woodward took a high position on this bench, and during a full term of fifteen years was esteemed one of its brightest ornaments, for the learning, ability, acuteness, and culture displayed in his judgments. It does not fall to the lot of any one of us to be always right, yet even when he dissented from the judgment of his brethren his opinions were marked by great force, vigor of thought, and excellence of style. One, I remember, was afterwards adopted, and became the ruling of the court in subsequent decisions. Being myself the only member of the present bench who sat with him, it falls to me, perhaps, more than others, to speak of him in his judicial career. In some things we differed widely, as is the case with those brought up in different schools of opinions. But I feel a great satisfaction, now that he has left the world and its exciting scenes, in declaring that, notwithstanding our differences on some great public questions, the utmost cordiality existed between us. In personal character he stood high. A man of marked qualities, he was open and free in expression, perhaps to a fault. When opposed to any public sentiment his opinions were not the less outspoken. He had little, indeed none, of that secretiveness which oftentimes attends the public career of men of less ability, and by his freedom of speech at times placed himself at a disadvantage. My entrance to this bench in 1863 was not my first introduction or first opportunity of studying his character. We were of the same age within three months, and but twenty-eight when we met together in the constitutional reform convention of 1837. I soon had occasion to notice him as one of no common ability. A very tall, slightly sallow, and then rather thin man, when he rose to address the chair his stature, deliberate manner, clear thought, vigorous language, and logical argument were striking in one of his years, and commanded the attention of every member. He rose rapidly, and soon took a front rank with those with whom he acted within party lines. In that convention were such gentlemen as Charles Jared Ingersoll, James Madison Porter, James Clarke, Thomas Earle, and others who were leaders on the same side; yet six weeks had scarcely passed away when George W. Woodward, the member from Luzerne, stood abreast with them, and became an acknowledged leader, and soon attracted to himself his party movements. Having indulged in these few personal recollections, I may now add that all my brethren unite with me in expressing our heartfelt sorrow for this sad event, which has removed an eminent jurist and distinguished man from our sight forever, and from the bosom of a family which loved and revered him. It is now ordered that the announcement of Mr. McClure of the death of the Hon. George W. Woodward, a former chief justice of this court, be entered on the minutes, and that his motion be granted that we do now adjourn, as a token of respect for his memory." For further information concerning the Woodward family see page 97.

CHARLES DENISON SHOEMAKER.

Charles Denison Shoemaker was appointed an associate judge of Luzerne county, Pa., August 21, 1830. For a sketch of his family see pages 45 and 128.

OVID FRASER JOHNSON.

Ovid Fraser Johnson, who was admitted to the bar of Luzerne county, Pa., April 6, 1831, was the grandson of Rev. Jacob Johnson, also of this city (see page 187), and the son of Jehodia Pitt Johnson, of this city. (See page 775). O. F. Johnson was born in Wilkes-Barre March 7, 1807. He was educated at the Wilkes-Barre Academy, and read law with John N. Conyngham. He practiced in this city from the time of his admission until the time of his marriage. On January 15, 1839, he was appointed attorney-general of Pennsylvania, which office he held until January 21, 1845. As an orator Mr. Johnson was brilliant, as a lawyer he had superior abilities and somewhat of a widely known reputation, being frequently employed to try cases in different states of the union. He had also high reputation as a political writer. He was the author of the celebrated "Governor's Letters," published during the administration of Governor Ritner, and which purported to give the ludicrous side to the political characters then figuring in the politics of the state. Mr. Johnson married, July 28, 1835, Jane Alricks, of Harrisburg, Pa. She was a descendant of Pieter Alricks, son of Pieter Alricks, who had been sent in 1658 by the Dutch government with instructions for New Netherlands and more than probable with the intention of remaining in the new country. In March, 1659, we find him carrying on trade in the "HoreKihl." In January, 1660, D'Hinayossa appointed him commander there. On September 6, 1664, New Amsterdam was captured by the English, and Governor General Stuveysant was expelled. Thirteen days after Sir Robert Carr appeared on the Delaware, and in a fortnight thereafter took the Dutch forts. The estate of Pieter Alricks was confiscated, but some years afterwards the Dutch again obtained possession not only of the banks of the Delaware but also of Fort Amsterdam, now New York city, and held possession until the English Governor Andross arrived, and then the annals inform us, "November 10, 1674, Fort Amsterdam, New York, was this day surrendered to Governor Andross, and all the magistrates in office at the time of the Dutch coming here, to be reinstated for the Delaware river, except Pieter Alricks, he having proffered himself to the Dutch at their first coming of his own motion, and acted very violent as their chief officer ever since." Commissary Alricks subsequently swore fidelity to the English and continued his trade on the South river. In August, 1672, he was appointed bailiff for New Castle, on the Delaware; in October, 1667, commissioned one of its justices and re-commissioned June 7, 1680, being one of the justices in commission when the proprietary government was formed. He was a member of the first assembly of the province, 1682 and 1683, and from 1685 to 1689 served as one of the provincial councillors. In 1685 William Penn bought out the title of the Indians in a large body of land lying between Philadelphia and Wilmington, extending back from the Delaware river as far as a man "can ride in two days with a horse." The first witness to this Indian deed is Pieter Alricks. He was commissioned one of the justices of the peace for the Lower Counties, April 13, 1690, and again May 2, 1693. On September 2, 1690, he was also appointed a judge of the provincial court, serving until 1693. He probably died about that time. From him for two generations it has been found difficult to trace the full descent, save that a son of Pieter last named was probably named Pieter and his son Wessels or Weselius Alricks. The latter was born in Delaware, afterwards removed to Philadelphia, where he became quite prominent in provincial affairs, and held several important offices. He died there, leaving a son Hermanus, born about 1730, in Philadelphia. He resided some years in his native city, but afterwards settled in Cumberland county. He was chosen the first member of the general assembly from that county, and was commissioned prothonotary of Cumberland county, and also a justice of the peace. Until his death he was a man of mark and influence in the valley west of the Susquehanna. Hermanus

Alricks was twice married. There was probably no issue by the first marriage. He married, second, Ann West, born 1733, in the north of Ireland; died November 21, 1791, in Donegal township, Lancaster county, Pa., and is buried in the old church yard there. Hermanus Alricks died December 14, 1772, in Carlisle. James Alricks, son of Hermanus Alricks, was born December 2, 1769, at Carlisle. He received a good education in the schools of his day, and was brought up to a mercantile life. In 1791–2 he was engaged in business in Maytown, Lancaster county, and in 1814 he removed with his family from Lost Creek Valley to Harrisburg. He was a man of extensive reading, passionately fond of books, and he regarded an honest man, of fine education and refined manners, as the most remarkable object on the face of the earth. After his father's death he was raised on a farm in Donegal township, and used to say that at that period no one could get an education for want of teachers. On March 10, 1821, he was appointed clerk of the Orphans' Court and Quarter Sessions, serving until 1824. He subsequently served as one of the magistrates of the borough. He married, July 21, 1796, at Harrisburg, Martha Hamilton, daughter of John Hamilton and Margaret Alexander. These were the parents of Jane Alricks, who was born at Oakland Mills, in Lost Creek Valley, now Juniata county, Pa., who married Ovid Fraser Johnson. Mr. and Mrs. Johnson had a family of four children—Fanny Alricks, who became the wife of Hon. Samuel Townsend Shugert, of Bellefonte, Pa., Hannah Ianthe Johnson, Martha Alricks Johnson, and Ovid Fraser Johnson, of Philadelphia. The last named is a lawyer, and the author of "Law of Mechanics' Liens in Pennsylvania," Philadelphia, 1884. O. F. Johnson, senior, died in the city of Washington, D. C., in February, 1854.

JOHN J. WURTZ.

John J. Wurtz, who was admitted to the bar of Luzerne county, Pa., August 2, 1831, was a descendant of Rev. Hans Conrad Wirtz, who came to this country from Zurich, Switzerland, in 1707.

He preached first at New Brunswick, N. J. He was pastor of the Egypt church, in White Hall township, Lehigh county, Pa., from 1742 to 1744. In 1747 he was the pastor of the Springfield Reformed church, in Bucks county, Pa. He removed to Rockaway, N. J., in 1751. In 1761 he removed to York, Pa., where he was pastor of the First Reformed church of that place. He died in York September 21, 1763, and is buried under the altar of the stone church, which was in process of erection during his pastorate. Dr. George Wurtz, of Montville and Boonton, N. J., was the son or grandson of Rev. Hans Conrad Wurtz. He was the father of John J. Wurtz, who was born at Longwood, N. J., February 2, 1801. His wife was Ann Barbara Norris, of Baltimore, Md. They had three children—Henry Wirtz, George Wurtz, and Eliza Ann, wife of Rev. Francis Canfield. Mr. Wurtz practiced in this city, and died here November 4, 1836.

VOLNEY LEE MAXWELL.

Volney Lee Maxwell, who was admitted to the bar of Luzerne county, Pa., November 11, 1831, was a grandson of James Maxwell, of the English navy, which he left at Halifax, N. S., long before the revolutionary war. Squire Maxwell, son of James Maxwell, was born in Warren, R. I. His wife was Phebe Rice, a native of New York. V. L. Maxwell, son of Squire Maxwell, was born in what is now Hamilton county, N. Y., June 12, 1804. He received his early education at Johnstown, N. Y., and later at the Aurora (N. Y.) Academy. In his early manhood he was a school teacher. He read law with Mr. Darlington, at West Chester, Pa., and was admitted to the Chester county bar November 1, 1831. From 1832 to 1839 he was a partner of the late Judge Conyngham. He married, September 15, 1840, at Paradise, Pa., Lydia M. Haines, a daughter of George Haines, who was a civil engineer in this city. The wife of George Haines was

Eliza Chapman, a daughter of Captain Joseph Chapman, who located in what is now Dimock, Susquehanna county, Pa., in 1798. He was a sea captain, from Norwich, Conn., who had made fifty voyages to the West Indies. He was the grandfather of C. I. A. Chapman, of the Luzerne county bar, and also the grandfather of the late Mrs. George W. Woodward. Mr. and Mrs. Maxwell had two children, only one of whom survives—Mary O. Maxwell, wife of W. W. Lathrope, of the Lackawanna county bar. V. L. Maxwell died in this city January 4, 1873. He was at the time of his death and for seven years previous the treasurer and accounting warden of St. Stephen's Protestant Episcopal church, and for thirty-eight years had been one of its vestrymen. He was also a member of the standing committee of the diocese of central Pennsylvania, and the president of the Luzerne County Bible Society.

WILLIAM WURTS.

William Wurts, who was admitted to the bar of Luzerne county, Pa., August 6, 1832, was born in Montville, New Jersey, November 25, 1809. He was educated at Amherst College, and read law with his brother, John J. Wurtz, in this city. His father was George Wurts, M. D., and his mother was Abagail Pettit, a daughter of Amos Pettit. His grandfather was John Jacob Wirtz, whose wife was Sarah Grandin. William Wurts married, March 17, 1836, Lucretia Jeanette Lathrop, a daughter of Salmon Lathrop and his wife Aurelia Noble. (See page 861.) Mr. and Mrs. Wurts had a family of eight children, five sons and three daughters—George Lathrop Wurts, Helen S. Wurts, Harriet L., wife of Rev. Franklin C. Jones, Theodore F. Wurts, Eliza A. Wurts, William A. Wurts, Frederick H. Wurts, and George Albert Wurts. Mr. Wurts practiced law in this city for many years, but some years before his death, which occurred at Carbondale, Pa., July 15, 1858, he removed to that city.

SAMUEL FREEMAN HEADLEY.

Samuel Freeman Headley, who was admitted to the bar of Luzerne county, Pa., April 3, 1833, was a native of Litchfield, Otsego county, N. Y., where he was born January 20, 1808. His grandfather was Isaac Headley, and his father was Samuel Headley, M. D., a native of Littleton, N. J. After the latter's marriage with Anna Fairchild, a daughter of Jonathan Fairchild, of Parsippany, N. J., he removed to Litchfield, N. Y. When the war of 1812 broke out he was elected surgeon of the Eighteenth Regiment New York Volunteers, and served during the war. He afterwards removed to Berwick, Pa., where he died in 1838. S. F. Headley's first tutor was Rev. Mr. Kirkpatrick, of Milton, Pa., who prepared him for Union College, at Schenectady, N. Y., where he graduated with the first honors in the class of 1831. He read law with Hon. Robert C. Grier (the father of Mrs. Doctor Mayer, of this city), at Danville, Pa., and was admitted to the bar of Columbia county in 1833. For many years Mr. Headley practiced in the courts of Columbia, Luzerne, Northumberland, and other adjoining counties in this state, pleading not only the cause of the rich client, but with equal earnestness that of the poor and oppressed who had nothing wherewith to compensate him. In 1839, 1840 and 1841 he represented Luzerne county in the senate of Pennsylvania, where his distinguished ability as a debater placed him among the leaders of the democratic party, to which he adhered until 1856, when he became a republican. In 1842 he was one of the commissioners to locate the county seat and public buildings of Wyoming county. Mr. Headley, while a resident of Pennsylvania, mostly resided in Berwick, but had large interests in this county, where he resided at times. In 1847 Mr. Headley and the Messrs. Wilson, of Harrisburg, erected a charcoal furnace, of water power, eight feet in the boshes, at Shickshinny, and for several years manufactured a considerable quantity of superior pig iron from the Columbia county and Newport ores, which they mixed. The charcoal iron of this furnace was sought after by the owners of foundries in

Bradford and other counties, as being superior for stove purposes. In 1852 Messrs. Headley & Wilson sold this furnace to William Koons. He was also interested in iron works in Nescopeck township. In 1854 he removed to Morristown, New Jersey, and accepted the superintendency of the Morris and Essex railroad, after which he was chosen assistant president and acting superintendent of the New York and Erie railroad, in which position, as in all others, he fully demonstrated his ability and qualification for any position that he might accept. The strong points in his character were a sound judgment, extraordinary perception, indomitable will, and untiring industry. He despised an idler, and his whole life was an example of industry and application worthy to be imitated by the young men of our day. He died at Morristown July 25, 1869. He was celebrated as a temperance lecturer, and spoke very frequently for the Sabbath school, tract and bible causes. Mr. Headley married, November 28, 1832, Marie Josepha Boyd, a daughter of John Boyd, of Scotch-Irish ancestry, who was born in Chester county February 22, 1750. When the war for independence came he entered into the service, and was a member of the committee of safety in 1776. He was subsequently commissioned second lieutenant in the Twelfth Regiment of the Pennsylvania Line. He was promoted to be first lieutenant, and transferred to the Third Pennsylvania Regiment as captain lieutenant. Under the rearrangement of January 1, 1781, he was retired from the service, but afterwards was appointed captain of a company of rangers on the frontiers, and was an excellent partisan officer. In June, 1781, while marching his men across the Allegheny mountains, he fell into an ambuscade of Indians, near the head waters of the Raystown branch of the Juniata, in Bedford county, Pa., and was made a prisoner with a number of his soldiers, and led a captive through the wilderness to Canada. One of the Indian chiefs who was instrumental in saving Captain Boyd's life, when asked why he did not put his prisoner to death, raised his eyes and pointing to the heavens said, "The Great Spirit protects him." He was confined, during his continuance in Canada, on an island in the St. Lawrence near Montreal. In the spring of 1782 an exchange of prisoners took place, and he returned to Philadelphia by water with a number of his fellow soldiers. He was engaged in the battles of White Plains, Germantown, Brandywine and Stony Point, and in all engagements with the enemy which took place previous to 1781. He was one of the "twenty" who composed the "forlorn hope," led by Anthony Wayne at Stony Point, who met within the fort. He was at West Point and saw the unfortunate Andre executed. He was one of the few surviving officers of the revolution who enjoyed the provisions of the act of congress of May, 1828. During the war he served one year as collector of the excise tax for Northumberland county. After the restoration of peace, in partnership with Colonel William Wilson, he entered into merchandizing at the town of Northumberland and in a mill at the mouth of Chillisquaque creek. They manufactured large quantities of potash, which they shipped to Philadelphia, where it met with a ready sale, but the difficulties of transportation compelled them to relinquish this enterprise. He served as a member of the supreme executive council of the state from 1783 to 1786. He was a member of the house of representatives from 1790 to 1792, and a presidential elector at the second election, in 1792, and was one of the original members of the Pennsylvania Society of the Cincinnati. He was also register and recorder of Northumberland county under appointment of Governor McKean. Mrs. Sarah Boyd, the mother of Captain Boyd, presented to the legislature of Pennsylvania a petition, which reads as follows, as extracted from the journal of the house of representatives: "A petition of Sarah Boyd, of the town of Northumberland, in the county of Northumberland, widow, was read, representing that, at an early period of life, she had the misfortune of being deprived of her husband, and was left to struggle with many difficulties to support herself and three sons, her only children; that at the commencement of the present war all of her said sons took an early and decided part in the grand contest, and she *cheerfully* consented to their serving their distressed country; that her youngest son, William Boyd, a lieutenant in the Twelfth Pennsylvania Regiment, fell in the battle of Brandywine, September 11, 1777; that her son Thomas Boyd, after having shared in all the dangers and fatigues of the Canada expedition, fell a sacrifice to Indian barbarity in the expedition commanded by General

Sullivan; and that her remaining son, John Boyd, now commands a company appointed for the defense of the frontiers of this state; and praying that she may be allowed the *depreciation* of the pay of her deceased sons, the same having been transferred to her by her surviving son." Captain Boyd died at Northumberland, Pa., February 13, 1831. He married, May 13, 1794, at Northumberland, Rebecca Bull, a daughter of John Bull, son of John Bull, who was born in 1730, in Providence township, now in Montgomery county, Pa. He was appointed captain in the provincial service May 12, 1758, and in June was in command of Fort Allen. The same year he accompanied General Forbes' expedition for the reduction of Fort DuQuesne, and rendered important service in the negotiations with the Indians. In 1771 he owned the Norris plantation and mill, now the borough of Norristown, Pa., and was residing there at the opening of the revolution. He was a delegate to the provincial conference of January 23, 1775, and of June 18, 1775, a member of the convention of July 15, 1776, that framed the constitution of the state, and of the Pennsylvania board of war, March 14, 1777. In 1775 he was appointed colonel of the First Pennsylvania Battalion, which he resigned January 20, 1776, on account of bad treatment from his officers. He was one of the commissioners at the Indian treaty held at Easton January 30, 1777; in February was in command of the works at Billingsport, and on July 16 was appointed adjutant general of the state. In October of this year his barns were burned and stock carried away by the enemy. In December, when General James Irvine was captured, General Bull succeeded to the command of the second brigade of the Pennsylvania militia, under General Armstrong. He was confirmed a justice of the courts by the assembly August 31, 1778. In 1778 and 1779 he was engaged in directing the defenses for Philadelphia, and in 1780 was commissary of purchases at that city. In 1785 he removed to Northumberland county, Pa., and in 1805 was elected to the assembly, and in 1808 was the federal candidate for congress, but was defeated. General Bull died at Northumberland August 9, 1824, aged ninety-four years. His wife Mary (*nee* Phillips) died February 23, 1811. Benjamin Rittenhouse, a brother of the celebrated philosopher, and who was commissioned by Governor

Mifflin in 1791 as one of the associate judges of the court of Common Pleas of Montgomery county, was married to a daughter of General Bull.

Mr. and Mrs. Headley had a family of three children—1. John Boyd Headley, born February 22, 1834; died August 6, 1870. He married, September 16, 1857, Helen M. Thomas, a daughter of Abraham Thomas, of Wilkes-Barre, Pa. (See page 835.) He had two children—William Thomas Headley and Nellie Boyd Headley. 2. Benjamin Franklin Headley, born May 25, 1836; married Rose J. McGoldrick, of Morristown, N. J., who died December 10, 1876. He had four children—Mary Elizabeth Headley, Maria Josepha Headley, Benjamin Franklin Headley and John Boyd Headley. 3. Elizabeth Boyd Headley, born May 19, 1842; married, first, James F. Bentley, second, Sayes J. Bowen. She has had four children—Charles Freeman Bentley, Bessie Boyd Bentley, Josepha Boyd Bentley, and Helen Louise Bentley.

MATTHEW HALE JONES.

Matthew Hale Jones was admitted to the Luzerne county, Pa., bar August 6, 1833. He was a native of Hebron, Conn., where he was born September 11, 1811. He was educated at the Wilkes-Barre Academy and at Rutgers College, New Brunswick, New Jersey, graduating in the class of 1830. He read law in this city with Chester Butler and with his brother, Joel Jones. (See page 1130.) He was admitted to the bar of Northampton county, Pa., August 22, 1833, where he practiced continually until his death, June 1, 1883. In his profession he was conspicuous for his comprehensive and exact knowledge, sound judgment, and keen and sensitive conception of honor. He magnified his calling by assiduous attention, constant vigilance, and a thorough intellectual honesty which never allowed the moral sentiment to be obscured or perverted. Mr. Jones was the son of Amassa Jones, and was a brother of Judge Joel Jones, Rev. Joseph H. Jones, D. D., at one time principal of the Wilkes-Barre

Academy, and Samuel Jones, M. D., all of whom are now deceased. Matthew Hale Jones married, in early life, Mary Elizabeth, daughter of Robert Innes, of Easton, Pa. He was the son of Robert Innes, sr., who came to America from Scotland. The children of Mr. Jones are Robert Innes Jones and Matthew Hale Jones, attorneys at law, Easton, and Elizabeth Huntington Jones, the wife of Hon. William S. Kirkpatrick, of the Northampton county bar, residing at Easton, Pa.

LUTHER KIDDER.

Luther Kidder was admitted to the bar of Luzerne county, Pa., November 5, 1833. He was the son of Luther and Phebe Kidder, and was born in Waterford, Vermont, November 19, 1808. Luther Kidder was a descendant of James Kidder, who was born at East Grinstead, in Sussex, England, in 1626. He may be considered as the patriarch of the family and the ancestor of all who bear the name in this country. In what year or by what ship he made his advent to New England cannot now be ascertained. It is certain that he was at Cambridge, Mass., as early as 1649. In that year he married Anna Moore, daughter of Elder Francis Moore. In 1653 he was occupying a farm of two hundred and eighty-nine acres in what is now known as West Cambridge. In the same year the general court granted Shawshire, now Billerica, to Cambridge, and for several years it continued to form a part of that town, many of its older residents receiving grants of land soon after removing there. It is most likely that James Kidder was among the first to take up his abode in that wilderness, and it is quite probable he may have gone there as early as 1653. It is certain that he was residing there with his family in 1656, and this place may be considered as the home of his family for over one hundred years. Both he and his wife were members of the church in Cambridge, and when a church was organized at Billerica they were the first to become members of it. In 1662 he was a juror of the court holden in Cambridge, and in the court records of that year we find the following entry: "James Kidder is allowed to be sergeant of the military company at Billerica." This may be thought to be a small affair for the courts to take cognizance of, but the organization of the military of that day was a matter of the first importance, and none but men of the most reliable character were entrusted with any office in it. He afterwards rose to the rank of ensign, his name often appearing in the town records of Billerica, where he was appointed on various committees. He was also selectman for six years. In 1675, when King Philip's war took place, he was in the public service, and kept guard over the small tribe of Indians at Wameset, now forming part of Lowell, and soon after was appointed to the command of a garrison house which contained seven families, including his own and that of his son James. He died April 16, 1676, in the midst of the war, aged about fifty years. John Kidder, son of James Kidder and Anna, his wife, was born in Cambridge about 1656. He moved to Chelmsford, Mass., when a young man, and in 1681 he bought of Jonathan Tyng five hundred acres of land lying on the west side of Concord river, in Chelmsford, where he afterwards resided. He married, December 3, 1684, in Chelmsford, Lydia Parker, daughter of Abraham Parker and his wife, Rose Whitlock, of Woburn. Thomas Kidder, son of John and Lydia Kidder, was born in Chelmsford October 30, 1690. He was admitted to the church in Westford April 7, 1728. He married Joanna Keyes, at Chelmsford, December 31, 1716. Aaron Kidder, son of Thomas and Joanna Kidder, was born in Chelmsford December 22, 1719; died in New Ipswich, N. H., November 16, 1769. He went to New Ipswich about 1750. He was one of the first commanders of the military company, and held some other town offices. He died very suddenly at the age of fifty years. He married Rachel Bush, at Marlboro, May 19, 1749. She died in 1815, aged ninety years. Luther Kidder, son of Aaron and Rachel Kidder, was born at New Ipswich June 29, 1767; died at Pike, Bradford county, Pa., September 2, 1831. He married Phebe Church, at Windham, Conn., September 25, 1788. She died at Worcester October 13, 1851, and was the daughter of Asa Church and Abia Pease. She was born in Stafford, Conn., November 11, 1768.

From 1841 to 1844 Luther Kidder was a member of the senate of Pennsylvania. From 1845 to 1851 he was president judge of the courts of Carbon, Monroe and Schuylkill counties. He married, October 13, 1835, in Wilkes-Barre, Martha Ann Scott, daughter of Judge David Scott. (See page 392.) Judge Kidder died September 30, 1854. His only surviving child is Rev. Charles Holland Kidder, of Asbury Park, N. J.

DWIGHT NOBLE LATHROP.

Dwight Noble Lathrop, who was admitted to the bar of Luzerne county, Pa., November 5, 1833, was a son of Salmon Lathrop and his wife, Aurelia Noble. (See page 857.) D. N. Lathrop was born July 28, 1811, at Sherburne, Chenango county, N. Y. He was educated at the Wilkes-Barre Academy, and read law with George Denison, in this city. He practiced principally in the city of Carbondale. He was appointed postmaster of that city in 1861 and held the office until 1864. From 1862 to 1865 he was district attorney, and from 1870 to 1872 recorder of the mayor's court of the city of Carbondale. The wife of D. N. Lathrop was Harriet Ridgway, a native of White county, Ill., and daughter of John Ridgway, who was born near Walnford, N. J. The wife of John Ridgway was Mary Grant, of Inverness, Scotland, daughter of John Grant. D. N. Lathrop died October 8, 1887. Mr. and Mrs. Lathrop had a family of five children— William W. Lathrope, a member of the Lackawanna bar; Thomas R. Lathrope; Mary G., wife of Israel Crane; Aurelia N., wife of Eugene Scates; and Harriet J. Lathrope.

DAVID WILMOT.

David Wilmot was admitted to the bar of Luzerne county, Pa., August 5, 1834. He was the son of Randall Wilmot and his wife, a daughter of James Carr, of Canaan, Wayne county, Pa. David Wilmot was born in Bethany, Wayne county, Pa., January

20, 1814. He was educated in the schools of his native town and at the Aurora (N. Y.) Academy. At the age of eighteen he removed to Wilkes-Barre and read law in the office of George W. Woodward. Soon after his admission to the Luzerne bar he removed to Towanda, Pa., where he immediately took a prominent position as a democratic politician. For several years he occupied a commanding position in the political affairs of the county, and won a wide reputation as an able and effective speaker. In 1844 Mr. Wilmot received the unanimous nomination of the democracy for congress in the district composed of the counties of Bradford, Susquehanna and Tioga, henceforth known as the "Wilmot district." He was elected by a large majority, and took his seat at the opening of the twenty-ninth congress in 1845, where, in common with the democratic party, he favored the annexation of Texas. On August 4, 1846, the president sent to the senate a confidential message asking an appropriation to negotiate a peace with Mexico. A bill was introduced in the house appropriating two million dollars for the purpose specified. It had now become so apparent that the proposition was intended to strengthen the pro-slavery influence in the general government, that, at Mr. Wilmot's suggestion, a consultation was held by a few of the northern representatives who were opposed to the extension of slavery, the result of which was the offering by Mr. Wilmot of the celebrated proviso which has been so generally known as the "Wilmot Proviso," which provided that in any territory acquired from Mexico "neither slavery nor involuntary servitude shall ever exist in any part of the territory except for crime," etc. This proviso was adopted in committee, and the two million bill containing the proviso was sent to the senate, where it was killed by John Davis, of Massachusetts, talking against time and preventing its passage. In 1846 Mr. Wilmot again received the unanimous nomination of his party for congress and was re-elected. In 1848 the question of slavery began to be agitated, and the free soil party was formed, which nominated Martin Van Buren for the presidency. Wilmot again received the unanimous nomination for congress, and was re-elected by a large majority. He was succeeded by G. A. Grow in 1850. On the formation of the republican party Mr. Wilmot very soon espoused its principles and identified himself with the movement. In fact, the very measures he had proposed in congress in 1846 had no small influence in leading to its existence. At the republican national convention held in Philadelphia in 1856 Mr. Wilmot was proposed as the candidate for vice president on the ticket with Fremont. He could have commanded the unanimous nomination, but was averse to it. He was chairman of the committee on resolutions, and drew up the platform adopted by that convention. The next year, 1857, Mr. Wilmot was nominated for governor. He had, under the provisions of the amended constitution creating an elective judiciary, been chosen president judge of the judicial district composed of the counties of Bradford, Susquehanna and Sullivan in 1851, but resigned the office for the purpose of entering the gubernatorial contest. Although defeated by William F. Packer, his speeches made throughout the state had awakened a deep interest in the principles of the republican party, and the party was strengthened by the canvass. In 1860 Simon Cameron was named in the Pennsylvania republican convention as their first choice for president, and according to usage Mr. Cameron selected Mr. Wilmot as delegate at large to the Chicago convention, of which he was made temporary chairman, and when Mr. Cameron's name was withdrawn, used his great influence to secure the nomination of Abraham Lincoln, whose confidence he enjoyed during his administration. The selection of General Cameron to be secretary of war created a vacancy in the United States senate, which Mr. Wilmot was elected to fill, and took his seat in that body March 18, 1861. He was a delegate to the peace convention the same year. A wide field of honor and usefulness seemed opened before him. But at the outset of his senatorial career his health began gradually to fail, until it was almost impossible for him to attend to the routine of his duties. He served two years on the committees of foreign affairs, claims and pensions, and was succeeded in 1863 by Charles R. Buckalew. At the conclusion of his senatorial term Mr. Wilmot was appointed by President Lincoln a judge of the court of claims, which office he held up to the time of his death, March 16, 1868. His wife was Ann, a daughter of Thomas W. Morgan, an old-time resident of Wilkes-Barre, who at one time kept the Arndt hotel, which stood on the ground now occupied by the residence of E. P. Darling, on River street. He was also proprietor of "Morgan's mill," on Solomon's creek, since known as "Petty's mill." Mrs. Wilmot died March 25, 1888. Of the Wilmot family no sons or daughters remain to transmit to posterity the honored name. One son born to the house died in boyhood, having been accidentally poisoned by eating the root of the wild parsnip, mistaking it for an edible root.

HENRY HILL WELLS.

Henry Hill Wells, who was admitted to the bar of Luzerne county, Pa., August 4, 1835, was a descendant of Gideon Wells, M. D., of Cottness, near Hull, England, by his wife Mary, daughter of Richard Partidge, of London, who was at one time agent of the colonies of Pennsylvania, New Jersey, Rhode Island, and Connecticut, in London. Richard Wells, son of Dr. Wells, emigrated to America, and became a merchant in Philadelphia. He was secretary of the American philosophical society, and a director of the library company of Philadelphia. He was a member of the Pennsylvania assembly and for a long while cashier of the bank of North America. He died February 13, 1801. His wife was Rachel Hill, a daughter of Henry Hill, who was one of the original members of the city troop of Philadelphia, and was made colonel of the Fourth Pennsylvania regiment in 1776. He took part in the convention which gave Pennsylvania the constitution which succeeded the proprietary government, and for several years served in the Pennsylvania legislature. His wife was Anne, daughter of Reese Meredith, and she was a sister of Samuel Meredith, at one time treasurer of the United States. William Hill Wells, son of Richard and Rachael Wells, was born in Philadelphia January 7, 1769. He was an attorney, but where and when admitted is not known. He first appeared in Dagsborough Hundred, Sussex county, Delaware, where he married Elizabeth the daughter of General John Dagsworthy. He resided part of the time at Dover and Georgetown and the remainder of the time at the Dagsworthy homestead, of which his wife came in possession. He succeeded Dr. Joshua Clayton in the United States senate for the state of Delaware January 18, 1799, resigned November 6, 1804, after which he resided in Tioga county, Pa. He was again elected United States senator from Delaware on May 28, 1813, to succeed James A. Bayard. He was a member of the house of representatives for Sussex county in 1794, 1795, 1796, 1797, 1798, 1810, 1811, and 1819, and in 1812 and 1813 was a member of the state senate. He died March 11, 1829, in Dagsborough, and is buried in Prince George's churchyard. He was the father of Henry Hill Wells. While the latter resided in Wilkes-Barre, one son, Richard Jones Wells, was born, June 23, 1843. Henry Hill Wells was born in Sussex county, Delaware, February 18, 1797, and died at Skaneateles, N. Y. He was secretary of the state of Delaware in 1823. His wife was Mary Putman.

PIERCE BUTLER MALLERY.

Pierce Butler Mallery was admitted to the bar of Luzerne county, Pa., January 5, 1836. He was born in Wilkes-Barre in 1812. He read law with his father, Garrick Mallery, and practiced for a short time in Philadelphia, but his health failed him and he was sent to Havana, Cuba, where he died in 1838 of consumption. (For particulars of his ancestry see page 1083). He entered Yale college but did not graduate. He was an unmarried man.

ISRAEL DICKINSON.

Israel Dickinson was admitted to the bar of Luzerne county, Pa., April 16, 1836. He was a teacher in the old Wilkes-Barre academy for several years. In 1851 he resided in Wheeling, W. Va., and in 1854 was a resident of Lafayette, Ind. The christian name of his wife was Lucia.

JONATHAN W. PARKER.

Jonathan W. Parker was admitted to the bar of Luzerne county, Pa., August 8, 1836. He read law with John N. Conyngham, and subsequently removed to Davenport, Iowa.

JONATHAN JOSEPH SLOCUM.

Jonathan Joseph Slocum, who was admitted to the bar of Luzerne county, Pa., August 12, 1837, was a native of Wilkes-Barre, Pa., where he was born January 27, 1815. He was educated at Dickinson college, Carlisle, Pa., and Kenyon college, Ohio, and read law with Ebenezer W. Sturdevant in this city, where he practiced up to a short time before his death. He was the son of Joseph Slocum, of this city. (See page 339.) He married, September 12, 1840, Elizabeth Cutter LeClerc. Her father was Joseph Philip LeClerc, and his wife Rachel Manning Cutter, of New York. (See sketch of Edward E. LeClerc for a further sketch of the LeClerc family.) Mr. Slocum removed to Philadelphia shortly before his death, which occurred in that city February 27, 1860. Mr. and Mrs. Slocum had two children, Sallie L. Slocum, married to John B. Love, of Philadelphia, and Edward LeClerc Slocum, married to Emily Carpenter, also of Philadelphia.

CHARLES HENRY SILKMAN.

Charles Henry Silkman was admitted to the bar of Luzerne county, Pa., January 1, 1838. He was born in Bedford, West Chester county, N. Y., July 24, 1809, and came to Luzerne county in the spring of 1835, locating at Providence (now Scranton), Pa. He read law here and at once took an advanced position among the lawyers as an advocate and counsel. Daniel Rankin, E. S. M. Hill and D. R. Randall, all deceased, and David S. Koon, of this city, all emerged from his office at Providence as young lawyers of acknowledged ability and integrity. In 1845, 1846, and 1847 the Lackawanna valley was agitated by two exciting projects of which Silkman, by his superior qualifications as a ready writer and debater, was recognized as the organic head. One was to frustrate the Delaware and Hudson Canal Company from extending their gravity railroad and coal works down the valley below Archbald, and the other was to form a new county from the upper end of Luzerne, to be called Lackawanna. A weekly newspaper was started in 1845 in Providence by F. B. Woodward, and its columns were marked by the keen, incisive and not over benevolent pen wielded by Silkman in reference to these and other matters. The old settlers, of whom few are left, can never forget the repeated public meetings held in Hyde Park, Providence, and Cannon's tavern in Blakeley during these years, in which the persuasive eloquence of this gifted gentleman appeared to great advantage. He married for his first wife Lucilla S. Tripp, a daughter of Holden Tripp, whose mother was Martha Tuttle, a daughter of John Tuttle, whose father was Henry Tuttle, born in Basking Ridge, N. J., November 24, 1733. (See page 461.) The wife of John Tuttle was Mary, daughter of Thomas Bennett, of Forty Fort, who was born August 15, 1772. (See page 630.) Mr. Silkman removed west in 1854, residing in Milwaukee, Wisconsin, for about ten years. He afterwards lived in the oil regions of Pennsylvania. He then returned to Scranton. Some three years before his death his bright and active brain began to weaken. The immediate cause of his death was softening of the brain. Mr. Silkman was a good friend—a dangerous man for an enemy. His power of sarcasm was tremendous. He could annihilate a foe by giving merely a ridiculous name. Controversy was his natural element. For this he had distinguished powers and went into the conflict with ardor and delight. His energy was untiring—the blows he dealt heavy and frequent. He died March 8, 1877. He left two children to survive him by his first wife—Charles P. Silkman, of Chicago, Ill., and Martha, wife of Lemuel Curtis, also of Chicago.

JOHN TRIMBLE ROBINSON.

John Trimble Robinson, who was admitted to the bar of Luzerne county, Pa., April 4, 1838, was a descendant of William Robinson, of Massachusetts, who had a son Samuel Robinson, who had a son Rev. John Robinson, of Duxbury, Massachusetts, who had a son John Robinson, who had a son Samuel Robinson, who had a son John W. Robinson, of Wilkes-Barre, whose wife was Ann Butler, whom he married January 12, 1808, daughter of Zebulon Butler by his third wife, Phoebe Haight. The other children by this wife were Lydia Griffin and Steuben Butler. (See page 326.) Faith Robinson, who was a daughter of Rev. John Robinson, married Jonathan Trumbull and had among other children Mary, wife of William Williams, one of the signers of the declaration of independence. John W. Robinson died in Wilkes-Barre in 1840, aged sixty-two years. John Trimble Robinson, son of John W. Robinson and Ann Butler Robinson, was born in Wilkes-Barre December 30, 1814. He was educated in this city and read law with John N. Conyngham and Hendrick B. Wright. He died unmarried August 28, 1848. He was a brother-in-law of Hendrick Bradley Wright, whose wife was Mary Ann Bradley Robinson.

FREDERICK M. CRANE.

Frederick M. Crane, who was admitted to the bar of Luzerne county, Pa., April 4, 1838, was born in Salisbury, Connecticut, in 1815. He practiced in this county, principally at Carbondale, until 1844, when he removed to Honesdale, Pa. In 1843 he was postmaster of Carbondale. In 1854 and 1862 he represented Wayne county in the legislature of the state. He died at Honesdale January 8, 1877.

WILLIAM JESSUP.

William Jessup, who was commissioned president judge of the eleventh judicial district of Pennsylvania April 7, 1838, succeeded Judge Scott. He presided here from April term, 1838, to January term, 1841, inclusive, when an exchange was effected between him and Judge Conyngham, as follows: In 1839 Judge Conyngham had been commissioned president judge of the thirteenth district, consisting of the counties of Bradford, Susquehanna and Tioga. By sections five and six of the act of April 13, 1840, it was provided that after the first day of the next April Luzerne county should be attached to the thirteenth district, and Susquehanna county should be attached to the eleventh district, and the courts of the respective counties should be presided over by their local judges and the president judges of the respective districts. Thus Luzerne county was transferred to the district presided over by Judge Conyngham. By virtue of this legislative exchange of counties Judge Conyngham continued to preside in the courts of Luzerne from April term, 1841, to January term, 1849, inclusive, when his commission expired, February 27, 1849. By act of April 5, 1849, several changes in the judicial districts were made, and Luzerne, together with Wyoming county, which had been erected out of it, was united with Susquehanna in forming the eleventh district, of which Judge Jessup was president judge. He again presided over the courts of Luzerne from April term, 1849, until November term, 1851, inclusive.

William Jessup was born at Southampton, L. I., June 21, 1797, and graduated from Yale College in 1815. He was a descendant of John Jessup, who is said to have come to Massachusetts in 1620; in 1637 he was in Hartford, Conn.; then, before 1640, of Wethersfield, from which he was one of the first settlers of Stamford in 1640; and thence, as early as 1649, of Southampton, L. I., New York. The cane carried by this early Puritan is now in the possession of ex-judge Jessup, of Montrose, Pa., his descendant. He had a son, John Jessup, of Oldtown, who married, June 16, 1669, who had a son, Henry Jessup, born March 12, 1681; died in 1736. His wife's name was Bethia. He had a son, Deacon Thomas Jessup, born February 28, 1721, and died May 20, 1809. He had a son, Major Zebulon Jessup, born September 15, 1755, and died June 8, 1822. He married, December 6, 1780, Zerviah Huntting, daughter of Samuel Huntting, a merchant of Southampton. They were the parents of William Jessup. Mrs. Zebulon Jessup died May 25, 1835. She was a descendant of Elder John Huntting, who resided in the east of England, probably in the county of Norfolk. He came to this country in August, 1638, and when the Rev. John Allen was ordained minister of the gospel in Denham, Mass., John Huntting was at the same time ordained a ruling elder of the church. He was one of the founders of the town of Denham. He died April 12, 1682. His wife was Esther Seaborn. He had a son, John Huntting, born in England, whose wife was Elizabeth, daughter of Thomas Payne, of Dedham. He had a son, Rev. Nathaniel Huntting, born November 15, 1675, and died September 21, 1753. He was a graduate of Harvard College, and from 1696 to the time of his death the faithful and laborious minister in East Hampton. He had a son, Samuel Huntting, born 1710, who was the father of Samuel Huntting, the father of Mrs. Jessup. Samuel Huntting was twice married, his first wife being Mary Gardiner; his second wife, the mother of Mrs. Jessup, was Zerviah Rhodes.

William Jessup removed to Montrose in 1818, and entered the law office of A. H. Read. The following winter he taught the first term of the academy in that place. He was admitted to the Susquehanna county bar February 2, 1820, and at once entered vigorously into the profession, and success attended him. Added to the labors of the office were those of register of wills and recorder of deeds, appointments conferred upon him by Governors Shultze and Wolf from January, 1824, to 1833. He declined a reappointment in the latter year. During this period in the history of Judge Jessup, and for the ten years ensuing, he was a man of note throughout northern Pennsylvania. He stood at the head of his profession; he was engaged in every case of importance in his own and the adjoining counties, and having a military turn of mind, he took great pride and pleasure in having his regiment, of which he was colonel, better drilled and disciplined than any other in the division. The name of Colonel Jessup was intimately known throughout this part of the state. He was a good judge, a spirited soldier, and a zealous and successful advocate. In 1851 Judge Jessup received the nomination of his party for the supreme bench, but was not elected. After this he resumed the practice of his profession, and continued in it, laboring incessantly, until disease laid him prostrate, and he was thus compelled to relinquish a profession which he had dignified and ennobled by a long life of unimpeachable integrity and an honesty of purpose. No client had cause of complaint for lack of industry and thorough preparation, of ability in management, or of personal or professional integrity; nor could his opponent, in the person of party or counsel, make accusations of deception or ungentlemanly practices. As a lawyer he had few equals, and very few superiors. Possessing a strong and a well-balanced judgment, and his memory fresh and overflowing with all the leading cases, with a strong physical frame, he possessed all the necessary elements for thorough preparation, and he had the power of endurance, and, coupled with this, good oratorical qualifications. The late Christopher L. Ward, of Towanda, and, by the way, good authority, says of the judge that "his style of oratory at the bar was perspicuous, flowing, and strongly impressive. One of his most brilliant forensic triumphs may be reckoned his defence of the Rev. Albert Barnes, of Philadelphia, upon the charge of heresy before the general assembly of the Presbyterian church. In his character or position as a judge, he was remarkable for clearness and readiness upon any subject within the range of the profession, and for a prompt and proper dispatch of business. The bar in both districts where he presided was admitted to be equal in point of character and intelligence to any other in the interior of the state, and with scarcely an exception Judge Jessup commanded not only their respect for his learning and impartiality, as exhibited on the bench, but also their affection and esteem in the highest degree, as a man and a christian." These words, written many years ago, and by one who knew him well and intimately, are truthful and to the point. There was a peculiarity in one or two personal characteristics in him as a judge. No official entrusted with the power of a judge of the Court of Common Pleas of this state ever held the balances with a deeper settled conviction to administer the law with purity and impartiality. There was no taint of bad faith; there was not the shadow of a shade of it. If there was any defect in his decisions, it was because he relied more on his own judgment than the decision precedent—like Scott in this particular, and very unlike Conyngham, who would follow the precedent, though in conflict with his own judgment. "*Stare decisis*" is all well enough, till some organic cause makes the necessity of change. And when that change becomes necessary, one man may do it as well as the seven. Judge Jessup was *the one* to do this. Upon the bench his unrelaxed features gave no clue to the working mind within. To counsel it is painful that he cannot read in the judicial face some index to the judicial mind. It could not be traced here. He had a way of tearing slips of paper from his notes, and chewing them rapidly, when his mind was in labor, but this only showed mental agitation; it gave no clue to the inside work, and counsel on both sides did not know the drift of the matter till it came in well-measured and strong utterances to the jury. Then there was no mistaking the character of the legal current, and there was this grand and consoling reflection, and which all lawyers can well appreciate, as well as endorse, that a cause that ought to be won was never lost under his administration of the law. Nor was there the least flinching from putting down the record of the charge that would prevent a higher court from having ample means to know what had been done below. He was an upright and learned judge; a fit compeer of his cotemporaries, Scott and Conyngham; and taking the three together, without disparagement to others, they may be severally classed as brilliant examples of judicial life. As to his every-day life, one related to him by family ties has truthfully said: "In his social and religious life he won the affection of the good and upright. His religious convictions were deep, and gave a charm to his intercourse with his fellow-men. He was affable and courteous in his bearing to the humblest of his acquaintances." The temperance movement, the interests of the oppressed, the cause of education, and the advancement of agriculture, received his early and continued hearty coöperation. He joined the Presbyterian church of Montrose September 3, 1826, and was ordained a ruling elder of the same August 2, 1829. He was widely known and highly honored throughout the Presbyterian church, but nowhere did his christian character shine with greater lustre than among those who knew him best. He became vice president of the A. B. C. F. M., and cheerfully gave up two sons as foreign missionaries— Rev. Henry Harris Jessup, D. D., and Rev. Samuel Jessup, who have long been connected with American missions in Syria. In early life Judge Jessup was a democrat. In the conflict between Jackson and Adams he took sides with Henry Clay and remained a whig. When that party assumed the name of Republican he went there. On the breaking out of the late civil war he was appointed by the governor of this state on a committee, in conjunction with a committee appointed on the part of Ohio and New York, to assure President Lincoln of the support of the people in suppressing it. This was the last of his official acts. Not long after this he was attacked by paralysis, from which he never recovered. He died at Montrose September 11, 1868. He married, July 4, 1820, Amanda Harris, of Southampton. She was a descendant of George Harris, who is first mentioned in the list of 1657 with the residents of North Sea, Southampton, L. I. He had a son George, who had a son Henry, who had a son Henry, whose daughter Amanda married William Jessup. Mr. and Mrs. Jessup left a family of ten children—Jane R., now deceased, wife of Colonel J. B. Salisbury, of New York; Mary S., wife of F. B. Chandler, of Montrose; Harriet A., wife of Isaac L. Post, of Scranton; William H. Jessup, of Montrose (W. H. Jessup is a member of the law firm of Jessups & Hand, of Scranton, consisting of himself, his son, W. H. Jessup, Jr., and Horace E. Hand, his nephew. He also practices in Montrose in connection with his brother, Huntting C. Jessup. In 1878 W. H. Jessup was appointed president judge of Susquehanna county, to succeed F. B. Streeter, deceased. In the election following Judge Jessup was the republican candidate, but was defeated by J. B. McCollum, democrat and greenback candidate.) Rev. Henry H. Jessup, D. D., a missionary at Beirut, Syria, since 1856; Rev. Samuel Jessup, a missionary at Beirut since 1862; Fanny M. Jessup, of Montrose; George A. Jessup, of Scranton; Phœbe A., wife of Alfred

Hand, of Scranton (she is now deceased); Huntting C. Jessup, of Montrose, a law partner of W. H. Jessup. W. H. Jessup, Rev. Henry H. Jessup and Huntting C. Jessup are graduates of Yale college. Rev. Samuel Jessup entered Yale, but left before graduation; he received the degree of M. A. with his class.

HARRISON WRIGHT.

Harrison Wright was admitted to the bar of Luzerne county, Pa., November 6, 1838. (For a sketch of his life and family see article headed Harrison Wright).

CYRENUS M. SMITH.

Cyrenus M. Smith was admitted to the bar of Luzerne county, Pa., August 6, 1839. His wife was Eliza Gay, daughter of Fisher Gay, of Wyoming, Pa. He left four children—one son and three daughters.

GEORGE H. WELLS.

George H. Wells was admitted to the Luzerne county, Pa., bar January 6, 1840. He subsequently removed to Susquehanna county, Pa., and represented that county in the legislature of the state in 1863 and 1864.

WILLIAM E. LITTLE.

William E. Little was admitted to the bar of Luzerne county, Pa., August 4, 1840. He was a native of Delaware county, N. Y., where he was born in 1818. He read law with Andrew T. McClintock, in this city. He removed from Wilkes-Barre to Joliet, Ill., where he practiced until his death, a few years since.

CHARLES DENISON.

Charles Denison, who was admitted to the bar of Luzerne county, Pa., August 13, 1840, was a grandson of Colonel Nathan Denison. (See page 1088.) Lazarus Denison, son of Colonel Denison, was born in Kingston, Pa., December 5, 1773, and died there March 15, 1841. He is said to be the first white child born in Wyoming. His wife was Elizabeth, daughter of Hon. Benjamin Carpenter, whom he married February 14, 1802. (See page 1047.) Charles Denison, son of Lazarus Denison, was born in Kingston January 23, 1816. He was educated at Dickinson college, Carlisle, Pa., from which he graduated in the class of 1838. He read law in this city with George W. Woodward. He was in continual practice in Wilkes-Barre from the time of his admission until 1863. From the latter year until his death, June 27, 1867, he represented this county in the congress of the United States. He married, May 7, 1845, Ellen E. Hulings, of Norfolk, Va. In the proceedings of the United States senate, when Mr. Denison's death was communicated, Hon. Charles R. Buckalew said:

"He was able to concentrate upon himself a large measure of popular favor, and possessed some marked qualities of mind and character for commanding it. His will was firm; his industry constant; his temper steady, though sometimes pronounced, and his courage unquestionable. He was of the men who pursue an object in private life with perseverance and zeal, and who, when placed in public stations, do not bend before the pressure of the times. But tenacity of purpose, resolute courage, and fidelity to conviction, important as they are to success in such a career as his, are not alone sufficient to secure it. He possessed, in addition, a sound judgment, a sense and love of humor, and fidelity to associates and friends. Hence he was able more perfectly to combine the elements of success as a professional and public man; to win and hold and use the confidence and attachment of client and voter.

"Mr. Denison's political convictions were extremely ardent and uncompromising. What he said in the house of representatives, and his votes there, mark this trait of his character distinctly. It was never doubted that his political convictions were sincere, and he always gave them unflinching support."

General Simon Cameron said in the same proceedings:

"I knew Mr. Denison very slightly. I knew his family well. He was born in the far-famed valley of Wyoming, perhaps the most beautiful part of Pennsylvania, if it is not of the United States. That valley was settled by some of the most intelligent people who came into Pennsylvania; certainly by the most heroic and gallant and patriotic men that ever lived in any portion of this country. The earlier settlers were from New England. They came there at an early day; they came when the boundaries of the state were not sufficiently known, and remained there a long time before their titles were properly settled. During the revolution the settlers were active in support of the cause of the country. After the revolution they were harassed by such troubles as the people of no other part of Pennsylvania were subjected to. They had great trouble about their titles, and they had to contend with a long series of Indian invasions and massacres of the most cruel kind. On one occasion nearly all the people had taken refuge in a block house, but were by some means surrounded and destroyed. In after years George Denison, the uncle of this gentleman, served several years in congress, and after having been in congress he served in our state legislature. He was a man known to everybody in Pennsylvania for his very high order of talents and for his very great integrity. No public man has ever lived in Pennsylvania who has made such a record for these two great qualities as George Denison, and no man, public or private, in his day did more by his services in the legislature to develop the region which gave him birth.

"The people of that valley, from their earliest history, paid more attention to the cultivation of their intellects and their manners than any other portion of our people. The first schools of any importance established in the state were in the valley of Wyoming; and in consequence of this the immediate descendants of the earlier settlers were people of culture, far advanced above other portions of our people. It is, besides, a section of country most highly favored by nature. The valley itself, in its agricultural luxuriance, is equal to any part of the far-famed valley of the Mississippi. Every rood of it is cultivatable soil, and below the surface the earth abounds in as fine mineral coal as can be found in any other part of the world. There is no equal amount of territory so rich in soil and minerals as the valley of Wyoming. It was there that Mr. Denison was born, and there lived and died his ancestors. It was there that his associations were made. He could, therefore, hardly fail to have been a man of marked ability and marked culture.

"He and I did not agree in political sentiment, but his uncle and myself did. I have always believed him to be not only a man of talent and culture, but a man of entire honesty and of the most pure life and high-toned sentiments. I knew, also, very well the family from which his wife sprang. They, also, were people who took part in the revolution and all the struggles of this country; but they resided in a different part of the state. I offer to his wife and children my most sincere sympathy for the loss of their husband and father."

In the house of representatives of the United States Hon. S. J. Randall said:

"It was my privilege to be his associate in the thirty-eighth and thirty-ninth congresses, and he was also present at the first session of the present congress in March.

"An acquaintance and association with him soon ripened into a regard and friendship, for I was not long in finding out his noble traits of character.

"As a legislator he was able, intelligent, and pure; as a citizen, of patriotic motives and unyielding and unbending purpose and intent; as a friend he was true; as husband and father he was affectionate and was beloved. In a word, he was a good man; so lived and so died.

"In the public councils he commanded unbounded respect, and at his home his three elections to this house indicate in what esteem he was held. His example should not be without its lesson. A public man who can yield this life with such a name to live after him as Charles Denison may indeed be imitated."

Mrs. Denison died in this city in 1882. Mr. and Mrs. Denison left a family of four children—Charles Denison, of New York;

Elizabeth Brett, wife of the late George Henry Brett, Isle of Wight, England; Maria Denison, Isle of Wight; and Mary, wife of Richard Winslow, formerly of Cleveland, Ohio, now residing in France.

EDWARD EMMELIUS LE CLERC.

Edward Emmelius Le Clerc, who was admitted to the bar of Luzerne county, Pa., November 3, 1840, was a native of Philadelphia, Pa., where he was born August 19, 1819. He was the eldest son of Joseph Philip Le Clerc and Rachel Manning Cutter, of New York. J. P. Le Clerc was postmaster of the borough of Wilkes-Barre from 1843 to 1845. His grandfather was Joseph P. Le Clerc, a native of France. He was a brother of General Le Clerc, who married Pauline Bonaparte. His father was president of Metz under the first empire. The family residence of the father of E. E. Le Clerc was at the northeast corner of Union and Franklin streets. After graduating from Dickinson college he studied law in this city with his brother-in-law, Jonathan J. Slocum. Soon after his admission to the bar war was declared against Mexico, and in a short time thereafter two regiments of volunteers were called for as Pennsylvania's quota for the conquest of our sister republic. The Wilkes-Barre company, under Captain Dana, at once offered its service, and was accepted. Le Clerc was anxious to join the army under General Scott, and being offered the position of lieutenant in a company being enlisted in Columbia county, entered the service and participated in nearly every engagement from the taking of Vera Cruz to the final assault on Chapultapec and the national capital. He was also an honorary aid to General Scott. He returned with the soldiers when the war was over, but broken in health, and, possessing but a delicate constitution, did not long survive the many hardships he had endured while in the service. He died at Mount Airy, Philadelphia, August 11, 1847. He was an unmarried man. He was a poet of considerable ability, and many of his fugitive pieces have been going around the press for many years.

AMZI WILSON.

Amzi Wilson was admitted to the bar of Luzerne county, Pa., November 7, 1840. He was a native of Pittston, where he was born December 17, 1795. He was a son of Isaac Wilson and grandson of Joseph Wilson. (See page 914.) He resided in Carbondale, Pa., the greater part of his life. In 1837 he was one of the school directors of Carbondale. In 1832 he established the *Northern Pennsylvanian* newspaper in Dundaff, Pa., and in December of the same year removed the establishment to Carbondale. His was the first newspaper published in that city. In 1837 he sold the paper to William Bolton. He was an alderman of the city of Carbondale for many years. He married, July 3, 1827, Lena Wetherly; on February 5, 1837, Esther Wetherly. They were the daughters of Nathaniel Wetherly and his wife, Susanna Hubbard, of Scott township, Luzerne (now Lackawanna) county. On April 24, 1850 he married his third wife, Louisa Ayres, of Carbondale. Eight children survived Mr. Wilson—Julian N., Roderick, Henrietta, Josephine, Flora, wife of George H. Squier; Roscoe, Jarvis K., and Angie L., wife of William Geary. Mr. Wilson died in Carbondale May 27, 1872.

MORRISON ELIJAH JACKSON.

Morrison Elijah Jackson, who was admitted to the bar of Luzerne county, Pa., January 5, 1841, was a native of Berwick, Pa., where he was born February 10, 1817. The father of M. E. Jackson was Joel C. Jackson, who was born February 4, 1796, at Goshen, N. Y. The name of his wife was Elizabeth Doane, a daughter of Benjamin Doane, of Chester county, Pa., who emigrated to Columbia county in the latter part of the last century, settled at Berwick, and followed his trade, that of a tailor, until his death in 1845. M. E. Jackson was educated in the schools of his native place, and read law with

Judge Cooper, at Danville, Pa., then the county seat of Columbia county, where he was admitted to the bar November 16, 1840. In 1852 he represented Columbia and Montour in the house of representatives at Harrisburg. After Mr. Jackson's admission to the bar he opened his office in Berwick, where he was in continuous practice until his death, appearing as occasion required before the several courts in Columbia, Luzerne, Montour, Sullivan, Wyoming, Carbon and Schuylkill counties, also before the district and circuit courts of the United States for the western district, and the Supreme Court of the state. He was at the time of his death the senior member of the bar of Columbia county and president of the bar association. He was a successful practitioner, and held deservedly high place among his associates. In politics he belonged to the democratic party, and was an active member of the organization in Columbia county, assisting in the yearly canvass with the force and effect that a positive man always exerts. His influence was also strong in its bearing on the borough government, and as a member of the council he served a number of terms to the advantage alike of the corporation and the taxpayers. In a business way he was a man possessed of more than ordinary good judgment, and amassed a large property. He was a director of the First National bank from its inception, being a considerable stockholder therein and the attorney thereof. He was a trustee in behalf of the state of the normal school at Bloomsburg. He stood well up in the masonic fraternity as a member of the Berwick lodge. He was a member of the Methodist Episcopal church for twenty-seven years, and was a class leader therein a number of years. The following named persons had been at one time and another students in his office: Hon. C. R. Buckalew, Hon. Aaron J. Dietrick, Silas Buzzard, Alfred Hall, Hon. A. H. Dill, W. A. Peck, L. T. Thompson, Milton Stiles, C. B. Jackson. Mr. Jackson married, July 4, 1843, Anne S. Gilmore, a daughter of Stephen Gilmore, born in Ireland in 1794, and Jane Gilmore, (nee Doane). They had a family of two children—Charles B. Jackson, who was admitted to the bar of Luzerne county October 18, 1875, and Anne G. Jackson, who married Andrew K. Oswald, who was admitted to the bar of Luzerne county November 29, 1881. Mr. Jackson was never a resident of our county, but living near the line in Columbia county, we have seen fit to name him as one of our lawyers. As a matter of fact he did more business in our county than he did in Columbia county. He died at Berwick, July 23, 1879.

JOHN I. ALLEN.

John I. Allen was admitted to the bar of Luzerne county, Pa., January 6, 1841. He established at Carbondale, Pa., January 1, 1855, the *Democratic Standard and Know Nothing Expositor*, which was continued until September 17 following, when the building in which it was printed, together with about twenty others, was burned, and the paper was never reëstablished. He also at one time owned and conducted the *Wayne County Herald*, at Honesdale, Pa. He was drowned in the canal at Honesdale. He had a son, George Allen, who became a lawyer, but is now deceased.

WILLIAM CHAMPION REYNOLDS.

William Champion Reynolds was commissioned an associate judge of Luzerne county, Pa., March 15, 1841, succeeding William S. Ross in that position. (For a sketch of Mr. Reynold's life see page 778).

HORATIO W. NICHOLSON.

Horatio W. Nicholson, who was admitted to the bar of Luzerne county, Pa., April 6, 1841, was a descendant of Ambrose Nicholson and his wife, Margaret Hill, of Glastonbury, Connecticut, who were married June 13, 1756. Francis Nicholson, eldest son of Ambrose Nicholson, was born in Glastonbury April 13, 1758. His wife was Rachel Loveland, daughter of David Loveland, of Glastonbury, whom he married February 7, 1781. Francis Nicholson served in the war of the revolution, and about the end of the last century removed to what is now Hamlinton, in Wayne county, Pa. He died soon after. Zenas Nicholson, son of Francis Nicholson, was born in Glastonbury November 21, 1795. His first wife, the mother of H. W. Nicholson, was Mary, daughter of George Goodrich, who was the son of Seth Goodrich, who came from Connecticut. (See page 123.) Horatio W. Nicholson was born at Salem Corners, now Hamlinton, Pa., December 4, 1817. He was educated at Harford academy, Susquehanna county, Pa., and read law with Luther Kidder in this city. He practiced here for some years and then removed to Waverly, Pa., where he died June 16, 1855. He married, March 4, 1838, Rhoda Stone. She was the daughter of John Stone, who removed to Abington, Luzerne (now Lackawanna) county, in 1810 from Rhode Island. She subsequently married Lathan Jones, M. D. Mr. and Mrs. Nicholson had a family of two children—Oscar E. Nicholson and George S. Nicholson. The latter is still living. Oscar F. Nicholson, of this city, and J. Milton Nicholson, of Kingston, are half brothers of Horatio W. Nicholson.

LYMAN HAKES.

Lyman Hakes was admitted to the bar of Luzerne county, Pa., April 6, 1841. He was a descendant of Solomon Hakes, who was of Westerly, Rhode Island, in 1709. The records of the town meeting held in April, 1709, show that Solomon Hakes and some others were proposed to be made freemen, and at the next meeting Solomon was admitted a freeman and was allotted one hundred acres of the vacant land. The next year he removed to Stonington, Connecticut. The wife of Solomon Hakes was Anna Billings, granddaughter of William Billings, who came from England in 1640 and settled in Stonington. Her father was Ebenezer Billings, whose wife was Anna Comstock. Solomon Hakes had a son George Hakes. George S. Hakes, son of George Hakes, was born January 27, 1751, in Stonington. He left Stonington and from 1770 to 1793 was settled in Berkshire county, Massachusetts. He removed from Berkshire to Herkimer county, N. Y., in 1793, and died about 1826 at Salisbury, Herkimer county. He married Zurvia Church, a descendant of Captain Church, in 1774. His occupation was that of a farmer. Lyman Hakes, son of George S. Hakes, was born at Hancock, Berkshire county, Massachusetts, May 26, 1788. He married his first wife, Nancy Dayton, of Watertown, Litchfield county, Connecticut, at Harpersfield, Delaware county, N. Y., where she was engaged in teaching school, September 22, 1813. She died in 1850, after raising a family of eight children. He married for his second wife Delinda Osborne. He was for several years supervisor of Harpersfield, and took an active part in building up schools and establishing useful libraries, and was of much value to young men in their debating societies. He was the leading spirit in favor of good roads and in the construction of a turnpike through Delaware and Schoharie counties about 1836. In 1841 he was commissioned by Governor Seward a judge of the courts of Delaware county. It was during his term that the antirent insurrection broke out, making much business for the courts. In the war of 1812 he was drafted into the military service and was stationed at New York. In those days bounties were unknown. Each man had to provide his own weapon and accoutrements. He was honorably discharged and started home without a shilling. About 1870 he was awarded a pension of one hundred dollars a year, every dollar of which he gave away as soon as he received it. He died at Harpersfield July 14, 1873. His sister Hannah was the grandmother of Hon. Charles E. Rice, now president judge of Luzerne county. Lyman Hakes, son of Lyman Hakes, was born at Harpersfield, N. Y., March 23, 1816. He came to Pennsylvania in 1837, and for some time taught school at Berwick, Columbia county, Pa. While thus engaged he commenced the study of law under the tuition of the late Hon. S. F. Headley. In 1839 he came to Wilkes-Barre and continued his legal studies under William Wurtz. Very early in his career Mr. Hakes gave evidence of his power as a criminal lawyer, which afterwards distinguished him. He had to contend against able men and powerful orators, who did little to help the struggling young attorney; but opposition only developed the powers of his mind, and his strength of will overcame every obstacle, until he stood the peer of the brightest, if not, indeed, peerless at the Luzerne bar. He was not a brilliant orator, but he had a mathematical mind, capable of condensing facts and presenting them to a jury in a most convincing manner. He excelled in clearness of statement and was always powerful before a jury. In the earlier years of his practice Mr. Hakes was a close student and was almost as successful in civil as in criminal cases, but in his later years his practice was principally criminal and books were in a great measure neglected. But even up to the last he was no mean antagonist in any case. In the midst of a large practice at the bar he found time to keep up with the current scientific literature of the day, and was greatly interested in all scientific discoveries. He had almost a passion for machinery and when riding on a railroad almost invariably took a position on the locomotive. In appreciation of this trait of his character the Lackawanna and Bloomsburg railroad company named one of their locomotives the "Lyman Hakes." Among the students of the deceased are to be found some of our most promising lawyers. The intercourse between Mr. Hakes and the young gentlemen who studied under him, of which we can truthfully testify, was ever of the most agreeable kind. So likewise the indulgence he manifested towards the younger members of the bar. He was not envious of any other's success but rather preferred giving aid to its further advancement.

While it is not possible in a notice such as this to comment on all that is worthy of remark, there is, nevertheless, a trait pertaining to legal ethics wherein this practitioner was always the most scrupulous. He stood steadfastly by his word. His fellow-attorney need not ask under his signature for the evidence of any agreement pertaining to any matter to come before court on trial. His word was sufficient. What he verbally agreed to do was with him a matter of professional pride to consummate.

In his private life Mr. Hakes had many admirers, and this not without cause. He was a true and faithful friend; in the capacity of a neighbor, justly noted. There were few men more ready to serve, to aid, to counsel. His generosity was noble and exalted. Perhaps the highest meed of praise that man can bestow upon man is that due to charity. And all who knew Mr Hakes freely accord to him the exercise of this heaven-born virtue. The last dime in the purse was never refused to the cry of the needy. If he did not always give with discrimination, he gave liberally; and whatever were his faults, there are many whom he befriended who sincerely mourned his loss.

In the estimation of human character we are accustomed to place most confidence in the evidence of those most qualified, from closest intimacy, to judge. And it is in this case well worthy of notice that all nearest allied to this man, in professional, social and domestic life, bear the same testimony to his many virtues, and most keenly feel the providence which has summoned him from amongst us.

We knew Mr. Hakes well. As a student in his office, for a while a member of his family, by our intercourse with him, we learned not only to respect him, but to love him, and we here drop a tear to his memory.

> "And the night dew that falls, though in silence it weeps,
> Shall brighten with verdure the grave where he sleeps."

Mr. Hakes was twice married. His first wife, whom he married in 1851, was Elizabeth J. Baldwin, of this city. She was the daughter of Jared R. Baldwin, who was clerk of the board of commissioners of Luzerne county from 1845 to 1850. His second wife, whom he married in 1868, was Margaret D. Cowley, of Pittsburg. He left no children by either wife. Mr. Hakes died in this city December 8, 1873. He was a brother of Hon. Harry Hakes of this city. (See page 134).

HENRY MILLS FULLER.

Henry Mills Fuller was admitted to the bar of Luzerne county, Pa., January 3, 1842. (For a sketch of his life see page 586.)

ZIBA BENNETT.

Ziba Bennett was commissioned an associate judge of Luzerne county, Pa., February, 21, 1842. He was a native of Weston, Connecticut, where he was born November 10, 1800. His grandfather, Thaddeus Bennett and Mary Platt, were married at Weston April 15, 1761. Platt Bennett, son of Thaddeus Bennett, was born at Weston July 28, 1770. His wife was Martha Wheeler. While quite young Mr. Bennett's father removed from his native state to West Chester county, N. Y., whence, after a brief stay, he removed to Newtown (now Elmira), N. Y. Young Mr Bennett's educational advantages were similar to those generally enjoyed by boys in the beginning of the present century, but, notwithstanding their limited nature, he profited by them far more than the average of his fellows. His superior intelligence, excellent moral character and good manners made him noticeable even when a mere boy, and particularly attracted the attention of the late Judge Hollenback, who had at that time a branch store at Newtown. Judge Hollenback easily persuaded Mr. Bennett's father that the boy was better adapted to a mercantile career than to farming, and shortly after entering his "teens" Mr. Bennett was given the position of junior clerk in Judge Hollenback's branch store. In 1815 he was transferred to the main store at Wilkes-Barre, and immediately entered upon his duties in the store on South Main street. He proved a valuable acquisition in every way, being apt, obliging and conscientious, and besides becoming a prime favorite with the general public, so impressed his employer that he was rapidly advanced from the position of a subordinate to that of chief clerk of the establishment. In 1821 Judge Hollenback admitted his son, George M. Hollenback, to partnership, and the business was removed to new quarters at the corner of River and Market streets, where John Welles Hollenback's building is in process of erection. In 1822 Mr. Bennett became the partner of George M. Hollenback, and their business relations were maintained until 1826, when Mr. Bennett purchased the property of Stephen

Tuttle, on North Main street, and branched out for himself as a merchant. By close application to business and carefulness in its management he speedily placed his venture on a sound footing, and although at an age when few men have even fully decided what to do for a living, he took his place among the leading business men of the community. He continued thus engaged up to the time of his death, when he was at the head of the hardware house of Z. Bennett & Co., and the oldest merchant in Luzerne county. Mr. Bennett's perceptions were unusually clear, and his judgment always sound, and in spite of the fact that he was one of the most cautious of men, readily discerned the avenues to wealth, and so boldly entered them that he succeeded in amassing a large fortune. It has been said of him that he was one of the most popular, successful and upright merchants that ever graced the mercantile circles of the Wyoming valley. During the years 1833 and 1834 he was a member of the legislature of the state. Being elected to the office, he discharged his duties with the same fidelity to the interest of his constituents and of the state as he exercised in the management of his commercial affairs. The last named year the bill for common schools passed both branches of the legislature. Mr. Bennett took a very active interest in the matter, and as his name was the first in the alphabetical list of members of the house, his was the first vote given to the bill. The act of 1834 inaugurated a new era in education in this state. From that time forward steady progress has been made. At times it was slow and to many imperceptible, but public sentiment was never stagnant and legislation never went backward. With this law the foundation of the system of common schools now in vogue was laid. It provided that a tax should be levied on all the taxable property and inhabitants; that townships, boroughs and wards should be school districts, and that schools should be maintained at public expense. The establishment and supervision of schools in each district were entrusted to a board of six school directors to be chosen by the legal voters. The people in each township were allowed to determine by an election whether the new school system should be adopted or rejected, and an election upon this question might be held once in three years. The secretary of the commonwealth was made superintendent of public schools, and the legislature was authorized to appropriate funds annually from the state treasury in aid of the work of education. Mr. Bennett was a member of the reform convention which met at Harrisburg, Pa., January 8, 1834. His associates from this county were Luther Kidder, Albert G. Broadhead and Ovid F. Johnson. This convention was preparatory to the constitutional convention of 1838. They recommended the following amendments to the constitution: "The abolition of all offices for life; the meeting of the legislature on the first Monday in January; members of the senate to be elected for two or three years only; the enjoyment and security of the right of universal suffrage; the judges of the Supreme Court and judges of the Court of Common Pleas to be appointed by the governor, and the appointment to be sanctioned by the senate, or to be elected by joint ballots of both houses, in either case for a term of five or seven years; associate judges, justices of the peace, prothonotaries, registers and recorders and county treasurers to be elected by the people for a term of years; all executive and judicial officers who shall be appointed by the governor to have their appointments sanctioned by the senate; the election of a lieutenant governor, to preside in the senate, and to act as chief magistrate in case of the death, refusal to act, removal or impeachment of the governor; the term of continued eligibility to the office of governor to be reduced or shortened; a provision for future amendments of the constitution, and a restriction of the pardoning power of the governor." Mr. Bennett had no taste for politics, and when his term had expired he set his face against renomination, and also declined every subsequent invitation to enter the political arena, including several offers of a nomination to congress. Although not caring for public honors, and avoiding prominence so far as lay in his power, he was by no means indifferent to public affairs; on the contrary, he was unselfishly interested in every question that concerned the people, and while not caring to appear at the front in dealing with them, he was not infrequently active in determining them one way or the other. Judge Bennett possessed the public confidence to a degree seldom exceeded. Every trust confided to him was administered with religious exactitude and never with an eye to his personal advantage. His careful and methodical business habits were carried into his public life with the happiest effect upon the affairs transacted. During his remarkably long and successful business career Mr. Bennett was identified with many enterprises in the Wyoming valley. He was one of the founders of the Wyoming bank, an institution which owes its prosperity and unblemished record largely to his personal supervision of its affairs. Of this institution he was a director from its organization in 1829 until his death, and its president for nearly ten years. He was also for some years president of the Wilkes-Barre Bridge Company and of the Hollenback Cemetery Association. He was an incorporator of the Wilkes-Barre Gas Company, the Wilkes-Barre Water Company, Miners' Savings Bank of Wilkes-Barre, of the Home for Friendless Children, and other associations. In 1862 he founded and became the senior member of the banking house of Bennett, Phelps & Co., of Wilkes-Barre, his associates being John C. Phelps, his son-in-law, and George S. Bennett, his son. Of this banking firm he remained the head until his death. Mr. Bennett became a professing member of the Methodist Episcopal church at the age of twenty-one, and immediately proceeded to identify himself with its work. For over half a century he was a useful and prominent officer in the church. As a young man he was chorister. A large part of his labors at a later period were in connection with the First Methodist Episcopal Sabbath school, which he succeeded in making one of the most flourishing in Wilkes-Barre. His zeal in religious work was unflagging, and as Sabbath school superintendent, steward and trustee of the First Methodist Episcopal church, he was able to give it free rein. He was truly a religious man, and it is not too much to say that his whole life was sweetened, ennobled and rounded out by his sincere christianity. He donated the land on Franklin street upon which the First Methodist Episcopal church is erected. He was in active sympathy with all reforms, and was particularly interested in the cause of temperance, which he believed to be a starting point toward the higher moral state. He was one of the originators of the first organized movement against intemperance in Luzerne county, and lived to see many beneficial results follow its inauguration. In 1872 he was elected by the layman's convention to the general conference of the Methodist Episcopal church, held at Brooklyn, N. Y., and was thus one of the first lay delegates to that body from the Wyoming conference. His connection with the church established in the early days of Methodism in the Wyoming valley was lovingly maintained till the closing hours of his life. He gave liberally of his ample fortune to sustain religious and charitable work, and not the least worthy of his kind deeds was his unfailing hospitality to all engaged in christian work. He assisted in founding the Luzerne County Bible Society, was a liberal contributor to its funds, and was for twenty-six years its treasurer. As early as 1828 he was its recording secretary. In the work of public education he was warmly interested, and in order to bring the advantages of higher education closer to the people with whom his lot was cast, he aided in establishing the Wyoming Seminary at Kingston, was one of its trustees for many years, and founded its ample and extensive library, which was named in his honor. He held other positions of honor and trust besides those named, and in all was able, prudent and faithful in the discharge of the duties devolving upon him. He was treasurer of the borough of Wilkes-Barre in 1824 and 1825, and a member of the town council in 1828, 1829, 1849 and 1850. One of his marked characteristics was his kind, conciliatory disposition. He resolutely avoided all wrangling and contention, and never took part in or countenanced disputes on any subject. The wealth he acquired was obtained honestly, and was used generously to promote the welfare of humanity. This old, widely known and greatly esteemed citizen died November 4, 1878, to the great regret of the people of this city. Mr. Bennett was twice married. His first wife, whom he married November 25, 1825, was Hannah Fell Slocum, the eldest daughter of Joseph Slocum. (See page 339.) This most estimable christian lady died February 5, 1855, leaving behind a precious memory, fragrant of noble virtues and good deeds. Their two surviving children are:

I. George Slocum Bennett, born August 17, 1842, in Wilkes-Barre, Pa. Φ. B. K.; A. B., Wesleyan University, 1864; A. M., 1867. Commencement orator. 1864, with his father in banking business, Wilkes-Barre, Pa.; 1864–1889, director of Wyoming National bank, Wilkes-Barre, Pa.; 1864–1889, secretary of board of directors of Wyoming National bank, Wilkes-Barre, Pa.; 1865–79, member of the firm of Bennett, Phelps & Co., Wilkes-Barre, Pa.; 1868–89, superintendent First Methodist Episcopal church Sunday school, Wilkes-Barre, Pa.; 1868–70, member of town council, Wilkes-Barre, Pa.; 1869, traveled extensively in Europe; 1869–89, manager of Wilkes-Barre Bridge Company; 1870–73, member of school board, Wilkes-Barre, Pa.; 1871, president of Young Men's Christian Association, Wilkes-Barre, Pa.; 1871–87, member of board of managers of Young Men's Christian Association, Wilkes-Barre, Pa.; 1873–89, trustee of Wyoming Seminary, Kingston, Pa.; 1874–89, trustee First Methodist Episcopal church, Wilkes-Barre, Pa.; 1876–89, manager Wilkes-Barre City Hospital; 1876–89, treasurer Wilkes-Barre Bridge Company; 1878–89, manager Hollenback Cemetery Association, Wilkes-Barre, Pa.; 1879–83, member of school board, city of Wilkes-Barre, Pa.; 1879–89, secretary Luzerne County Bible Society; 1883, president school board, Wilkes-Barre, Pa.; 1886, vice president Wilkes-Barre Lace Manufacturing Company; 1886–88, treasurer Sheldon Axle Company, Wilkes-Barre, Pa.; 1887–88, president Wilkes-Barre Lace Manufacturing Company; 1888–89, trustee of Wesleyan University, Middletown, Conn.; 1888–89, trustee of Drew Theological Seminary, Madison, N. J.; 1888–89, president board of trustees of Wyoming Seminary, Kingston, Pa. He married, September 7, 1871, Ellen W. Nelson, daughter of Rev. Reuben Nelson, D. D., of Kingston, Pa. Their children are: 1. Martha Phelps Bennett, born October 16, 1873; 2. Reuben Nelson Bennett, born December 12, 1875; 3. Ziba Platt Bennett, born March 22, 1881.

II. Martha Wheeler Bennett, born in Wilkes-Barre, Pa., August 2, 1833. She married, September 20, 1854, John C. Phelps, a native of Granby, Conn., where he was born April 20, 1825. Their children are: 1. Anna B. Phelps, born January 1, 1856. 2. William G. Phelps, born August 17, 1857; married, November 17, 1880, Caroline I., daughter of Hon. L. D. Shoemaker. 3. Francis A. Phelps, born May 4, 1859. 4. Grace L. Phelps, born March 31, 1863; married November 9, 1887,

Henry B. Platt, son of Hon. Thomas C. Platt. 5. Ziba Bennett Phelps, born December 7, 1870.

The second wife of Ziba Bennett, whom he married November 18, 1856, was Priscilla E. Lee, daughter of the late James Stewart Lee, of Nanticoke. He was a brother of Colonel Washington Lee. (See page 1079.) She erected the chapel connected with the First Methodist Episcopal church of this city at a cost of $26,000, and presented the same to that society. She might also be called the foundress of the Home for Friendless Children on South Franklin street in this city. On March 22, 1862, a number of ladies interested in benevolent work met at the house of Mrs. Bennett. A board of lady managers were chosen, and Mrs. Bennett was appointed the treasurer. The society was subsequently incorporated. The management of the Home is in the hands of twenty-four ladies, who meet once a month for consultation. For a large number of years Mrs. Bennett has been the president. She has been connected with the First Methodist Episcopal Sabbath school of this city for the past thirty years, and for the past fifteen years she has been the assistant superintendent. She still survives, and the hope and prayer of all christian people is that her life may long be spared to bless this community with her charitable and benevolent work. Her large benevolences and noble christian character have made her name familiar, and her "praise is in all the churches."

JAMES HOLLIDAY.

James Holliday was admitted to the bar of Luzerne county, Pa., April 4, 1842. In the latter part of the following year he removed to Milwaukee, Wisconsin, where he remained until his death several years since. He died in the court room there while engaged in trying a case. His wife was Mary Sterling, a granddaughter of Samuel Sterling, who came with his family from Bridgeport, Conn., prior to 1800, and settled in what is now Meshoppen township, Wyoming county, Pa., where he died about

1830. He was a descendant of David Sterling, who was born in Hertfordshire, England. He came to this country in 1651 and settled in Charlestown, Mass. The father of Mrs. Holliday was Major Daniel Sterling, son of Samuel Sterling, who came from Bridgeport with his father's family. He was born there July 8, 1776. He early opened a store and hotel at Black Walnut, and bought land on Meshoppen creek near its mouth, where he was for many years extensively engaged in lumbering, grist milling, merchandizing, and farming. He removed about 1837 to Illinois, where he died August 25, 1839. He was married three times, his third wife, the mother of Mrs. Holliday, being Rachel Brooks. Mr. and Mrs. Holliday had two children, Walter Holliday, now deceased, and Elizabeth Holliday. Mrs. Holliday subsequently married James P. Whaling, auditor of the Chicago, Milwaukee and St. Paul railroad. She now resides at Milwaukee, Wisconsin.

AARON KINGSLEY PECKHAM.

Aaron Kingsley Peckham was admitted to the bar of Luzerne county, Pa., August 1, 1842. He was the second child of Kingsley Peckham and Hannah Retta Rounds, and was born at Bristol, Rhode Island, October 15, 1815. His father was a farmer and while residing in Rhode Island made a bare competence for himself and family. Learning of the cheapness and facility with which land could be acquired in Pennsylvania, he left Rhode Island in the spring of 1829, and after a long and tedious journey, fraught with the dangers, difficulties and discouragements incident to the season and mode of travel, arrived and settled early in the spring in Columbia, Bradford county, Pa. The expenses of the trip left his father little to begin with, but he went earnestly to work in the heavily timbered forest, soon made a clearing, and erected habitable buildings. At this time the subject of our sketch was fourteen years old, just the age when he should have been placed at school and had opportunities for fitting himself better for his after work. He remained with his father until about the age of nineteen, assisting in clearing, working the land

and making improvements in spring, summer and fall, and attending the common schools of the neighborhood in the winter. He then procured a tract of land in Armenia township, Bradford county, and went to work for himself. Not a tree had been cut upon this tract when he went upon it. He cut and cleared a number of fallows, set up a good sugar bush, and made sugar several seasons. He remained there until the spring of 1838, when he rented a pail factory. It was shortly after be began manufacturing pails that he determined to study law. He entered his name as a student with John C. Adams, of the Towanda, Pa., bar, meanwhile carrying on his business, and in addition taught school winters. In 1842 he was admitted to the Bradford county bar. He located at Tunkhannock and practiced there. This was a short time before Wyoming county was separated from Luzerne county. He immediately obtained a fair share of business, and by his industry, application and perseverance worked his way into a good practice. In 1860 the late Warren J. Woodward, the then presiding judge of the twenty-sixth judicial district, comprising among others Wyoming county, was elected president judge of the twenty-third judicial district, and surrendered his commission as the presiding judge of the twenty-sixth. Governor Curtin commissioned A. K. Peckham to fill the vacancy, in the fall of 1861, which position he held until December 1, 1862. He resumed the practice of his profession at Tunkhannock, continuing there until his death, March 22, 1865. He married Jane A. P. Manville, at Towanda, February 21, 1845. She died at Tunkhannock July 5, 1855. By her he left one daughter, Mrs. N. P. Hicks, of Towanda. Mr. Peckham married a second time —Jane E. Knowles, of Chittenango, N. Y.—November 24, 1858. By her he left one daughter, Mary.

WARREN JAY WOODWARD.

Warren Jay Woodward, who was admitted to the bar of Luzerne county, Pa., August 1, 1842, was a descendant of Richard Woodward, who was admitted a freeman September 2, 1635, and whose name is on the earliest list of the proprietors of Water-

town, Massachusetts. (See page 97.) His grandfather, Abishai
Woodward, was the father of the late George W. Woodward.
He was an associate judge of Wayne county from 1814 to 1829,
and sheriff from 1807 to 1810. The father of W. J. Woodward
was John K. Woodward. He was the son of Abishai Woodward. J. K. Woodward was a surveyor, draftsman and a good
mathematician. When Pike county was created John K. Woodward ran the division line of the new county. He was prothonotary and clerk of the several courts from 1823 to 1827. The
wife of John K. Woodward was Mary Kellogg, a daughter of
Silas Kellogg, who removed to Wayne county in 1792, from the
state of New York. He was sheriff of Wayne county from 1813
to 1816. Warren J. Woodward was born September 24, 1819,
near Bethany, Wayne county, Pa.; secured in his youth an academic education at Wilkes-Barre; taught school several terms
in his native county; entered the printing office of the Wayne
county *Herald*, at Bethany, and conducted that newspaper for a
time in the absence of its proprietor, and was then for about two
years connected with the *Pennsylvanian*, at Philadelphia, in an
editorial capacity. He studied law at Wilkes-Barre with his
uncle George W. Woodward, and E. L. Dana, and then practiced
for about fifteen years with eminent success, holding at the time of
his appointment to a judgeship the leading practice at the Luzerne
bar. He had the habits and tastes of a student, and was one of
the most laborious of men, always disposed to master difficulties
and go to the bottom of a subject. A conscientious performance
of judicial duty involves much of concentrated attention and
effort, quite unknown to the outer world because performed
mostly in private. Even in the long run results only become
evident; it comes to be known that the faithful judge is a great
or accomplished lawyer; that his work is correctly and promptly performed; that sound law is pronounced, and impartial justice administered by him; but little is known by the general public of the days or weeks or years of patient toil and of self-discipline
which have made him what he is—an accomplished minister of
justice. The immediate cause of the judge's death was nervous
exhaustion, accompanied by an enlargement of the liver. For
twenty years he had been subject to recurring bilious attacks,

which, with overwork, appear to have caused his final sickness
and death. His walk was remarkably erect; his limbs and face
clothed with little flesh; but his frame was of fair size, his body
substantial, and his head showed intellectual development and
power. His eye was kindly, and kindled in familiar discourse;
his conversation was emphatic, without violence, and had the
charms of earnestness and variety in intercourse with friends.
He read much of general literature, and obtained larger views of
mankind and affairs than those of the mere lawyer or plodding
judge. But of all his characteristics, conscientiousness was, perhaps, the most commanding and constant. This was the spur
to labor and study throughout his career, carrying him with tireless activity through all the obscurities and difficulties of every
case, and presenting to him at all times a wholesome apprehension that some man's right or some principle of justice might be
overlooked or neglected. He was never a candidate for political
office in the ordinary sense of that term, but by devotion to his
profession of the law he qualified himself for high judicial positions, and obtained them without personal solicitations or effort.
Although a democrat of the straightest sect, he was appointed
by Governor Pollock to be president judge of the judicial district composed of Columbia, Sullivan and Wyoming counties
upon a general request of the members of the bar of both parties, and was afterwards elected to the same position by the people without opposition. Upon the bench he exhibited great
ability and impartiality, united with a faithful devotion to the
duties of his office. All business before him was promptly disposed of, and the intrusion of political feelings or other sinister
influence into his courts was sternly prevented. He brought to
the bench qualities which had received their training and discipline under Judge Conyngham, of this county, before whom his
professional life at the bar had been passed—an admirable judge
and a finished gentleman, whose memory yet holds the respect
of the people of all the courts in which his judicial duties were
discharged. These qualities, constituting high qualifications for
a judge, were great integrity of purpose, great industry, and a
most sincere, unassuming devotion to justice. And in social
intercourse off the bench his temper was genial and kindly, and

his friendship was considered a proper object of just and honorable effort. In 1861 Judge Woodward was nominated by the democrats of the Bucks and Montgomery district as their candidate for the president judgeship, but he declined. He was then invited to accept a nomination for president judge of Berks county, and was chosen to that position at the general election of that year by a large majority. In 1871 he was reëlected without opposition, for he had then become known to the people of that county as a most admirable judge and an estimable man, and his retention upon the bench was considered an object of the utmost importance to the people of that county. From that position of usefulness, however, he was called to the bench of the Supreme Court by an election in the fall of 1874, taking his seat on the first Monday of January following, so that at the time of his death he had served as a justice of the Supreme Court something more than four years and a half. His opinions, to be found in the books of reports, will remain to bear evidence of his ability, and their language and composition to gratify all readers of sound taste and learning. Judge Woodward was married to a daughter of Judge Scott, of this city. She died many years since. He was a great reader of current literature, and was constantly keeping up with all the magazines and new books. He possessed a fondness for literary pursuits, and while still a law student was an editorial contributor to the *Pennsylvanian*. He was also much devoted to agriculture and horticulture, and on his farm in New York he had all of the best varieties of fruit in cultivation. He was a liberal contributor to charitable objects, and was identified with every movement in the city of Reading calculated to relieve distress. He was president of the Reading benevolent society for a number of years, and presided over the annual meetings. He was a director of the Reading dispensary up to the time of the reorganization of the institution. He was also a liberal contributor to the Reading relief society. He took a prominent part in the reorganization of the Reading library company, and was one of the founders of the reading room association. Judge Woodward was the law preceptor of Governor Hoyt, and occupied a seat with the latter in a barouche in the inaugural procession in Harrisburg. He also publicly administered the oath to

Governor Hoyt upon his inauguration. Many anecdotes could be related of Judge Woodward. He presided with great dignity in the trial of cases; while off the bench he was a pleasant companion. When a young man, like many other lawyers, he fell into the habit of writing an execrable hand, but upon finding one day that he was unable to decipher some notes which he had taken, he determined to improve his penmanship. He adopted the rule to write so that each letter would be perfectly plain, and he persevered until his chirography became a model of elegance. His judicial dockets are remarkable for the neat and legible manner in which they were kept, the entries being as easily read as printed matter. In 1875 he received the honorary degree of doctor of laws from Franklin and Marshall college, of Lancaster. The severe labors which he had undergone in his long judicial service had, before his elevation to the supreme bench, enfeebled a constitution always frail and delicate. The death of his eldest son, Henry, in 1878, added to his sufferings. In the summer of 1879 he was compelled by ill health to retire to his farm near the village of Hamden, Delaware county, N. Y., and there died, September 23, 1879, and is buried in Hollenback cemetery in this city. Two children survived him—Warren Woodward, a member of the Lackawanna county bar, who died in 1881, and Katharine Woodward, since married to Frank Perley Howe, of Danville, Pa., a son of Bishop Howe, of the Protestant Episcopal church.

WILLIAM HENRY MILLER.

William Henry Miller, who was admitted to the bar of Luzerne county, Pa., November 11, 1842, was born near Middletown, Adams county, Pa., January 13, 1820. He studied law with Hon. John Reed, at Carlisle, Pa., and was admitted to the bar at that place in August, 1842, and soon after removed to Luzerne (now Wyoming) county, and located at Tunkhannock, where he practiced law until the latter part of 1843, when he removed to Carlisle and practiced there the remainder of his life. He married, May 30, 1843, Jane R. McDowell, who still survives him. Mr. and Mrs. Miller have no children living. Mr. Miller at one time filled the office of district attorney for Cumberland county, Pa. He died in June, 1877. "He lived a long and useful life—an honored citizen, a good lawyer, and an upright man."

MINER S. BLACKMAN.

Miner S. Blackman, who was admitted to the bar of Luzerne county, Pa., January 2, 1843, was a native of Wilkes-Barre, Pa., where he was born August 14, 1815. He was a descendant of John (?) Blackman, who was born in England about 1600 and emigrated to Massachusetts or Connecticut about 1635. He had a son John (?), who was born in Connecticut in the latter year. He had a son Elisha, who was born in Connecticut about 1687, married, lived, and died about 1768, in Lebanon, Connecticut. Elisha Blackman, son of Elisha Blackman, was born in Lebanon in 1717; married Lucy Polly, who was a widow Smith; emigrated with his family to Wilkes-Barre early in the spring of 1772; was in the battle at Nanticoke and defeat of Plunkett in 1775; was in the skirmish with the Indians at Exeter on July 1, 1778; returned to Lebanon after the battle and massacre of July 3, 1778; returned to Wilkes-Barre in 1790; owned a farm extending on both sides of Main street; one lot west of Academy street; died there in 1804. Ichabod Blackman, son of Elisha Blackman, was born in Lebanon, Connecticut, in 1762; came to Wilkes-Barre with his father's family in 1772; was in the skirmish at Exeter, July 1, 1778, together with his father and brother Elisha; fled with his father, mother, sisters and brother Eleazer, on July 4, 1778, through the woods to Stroudsburg, and from thence to Connecticut; returned to Wilkes-Barre about 1784. (See page 931.) In 1786 he married, at Goshen, N. Y., Elizabeth Franklin, daughter of Jonathan Franklin. The Franklins were a large and respectable family, distant relatives of Dr. Benjamin Franklin. Of the Wyoming family there were seven brothers, all of whom had large families, from whom a numerous progeny has sprung. John was killed in the battle and massacre of Wyoming. Mr. Blackman removed to Sheshequin, Bradford county, in 1794. He went up the river on a boat with Judge Hollenback and brought the first cart used in the township. In the month of April, 1798, he was drowned while crossing the river in a canoe on a very dark night. Ichabod Blackman had three sons—Colonel Franklin Blackman, Rev. David S. Blackman, a Presbyterian minister, and Elisha Blackman. The latter was born in Horn Brook, Bradford county, in 1791. His first wife was Mary Searle. The two latter were the parents of Miner S. Blackman. Mr. Blackman was educated in his native town. He read law with H. B. Wright, in this city He served an apprenticeship to the printing business with Asher Miner, at Doylestown, Pa., in his young manhood, and in connection with Dr. Thomas W. Miner published the *Wyoming Republican*, in Kingston, from 1837 to 1839. In 1844, 1845 and 1846 he was one of the trustees of the Wyoming seminary, at Kingston. He was also district attorney of Luzerne county during the years 1841, 1842 and 1843. He was a member of the town council of the borough of Wilkes-Barre at the time of his decease. He was a class leader in the Methodist Episcopal church for a number of years. Mr. Blackman married, September 26, 1843, Ann Elizabeth Drake, of this city. She was the daughter of Benjamin Drake, a native of Mendham, Morris county, N. J., where he was born April 22, 1778, and his wife Nancy S. Ely, a native of Abington, Montgomery county, Pa., where she was born February 10, 1788. They were married March 2, 1817. Mr. and Mrs. Blackman had two children, but neither survived. Mr. Blackman died by his own hands, May 25, 1848, while suffering from a severe attack of small pox. His wife is also deceased. They left no children.

EDWARD M. COVELL.

Edward M. Covell, who was admitted to the bar of Luzerne county, Pa., January 2, 1843, was a native of Wilkes-Barre, Pa. He was the grandson of Matthew Covell, M. D., who was a resident of Wilkes-Barre prior to 1800, and in 1798 he was a justice of the peace for Wilkes-Barre township. In 1811 he was one of the commissioners of the Wilkes-Barre meeting house and bank lottery. The wife of Dr. Covell was Aurelia Tuttle. She was a descendant of Joseph Tuttle, who was baptized in New Haven, Conn., November 22, 1640; married, May 2, 1667, Hannah, daughter of Captain Thomas Munson, born June 11, 1648. Captain Munson came in the Elizabeth to Boston in 1634; removed to Hartford, and was of the Hartford contingent under Captain Mason at the destruction of the Pequot fort; removed to New Haven 1642; offered one-third of an unclaimed allotment in the governor's quarter on conditions that he never complied with, namely, that he would build a house thereon and devote himself to making wheels and ploughs for the good of the colony. In 1669 he was a commissioner with Samuel Bishop and three others to meet five commissioners from Branford to establish boundaries. In 1675 he commanded the New Haven troops that, at Norrituck, defended the plantation against the Indians. He was a representative in the general assembly twenty-four sessions, from 1666 to 1683. A complaint against Joseph Tuttle and John Hold was made August 7, 1666, for "tumultous carriage and speaking against the infliction of punishment upon two delinquents;" fined twenty shillings. "He was excused from 'watching in 1685,'" being an impotent man, having lost the use of one of his feet, and now having two sons in the public service." The same year he was appointed constable, but declined on account of lameness. Stephen Tuttle, son of Joseph Tuttle, was born May 20, 1673; removed to Woodbridge, N. J., where his name first appears on land record April 17, 1695, as grantee of six acres of high land, which was laid out to him December 21 of same year. At town meeting January 1, 1697, Stephen Tuttle was chosen constable for the year ensuing. His name stands fourth on the list of church members. He was married in Woodbridge by Samuel Hale, justice of the peace, September 12, 1695, to Ruth Fitz Randolph, of Woodbridge, of the family from which Governor Randolph is a descendant. Stephen Tuttle, son of Stephen Tuttle, was taken young with his father's family to Woodbridge, but returned to Connecticut and lived with Theophilus Munson at New Haven.

He afterwards lived in Farmington, Conn., perhaps with his uncle, Samuel Tuttle. He was killed by lightning while standing under a tree on the Farmington meadows, June 23, 1735. He married, January 23, 1735, Sarah, daughter of Nathan Stanley, of Farmington. Stephen Tuttle, son of Stephen Tuttle, was born October 19, 1735, posthumous; was taken into the Stanley family, and in 1742 removed with his grandfather, Stanley, to Goshen, Conn., where he married, March 23, 1758, Lydia, daughter of Ebenezer Lyman, of Torrington, Conn. He owned land in Goshen, but removed, probably about 1773, to Palmyra, Tioga county, N. Y., thence to Wilkes-Barre, where he died in 1809. His wife was a cousin of Esther, mother of Dr. Lyman Beecher. Aurelia Tuttle, daughter of Stephen Tuttle, who was born June 29, 1764, at Goshen, was the wife of Dr. Matthew Covell. Edward Covell, son of Dr. Covell, was born in Wilkes-Barre May 12, 1792; graduated from Princeton college, N. J., in 1812; studied medicine in Philadelphia with Dr. Benjamin Rush, and practiced his profession in this city. He was greatly loved and respected. Married in Wilkes-Barre, May 7, 1717, Sarah S. Ross, a daughter of General William Ross. (See page 293.) Edwin M. Covell, son of Edward Covell, M. D., graduated from Princeton college and studied law in this city. His health failed him and he died at Clifton Springs, N. Y., September 8, 1864. He married, June 4, 1845, Mildred S. Glassell, of Culpepper, Va., a daughter of John Glassell.

EDWARD GARRICK MALLERY.

Edward Garrick Mallery, who was admitted to the bar of Luzerne county, Pa., August 14, 1843, was a son of Garrick Mallery and his wife, Sylvina Pierce Butler, daughter of General Lord Butler. (See page 335.) E. G. Mallery was born at Wilkes-Barre, Pa., in 1824, was educated at Lafayette college, where he was the junior orator in 1837, and read law with his father. He practiced law in this city and at Philadelphia, Pa. He was the author of the following inscription on the Wyoming monument:

> Near this spot was fought,
> On the afternoon of Friday, the third day of July, 1778,
> THE BATTLE OF WYOMING,
> In which a small band of patriotic Americans,
> chiefly the undisciplined, the youthful, and the aged,
> spared by inefficiency from the distant ranks of the republic,
> led by Col. Zebulon Butler and Col. Nathan Denison,
> with a courage that deserved success,
> boldly met, and bravely fought,
> a combined British, Tory, and Indian force
> of thrice their number.
> Numerical superiority alone gave success to the invader,
> and widespread havoc, desolation and ruin
> marked his savage and bloody footsteps through the valley.
> THIS MONUMENT,
> commemorative of these events,
> and of the actors in them,
> has been erected over the bones of the slain,
> by their descendants and others, who gratefully appreciate
> the services and sacrifices of their patriot ancestors.

Mr. Mallery was an unmarried man, and died May 27, 1852.

CHARLES PHILLIPS WALLER.

Charles Phillips Waller, who was admitted to the bar of Luzerne county, Pa., August 7, 1843, was a native of Wilkes-Barre, Pa., where he was born August 7, 1819. He was the son of Captain Phineas Waller, a native of Massachusetts, who moved into the Wyoming valley in 1774 with his father's family. Captain Nathan Waller, his father, a farmer, settled in the Wyoming valley when Phineas was a young man. The mother of C. P. Waller was Elizabeth Jewett, a daughter of Dr. David Hibbard Jewett, of Montville, Conn. (See page 842.) Mr. Waller spent his youth at home and in the schools of Wilkes-Barre until he entered Williams college in 1838, where he was a student for two years, but owing to weakness of his eyes he was obliged to discontinue his studies. In 1839 and 1840 he was principal of the Bloomsburg, Pa., academy, and was the first to organize a classical school there. He studied law with Judge Collins in this city, and soon after his admission here he removed to Honesdale, Pa., where he successfully carried on his profession until 1874, when he was elected president judge of Wayne county, Pa. He married, April 3, 1845, Harriet W., daughter of Henry W. Stone, of Mount Pleasant, Pa.

STEPHEN SEVERSON WINCHESTER.

Stephen Severson Winchester was admitted to the Luzerne county, Pa., bar November 6, 1843. He was a native of Baltimore, Maryland, where he was born in October, 1817. When he reached his majority he came to this city and was domiciled in the family of Thomas Myers, who at that time was sheriff of the county. For some years he continued with Sheriff Myers, acting in a clerical capacity in his office. He subsequently served for a short time as a teacher in the old Wilkes-Barre academy. He began his legal studies with the late Hon. Luther Kidder in 1841, and shortly after removed to Tunkhannock, Pa., and completed his legal studies under the tuition of Hon. R. R. Little. He was admitted to the bar of Wyoming county at September term, 1843, and was shortly after appointed deputy attorney-general of Wyoming county, Pa. He served with distinction as Wyoming's attorney, and subsequently entered upon a very vigorous and promising practice at Tunkhannock. In 1846 he purchased the *Wyoming Democrat* of William Bolton, and became its editor and publisher up to 1853, when the paper was disposed of to W. M. Piatt and John Brisbin. In the same year he was induced to return to Luzerne to accept the editorial management of the *Luzerne Union* (since merged in the *Union Leader*), which had just been started. In his editorial labors he found congenial employment, for he was naturally a newspaper man, and was as ready with his pen as he was with his speech in the defense of the principles of a political faith which he clung to until the last: It was while he was in charge of that paper that he was commissioned a brigadier general of the state militia, and put in command of a military district in this section of the commonwealth. About 1855 General Winchester entered the political arena, having accepted the nomination of district attorney. His opponent was Henry M. Hoyt, whom he defeated by a neat majority. He served the office with honor to himself and his party, and with true fidelity to the interests of the people. General Winchester was a hard, earnest worker. He had a powerful will, which enabled him to fight a malady which would have laid many another man aside. As a lawyer he was keen, shrewd and intelligent; as an editor he was ardent, honest and vigorous. In his relations with others he was ever suave, kindly, generous and benignant. In address he was pleasant and in manners polished. In debate he was ever earnest, his style being bold and aggressive. He was a firm believer in the political doctrines of Jefferson, and his position was never mistaken. Ten years before his death General Winchester had amassed a comfortable fortune, but unfortunately it was in real estate, which depreciated in value with the passage of time, and so, in a measure, wrecked him. He passed away at a day when a loving family could illy afford to lose him, but followed by the heartfelt regret of relatives, associates at the bar and friends. He married, February 26, 1857, Anna L. C. Burdett, daughter of Jacob Burdett, and granddaughter of Stephen Burdett. Mr. Winchester died June 26, 1881, leaving to survive him his widow and two children, Martha C. Winchester, now the wife of William E. Speakman, of Woodbury, N. J., and Byron Burdett Winchester, now a young law student.

SAMUEL HODGDON.

Samuel Hodgdon, who was admitted to the bar of Luzerne county, Pa., November 6, 1843, was the son of Major Samuel Hodgdon, quartermaster general and commissary general of military stores in the continental army, and Mary Hodge, his wife.

She was the granddaughter of William Hodge and Margaret, his wife, who lived in the north of Ireland. They were the parents of four boys and two girls, of whom two died in early childhood, and one surviving to maturity left no record. The father died January 4, 1723, and the mother October, 15, 1730. Soon after the death of their mother the three remaining children—William, Andrew and Hugh—emigrated to America and settled in Philadelphia, where they became successful merchants and men of influence in the community. Andrew Hodge, the second in order of age of the immigrant brothers, born in Ireland March 28, 1711, was the father of Mrs. Hodgdon. He soon became a successful merchant and acquired considerable property. His wharf and store and city residence, in which he spent his life, were on Water street, to the south of what is now termed Delaware avenue. His country seat was on Mead lane, now Montgomery avenue, and he possessed one of the only six carriages then in the city. He was active and influential in all the affairs of the church and of the community, one of the founders of and a liberal contributor to the Second church, and a member of its board of trustees to the day of his death. In 1739 he married Miss Jane McCulloch. Mr. and Mrs Hodge were the parents of fifteen children, of whom Mary was the fourth daughter. Hugh Hodge, brother of Mrs. Hodgdon, was the grandfather of Rev. F. B. Hodge, D. D., of this city. Samuel Hodgdon, son of Samuel Hodgdon and Mary Hodge, his wife, was born in Philadelphia, Pa., September 3, 1793. He was educated in the schools of Philadelphia and at Rutgers college, New Brunswick, N. J. Early in life he entered into the mercantile business in Philadelphia. About the year 1814 he married and removed to Silver Lake, Susquehanna county, Pa., where he undertook the management and development of his father's lands. Subsequently he resided and carried on business as a merchant successively in Montrose and Carbondale, Pa. After reading law and his admission to the bar he practiced in Carbondale. At the organization of the Presbyterian church in Carbondale, June 27, 1829, he and his wife joined the same by letters, and Mr. Hodgdon was made a ruling elder. He also filled the same position in one of the Presbyterian churches of his native city. He was elected prothonotary of Luzerne county in 1849, and held the office from December 1, 1849, to December 1, 1852. In 1853 he removed to Scranton from Wilkes-Barre, where he had resided during the time he held the office of prothonotary, and resumed the practice of his profession. Failing health induced Mr. Hodgdon to return to his native city, where he died January 17, 1865. Mr. Hodgdon was married three times. His children by his first wife were Samuel Hodgdon, late of Port Blanchard, and Captain James H. Hodgdon, U. S. N., of Philadelphia, both of whom died in consequence of disease contracted in the late civil war; also Edward, Alexander H. and Thomas H. Hodgdon, all of whom died unmarried in early manhood. By his second wife, Ann, daughter of Captain Henry Harris, of Long Island, he had eight children, the survivors being Mary A. Urquhart, wife of Dr. George Urquhart, of Wilkes-Barre; Hattie E. Meylert, wife of Dr. Asa P. Meylert, of New York; and Captain Henry C. Hodgdon, also of New York. His third wife, Margaret Keene, of Newark, N. J., survived him nearly ten years, dying December 17, 1876. Mr. Hodgdon is well remembered as an upright and honorable counsellor, a wise and prudent man, and in all points the gentleman. Timothy Pickering on leaving the army in 1785, went into business in Philadelphia with Major Samuel Hodgdon as a commission merchant.

NATHANIEL JONES.

Nathaniel Jones was admitted to the bar of Luzerne county, Pa., January 2, 1844. He read law with A. T. McClintock, and soon after his admission removed to Schuylkill county, Pa.

JAMES ROBB STRUTHERS.

James Robb Struthers, who was admitted to the bar of Luzerne county, Pa., August 6, 1844, was a native of Paisley, Scotland. His grandfather, James Struthers, whose wife was Margaret Wallace, and his father, Alexander Struthers, whose wife was Jean Sim, a daughter of John Sim and Jean Robb, were also natives of Paisley. James Struthers, the grandfather, came to this country in 1816, where he and his brother John engaged in business as bakers in Baltimore. Alexander Struthers, the father, with his family, removed to Baltimore in 1818, where they continued to reside until 1823, when they removed to Philadelphia. James R. Struthers was born August 3, 1815, and graduated from Lafayette college, Easton, Pa., among its first students. He then entered the law office of James Madison Porter, at Easton, and was admitted to the Northampton county bar. He first practiced law at Stroudsburg, and removed to Mauch Chunk in 1840, where he became a teacher. From 1843 to 1846 he was district attorney of Carbon county, and represented the same county in the legislature of the state in 1844 and 1845, and also in 1852 and 1853. In 1849 and 1850 he was treasurer of Carbon county. He frequently changed his locality and business, and resided at times in Iowa, Wisconsin, and New Jersey, sometimes following the profession of the law, sometimes publishing a newspaper, and at other times he engaged in farming. Mr. Struthers married, April 28, 1839, Ellen B. Tolan, a daughter of Hugh Tolan, who was born May 24, 1788, whose wife, Hannah Tolan, was born November 19, 1787. Mr. and Mrs. Struthers had a family of thirteen children. Simon Cameron Struthers, of this city, is one of his sons. James Robb Struthers died in this city May 8, 1885.

CHARLES BENNET.

Charles Bennet was admitted to the bar of Luzerne county, Pa., April 7, 1845. He was the only son of John Bennett, who was a son of Andrew Bennett, and grandson of Thomas Bennett, of Kingston. (See page 361.) Charles Bennet was born in Kingston February 28, 1819. He received a liberal education, and read law with E. W. Sturdevant in this city. Preferring a life of out-door activity, he did not devote himself entirely to the practice of his profession, but turned his knowledge of its principles to good account in every day life. He commenced his career of usefulness at a time when coal had to be utilized for fuel instead of wood, which had nearly been exhausted. The mineral wealth was to be developed; shafts were to be sunk and breakers built to prepare the new fuel for market; railroads and other ways of transportation must be started in all directions, and the difficulties to be overcome were formidable. Men were required to overcome these difficulties, and such a man was Charles Bennet, who, by his pleasant manners and address, his thorough knowledge of human nature and his persuasive powers, enlisted capitalists in the large cities in the enterprise. The right of way for the various railroads was to be secured and the routes ascertained. Mr. Bennet took hold of the work with his characteristic energy and persistence, and success crowned his efforts. The valley which had been well nigh isolated and inaccessible, was thrown open, property advanced in value, and many in moderate circumstances became suddenly rich. The actors in such scenes had need of well balanced minds, and such was Mr. Bennet's. Not elated by prosperity nor depressed by adversity, but hopeful in the midst of discouragement, he had the faculty of making friends and attaching them to him. He was liberal in his expenditures, generous in his benefactions, and abundant in his hospitalities. Mr. Bennet died August 6, 1866. His wife was Sarah Sly, a native of Franklin, Michigan, who died in this city June 16, 1887. Two children survive this union—Miss Martha Bennet and Miss Sarah Bennet, of this city.

WASHINGTON LEE.

Washington Lee, who was admitted to the bar of Luzerne county, Pa., August 4, 1845, was a native of Hanover township, Luzerne county, Pa., where he was born May 8, 1821. He was the son of James Stuart Lee, who was the son of Captain Andrew Lee. (See page 1079.) James S. Lee was born in Harrisburg in 1789, and came to Hanover with his father's family in 1804. His wife was Martha Campbell, who was a daughter of James Campbell and his wife, Margaret Stewart. She was the daughter of Captain Lazarus Stewart. (See page 844.) Washington Lee was educated in the public schools of his neighborhood, and at Dickinson college, Carlisle, Pa., from which he graduated in the class of 1843. He read law with Charles Denison, in this city, and practiced his profession for a few years in Wilkes-Barre. While at the bar here he was elected district attorney of the county. He subsequently left the bar and engaged in business enterprises elsewhere; first with his uncle, Colonel Washington Lee, in the operation of coal mines at Nanticoke. He then removed to Baltimore, and afterwards to New York, where he died March 26, 1883. Mr. Lee married, June 29, 1846, Emily Laura Thomas, daughter of Abraham Thomas. (See page 835.) Mr. and Mrs. Lee had a family of five children. They are all married and reside elsewhere, except Charles W. Lee, who resides in this city. His wife is Priscilla Lee Doolittle, a daughter of Dr. J. L. Doolittle, of Ballston, N. Y.

ASHER MINER STOUT.

Asher Miner Stout, who was admitted to the bar of Luzerne county, Pa., August 4, 1845, was a native of Bethlehem, Pa., where he was born in September, 1822. He was educated in Philadelphia, and at Yale college, from which he graduated in the class of 1842. He read law with Chester Butler, in this city, where he practiced until his death, in April, 1860. His father was Abraham Stout, M. D., of Bethlehem, and his mother was Anna Maria, daughter of Asher Miner. (See article headed Joseph Wright Miner.) Asher Miner Stout married, January 31, 1849, Ellen C. Gildersleeve, daughter of Rev. Cyrus Gildersleeve, born in South Orange, N. J., son of Ezra Gildersleeve, of Orange. (See page 721.) The mother of Mrs. Stout, wife of Rev. Cyrus Gildersleeve, was Frances Caroline Kennedy, born and educated in

Newbern, N. C., whose father, John Kennedy, was born and educated in the north of Ireland. Three children—John Stout, Kennedy Stout, and Katharine H., married to Henry M. McCartney,—survived Mr. Stout. Mrs. Stout resides in Spokane Falls, Washington Territory.

JACOB WAELDER.

Jacob Waelder, who was admitted to the bar of Luzerne county, Pa., August 4, 1845, was a native of Weisenheim, province of the Rhine, Germany, where he was born May 17, 1820. His father emigrated to this country in 1823 and settled in this state. Mr. Waelder emigrated with his parents, and continued his studies here until he was fifteen years of age, when he was placed in a printing office to learn the art preservative. He continued in this position for two years. He then received an appointment as proof reader for the constitutional convention of Pennsylvania in 1837. In 1838 he returned to Germany, where he remained over two years and completed his general education. In 1841 he returned to America and established the *Democratic Waechter*, a German newspaper, in this city, of which he was editor and proprietor. This publication has been continued until the present, under the proprietorship of Robert Baur. From 1855 to 1858 his brother, Charles Waelder, and Mr. Niebel were the editors and proprietors of the *Luzerne Union*, a democratic newspaper, in this city. In 1842 he began studying for the bar in the office of L. D. Shoemaker. Shortly after he began the practice of the law the Mexican war was engaging the attention of the country, and he enlisted in the First Pennsylvania Volunteers, serving through the war. He was elected second lieutenant of Company I of that regiment. He was afterwards appointed adjutant of battalion, then acting assistant adjutant general of the army, by General Childs. After the war ended he returned to his practice in this city, and was elected district attorney of Luzerne county. He was also brigade inspector of the militia. In 1852 he removed to San Antonio, Texas, on account of the failing health of his wife. In 1855, 1857 and 1859 he was a member of the Texas legislature. During the late civil war he was a major of the Confederate army, serving first as general enrolling officer, afterwards as assistant purchasing commissary. In 1875 he was a member of the convention which framed the present constitution of Texas, and exerted a prominent influence in the formation of that instrument, which ended his political career. After the war he returned to this city, and subsequently removed to New York, where he practiced one year with M. C. Riggs in Wall street. In 1868 he returned to San Antonio and entered into partnership with Hon. C. Upson, under the firm name of Waelder & Upson. Mr. Waelder was married twice. His first wife was Lizzie Lamb, of this city, a daughter of the late Colonel Henry F. Lamb. One child was the fruit of this union—Mary Louise, now the wife of E. B. Chandler, a prominent citizen of San Antonio. His second wife was Mrs. Ada Maverick, the widow of Louis Maverick, (*nee* Ada Bradley). Mr. Waelder died at White Sulphur Springs, in Virginia, August 28, 1887. The immediate cause of his death was a throat affection. Eight sons and daughters survive Mr. Waelder. He was a prominent member of the Protestant Episcopal church of San Antonio, and was buried according to the ritual of that church. He was for thirty years a vestryman in the above named church. He had a military funeral, the long cortege comprising a battery of artillery, three troops of cavalry, besides numerous civic, beneficial and musical associations. The Beethoven Maennerchor sang at the grave, and the Belknap rifles fired a farewell salute.

JOHN WILLIAM MYERS.

John William Myers, who was admitted to the bar of Luzerne county, Pa., April 7, 1846, was a native of Wilkes-Barre, Pa., where he was born October 7, 1824. He was the son of John Myers, and grandson of Philip Myers, whose wife was Martha Bennett Myers. (See page 630.) His mother was Sarah Stark

Myers, a daughter of Henry Stark, who was born April 19, 1762, and who was driven from the valley at the time of the massacre, but returned and became the owner of a large tract of land in the now township of Plains, in this county. Henry Stark was the son of James Stark, who was the son of Christopher Stark, who removed to the Wyoming valley in 1769. (See page 566.) J. W. Myers was educated in this city, and at Wyoming seminary, at Kingston, Pa. He read law with Charles Denison, in this city. When the Mexican war broke out he enlisted as a private in company I, First regiment, Pennsylvania volunteers, captain, E. L. Dana. He died at Perote, Mexico, November 25, 1847. He was a brother of Lawrence Myers, of this city.

JOHN KOONS.

John Koons, who was commissioned an associate judge of Luzerne county, Pa., April 22, 1846, was a native of Monroe county, Pa., where he was born August 23, 1795. He was the son of Daniel Koons, who removed from near Stroudsburg, Northampton (now Monroe) county, in 1816, to Huntington township, in this county. John Koons removed to what is now the borough of New Columbus, in this county, in 1819, and soon after commenced to clear up the wilderness on the site of the now borough. He became one of the most prominent men in the lower part of the county. In his early days he was largely interested in the Nanticoke and Hughesville and the Susquehanna and Tioga turnpikes. In 1836 he was appointed postmaster of New Columbus, and in 1858 he became interested in the building of the academy and normal institute at that place. He built that portion of the Wyoming canal from Shickshinny to the Search farm. He was a justice of the peace of the borough of New Columbus from 1866 to 1876. He was a merchant and also a surveyor. In 1830 the North Branch canal was completed to the Nanticoke dam, and the first boat, named "The Wyoming," built by John Koons at Shickshinny, was launched and towed to Nanticoke, where she was laden with ten tons of anthracite coal, a quantity of flour and other articles. Her destination was Philadelphia. The North Branch canal being new and filling slowly with water, the "Wyoming" passed through the Nanticoke chute and thence down the river to Northumberland, where she entered the Susquehanna division of the Pennsylvania canal and proceeded with considerable difficulty by the way of the Union and Schuylkill canals to Philadelphia. The "Wyoming" received in the city fifteen tons of dry goods, and commenced her return trip; was frozen up in the ice and snow at New Buffalo in January, 1831. From this place her cargo was transported to Wilkes-Barre on sleds. The voyage of the "Wyoming" was attended with many difficulties and detentions, and embraced a period of upwards of three months. Mr. Koons married, June 21, 1819, Anna A. Fellows, a daughter of Abiel Fellows by his second wife. (See page 711.) Mr. and Mrs. Koons raised six children —Elvira, wife of Rev. J. S. Haynes; Eveline, wife of Amos J. Hess; Marquis L. Koons, F. A. B. Koons, E. L. Koons, and J. R. Koons. Judge Koons died February 13, 1878. William Koons, who was sheriff of Luzerne county from 1847 to 1850, and one of the commissioners of the county in 1837, 1838 and 1839, was a brother of John Koons.

PETER J. BYRNE.

Peter J. Byrne, who was admitted to the bar of Luzerne county, Pa., August 3, 1846, was a native of Eniscorthy, Wexford county, Ireland, where he was born in the year 1799, and graduated at St. Peter's college. After coming to America he resided in the city of New York, where he held numerous positions of trust. He was commissioned by Governor Marcy, in the year 1835, first lieutenant of the Eleventh regiment of artillery of that state, and in the following year captain of the same regiment. Having removed with his family to Silver Lake, Susquehanna county, Pa., he was elected a justice of the peace of that township in 1840 without solicitation on his part. In 1844 he was tendered by Governor Porter the commission of captain in the Montrose and Bridgewater artillery, which he held for many years during his residence at Montrose, as well also the position of notary public of the commonwealth. In the year 1841 he was admitted to the bar at Montrose before Judge Conyngham. The same year he was appointed by Governor Shunk aid-de-camp to his excellency, with the rank of lieutenant-colonel, by which honorable title he was known during the remainder of his life. In the year 1853 the Christian college, at New Albany, Indiana, conferred upon him the degree of doctor of laws. He was elected to the legislature of this state in the year 1860, and also in 1861, and served with credit to his constituents, to himself, and to the land of his nativity, being the first Irishman elected to the position from Luzerne county. That being the time of the commencement of the late civil war, his voice was among the first to advocate vigorous means for its suppression. He was tendered a commission by Governor Curtin, but old age and its infirmities compelled him to decline. As a lawyer for many years he stood at the head of his profession, advocating the rights of his client with energy and zeal. As a counselor he was profound, able, and strictly conscientious, always preferring the interests of his client to that of his own. Although a man over seventy years of age, he was, up to the time of his death, in the fullest enjoyment of mental and bodily vigor. His education was far better than most men of his time. His culture was proverbial, and his urbanity and courteous demeanor won for him a distinction in the elegances of life which few men hold. He was naturally a gentleman, and he never allowed himself to be carried away from his strict notions of gentility by even the most aggravating circumstance. He died at Carbondale, Luzerne (now Lackawanna) county, June 30, 1875.

JOHN MARION ALEXANDER.

John Marion Alexander was admitted to the bar of Luzerne county, Pa., August 4, 1846. He was a native of Cortland county, N. Y. When a young man he removed to Wayne county, Pa., where he taught school for a number of years. He married a Miss Atwater, of Mount Pleasant, in that county, and had a family of two daughters. He read law in Honesdale, Pa. In 1853 and 1854 he was clerk for the commissioners of Luzerne county. In 1846 he settled in Providence, now a portion of the city of Scranton, and advertised his office "in the cave at Cottrill's hotel." He subsequently removed to Leavenworth, Kansas.

ALFRED DARTE.

Alfred Darte, who was admitted to the bar of Luzerne county, Pa., November 2, 1846, was a native of Bolton, Tolland county, Conn., where he was born July 14, 1810. His father was Elias Darte. (See page 130.) In 1829 Alfred Darte left his native state and settled in Dundaff, Susquehanna county, Pa. On December 30, 1830, he married Ann E., daughter of Dorastus Cone. He was a teacher for a number of years, and when not so employed built the Meredith saw mill, one of the first buildings erected in Carbondale. In 1844, while having a wife and three children, he concluded to study law. As it was necessary under the rules of court of Susquehanna county to remain in a lawyer's office for one year, which he could not afford to do with his young family, he went to the state of Kentucky, where he passed an examination and was admitted to the Supreme Court of that state. Upon the certificate of his admission in Kentucky he was admitted to practice in the courts of Susquehanna county. In 1845 he removed to Carbondale, Luzerne (now Lackawanna) county, where he practiced his profession (except during the time he was in the army and while on the bench) until his death, which occurred August —, 1883. He ranked as colonel in the state militia thirty years ago. On April 18, 1861, he was commissioned a captain of company K, in the Twenty-fifth regiment, Pennsylvania volunteers, and as such served in the three months regiment that was called out at the outbreak of our late civil war. His son, Alfred Darte, was first lieutenant in his father's company. They were mustered out August 1, 1861, and on October 30,

1861, Alfred Darte was commissioned as captain of company M, Sixty-fourth regiment, fourth cavalry, Pennsylvania volunteers, and served as such until December 4, 1862, when he resigned. He was wounded at the battle of Antietam. His son, Alfred Darte, was second lieutenant of the same company, and on his father's resignation was commissioned captain in the company. In 1863 Colonel Darte was sent to Fort Leavenworth, Kansas, where he organized and commanded a regiment of Sioux Indians. He was an abolitionist in every sense of the word. In the early days of the late civil war he placed a musket in the hands of his colored servant, one Henry Brown, who is now a resident of this city, telling him that in case any one questioned his authority to carry arms, to refer such persons to the colonel. Many old soldiers remember Brown as the first colored man they ever saw with a musket. Judge Darte was an active republican, and was one of the organizers of the party in Luzerne county. He was a delegate to the first republican convention held in the county. He was district attorney of the mayor's court of Carbondale, in 1871 and 1873, and recorder of the same court in 1872 and 1874. Mr. Darte was a patriot through and through. He was remarkable for his independence of thought and expression, and his contempt for that which people call policy. He hated shams and cant, and liked the society of those who had opinions and independence enough to express them. Mr. Darte died August 13, 1883, at Carbondale. He left four children to survive him—Mrs. James Thompson, of Carbondale; Mrs. William Herring, of Detroit, Michigan; Alfred Darte, a member of the Luzerne county bar, who is serving his second term as district attorney of the county; and L. C. Darte, ex-commissioner of Luzerne county.

MILTON DANA.

Milton Dana, who was admitted to the bar of Luzerne county, Pa., November 6, 1846, was the great-grandson of Anderson Dana, a lawyer from Ashford, Connecticut. (See pages 31 and 240.) Milton Dana was born in Eaton, Luzerne (now Wyoming) county, Pa., February 27, 1822. He was educated in this city and read law with George W. Woodward. He practiced in this city, at Tunkhannock, and in the state of Texas. During the late civil war he was quartermaster of the One hundred and forty-third regiment, Pennsylvania volunteers, of which his brother, Edmund L. Dana, was colonel. On May 17, 1865, he was appointed assistant quartermaster United States volunteers, with the rank of captain. His wife was Sarah Warren, of Freyburg, Maine. She was the granddaughter of Ichabod Warren, of Berwick, Maine, and daughter of Isaiah Warren, of Denmark, Maine. Mr. and Mrs. Dana had no children, but adopted a son, Perceival Walker Dana. Milton Dana died at Conway, New Hampshire, February 18, 1886.

ELLIOTT SMITH MILLER HILL.

Elliott Smith Miller Hill, who was admitted to the bar of Luzerne county, Pa., August 3, 1847, was a native of Carmel, Putnam county, N. Y., where he was born December 20, 1822. He was educated in his native village, and subsequently removed to where Scranton is now located, and there read law with David R. Randall. He married, about 1846, Lucy Newbury, and left several children surviving him. Mr. Hill died in 1874. He established, in 1860, the *Luzerne Legal Observer*, which he published for nearly four years. He also established, about 1865, the *Scranton Daily Register* and *Scranton Register*, which were discontinued in 1868. In 1866 he became the first mayor of Scranton, which office he held for three years. His father was Noah Hill, and his maternal grandfather was Benjamin Miller.

HENRY METCALF.

Henry Metcalf, who was admitted to the bar of Luzerne county, Pa., August 3, 1847, was a native of Yorkshire, England, where he was born August 24, 1821. He was a son of Richard Metcalf and Mary Metcalf, (*nee* Harper). Mr. Metcalf was educated at Dana's academy, in this city, and at Yale college. He read law with Andrew T. McClintock, of Wilkes-Barre, and after his admission here practiced in the counties of Luzerne, Sullivan, and Wyoming. He was elected district attorney of Sullivan county and served several terms. During the late civil war he was a major of the Fifty-eighth regiment, Pennsylvania volunteers. Mr. Metcalf married, November 14, 1848, Sarah A. Dana. She is the daughter of Asa S. Dana and his wife Ann Pruner, and a sister of the late General E. L. Dana, of the Luzerne bar. (For further particulars concerning the Dana family see page 31). Mr. and Mrs. Metcalf had a family of three children—Mary G. Metcalf, Henry F. Metcalf, and Emma H. Metcalf. Mary G. was married, June 4, 1874, to Bradley W. Lewis, of the Wyoming county bar. Mr. Metcalf died December 23, 1864.

ELISHA BOANERGES HARVEY.

Elisha Boanerges Harvey was admitted to the bar of Luzerne county, Pa., November 4, 1847. (For a sketch of his life see page 508).

DAVID RICHARDSON RANDALL.

David Richardson Randall, who was admitted to the bar of Luzerne county, Pa., November 4, 1847, was a native of Richmond, Cheshire county, N. H., where he was born August 21, 1818. He was the son of Joseph Randall, who was born in Cheshire county in 1795, and the grandson of Levi Randall, who was born in the same county December 22, 1761. Joseph Randall was a farmer, and removed to McDonough, Chenango county, N. Y., when David was about six years old. Some years after his father died, leaving him the oldest child and only son of a family of eight children, and but little property. Young Randall thus found himself at the age of fifteen the head of a family who looked to him for support and protection, with nothing to assist him in the struggle of life but his own indomitable determination, fortitude, and perseverance of character, guided by the affectionate counsel of a devoted mother, and the kind hand of a beneficent providence. Left thus with seven sisters, he struggled on to support the family and educate himself. Daylight found him at his work on the farms of the neighborhood, or any other labor that he could find to do that was honorable, and the night time found him at his books by the light of pine fagots. In this way he educated himself and supported a widowed mother and his sisters till he arrived at the age and acquired the necessary education to enable him to become a teacher, he having passed a most flattering graduation from Oxford (N. Y.) academy, at that time one of the most thorough and popular institutions of learning in the state. As a teacher he labored with the same energy that had characterized him from early boyhood, and at the age of twenty-six he was elected superintendent of common schools for the county of Chenango. His rare fitness for the position and eminent usefulness in it was universally conceded. Indeed, in later years, while in the practice of his chosen profession, he gave some of his best thoughts and efforts to promote the cause of popular education. His labors in behalf of the common schools in Luzerne county will ever be gratefully remembered by our people. Devoting his time and efforts to the cause of education in this capacity for two years, he then concluded to enter upon the study of the law. He accordingly entered his name as a student in the office of Ransom Balcomb, later one of the judges of the Supreme Court of the state of New York. This was in 1843, and he continued to read law with Judge Balcomb until 1846, being obliged, however, to devote much time to teaching to support the family. Judge Balcomb became so much interested in his student that he frequently visited him at his home, after young Randall had settled in this county. In 1846 Mr. Randall left his home and went to Hyde Park, now a portion of the city of Scranton, in this county, commencing there to build up his fortune by teaching, and soon afterwards entered his name as a law student with Charles H. Silkman, Esq., of Providence, also a portion of the city of Scranton. There, as in the state of New York, he was obliged to teach daytimes and study nights, for there was ever before him the dependence of his mother and sisters. Struggling along with persistent energy, he was admitted to the bar of Luzerne county, as we have already stated, on November 4, 1847. He opened an office at Providence, and soon his studious habits, frank manners, and ready business tact brought him clients, the number of whom increased up to the time of his sickness.

Mr. Randall had all his life been a steady, consistent and thorough democrat, and in the fall of 1860 he was nominated as a candidate for congress by the democracy of the Twelfth congressional district of Pennsylvania, composed of the counties of Luzerne, Wyoming, Columbia, and Montour. His opponent was Hon. George W. Scranton, the strongest man by all odds in his party, and who defeated Mr. Randall by a majority of six hundred and ninety-five in the district. It the town of Providence Mr. Randall had a majority of twenty-four, where Colonel Scranton had two years before received a majority of eighty-two, and a majority of three thousand, nine hundred and eighty in the district. Upon the death of E. B. Chase, the district attorney of Luzerne county, Mr. Randall was appointed on February 18, 1864, by Judge Conyngham, district attorney of the county until the next annual election. When the democratic convention met in the fall of the same year he was unanimously nominated as the candidate for district attorney. So great was his popularity as a lawyer among the people with whom he had spent so many years of his life that he received a majority of fifty-three votes in the town of Providence, and this was at a time during the war when party spirit was running rampant, and his town at that time gave a majority of seventy-three votes to the republican candidate for congress. Mr. Randall was triumpantly elected district attorney by a majority of two thousand, two hundred and thirty-five in the county. This was the last time Mr. Randall ever suffered his name to go before the people as a candidate for office. Upon the incorporation of the city of Wilkes-Barre in 1871, Mr. Randall was appointed chief assessor of the city by Garrick M. Harding, a republican judge, upon the unanimous recommendation of the members of the city council and the commissioners of the county. He so faithfully performed the duties of this office that upon the expiration of his term in 1874 he was reappointed, and continued to perform the duties of his office up to the time of his death.

Mr. Randall was twice married. On August 25, 1849, to Mary Child, by whom he had four children, none of whom are now living. She died February 7, 1855. On March 5, 1856, he married Elizabeth S. Emerson, of McDonough, N. Y., who still survives him. She is the great-granddaughter of Thomas Emerson, granddaughter of Samuel Emerson, and daughter of Moses Sargent Emerson, all of whom were born in New Hampshire. Mr. Randall died August 31, 1875, leaving six children to survive him. The qualities of the deceased endeared him to his friends and commanded the respect of all who knew him. He was a true friend and generous foe. Bluff, hearty, and outspoken in his dealings with his fellows, he went in and out among them through the years of his busy, useful life honored and beloved, and left to his children the priceless legacy of an unstained name.

GEORGE BYRON NICHOLSON.

George Byron Nicholson was admitted to the bar of Luzerne county, Pa., November 10, 1848. He was a native of Salem, Wayne county, Pa., where he was born May 31, 1826. He was a son of Zenas Nicholson and his wife Nancy Goodrich, daughter of Seth Goodrich. (See pages 123 and 539.) His wife was Mary A. Stone. Mr. Nicholson died in this city February 12, 1873. He left two daughters to survive him—Mary Emma Nicholson, now the wife of Ernest Jackson, and Ruth Nicholson.

JOHN BUTLER CONYNGHAM.

John Butler Conyngham was admitted to the bar of Luzerne county, Pa., August 6, 1849. He was a son of John N. Conyngham, and was born in this city September 29, 1827. In 1842, when not quite fifteen years of age, he entered Yale college. As a student he stood well and took several honors. In 1844 he, with fourteen of his class mates, started a Greek letter fraternity. Those fifteen members of the class of 1846 builded better than they knew when they founded the brotherhood to which good fellowship has ever been a passport not less requisite than learning. To-day the fraternity has chapters in twenty-nine of the leading colleges of the United States, and stands at the head of the Greek letter college societies. Graduating from college in the summer of 1846, Mr. Conyngham returned to Wilkes-Barre and immediately began the study of the law in the office of A. T. McClintock. In 1852 he established himself at St. Louis, Missouri, as a lawyer, and remained there with great credit to himself until 1856, when he returned to Wilkes-Barre. Upon the breaking out of the late civil war he enlisted in Captain William Brisbane's company, of Wilkes-Barre, for the three months' service. This company became C company of the Eighth Pennsylvania Regiment, and Mr. Conyngham was elected and served as its second lieutenant. When the Fifty-second Regiment Pennsylvania Volunteers, for three years' service, was organized in the fall of 1861, Lieutenant Conyngham was made major of the regiment. On January 9, 1864, he was promoted to lieutenant colonel, and soon after his regiment was ordered to South Carolina. During the attack on Fort Johnson, before Charleston, July 4, 1864, he was taken prisoner and confined first in Charleston and then in Columbus, Georgia. After his release he was, on June 3, 1865, promoted to the coloneley of his regiment. At the close of the war Colonel Conyngham was honorably mustered out of the service, and returned to Wilkes-Barre. On March 7, 1867, he was appointed captain in the Thirty-eighth United States Infantry, and in November, 1869, he was transferred to the Twenty-fourth United States Infantry. In 1871 he was brevetted lieutenant colonel for gallant services in the field. Mr. Conyngham was an unmarried man. He died at Wilkes-Barre May 27, 1881. (See pages 203 and 1114.)

WINTHROP WELLES KETCHAM.

Winthrop Welles Ketcham, who was admitted to the bar of Luzerne county, Pa., January 8, 1850, was a native of Wilkes-Barre, Pa., where he was born June 29, 1820. He was the grandson of Daniel Ketcham and his wife Alice Holmes, who were married March 28, 1771. His father was Lewis Nesbet Ketcham, who was born in Philadelphia February 3, 1795, and his wife Deborah Eldridge, who was born in the same city November 20, 1800. They were married April 17, 1819. Lewis N. Ketcham was a painter and cabinet maker. At an early age Winthrop assisted his father and painted many buildings in this city, and also a number of the lock houses along the canal. As a boy he was always hard working and industrious, and seemed to understand that he had his own way to make in the world. He determined to obtain an education, and attended school whenever opportunity offered. As an instance of his energy and perseverance, it is said that when at work painting he would carry his books with him and learn his lessons during the noon-day hour. In 1844, when the Wyoming Seminary, at Kingston, was first opened, he secured the position of a teacher under the late Rev. Reuben Nelson, D. D. He devoted himself to study and his duties as teacher until 1847. After leaving the seminary Mr. Ketcham studied law in the offices of Lazarus D. Shoemaker and the late Charles Denison. On September 15, 1847, while yet a teacher in Kingston, he married Sarah Urquhart, a daughter of John Urquhart, of this city, and a native of Readington, Hunterdon county, New Jersey. His father, George Urquhart, was born in Scotland January 17, 1767, and came to America in 1786. He was for nearly his whole lifetime a school teacher. Two children were born to Mrs. Ketcham—Ellen U., who died in Pittsburg, and John Marshall Ketcham. In 1848 Mr. Ketcham went to Philadelphia and became a teacher in Girard College, of which institution Joel Jones was then president. Here he remained until the latter part of 1849, constantly studying and fitting himself for the career that lay before him, and then returned to

Wilkes-Barre and soon thereafter was admitted to the bar. To
his new profession he brought all the energy and zeal which had
always characterized him, and rapidly rose into popularity. His
first public office was that of prothonotary of Luzerne county,
to which he was elected in 1855. This he held during the term
of three years. In 1858 he was elected a member of the house
of representatives and served one year. In 1859 he was chosen
state senator for three years. President Lincoln appointed him
solicitor of the United States court of claims in 1864, and he
removed to Washington. In the fall of 1866 Mr. Ketcham
resigned this office, as he was not in accord politically with President Johnson. Mr. Ketcham became a republican when that
party was first organized, having been a whig prior to that time.
He was a delegate to the Chicago convention of 1860 which
nominated Mr. Lincoln, and a delegate at large to the Baltimore
convention of 1864, when Mr. Lincoln was re-nominated. In 1868
he was a presidential elector from this state and cast his vote for
General Grant. In 1866, 1869, and 1872 he received flattering
votes in the republican state convention for governor. He was
elected to congress from this district over Hendrick B. Wright
in 1874. Before Mr. Ketcham's term in congress had expired
he was appointed judge of the United States circuit court for the
western district of Pennsylvania, and retained that high position
until his death. President Lincoln, in 1863, appointed Mr.
Ketcham to the position of chief justice of the territory of Nebraska, but, although pressed to accept that high position, he
declined. In 1867, when the act was passed authorizing an additional law judge for this district, Mr. Ketcham was appointed the
judge by Governor Geary. This office he also declined. Mr.
Ketcham died December 6, 1879. At his funeral Rev. W. H. Olin,
D. D., of the Methodist Episcopal church, spoke thus of Mr.
Ketcham: "He was a notable example of successful endeavor as
a self made man. He demonstrated the fact that a poor young
man may lay hold on the possibilities of life and win; that no
position was too high but integrity and fidelity may attain it.
He was always an attentive, respectful, and candid hearer of
the preached word. He had a broadness of soul that respected
truth wherever found. He leaves his work, worth, and example

as things to be proud of. He was a grand specimen of an American citizen. His sympathy for young men struggling for success was remarkable. There was nothing selfish in him, no jealousy lest another might surpass him. He desired to bring all up to his standard. It is a privilege to mourn for such a man —like Cæsar—whose good deeds done the state Marc Antony emblazoned—he has given the state so much of worth that its people love him. His example is one to be followed and his death, like his life, is an example to all. His self denial, intense labor, integrity, judicial fairness and impartiality commend him for imitation. Out of these came a successful life, a triumphant death, and a blessed hereafter." Mrs. Ketcham and her son, J. M. Ketcham, reside in Grand Rapids, Michigan.

EDMUND TAYLOR.

Edmund Taylor, who was commissioned an associate judge of Luzerne county, Pa., January 15, 1850, was a native of Allyngford, in the county of Herefordshire, England, where he was born August 4, 1804. He was the youngest of the fourteen children of his father, John Taylor, and was the twelfth son. He emigrated to this country with his father's family in 1818, and located in this city the same year, where he remained until his death, February 8, 1881. He was married, December 28, 1828, by Rev. Samuel Carver, to Mary Ann, daughter of Elnathan Wilson, who was the son of Uriah Wilson, who resided near New London, Connecticut. The Wilson family at one time owned a great part of the land upon which New London now stands. The day Elnathan Wilson was sixteen years of age he enlisted in the continental army. A few days after a sergeant's squad of twelve men, of whom he was one, were detailed to guard a cross-roads where stood an old school house, in which the sergeant and his men took up their night's quarters. After stationing one of the number at the corner of the roads to look out for any straggling enemy that might happen to pass that way, the rest of the squad had the hard floor to sleep on. Elnathan had not yet got hardened to that kind of bed, he was restless and could not sleep, so he got up just before daybreak and told the sentinel that he would relieve him, for he could not sleep on the soft side of a board. The sentinel gave him his old musket that would not go off, or if it did would not hit a barn door five rods off, and went into the school house. He had not stood long at his post when he heard the clatter of horses' feet, and soon discovered a horseman coming towards him. When he came up within a few rods it was just light enough to see that the rider, who was jogging slowly along, had on the uniform of a British officer, who seemed to be more asleep than awake. Mr. Wilson stood behind a post and the officer did not see him till he sprang right before the horse, grabbed the bridle rein, and shouted to the astonished redcoat to halt, dismount, and surrender or he would blow him through, and then pulled the officer off his horse. The men in the school house rushed out and escorted their prisoner into their quarters. Mr. Wilson was very proud of his first success in war. The horse and trappings were valued at one hundred and eighty dollars, which, according to usage, belonged to him, but he never received a penny. The prisoner in a few hours made his escape, probably by the connivance of some of the men, who might have been tories and willing to take any fee the officer might give for permission to escape. In 1787 Elnathan Wilson left his native state and removed to Stroudsburg, Pa., where he remained four or five years, and then removed to Forty Fort. He employed himself at any kind of labor that presented a chance of making money, and always had something to do. In those primitive times the village of Wilkes-Barre had no better way of getting their salt, sugar, molasses, and such heavy articles of household use than to send down the river by boats to pick up their supplies from the lower river towns. They had a kind of craft called Durham boats, long, slim, low boats, with running planks on each side from stem to stern, for the boats were propelled by three or four polemen on each side, walking backward and forward the whole length of the boat, with the ends of their long ash poles against their shoulders, pushing in a bent position with all their might when loaded and coming up the river in swift water. At the stern of the boat was a long oar for steering and keeping the boat steady while the polemen were walking up and down. The steerman was the captain and a man of no little consequence. He had a trumpet or horn—a loud sounding affair that sent its musical notes from hill to hill as he approached the towns along the river. At the sound of the boat horn all the boys and girls within hearing would rush to the river shore, for the sight of a Durham boat was as exciting to the juvenile of that day as Barnum's circus would be now. Mr. Wilson for a time had an interest in one of these boats, and went with it as captain. About the time Mr. Wilson was engaged in the boating business a family by the name of Baker removed from Connecticut and settled in Forty Fort, near where Mr. Wilson lived. Stephen Baker and his wife were members of the first Methodist class in Wyoming, at Ross Hill. In Doctor Peck's "Early Methodism" he says: "On December 2 (1793), Mr. Colbert is at Stephen Baker's, in Kingston, where he preached, and Brother Turck formed four bands. Baker lived on the old road between Forty Fort and Wilkes-Barre, on what is now called the Church place. This was thenceforth a place of resort and rest for the preachers, and frequently a preaching place." Mrs. Baker soon after was killed by lightning while sitting in her house on the side of her bed. Elizabeth Baker, daughter of Stephen Baker, and Elnathan Wilson were married in May, 1798, by Rev. Anning Owen, the first Methodist preacher at Wyoming. She was but fifteen years of age at the time. Mrs. Baker was a sister of the celebrated American traveler, John Ledyard, who sailed around the world with Captain Cook, and was on the shore with Cook when he was killed by the savages of the Sandwich Islands. He died in Cairo, Egypt, while on another trip around the world. In 1811 Mr. Wilson leased the old ferry house, about five acres of land and the ferry with its equipments of flats and skiffs, for one hundred dollars per year. He took in the first year three thousand dollars, besides his living. He often took in thirty and forty dollars a day in summer time. He also kept a hotel. The trouble brewing between Great Britain and this country, that resulted in the war of 1812, caused thousands of families of the

Yankee states to move to the far west, which by the way is not the far west of our day. The great bulk of immigration was to what was then called "The Holland Purchase," a large piece of good land in the western part of the state of New York that had been bought many years before by a company of Hollanders who now offered it for sale at a low price to settlers. Thousands took advantage of this offer, traveling mostly by the route that led them to cross the Susquehanna river at Wilkes-Barre. Mr. Wilson also had the ferry in 1812, and took in an additional three thousand dollars. At the end of this time travel began to decrease, and Mr. Wilson gave up the ferry. He then built a store house and dwelling in Kingston and commenced the mercantile business. Trade was brisk and profits large. The price of goods began rapidly to decline after the treaty of peace in 1815, and Mr. Wilson disposed of his goods for lumber and carpenter work and built a large hotel in Kingston. Three-fourths of those in the mercantile business in the valley failed. Mr. Wilson sold his dwelling and store house to Gilbert Lewis and moved into the hotel, which was the largest building in Kingston. He also built another two-story house and boarded the hands who built the large stone house of James Barnes, which is still standing across the street a hundred feet below the hotel which Mr. Wilson kept. He kept the hotel for several years. Napthali Hurlbut also kept a hotel in Kingston at the same time. The Wilson house for years was the home of the itinerant Methodist preachers. Rev. Benjamin Bidlack, Rev. George Lane, Rev. Marmaduke Pearce, Rev. George Peck, and a score of others liked, in their travels round their circuits, to stop with brother and sister Wilson. He afterwards sold his hotel and other real estate in Kingston and moved to the Wilkes-Barre bridge house, where he lived until his death. Mr. Wilson was born February 23, 1762, and died in March, 1837. His wife, Elizabeth Baker, was born December 19, 1782, and died October 10, 1840. Their daughter, Mary, the wife of Judge Taylor, was born August 11, 1804, and died May, 1883. Judge Taylor in early life connected himself with the Methodist Episcopal church, in which he was a class leader. In 1838 he joined the Presbyterian church and continued in that communion until his death. He learned the saddlers' trade with his brother, Arnold Taylor, in Kingston, and he carried on that business in this city from 1828 up to within a few years of his death. Judge Taylor was treasurer of Luzerne county from November, 1857, to 1859. He left to survive him five children—Thomas Taylor; Elizabeth, wife of E. H. Chase of this city; John Taylor; Bethlehem, Pa.; Edmund Taylor, New York; and Mary A. White, wife of Samuel White, Lawrence, Massachusetts.

ANGELO JACKSON.

Angelo Jackson was admitted to the bar of Luzerne county, Pa., April 1, 1850. (For a sketch of his life see page 538.)

JOSEPH WRIGHT MINER.

Joseph Wright Miner was admitted to the bar of Luzerne county, Pa., August 5, 1850. "Edward III, in going to make war against the French, took a progress through Somersett, and coming to Mendippi *colles minerari* Mendippi Hills, in Somersett, where lived one Henry Miner his name being taken rather *a denominatione lo ci et ab officio*, who with all carefullness and loyaltie, having convened all his domesticall and meniall servants, armed with battle axes, profered himself and them to his master's services, making a compleat hundred. Wherefore he had his coat armoriall gules, signifying *miner*, red another demonstration of the original of the surname a *fesse* (*id est cingulum militaire*, because obtained by valor,) betwixt three plates *argent*, another demonstration of the arms, for there could be no plates without mines." Henry died in 1359. He had a son William, who had a son Thomas, who married in 1399, who had a son Lodowick, died in 1480, who had a son Thomas, born in 1436, who had a son William, who had a son William, died in 1585, who had a son Clement, died in 1640, who was the father of Thomas. He was evidently a man of note and influence. Thomas Miner was born in England in 1608, and came to Connecticut in 1643. He had a son Clement, born in 1640, died

1700, who had a son Clement, born 1663, died 1747, who had a son Hugh, born 1710, died 1753, who had a son Seth Miner, born 1742, of Norwich, Conn. He was a commissioned officer in the militia, a zealous whig, and at the first alarm hastened to Boston with journeymen and apprentices. A man of strong mind and ardent feelings, he entered upon the expedition with zeal, and he used to tell of attending General Jedediah Huntington when visiting the outposts on Dorchester Heights in the early morning when the enemy from the town opened fire from their cannon and several times covered them with earth thrown up by the balls. As a member of the Connecticut-Delaware Land Company, Seth Miner had a claim in the territory so long in dispute between the proprietaries of Pennsylvania and the colony and state of Connecticut under the charter of King Charles II, and his son, Charles Miner, was deputed to come out to the Susquehanna to look after his interests there. Charles Miner was the father of William Penn Miner, of the Luzerne bar. (See page 42.) The wife of Seth Miner was Anna Charlton. Asher Miner, son of Seth Miner, was born in Norwich, Conn., March 3, 1778. He served an apprenticeship of seven years in the office of the *Gazette and Commercial Intelligencer*, at New London, Conn., and afterwards worked as a journeyman a year in New York. In 1799 his brother, Charles Miner, who had already pitched his fortunes on the semi-savage frontier of Wyoming, wrote to him, "Come out here and I will set you up," without having a dollar to make good his promise. Nevertheless, Asher Miner migrated to the Susquehanna. In 1795 two young men came to Wilkes-Barre from Philadelphia with a small press and a few cases of type. They printed the *Herald of the Times*, the first newspaper published in the county. It was issued for a short time and was then sold to Thomas Wright, and published by Josiah Wright under the name of the *Wilkes-Barre Gazette*. The first number was dated November 29, 1797. In 1801 it ceased to be published. Asher Miner worked in the office of the *Gazette*, and in a short time afterward established the *Luzerne County Federalist* in this city, the first number being issued January 5, 1801. In April, 1802, he took his brother Charles into copartnership, which continued until May, 1804, when Asher relinquished his interest to

Charles. The press on which the *Federalist* was printed was brought from Norwich on a sled. In severing his connection with the *Federalist* an invitation was given to exchanges to send copies to him at Doyles-Town, Pennsylvania, where he had already resolved to establish a newspaper. He went immediately to Doylestown, where he found (what is now a beautiful town of twenty-five hundred inhabitants) a cross-road hamlet with less than a dozen dwellings along the Easton road and the road from Swede's ford to Coryell's ferry, now State street. The first issue of the new paper, *Pennsylvania Correspondent and Farmers' Advertiser*, which afterwards became the *Bucks County Intelligencer*, appeared July 7, 1804. Mr. Miner said, in his address to the public: "The editor is by birth an American, in principles a federal republican. His private sentiments with regard to the administration of the government of his country, he will maintain and avow as becomes a freeman. In his public character as conductor of the only newspaper printed in the county he will act with that impartiality which prudence and duty require." It was a small medium sheet, and the appearance of the paper created quite a sensation. The first issue was largely given away. It was left at a few points in the central part of the county by carriers, and subscribers were charged twenty-five cents additional for delivering their papers. The aforesaid newspaper proved a success, and its founder remained in charge of it twenty-one years. Prosperity authorized the enlargement of the paper, in July, 1806, from a medium to a royal sheet. On September 22, 1806, Asher Miner announced that he intended to issue a prospectus for a monthly magazine, literary, moral and agricultural, which probably was never published. For several years the advertising was light, but there was a notable increase between 1815 and 1820. In 1816, when preparations were making to commence the publication of the Doylestown *Democrat*, Mr. Miner protested against it in an address to the public, which he thought "may not be ill-timed," on the ground that the parties were nearly equally divided and a party paper was not needed. In the spring of 1816 Mr. Miner contemplated publishing a "monthly literary and agricultural register," to be called the *Olive Branch*, and sent out his subscription papers, but as they were not returned with enough names to warrant it, the project was given up. In April, 1817, he opened a branch office at Newtown in charge of Simon Siegfried. He proposed to issue from that office a weekly paper, to be called *The Star of Freedom*, to be devoted principally to "agricultural, biographical, literary and moral matters." The first number appeared May 21, 1817. This was a movement to keep competition out of the county. A printer at Newtown had a pamphlet in press for the Friends, but being intemperate, he failed to meet his contract, and gave up business. Miner sent Siegfried, an apprentice in his office, down to finish the work. This led to the purchase of the materials and the establishment of a paper there. The size was eighteen by eleven and a half inches, and consisted of eight pages. It was published weekly, "at $2 per annum if taken from the office, or $2.25 if delivered by post." It contained little news and but few advertisements. The publication was suspended April 7, 1818. Mr. Miner was postmaster of Doylestown several years, and kept the office at the printing office, and he had also a small book store, where he kept various articles for sale besides, and among them physic in the shape of "antiseptic pills," which he retailed. He gave up the post office in March, 1821. In 1818 the name of the paper was changed to *Pennsylvania Correspondent*, making one line reaching entirely across the head. On September 24, 1824, after an active editorial life of twenty years, Mr. Miner sold the *Correspondent* to Edward Morris and Samuel R. Kramer, of Philadelphia. The sale was hardly concluded before he repented and begged to have it annulled, but did not succeed. Mr. Miner removed from Doylestown to West Chester, Pa., and formed a partnership with his brother Charles in the publication of the *Village Record*. In 1834 they sold out to the late Henry S. Evans, when the brothers returned to Wilkes-Barre, where Asher Miner died March 13, 1841. He was a devout christian and a member of the Presbyterian church. Asher Miner was an able writer and besides a prominent business man. He had the faculty of making friends, and when once made they were retained.

The wife of Asher Miner, whom he married May 19, 1800, was Mary Wright, a daughter of Thomas Wright, born in county Down, Ireland, in 1747, a wealthy merchant and land owner of

Wilkes-Barre. Thomas Wright was a good-looking young Irishman, who, landing at Philadelphia about 1763, was soon in charge of a school at Dyerstown, two miles north of Doylestown. Securing a home in the family of Josiah Dyer, he taught the rudiments of English to the children of the neighborhood and love to Mary, the daughter of his host. One day they slipped off to Philadelphia and were married, which relieved the case of a deal of difficulty, for in that day Friends could not consent to the marriage of their daughters out of meeting. Mr. Wright in a few years removed to Wilkes-Barre, and became the founder of Wrightsville, now the borough of Miner's Mills. He built a mill there in 1795, which has been in the possession of his descendants since—2, Asher Miner; 3, Robert Miner; 4, C. A. Miner; 5, Asher Miner—five generations. In 1795, 1796, 1800 and 1801 Thomas Wright was one of the commissioners of Luzerne county, and was one at the time the early court house and jail was erected.

The following is a copy of the marriage certificate of Asher Miner and Mary Wright. The original is in the possession of Hon. Charles A. Miner, their grandson. General William Ross, who performed the marriage ceremony was a justice of the peace in this city, and was the grandfather of Mrs. Charles A. Miner.

"This may certify that Asher Miner and Mary Wright, both of Wilkes-Barre, having the consent of friends and no objections appearing, were joined in marriage, each to the other, before me, on the nineteenth day of May, one thousand eight hundred. Witness my hand and seal.

WM. ROSS, [L. S.]

In presence of the undersigned witnesses.

THOMAS WRIGHT,	MARY WRIGHT,
JOSEPH WRIGHT,	JOSIAH WRIGHT,
WILLIAM WRIGHT,	THOMAS WRIGHT, JR.,
LORD BUTLER,	WILLIAM CALDWELL,
ROSWELL WELLS,	BENJAMIN DRAKE,
LUTHER WRIGHT,	HANNAH WEILL,
ELIZA ROSS,	SARAH WRIGHT,
ANNA WRIGHT.	

In confirmation whereof they have hereunto set their hands, she, according to the custom of marriage, assuming the name of her husband.

ASHER MINER,
MARY MINER."

Mr. and Mrs. Miner had a family of thirteen children. His eldest son was the late Thomas Wright Miner, M. D., of this city. His next eldest son, Robert Miner, was the father of Hon. Charles A. Miner, of this city. His twelfth child was Joseph W. Miner, who became a member of the Luzerne bar. J. W. Miner was born at Doylestown January 29, 1825, and was the son of Asher Miner. He read law with Harrison Wright, in this city. During the Mexican war he was a member of Company I, First Regiment Pennsylvania Volunteers, going as fourth sergeant and returning as first lieutenant. In 1853, in connection with his cousin, William P. Miner, he established the *Record of the Times* newspaper. Mr. Miner was an unmarried man, and died in Plains township February 5, 1859.

Robert Miner, a brother of J. W. Miner, was the third child and second son of Asher Miner, and was born in Doylestown August 8, 1805. At the age of fourteen years his father had so much confidence in his ability, which was inspired by his uncommon seriousness and stability of character, that he sent him to Wilkes-Barre to take charge of his agricultural, milling and mining interests in the Wyoming valley. During the following year, while visiting a camp meeting near Kingston, the opportunity his serious and religious nature longed for presented itself, and he joined the Methodist Episcopal church. Doctor Peck, in his History of Early Methodism, says: " Robert Miner, son of Asher Miner, Esq., was a beautiful little boy when he was converted and united with the church ; but even then he had about him the gravity and the dignity of mature years. He was a devoted and consistent christian, and for years class leader and steward in the Wilkes-Barre charge. He died in great triumph in the prime of life, and was universally lamented. He was one of the few of whom no one ever said anything but good." He married, January 3, 1826, Eliza Abbott, a daughter of Stephen Abbott, of Wilkes-Barre (now Plains) township. Charles Miner, in his Hazleton Travellers, has the following in regard to the Abbott family :

"On the other side of the river, opposite Forty Fort, lives Stephen Abbott, a respectable and independent farmer. His father, John Abbott, was an early settler in Wyoming. There was one cannon, a four-pounder, in the Wilkes-Barre fort, and it had been agreed upon that, when certain information came that the enemy was dangerously near, the gun should be fired as a signal. At work on the flats, with his son, a lad eight or nine years old, he heard the terrific sound come booming up. Where, or how near the enemy might be, of course he could not tell; but loosening the oxen from the cart, he hastened to the rendezvous. He was in the battle, and fought side by side with his fellows to defend their homes. It makes my heart bleed to recur, as in these sketches I am obliged to do so often, to the retreat of our people. Again and again I aver there was no dishonor in it. I do not believe a braver or more devoted set of men ever marched forth to battle; but remember, a great part of the fighting men, those fit for war, raised for the defence of Wyoming, were away, defending the country, to be sure—fighting in the thrice glorious cause of independence, most certainly—but leaving their own homes wholly exposed, so that our little army was made up of such of the settlement as were left, who could carry a gun, however unfit to meet the practiced and warlike savage, and the well trained rangers of the British Butler. Mr. Abott took his place in the ranks. He had a wife and nine children (the eldest boy being only eleven) depending on his protection, labor and care. If a man so circumstanced had offered his services to Washington, the general would have said, 'My friend, I admire your spirit and patriotism, but your family cannot dispense with your services without suffering—your duty to them is too imperious to permit you to leave them, even to serve your country.' Such would have been the words of truth and soberness. But the emergency allowed no exemption. In the retreat Mr. Abbott fled to the river at Monocasy Island, waded over to the main branch, and, not being able to swim, was aided by a friend and escaped. In the expulsion which followed, taking his family he went down the Susquehanna as far as Sunbury. What could he do? Home, harvest, cattle—all hopes of provision for present and future use were at Wyoming. Like a brave man who meets danger and struggles to overcome it—like a faithful husband and fond father —he looked on his dependent family and made his resolve. Mr. Abbott returned in hopes of securing a part of his excellent harvest which he had left ripening in his fields. I am somewhat more particular in mentioning this, my friend, for I wish, as you take an interest in this matter, to impress this important fact upon your mind—that our people, though sorely struck, though suffering under a most bloody and disastrous defeat, did not lie down idly in despair without an effort to sustain themselves. No; the same indomitable spirit which they had manifested in overcoming previous difficulties still actuated them. Mr. Abbott came back, determined, if possible, to save from his growing abundance the means of subsistence. He went upon the flats to work with Isaac Williams. Mr. Abbott and Mr. Williams were ambushed by the savages, and both murdered and scalped. There is a ravine on the upper part of the plantation of Mr. Hollenback, above Mill Creek, where they fell. All hope was now extinguished, and Mrs. Abbott (her maiden name was Alice Fuller), with a broken heart, set out with her nine children (judge ye how helpless and destitute!) to find their way to Hampton, an eastern town in Connecticut, whence they had emigrated. Their loss was total. House burnt, barn burnt, harvests all devastated, cattle wholly lost, valuable title papers destroyed—nothing saved from the desolating hand of savage ruin and tory vengeance. 'God tempers the wind to the shorn lamb.' They had between two and three hundred miles to travel, through a country where patience and charity had been already nearly exhausted by the great number of applicants for relief. But they were sustained, and, arrived at their native place, the family was separated, and found homes and employment among the neighboring farmers. Here they dwelt for several years, until the boys, grown to manhood, were able to return, claim the patrimonial lands, again to raise the cottage and the byre, and once more to gather mother and children around the domestic hearth, tasting the charms of independence and the blessings of home."

"An interesting case, most certainly. Besides the loss of a father, the direct loss of property must have been considerable—more than a thousand dollars, I should suppose. I confess it appears to me very plain, that the continental congress, having drawn away the men of war raised for the defence of Wyoming, thereby brought down the enemy on a defenceless place, and were the cause of its sufferings and losses, and that the national government is, therefore, by every consideration of justice and honor, though late postponed, bound to make good to the sufferers the losses sustained. Did you say that Mrs. Abbott, the widow, also returned?"

"Yes, and long occupied the farm where her husband fell. She was afterwards married to a man whose name was known as widely as the extent of the settlement; a shrewd man, a great reader, very intelligent, distinguished far and near for the sharpness of his wit, the keenness of his sarcasm, the readiness of his repartees, and the cutting pungency of his satire; withal not unamiable, for in the domestic circle he was kind and clever, and she lived happily with him. But his peculiar talent being known for many years, every wit and witling of the country 'round about thought he must break a lance with him. Constantly assailed, tempted daily 'to the sharp encounter,' armed at all points like the 'fretful porcupine,' cut and thrust, he became expert from practice as he was gifted by nature for that species of warfare. All the old people, in merry mood, can tell of onslaught and overthrow of many a hapless wight who had the temerity to provoke a shaft from the quiver of old Mr. Stephen Gardiner."

"You began by speaking of Mr. Stephen Abbott. Did he marry before he returned from Connecticut, or did he take a Wyoming girl to wife—a daughter, as he was the son, of one of the revolutionary patriots?"

"You shall hear. He married a Searle. Having resettled on the patrimonial property, a fruitful soil, industry and economy brought independence in their train. Could you look upon the expelled orphan boy of 1778, pattering along, his little footsteps beside his widowed mother and the other orphan children, as they were flying from the savage, and contrast his then seemingly hopeless lot with the picture now presented, you would say, 'It is well.' In a very neat white house himself, his four children living near, each also occupies a white house, all of which are the abodes of agricultural independence and comfort. Mr. Abbott has a second wife, having married Sarah a daughter of Colonel Nathan Denison. Now past seventy, the old gentleman enjoys excellent health. The canal passes through his farm, and a coal mine opened near its banks yields him a revenue equal to every reasonable desire. Long may they live to enjoy it."

The Hazleton Travelers also contains the following in relation to the Searle family:

"In reply to your question, I said that Mr. Stephen Abbott married a Searle—Abigail, daughter of William Searle, who was the son of Constant Searle. The last named (Mrs. Abbott's grandfather) was in the battle. He was a man advanced in age, having several sons and daughters married, and being the grandfather of a number of children."

"What! Old men! Grandfathers! Were such obliged to go out?"

"They were; the able-bodied men, fit for war, being marched away, the direful necessity was created which drew to the battle-field old and young. Mr. Searle was there, and a son of his, Roger Searle, quite a young man. His son-in-law, Captain Deathic Hewett, commanded the third company raised at Wyoming, by order of congress, a very short time before the invasion. So there were three of the family in the engagement; and the fourth (William Searle) would also have been there, but was at the time confined to the house by a wound received from a rifle shot while on a scouting party a few days previous to the battle. How unsuitable it was that a man like old Mr. Searle should go out will further appear from the fact that he wore a wig, as was not unusual with aged men in those days. The bloody savages, in their riotous joy after their victory, made this wig a source of great merriment. A prisoner (adopted, I have reason to think, after the Indian fashion) was painted and then permitted to go down from Wintermoot's to Forty Fort, under a guard, to take leave of his mother. When near the brook that runs by Colonel Denison's he saw a group of savages in high glee. On coming nearer he beheld an Indian on a colt, with a rope for a bridle, having on his head, hind side before, the wig of Mr. Searle. The colt would not go, and one of the wretches pricked him with his spear; he sprang suddenly, the Indian fell on one side, the wig on the other, and the demons raised a yell of delight. Mr. Searle, before he went out to battle, took off a pair of silver knee buckles which he wore—gave them to his family, saying they might impede his movements; if he fell, he would not need, and if he returned, he could get them. There was evidently a strong presentiment on his mind—'I go to return no more.' The foregoing incident I find myself reluctant to relate; it appears like awakening light thoughts in the midst of anguish, sorrow and despair; but it seems proper that those things should be set forth which make deep impressions of material facts, and I deem it a very important matter, in considering the battle, the defeat, and the present claim of our people, to show that *old men, unfit for war*, were, by the necessity of the case, forced into the field against trained, youthful and expert warriors. The very young also were there. Roger Searle, the son of Constant, a young man of eighteen or nineteen, stood by the side of William Buck, a lad of fourteen; they fought together, Buck fell, and Searle escaped. William Searle, Mrs. Abbott's father, went out through the wilderness with the family, having twelve women and children under his care. I have seen a memorandum book kept by him. It runs thus: 'Battle of Westmoreland, July 3, 1778. Capitulation ye 4th. Prisoners obtained liberty to leave the settlement ye 7th.' It proceeds to the 25th, when they arrived at their former residence in Stonington, Connecticut. On the 13th they got to Fort Penn, on the Delaware, and here they received from Colonel Stroud a pass and recommendation, a copy of which may not be unacceptable as a memorial of old times:"

"'Permit the bearers, Serg't Wm. Searle with twelve women and children, in company with him, to pass unmolested to some part of the State of Connecticut, where they may be able, by their industry, to obtain an honest living, they being part of the unhappy people drove off from Wyoming by the Tories and Indians, and are truly stripped and distressed, and their circumstances call for the charity of all Christian people; and are especially recommended by me to all persons in authority, civil and military, and to all continental officers and commissaries, to issue provisions and other necessaries for their relief on the road.

"'Given under my hand at Fort Penn, July 14, 1778.

"'JACOB STROUD, Col.'

"Four of the name, to wit, Roger, William, Constant and Miner Searle, were forty-five years ago among the most intelligent and influential citizens upon the Lackawanna, but they all departed in mid-life. Constant, who was in the battle, died at Providence, Pa., August 4, 1804, aged 45 years. Their descendants retain, or possess, several of the most valuable farms in old Westmoreland, while one at least, whom we could name, from a female branch of the family, is winning his way to distinction in an arduous and honorable profession."

Robert Miner was engaged at the mill of his father at Wrightsville for several years after his marriage. It had burned down either early in 1826 or late in 1825, and Mr. Miner rebuilt it for his father. In 1833, in connection with Eleazer Carey, Mr. Miner purchased the *Wyoming Herald* newspaper. These gentlemen conducted the paper until 1835, at which time it was merged in the *Wyoming Republican*, which was then published in Kingston. The Hazleton Coal Company was incorporated March 18, 1836. From Mr. Miner's diary we have the following:

"1836, Nov. 1. Came to Hazleton to be clerk for company on trial; no terms fixed. Board at the old Drumheller house tavern kept by Lewis Davenport. The company's office is the lower room of an addition built on the east end of old house. Railroad located and contracts just assigned. Village laid out.

"Nov. 10, 1836. Town lots were laid out and sold by company. Wages offered for 'good hands' are: $16.00 a month with board on Sundays. Fresh pork is, by the hog, 8c.; corn meal, $1.12½; rye chop, $1.25; Oats, 50c.; coal, $1.75 ton.

"1837. First dwelling put up and occupied by Chas. Edson; lot No. 9, sq. 11. Then by S. Yost, F. Santee, T. Peeler. Store and house by L. H. and J. Ingham. R. Miner; Hotel.

"4th of July (1837), moved my family from Wyoming valley —Plains—to Hazleton, in house I have just finished on corner of Broad and Poplar streets.

"L. Davenport moved to hotel 23d October, W. Apple taking the old house.

"First birth of child in Hazleton Oct. 9—W. Apple's, born in house at junction of old state road and turnpike—daughter. 2d, child of F. Santee, blacksmith. 3d, my son—John Howard Miner.

"First corpse interred in grave yard was wife of Th. B. Worthington, in the fall of 1837.

"Locomotive 'Hazleton' first one on the railroad."

The position of Mr. Miner at Hazleton was secretary of the Hazleton Coal Company. He kept the books, paid out money, and made purchases. The company commenced shipping coal in May, 1837, Mr. Miner, secretary, and A. Pardee, superintendent. This continued until 1840, when the firm of Pardee, Miner & Company was formed. The company part of the firm was Mr. Hunt, a miner. They mined coal by contract and delivered it into boats at Penn Haven. Mr. Miner's health failed in 1841, when Mr. Pardee bought him out, and he removed to his old home in Plains township. The next year Mr. Hunt's health also failed, and Mr. Pardee bought him out also. After that J. G. Fell came in, and the firm of Pardee & Co. was formed. In November, 1842, Mr. Miner had business of importance to attend to in Easton and Philadelphia. He traveled in a private carriage with his brother, Joseph W. Miner, and they returned home December 9. That night Robert Miner was taken violently ill and died before morning. He has been described as of "peculiar and substantial worth," "at all times cheerful and happy, with power to raise those emotions in others. His life was an exemplification of the true greatness to which many may attain through a mastery over self. His piety, charity and urbanity became a part of his existence; to do good to his fellow creatures was the pleasure of his life." "He was polite without show, charitable without ostentation, and religious without bigotry." "In business he was punctual and exact, and such was the burthen he took upon himself in whatever he engaged in, that those coming after him found little to do." This is the description given of him by one who appeared to have known him long and had an extended intercourse with him. In an obituary notice by Rev. J. Seys he is spoken of as having manifested "from a child one of the mildest and most amiable dispositions," and as being "admired and loved by all who knew him." Mr. Miner had three children, only one of whom, Charles Abbot Miner, survives. The other two died in infancy. Helen Elizabeth lived less than a year, and John Howard died at the age of six years.

Charles A. Miner was born in Plains township August 30, 1830, and received his education at the academy in this city and at West Chester, Pa. Since attaining his majority he has been engaged in the milling business. The first grist mill erected at Wrightsville, now the borough of Miner's Mills, was built by Mr. Miner's great-grandfather, Thomas Wright. His partner is his son, Asher Miner. Mr. Miner has been connected with most of the successful business enterprises of Wilkes-Barre. For fifteen years he has been the president of the Coalville (Ashley) Passenger Railway Company, and for twenty years a director. For fifteen years he was president of the board of directors of the Wilkes-Barre City Hospital. . He was president for eleven years of the Wilkes-Barre and Harry Hillman academy in this city. For twenty-one years he has been a director of the Wyoming National bank. He was also a director in the People's bank of this city. He is a vestryman in St. Stephen's Protestant Episcopal church. He is chairman of the committee on legislation and taxation in the Wilkes-Barre Board of Trade, and a director and member of the executive committee of the Wilkes-Barre City Hospital. For a number of years he was a member of the city council of Wilkes-Barre, and has been president of that body. He has been president of the Luzerne County Agricultural Society and of the Pennsylvania Millers' State Association, and in 1873 he represented this state as honorary commissioner at the world's exhibition at Vienna, Austria. From 1875 to 1880 he represented this city in the legislature of the state. In 1881 he was the candidate of the republican party of the county for state senate, but was defeated by Eckley B. Coxe. Wilkes-Barre contains no more popular citizen within its limits that Mr. Miner. He married, January 19, 1853, Eliza Ross Atherton, a daughter of Elisha Atherton (see page 528) and his wife, Caroline Ross Maffet. (See page 295.) Mr. and Mrs. Miner have a family of four children—Asher Miner, a partner of his father in the milling business—was educated at the Wilkes-Barre academy and Williston seminary, Easthampton, Mass.; Elizabeth Miner; Sidney Robic Miner, a graduate of Harvard university in the class of 1888, now a law student in the office of L. D. and R. C. Shoemaker; and Charles Howard Miner, a student at Princeton university in the class of 1890.

ARNOLD COLT LEWIS.

Arnold Colt Lewis, who was admitted to the Luzerne county bar August 5, 1850, was a descendant of Hon. William Lewis, of Philadelphia, being his great-grandson. (See page 817.) His grandfather was Josiah Lewis, and his father was the late Sharp Delaney Lewis, a native of Philadelphia, where he was born January 2, 1805, who was a printer by trade, a knowledge of which craft he acquired in the office of Samuel Maffett, publisher of the *Susquehanna Register.* From 1824 to 1831 S. D. Lewis, in connection with Chester A. Colt, published the *Susquehanna Democrat*, in this city. In 1832 Mr. Lewis established the *Wyoming Republican*, in Kingston, and edited it with ability until 1837, when the press and material was sold to Dr. Thomas W. Miner, who removed it to Wilkes-Barre. Stewart Pearce, in his "Annals of Luzerne County," says: "We feel that we hazard nothing in saying that the *Republican*, from its birth until its death, was one of the best and most ably conducted papers in the county, and no one can peruse its old files without lively interest and admiration." In 1843 Mr. Lewis purchased the *Wilkes-Barre Advocate* and continued to publish it until 1853, when he sold the paper to W. P. and Joseph W. Miner, who changed the name to *The Record of the Times.* "The History of Wyoming," by Isaac Chapman, a resident of the valley, was printed and published at Wilkes-Barre in 1830, by S. D. Lewis. It contains two hundred and nine pages. It is of the 12 mo. style, and is rarely met with. For a country publication of nearly sixty years ago, it exhibits a fair degree of mechanical skill in respect both to printing and binding. From 1847 to 1849 Mr. Lewis was treasurer of Luzerne county. He was also a justice of the peace and alderman in this city for many years. He was also a prominent member of the Methodist Episcopal church. He was a trustee and class leader of the Franklin street M. E. church, and was also a local preacher. In 1835 he was elected a justice of the peace for the townships of Dallas, Kingston, and Plymouth. The wife of S. D. Lewis, and the mother of Arnold C. Lewis, was

Mary B. Colt, a daughter of Arnold Colt. (See page 495.) He married for a second wife Deborah Chahoon, the widow of Anning O. Chahoon, and the daughter of Joseph Slocum, of this city. S. D. Lewis died in this city. Arnold Colt Lewis, son of S. D. Lewis, was born in this city, March 2, 1829. He read law with E. G. Mallery, in this city. Soon after his admission to the bar he went to California, where he was an associate judge at Mokelumne Hill. He enlisted in the Mexican war in Company I, First Regiment, Pennsylvania Volunteers. He was first sergeant, and returned with his company at the close of the war as second lieutenant. During the late civil war he was major of the Forty-sixth Regiment, Pennsylvania volunteers. For a punishment given to one of the men of his regiment he was shot by him at Darnellstown, Maryland, September 22, 1861. Mr. Lewis established, in 1859, the *Pittston Free Press*. It had a short existence of a few months. He subsequently removed to Catasauqua, Pa., where he was elected burgess in 1860. He was also postmaster. He also edited the *Catasauqua Herald*. He married, March 19, 1861, Amanda M. Rohn, a daughter of William and Sarah Rohn. Mr. and Mrs. Lewis had one son—Arnold Rohn Lewis—who married Clara M. Hersh, a daughter of Franklin and Emma Hersh.

CALEB FRANKLIN BOWMAN.

Caleb Franklin Bowman, who was admitted to the bar of Luzerne county, Pa., August 5, 1850, was a native of Berwick, Columbia county, Pa., where he was born February 21, 1822. He was a descendant of George Christopher Bauman and his wife, Susan Banks. (See pages 695 and 713.) A tradition in the family is that the Baumans or Bowmans were German-Swiss, who emigrated to Alsace—a province recently ceded by France to Germany, to which it anciently belonged—and that they finally settled in Prussia; first at Weisbaden, on the Rhine, and subsequently at Ems, on the Lahn. Rev. Thomas Bowman, son of Christopher Bowman, was born in Bucks county, Pa., December

6, 1760. In 1782 he married Mary Freas, a young lady residing in the neighborhood of the old Bowman farm in Northampton county. When five children were born to them he resolved to remove to the interior of the state. Accordingly, in April, 1793, he and his family left the old farm at Mount Bethel, travelling by wagon by way of Nazareth, Lehighton and Mauch Chunk, to make their new home under trying disadvantages in a wilderness country. Upon their arrival in Briar Creek, in Columbia county, they occupied, temporarily, a log house situated upon the public road leading from Berwick to Orangeville. At this time Rev. Thomas Bowman was a local preacher. He was accustomed to take his horse and saddle-bags and traverse the country from Canada to Baltimore, preaching the Saviour of men in the settlements and villages along the Susquehana river, and not unfrequently he was long delayed from home at various places, conducting revivals, gathering converts, organizing societies, visiting from house to house, and so helping to plant the church of his choice abroad the land from lake to sea. He was ordained a regular preacher at Forty Fort by Bishop Asbury July 19, 1807. Soon after he helped to build the Methodist Episcopal Briar Creek stone church, the first and only edifice within a hundred miles of the place at the time. He died at the age of sixty-three years April 9, 1823. His wife died July 4, 1829. Jesse Bowman, son of Thomas Bowman, was born in 1788, married Anna Brown, of Berwick, in 1809, and died October 30, 1880. In 1842 he visited England. He was recognized as a pioneer in the matter of giving his children a classical education, being among the first in all that community. He was elected a member of the board of trustees of Dickinson college in 1847, which position he held until 1857, when he resigned. He was director of a state bank in Danville, and afterwards also of the National bank of Berwick. In 1839 he was appointed a justice of the peace by Governor Wolf, which appointment was for life, or "so long as he should behave himself well." He was also a captain in the state militia. He contributed largely to the erection of the Methodist Episcopal church in Berwick, and also contributed largely to the erection of other churches. He was a class leader for about sixty years. Anna Brown Bowman, wife of Jesse Bowman, was born March 25, 1791, and was the second child born in Berwick. She was the daughter of Bobert Brown, a native of Norwich, England, and Mrs. Mary Barrett (*nee* Macintosh), a native of the north of Ireland. Mrs. Bowman was the first person married in Berwick. She died December 31, 1876. Bishop Thomas Bowman is the nephew of Jesse Bowman. Caleb F. Bowman, son of Jesse Bowman, was educated at the academy at Berwick and at Harford academy, in Susquehanna county, Pa. He read law with James Armstrong, at Williamsport, Pa. Soon after his admission to the Lycoming county bar he removed to Pottsville, Pa., and opened an office there. He subsequently came to this county and opened an office in Pittston, and in the course of a year he removed to this city, where he resided and continued in the pursuit of his profession to the time of his death, January 25, 1874. In 1872, in company with his wife, he visited England, Ireland, Belgium, France, Germany, Switzerland and Italy. As a man of business he was successful, and most scrupulously honest. He was for many years clerk of the old borough council. He married, December 8, 1846, Isabella W. Tallman, of Williamsport. She is the daughter of the late Jeremiah Tallman, a civil engineer and surveyor, a native of New Jersey, and his wife, Maria Brown, a native of White Deer valley, Pa. They resided for many years in Williamsport, and were a prominent and prosperous family. The late General Samuel M. Bowman, of the United States Volunteers, was a brother of Caleb F. Bowman. Mr. and Mrs. Bowman had no children.

DANIEL RANKIN.

Daniel Rankin was admitted to the bar of Luzerne county, Pa., August 7, 1850. He was originally from Montgomery county, Pa. He removed to Providence, now a portion of the city of Scranton, and was a journeyman tailor. He read law in Providence with Charles H. Silkman. In 1858 he was a candidate for the legislature on the democratic ticket, but was defeated. At the organization of the mayor's court in Scranton he was elected the clerk of that court. His wife was Sarah A. Chapin, of Wyoming, Pa. He left one son to survive him—Foster Rankin—who died February 19, 1889.

On April 15, 1851, an act entitled "An act to provide for the election of judges of the several courts of this commonwealth, and to regulate certain judicial districts," was passed, and in its last section constituted the eleventh judicial district out of the counties of Luzerne, Wyoming, Montour, and Columbia. Under the provisions of this act Judge Conyngham was elected president of the district, and was commissioned, November 6, 1851, for the term of ten years, from the first Monday of December, 1851. He was reëlected in the year 1861, and was recommissioned for a further period of ten years. In the meantime Montour had been annexed to the eighth district, and the counties of Columbia, Sullivan, and Wyoming had been erected into a separate district—the twenty-sixth. Thus in 1856 Luzerne became a separate judicial district, with Judge Conyngham as president judge. By act of June 27, 1864, Luzerne was authorized, at the next election, to elect an "additional judge," learned in the law. He was required to possess the same qualifications, hold his office by the same tenure, was given the same power, authority and jurisdiction, was subject to the same duties, penalties and provisions, and was to receive the same compensation as the president judge. The governor was directed to appoint until the election, etc. Under this act Henry M. Hoyt, since elected governor, was appointed to and held the office of additional judge until the first Monday of December, 1867. In the fall election Edmund L. Dana was elected, and was commissioned for the term of ten years from the first Monday of December, 1867. Judge Conyngham resigned in the summer of 1870, and on July 8, 1870, Garrick M. Harding was appointed and commissioned president judge in his stead. He took the required oath on July

12, 1870. He was elected in the fall, and on November 4, 1870, was commissioned as president judge for the term of ten years from the first Monday of December, 1870. The changes wrought by the constitution of 1874, so far as they are material here, are as follows:

"Whenever a county shall contain forty thousand inhabitants it shall constitute a separate judicial district, and shall elect one judge, learned in the law; and the general assembly shall provide for additional judges as the business of the said district may require. * * * "

"All judges required to be learned in the law, except the judges of the Supreme Court, shall be elected by the qualified electors of the respective districts over which they are to preside. * * * "

"Any vacancy happening by death, etc., or otherwise, in any court of record, shall be filled by appointment by the governor, to continue till the first Monday of January next succeeding the first general election, which shall occur three or more months after the happening of such vacancy."

"The general assembly shall, at the next session after the adoption of this constitution, designate the several judicial districts, as required by this constitution, etc."

"The general assembly shall, at the the next succeeding session after each decennial census, and not oftener, designate the several judicial districts, as required by this constitution."

"Judges learned in the law of any court of record, holding commissions in force at the adoption of this constitution, shall hold their respective offices until their successors shall be duly qualified."

"After the expiration of the term of any president judge of any Court of Common Pleas, in commission at the adoption of this constitution, the judge of such court, learned in the law, and oldest in commission, shall be president judge thereof, * * * but when the president judge of a court shall be reëlected, he shall continue to be president judge of that court."

As has already appeared, Judge Harding as president judge and Judge Dana as additional judge were in commission at the adoption of the constitution. The act of April 9, 1874, designated Luzerne as composing the eleventh district, authorized the election of another additional judge, learned in the law, at the next general election, and provided for the election of a successor to the additional judge already in commission, when his term should expire. At the first election held after the passage of this act John Handley was elected additional judge, and in pursuance of the provisions of the general act of April 30, 1874, was commissioned for the term of ten years from the first Monday of January, 1875. At the general election in 1877, William H. Stanton was elected as a successor to Judge Dana, whose term was about expiring, and was commissioned for the term of ten years from the first Monday of January, 1878. Hence, at the time of the erection of the county of Lackawanna, Hon. Garrick M. Harding was president, and Hon. John Handley and Hon. William H. Stanton were additional judges of the Court of Common Pleas of the district. The act of April 17, 1878, provided for the division of and the erection of a new county out of any county containing one hundred and fifty thousand inhabitants. Section thirteen of the act provided that the judicial, senatorial, and representative districts shall remain the same, and that the judges of the several courts of said county, or a majority, shall meet and organize the courts thereof. The county of Lackawanna was erected under the provisions of this act. The election was held August 13, 1878, and the final proclamation of the governor was made August 21, 1878. Notwithstanding the express provisions of section thirteen of the act, it was claimed that, as the new county had more than forty thousand inhabitants, it became at once a separate judicial district. Recognizing this claim, Governor Hartranft, August 22, 1878, appointed and commissioned Benjamin S. Bentley president judge of the new county, who proceeded to open the court at the time designated in the act. In order to avoid a conflict, Judges Harding, Handley, and Stanton declined to interfere, but in order to test the validity of Judge Bentley's commission, an application was made to the Supreme Court for a mandamus against the former judges. On October 14, 1878, the Supreme Court, holding that the appointment of Judge Bentley was unauthorized, issued a peremptory writ against the judges above named, commanding them to open and organize the court, as directed by the act of April 17,

1878, *supra*. In obedience to this decision, Judges Harding, Handley, and Stanton opened the courts of Lackawanna county, October 24, 1878. Judge Bentley no longer assumed to hold the office. Judge Stanton resigned, February 25, 1879, and on March 4, 1879, Alfred Hand was appointed and commissioned to fill the vacancy. By a supplement to the above act, with relation to the division of counties, it was provided that in case the new county contained forty thousand inhabitants, the governor should, by proclamation, declare it to be a separate judicial district. The president judge of the old county was thereupon directed to elect to which district he would be assigned, and the other law judge or judges were to be assigned to the other district. If more than one additional law judge, the oldest in commission should be commissioned president judge of the new district and the other as additional law judge. Under this act Judge Harding, March 25, 1879, elected to remain in the old district of Luzerne, and Judges Handley and Hand were assigned to the new district—the forty-fifth. The former was commissioned president judge thereof, March 27, 1879, and the latter additional law judge. From that time on Judge Harding ceased to act in Lackawanna county, and the other two judges ceased to act in Luzerne.

In June of the same year another act was passed providing for the election of a judge in a new district created as above. It contains the *proviso* "that this act shall not take effect in case the president judge of the old county shall have selected to be assigned to and reside in the new district, and in case any other person shall have been commissioned president judge for such district, the judge elected by virtue of this act shall be commissioned an additional law judge." Under this act, at the general election in 1879, Judge Hand was elected in Lackawanna county as additional law judge of the forty-fifth district, and as such was commissioned for the term of ten years from the first Monday of January, 1880. It was claimed that the right of Luzerne to elect an additional law judge under the acts of 1867 and 1874 (*supra*) was not affected by the preceding legislation, and at the fall election of 1879 Charles E. Rice was elected additional law judge of Luzerne, composing the eleventh district, and as such was commissioned, December 4, 1879, for the term of ten years from the first Monday of January following. The resignation of Judge Harding took effect December 31, 1879. Judge Rice went into office under his commission as additional law judge January 4, 1880. On the day following, by reason of his holding the oldest commission, he was commissioned as president judge for the term of ten years from the first Monday of January, 1880. The vacancy thus existing was filled by Governor Hoyt, by appointing and commissioning Stanley Woodward additional law judge, vice Rice, who had become president judge by operation of law. The date of Judge Woodward's commission was January 9, 1880. At the general election following Judge Woodward was elected, and December 2, 1880, was commissioned additional law judge for the term of ten years from the first Monday of January, 1881.

SEPARATE ORPHANS' COURT.—The constitution of 1874 provided that in counties containing one hundred and fifty thousand inhabitants the legislature *shall*, and in other counties may, establish separate Orphans' Court, to consist of one or more judges learned in the law. By the same section separate registers' court was abolished, and the jurisdiction conferred upon the Orphans' Court. Under this constitutional mandate, the separate Orphans' Court of Luzerne was established by act of May 19, 1874, with one judge, to be elected and commissioned for the same term and in the same manner as judges of the Common Pleas. At the general election following Daniel L. Rhone was elected and was subsequently commissioned judge of the Orphans' Court for the term of ten years from the first Monday of January, 1875. Under the act of May 24, 1878, he is now styled and commissioned president judge of said court. Judge Rhone was included in the application for mandamus above referred to, but as to him it was refused, for the reason that under the act of 1878, *supra*, there could be no separate Orphans' Court in the new county of Lackawanna, the jurisdiction being vested in the judge of the Common Pleas.

Hon. D. L. Rhone was reëlected a judge of the Orphans' Court in 1884, and was commissioned December 17, 1884, for a further term of ten years from the first Monday of January, 1885.

MAYOR'S COURTS.—The mayor's court for the city of Carbondale was established by act of March 15, 1851. Its jurisdiction originally extended over the city of Carbondale, and the townships of Carbondale, Fell, Greenfield, and Scott. The latter township was excluded from its jurisdiction by act of April 11, 1853. By act of June 2, 1871, the north district of the township of Blakeley and the borough of Gibsonburg were authorized to vote upon the question of annexation to the jurisdiction of the mayor's court. The mayor's court of Scranton was established by act of April 23, 1866. Its jurisdiction was extended over the townships of Covington, Jefferson, Madison, Spring Brook, and the borough of Dunmore, by act of April 5, 1870. By the original acts these courts, with certain limitations, had the jurisdiction of courts of Common Pleas and Quarter Sessions. They were courts of record, and their judgments were reviewable in the Supreme Court. Their judges were the mayors of the respective cities, the aldermen, and a recorder. By express direction of the statutes, the president judge of Luzerne was directed to act as recorder in each of the courts. In December, 1869, quo warranto proceedings were begun by the attorney general, in the Supreme Court, against Judge Conyngham, to test his right to act as recorder in the mayor's court of Scranton. July 7, 1870, judgment was entered for the commonwealth, the Supreme Court holding that the legislature in creating a new court within part of the district or county occupied by an old court cannot legislate upon the bench of the new court the judge of the old court. The judge of the new court must be chosen by the people of his district. After this decision the president and additional law judge of Luzerne ceased to preside in either of the mayors' courts. In pursuance of acts of assembly, recorders of the several courts were thereafter elected. By section eleven of the schedule to the constitution of 1874, and the act of May 14, 1874, passed to carry the same into effect, both of these courts were abolished, December 1, 1875; the jurisdiction of the courts of Common Pleas, etc., of Luzerne was revived, and the records, etc., transferred thereto.

By the amendments to the constitution adopted October 9, 1838, and which went into effect January 1, 1839, the term of the judges of the Supreme Court was made fifteen years, and that of the president and other law judges of the Common Pleas was made ten years. The judges were to be nominated by the governor, and by and with the consent of the senate appointed and commissioned by him. The schedule provided that the commissions of the law judges of the Common Pleas "who shall not have held their offices for ten years, adoption of the amendments to the constitution, shall expire on February 27 next after the end of ten years from the date of their commissions." Under this provision of the schedule the commission of Judge Jessup expired February 27, 1849. By joint resolution passed 1849 and 1850, it was proposed to amend the second section of the judiciary article so as to make the judges elective. This amendment was adopted by vote of the people on the second Tuesday of October, 1850. The amendment provided that "the first election shall take place at the general election of this commonwealth next after the adoption of this amendment, and the commissions of all the judges who may be then in office shall expire on the first Monday of December following, when the terms of the new judges shall commence." The act of April 15, 1851 (referred to in another place), was passed to carry the amendment into effect, and the first election thereunder was held in the fall of that year.

CHARLES MINER STOUT.

Charles Miner Stout was admitted to the bar of Luzerne county, Pa., April 7, 1851. He was a brother of Asher Miner Stout. (See page 1226.) His wife was Lizzie Schropp, of Bethlehem, Pa. They left no children. During the Mexican war he entered as third corporal in Company I, First Regiment Pennsylvania Volunteers. He was subsequented appointed lieutenant in the Eleventh Infantry. Mr. Stout, at the commencement of the late civil war, entered into the service, and died in that service.

CROMWELL PEARCE.

Cromwell Pearce was admitted to the bar of Luzerne county, Pa., April 8, 1851. His ancestors were Protestant soldiers who entered Ireland from England with the army of Cromwell in 1649. Receiving confiscated lands in part pay for military services, a portion of the family settled near Enniskillen, in the province of Ulster. In 1690 his great-great-grandfather, in company with four brothers, entered the army of William III, and fought shoulder to shoulder with Huguenots and English Blues against King James II at the celebrated battle of the Boyne. Edward Pearce, the great-grandfather of Cromwell Pearce, was born in Enniskillen August 6, 1701, and married Frances Brassington, of Dublin. They had three children born in Ireland, with which little family they sailed for America in May, 1737. Two of the children died of small pox on the voyage. Mr. Pearce arrived in Philadelphia in August, having been thirteen weeks in crossing the ocean. Cromwell Pearce, the surviving child, was born in December, 1732, and was near five years old on his arrival in Pennsylvania. The family remained in Philadelphia until the spring of 1738, when they removed to the neighborhood of St. David's church, in Radnor township, Chester county, Pa. Edward Pearce was by trade both a mason and carpenter. In 1744 he built St. Peter's church, in the Great Valley. On April 15, 1745, he was chosen its first senior warden. In 1750 he purchased the farm in Willistown where, twenty-seven years afterwards, the memorable "Paoli massacre" occurred, and on which the monument now stands. Upon this farm he spent the remainder of his days, and died there March 6, 1777. He and his wife (who died March 26, 1783) were interred at St. David's church in one grave.

Cromwell Pearce, son of Edward Pearce, was the grandfather of Cromwell Pearce. On May 8, 1758, he was commissioned a lieutenant in the battalion of Pennsylvania's regiment of foot, and served under General Forbes, the successor of General Braddock. Among other services in the French and Indian war, the company to which he belonged built a fort at Shamokin, now Sunbury, Pa. On May 6, 1777, he was appointed major in the continental army, and May 20, 1779, colonel of the fifth battalion of Chester county militia. The extent of his services is not known beyond the fact that he went on a tour of duty to Amboy, N. J. On May 1, 1781, he was commissioned major of the second battalion of Chester county militia. He married Margaret, daughter of John and Margaret Boggs, who owned a large tract of land in Willistown. Her parents were members of the Presbyterian church, and several of their sons served as soldiers in the war of the revolution. She died December 28, 1818, aged seventy-eight years. Cromwell Pearce, after his father's death, became the owner of the farm in Willistown, where he passed the remainder of his days, and died August 4, 1794.

Marmaduke Pearce, son of Cromwell Pearce, and father of Cromwell Pearce, the subject of this sketch, was born at Paoli, Willistown township, Chester county, Pa., August 18, 1776. His opportunities for acquiring a complete education were very limited. He possessed a natural taste for books and study, and by improving himself became qualified to teach a country school. In 1805 he removed to Bellefonte, Pa., where he continued to reside for several years. Having determined to preach the gospel, he was in 1811 licensed to preach by Rev. Gideon Draper, presiding elder of the Susquehanna district of the Methodist Episcopal church. As a preacher he had few equals, and his sermons were the embodiment of sound common sense. Reason and logic were the weapons which he employed. His sermons did not generally exceed thirty minutes, but in that period, by reason of his unusual powers of condensation, he would say as much as most men in double that time. He was a master of English style, and a most able critic in grammar, logic and rhetoric. He made no display of his learning. He sought the shade, wishing, as he once expressed himself, if he could not be *little*, to be *unknown*. He was an immense man physically, about six feet in height, and weighing in ordinary health about three hundred pounds. He died in Berwick, Pa., August 11, 1852. Colonel Cromwell Pearce, of the Sixteenth United States Infantry in the war of 1812, and subsequently sheriff and associate judge of

Chester county, Pa., was a brother of Rev. Marmaduke Pearce. The mother of Cromwell Pearce, and wife of Rev. Marmaduke Pearce, was Hannah Stewart (*nee* Jameson). She was a descendant of John Jameson, and great-granddaughter of Robert Jameson and his wife, Agnes Dixon, daughter of Robert Dixon. Robert Jameson and his father-in-law, Robert Dixon, were among the original petitioners to the Connecticut legislature in 1753, asking for the organization of the Connecticut Susquehanna Land Company. The preamble of their petition was as follows: "Whereas, there is a large quantity of land lying upon a river called Susquehanna, and also at a place called Quiwaumuck, and that there is no English inhabitant that lives on said land nor near thereunto, and the same lies about seventy miles west of Dielewey river, and, as we suppose, within the colony of Connecticut, and there is a number of Indians that live on or near the place or land aforesaid who lay claim to the same, and we, the subscribers, to the number of one hundred persons, who are very desirous to go and inhabit the aforesaid land and at the place aforesaid, provided that we can obtain a quiet or quit claim of the honorable assembly of a tract of land lying at the place aforesaid, and to contain a quantity sixteen miles square, to lie on both sides Susquehanna river, and as the Indians lay claim to the same, we purpose to purchase of them their right, so as to be at peace with them, whereupon we humbly pray that the honorable assembly would grant to us a quit claim of the aforesaid tract." The company was organized and the Indian title extinguished at the treaty of Albany in 1754. John Jameson was the son of Robert Jameson, and his wife was Abagail Alden. (See page 301.) Mrs. Hannah Pearce, the mother of Cromwell Pearce, was born about two months after the death of her father, John Jameson. She married, in 1799, James Stewart, son of Captain Lazarus Stewart, who commanded the Hanover company in the battle and massacre of Wyoming, where he fell bravely fighting in the defense of his country. James Stewart died in 1808. In 1819 his widow married Rev. Marmaduke Pearce. She died in Wilkes-Barre October 21, 1859.

Cromwell Pearce was born in Wilkes-Barre, Pa., July 1, 1823, and read law with M. E. Jackson, in Berwick, Pa. He left the practice of the law in 1859, when he became a minister of the Methodist Episcopal church. He married, November 27, 1861, Sarah H. Taylor, a daughter of David Taylor. Mr. and Mrs. Pearce had one child—Carrie H., now the wife of M. Lincoln, M. D. Mr. Pearce died June 16, 1872. The late Hon. Stewart Pearce, of Wilkes-Barre, was his brother, as is also Rev. John J. Pearce, of the Central Pennsylvania Conference of the Methodist Episcopal church, who, in 1854, was elected to the congress of the United States.

WILLIAM HENRY BEAUMONT.

William Henry Beaumont was admitted to the bar of Luzerne county, Pa., April 8, 1851. He was a descendant of William Beaumont, of Carlisle, England, who settled in Saybrook, Conn., about 1648, and was made a freeman in 1652. Isaiah Beaumont, a descendant of William Beaumont, was a soldier of the revolution, fighting with Washington at Trenton and at Princeton. In the latter battle he was severely wounded, and was discharged from the service on a pension. He removed in 1791 to the neighborhood of the Wyalusing creek, in Susquehanna county, Pa. The wife of Isaiah Beaumont was Fear Alden. Captain Jonathan Alden, fourth son of John and Priscilla (Mullins) Alden, had four children. Andrew, his eldest child, married Lydia Stanford February 4, 1714, and they had eight children. They all resided in Lebanon, Conn., and there Fear Alden, one of his children, married Isaiah Beaumont. Prince Alden, third child of Andrew and Lydia Alden, married Mary Fitch, of New London, Conn., who bore him ten children. Prince removed to the Wyoming valley in 1772 and settled in Newport township. He subsequently removed to Meshoppen, Luzerne (now Wyoming) county, where he died in 1804. (See page 306.)

Andrew Beaumont, son of Isaiah Beaumont, was born in Lebanon, Conn., in 1791. In 1808 he came to this city, determined to obtain an education, and attended schools for several terms, paying for his tuition by the product of his labor. He was afterwards engaged in teaching, and at the same time completing his studies in his home neighborhood and at the Wilkes-Barre academy (where he subsequently taught), when, having thoroughly mastered a classical course, he entered the office of Garrick Mallery, in this city, as a student at law. At the termination of the usual period of study he passed the examination required, but was denied admission to the bar by Judge Scott, the presiding judge, on the ground that he had not read the necessary time. This was a mere pretext, as Mr. Beaumont thought, and it had the effect of driving the candidate from the profession. In January, 1814, he was appointed, under the administration of President Madison, collector of revenue, direct taxes and internal duties for the twentieth collection district of Pennsylvania, which included Luzerne county. This office he held until 1816, when he was appointed prothonotary and clerk of the courts of Luzerne county. Mr. Beaumont held these offices until 1819. In 1821 he was elected to the legislature of the state, and reëlected in 1822. In 1826 he was appointed postmaster of Wilkes-Barre and held the office until 1832. During the latter year he was a candidate for congress in the district composed of the counties of Luzerne and Columbia. The candidates were Mr. Beaumont, Thomas W. Miner, M. D., whig, and James McClintock, also a democrat, as Mr. Beaumont was. The fight was a bitter one, and the result was not known for a week afterward, and then it was ascertained that Mr. Beaumont was elected by a majority of eighty-eight votes. He was reëlected to congress in 1834. During his service in congress the celebrated contest of President Jackson against the United States bank occurred, and he took strong grounds with General Jackson as opposed to private institutions supported by the government. His course in this contest was sustained by his constituents by his reëlection. He opposed and steadily voted against the bill which distributed the surplus revenue among the states. He enjoyed the close confidence and intimacy of Presidents Jackson, Van Buren and Polk, Vice President King, General Lewis Cass, and others of his political party. In 1840 he was tendered, by President Van Buren, the appointment of treasurer of the United States mint at Philadelphia, which, however, he declined, believing that he could be of better service at his home. In 1847 he was tendered the appointment by President Polk of commissioner of public buildings and grounds for the District of Columbia, at that time an office of great responsibilty and requiring great executive ability in the incumbent. He accepted the office and continued therein until his nomination was rejected by the United States senate, through the influence of Senator Benton, of Missouri, who opposed him on personal grounds. During 1849 he suffered from protracted illness, and, when partially recovered, exposed himself endeavoring to extinguish a fire in this city, thus sowing the seeds of the disease which finally carried him off. During his illness in the latter year he was again elected to the legislature of the state. During this service he urged the necessity of direct relations between the state and the general government, and through his exertions and speeches the first committee on federal relations was created, of which he was chairman, and he made the first report on that subject ever presented to the Pennsylvania legislature. He was one of the organizers of St. Stephen's Episcopal church of this city in 1817, and was one of its first vestrymen. He was one of the founders of the Luzerne Bible Society in 1819, and for a number of years was one of its officers. A contemporary, writing of him, says: "With a friend who could appreciate the force and depth of his remarks, the corruscations of wit, fancy, eloquence and pathos, adorned with the wealth which a tenacious memory had extracted from classical and contemporary literature, would pour from his lips apparently unconscious of hours. In figure of speech, ready, trite and apposite comparisons, we never knew his equal." He was well known for a period of forty years in Pennsylvania as a political writer, and his writings on subjects of political economy would fill volumes. He married, in 1813, Julia A. Colt, second daughter of Arnold Colt. (See page 495.) She survived her husband and died at Wilkes-Barre October 13, 1872. Andrew Beaumont died at the same place September 30, 1853. John Colt Beaumont, his eldest son, became a midshipman in 1838. He died in 1882, a rear admiral in the United States navy. Eugene Beauharnais Beaumont, his youngest son, graduated from West Point May 6, 1861. He is now major of the Fourth United States Cavalry, and lieutenant colonel by brevet.

He also served as an adjutant general during a portion of the late civil war, and was brevetted colonel of volunteers. Andrew Beaumont's eldest daughter married Samuel P. Collings, father of John B. Collings, of the Lackawanna bar.

William Henry Beaumont, the second son of Andrew Beaumont, was born in Wilkes-Barre November 27, 1825, and read law with Charles Denison in this city. He served throughout the whole of the Mexican war, and was first sergeant of Company I, First Regiment Pennsylvania Volunteers. In connection with M. B. Barnum he started, in 1852, *The True Democrat*, a democratic newspaper. The paper existed for about a year. Mr. Beaumont died in this city June 19, 1874. He was an unmarried man.

JOSEPH SLOCUM.

Joseph Slocum was commissioned as an associate judge of Luzerne county, Pa., April 28, 1851. (For a sketch of his life see page 339.)

WILLIAM HANCOCK.

William Hancock, who was commissioned an associate judge of Luzerne county, Pa., November 10, 1851, was the son of Jonathan Hancock, a native of Snow Hill, Maryland, who removed to this city at an early day. His wife was Catharine Young. Mr. Hancock was a hotel keeper in this city for many years, and kept a hotel on the Public Square on lands now occupied by the Luzerne house. William Hancock, son of Jonathan Hancock, was born in Wilkes-Barre December 18, 1799. He was a tanner and currier by trade, and resided the greater part of his life in what is now the borough of Luzerne, in this county. He married, February 13, 1821, Laura Smith, daughter of Obadiah Smith, of

Wethersfield, Connecticut. By her he had six children. She died November 4, 1846. He married a second time, February 15, 1848, Elizabeth Denison, a sister of Hon. Charles Denison, and daughter of Lazarus Denison. (See pages 1087 and 1191.) By her he had three children. She died in May, 1855. William Hancock died at his residence, in Luzerne, Pa., January 7, 1859. James Hancock, of Plains, was a brother of William Hancock. Colonel E. A. Hancock, of Philadelphia, is one of his sons.

MARTIN CANAVAN.

Martin Canavan, who was admitted to the bar of Luzerne county, Pa., August 10, 1852, was born in the county Sligo, Ireland, in 1802. He was the son of John Canavan and his wife Catharine Canavan (*nee* Rogers). Martin Canavan emigrated to this country in early life and read law with Peter J. Byrne, LL. D., in Carbondale, Pa. He practiced in Scranton and Patterson, N. J. While in Patterson he was surrogate, recorder of deeds and associate judge. He married, in 1844, Catharine Corcoran, a daughter of Loughlin Corcoran and his wife Jane Corcoran (*nee* Cullen), natives of Kings county, Ireland. Mr. and Mrs. Canavan had a family of three children—Mary A. Canavan, Thomas I. Canavan, and Frank P. Canavan.

CHARLES PIKE.

Charles Pike was admitted to the bar of Luzerne county, Pa., April 4, 1853. He was born in Northmoreland township, Luzerne (now Wyoming) county, Pa., February 1, 1830. He was a son of James Pike, a native of Brooklyn, Windham county, Connecticut, who emigrated to Pennsylvania in 1819. Charles Pike read law in the office of Harrison Wright, and soon after his admission took a prominent position in his profession, and a few years afterwards entered into partnership with Hendrick B.

Wright, a business connection which continued through many years, bringing profit and distinction to each of its members. He was a natural lawyer, if such a thing can be. His mind was of that penetrating, analytical, and judicial order which comprehends all that is in a dispute, however manifold its ramifications, and goes to the heart of it without any indirectness, and decides as to its merits with promptitude and almost unerring clearness and fairness. Our ablest attorneys freely confessed him a foeman worthy of their best steel. It was seldom that he was worsted in a cause in which his sympathies were really enlisted. He had a thorough contempt for shams of every description, and many and amusing are the stories in which his keen criticisms under this head are recorded. Mr. Pike was a man of unswerving integrity in all his business transactions, and no one can be found to say aught against his integrity as a man and lawyer. He never held a political office of any kind, but might have filled many had his ambition led him in that direction. He died at his residence in this city September 12, 1882. Mr. Pike married, in 1868, Bridget O'Brien, daughter of the late Anthony O'Brien, of Pittston, who survives him. He left no children.

SAMUEL SHERRERD.

Samuel Sherrerd, who was admitted to the bar of Luzerne county, Pa., April 4, 1853, was a native of Philadelphia, Pa., where he was born April 25, 1819. He was a descendant of John Sherrerd, a merchant of London, England, who came to this country and settled near Washington, N. J., about 1750. Samuel Sherrerd was a son of John Sherrerd. On a tombstone in Greenwich churchyard, Warren county, N. J., is this inscription: "In memory of John Maxwell, second son of John and Anne Maxwell. He was born in county Tyrone, Ireland, November 25, 1739, and at an early age emigrated with his father to New Jersey. He was a lieutenant in the first company raised in Sussex county, for the defense of his adopted country in the revolutionary war, and soon after, in the darkest hour of her fortunes, joined the army of General Washington as a captain of a company of volunteers. He was engaged in the battles of Trenton, Princeton, Brandywine, Germantown, Monmouth, and Springfield, and ever distinguished himself as a brave and able officer. Having served his country in various civil and military offices, and faithfully discharged his various duties as a soldier, citizen, and christian, he closed a long and useful life at his residence at Flemington, N. J., February 15, 1828, in the eighty-ninth year of his age." His daughter, Ann, married Samuel Sherrerd. William Maxwell, brother of John Maxwell, was a general in the revolutionary war. John Maxwell Sherrerd, son of Samuel Sherrerd and Ann Sherrerd, was born, September 6, 1794, at Pleasant Valley, N. J. He graduated from Nassau Hall, Princeton, N. J., in 1812. He commenced the study of law with his uncle, Hon. John Maxwell, and was admitted to the bar from the office of Chief Justice Charles Ewing (his uncle having died in the meantime), in 1816, and practiced in New Jersey until his death, May 26, 1871. When Warren county was created he was appointed the first surrogate of that county. The wife of J. M. Sherrerd was Sarah Browne, of Philadelphia, whom he married May 19, 1818. She was a descendant of Nathaniel Browne, who was overseer of Wellodge shipyard, England, about 1725. His son Peter, a Quaker, was also a shipbuilder, coming to this country about 1730. His son Nathaniel was interested in shipbuilding and property in Philadelphia, also his son Peter after him. The latter was also a merchant and was the father of Mrs. Sherrerd. Samuel Sherrerd, son of John Maxwell Sherrerd, graduated from the college of New Jersey, at Princeton, in the class of 1836, and from the Rensselaer Polytechnic Institute, at Troy, N. Y., in 1838. He read law with Henry D. Maxwell, of Easton, Pa., and was admitted to the Northampton county bar in 1842. He practiced in Belvidere, N. J., until his removal to Scranton, in 1853. After practicing in Scranton a number of years, he returned to Belvidere in 1868. He was president judge of the court of Common Pleas of Warren county, N. J., from 1872 to 1875. Mr. Sherrerd married, May 6, 1847, Frances M. Hamilton. She was the granddaughter of John Hamilton and Phoebe Ross (daughter of John Ross, of Elizabeth, N. J.), who lived on a large estate at Princeton, N. J. One of their sons, Samuel Randolph

Hamilton, father of Mrs. Sherrerd, was born about 1790, graduated at Nassau Hall, Princeton, and studied law with Governor Williamson, at Elizabeth, N. J. He was a lineal descendant of Miles Standish. He was prosecutor of the pleas of Mercer county, N. J., and was quartermaster general for a number of years. He died at Trenton, N. J., in 1857. The wife of Samuel R. Hamilton was a descendant of Jonathan Robeson, a Quaker, who came from England about the time of William Penn and settled near Philadelphia. In 1741 he built the first iron furnace, which he named Oxford, in compliment to his father, Andrew Robeson, who had been educated at the University of Oxford. *Edsall's Centennial Address* says: "Jonathan Robeson was one of the first judges of Sussex county, N. J. His father and grandfather both wore the ermine before him in Pennsylvania, while his son, grandson, and great-grandson, each in his turn, occupied seats on the judicial bench. William P. Robeson (father of ex-secretary of the navy, George M. Robeson,) of New Jersey, was the sixth judge in regular descent from his ancestor, Andrew Robeson, who came to America with William Penn, and was a member of Governor Markham's privy council." Morris Robeson, son of Jonathan Robeson, married Anna Rockhill April 25, 1750. Their son, David Maurice Robeson, married Tacy Paul, of Philadelphia, about 1790. Their daughter, Elizabeth Robeson, married Samuel Randolph Hamilton. Their daughter, Frances M., married Samuel Sherrerd. Mr. Sherrerd died at Belvidere, N. J., June 21, 1884, leaving three sons to survive him—Alex. H. Sherrerd and Morris H. Sherrerd, of Scranton, Pa., and John M. Sherrerd, of Troy, N. Y.

THEODORE L. BYINGTON.

Theodore L. Byington, who was admitted to the bar of Luzerne county, Pa., November 7, 1853, was a son of Roderick Byington, M. D., a native of Stockbridge, Mass., where he was born October 27, 1799, and died at Belvidere, N. J., August 18, 1872. He read medicine in Johnsonburg, N. J., and subsequently graduated from the Jefferson medical college. He practiced in Johnsonburg from 1825 to 1841, and at Belvidere until his death. The wife of Dr. Byington was Caroline Linn, a daughter of John Lynn, a native of Hardwick township, Sussex (now Warren) county, N. J. In 1805 he was appointed judge of the Court of Common Pleas, and reappointed in 1810, 1815 and 1820. He represented the fourth district of New Jersey in the congress of the United States two terms, and while in congress in the winter of 1823 he was taken ill and died of typhoid fever.

Theodore L. Byington was born in Johnsonburg March 15, 1831. He was graduated from the college of New Jersey, at Princeton, in the class of 1849. He then came to this city and read law in the office of A. T. McClintock. After practicing a short time in Scranton the whole course of his life was changed. After studying theology at the Union Theological seminary he entered the ministry of the Presbyterian church. He married, May 30, 1858, Margaret Esther Hallock, a native of Smyrna, in Turkey, Asia. Her parents were Rev. Homan Hallock, born in Plainfield, Mass., and his wife, Elizabeth Flett, born in London, England. Rev. Homan Hallock was a son of Rev. Moses Hallock, of Plainfield, Mass. Soon after his marriage Rev. T. L. Byington was sent as a missionary to Bulgaria, Turkey, by the American board, and was one of their pioneers. His wife accompanied him to Turkey and took part in the missionary work. He returned to this country in 1868, and from 1869 to 1874 he was pastor of the Presbyterian church at Newton, N. J. The American board, however, prevailed on him to return to the mission field in 1874, and he became the editor of a weekly paper at Constantinople, published in the Bulgarian language, under the auspices of the board. His health became broken and he was obliged to return home in May, 1885. After an illness of three and a half years he died at Philadelphia June 16, 1888. He received the degree of doctor of divinity from Princeton college in 1878. He left a widow and two sons—Rev. Edwin H. Byington, pastor of the Eastern avenue church, Springfield, Mass., Roderick Byington, counsellor at law, Newark, N. J.—and three daughters, the eldest of which, Caroline Margaret, is the wife of Rev. Orville Reed, of Springfield.

JAMES SUTTON BEDFORD.

James Sutton Bedford was born at Waverly, Pa., October 16, 1839. He was educated at Madison academy, Waverly, and at Amherst college. He read law with G. Byron Nicholson, and was admitted to the bar of Luzerne county January 10, 1854, and practiced in this city and Brownsville, Nebraska. He died in the latter place December 2, 1865. He was an unmarried man and a brother of George R. Bedford, whose biography will be found on page 208.

GEORGE SCOTT.

George Scott, who was admitted to the bar of Luzerne county, Pa., January 10, 1854, was a son of Judge David Scott. (See page 392.) Mr. Scott was born in Wilkes-Barre, Pa., June 30, 1829. He was educated in the schools of his native city, and during the years 1840, 1841 and 1842 attended the Moravian school at Nazareth, Pa. He then learned the trade of a printer in the office of Strange Palmer, in Pottsville, Pa., and subsequently read law in the office of his brother-in-law, Luther Kidder, in this city. In 1860 he was register of wills of Luzerne county. Mr. Scott was an unmarried man. He died in Wilkes-Barre September 26, 1861.

LYMAN RICHARDSON NICHOLSON.

Lyman Richardson Nicholson was admitted to the bar of Luzerne county, Pa., April 6, 1855. He was a native of Salem, Wayne county, Pa., where he was born April 12, 1832. He was the son of Zenas Nicholson and Nancy Goodrich, his wife. (See page 123.) He died July 13, 1863, of wounds received in the battle of Gettysburg, July 1, 1863. He was lieutenant in Company G, One Hundred and Forty-third Regiment Pennsylvania Volunteers. Mr. Nicholson was an unmarried man. His remains were brought home and he was buried in the Salem cemetery.

SAMUEL PRICE LONGSTREET.

Samuel Price Longstreet was admitted to the bar of Luzerne county, Pa., August 6, 1855. He was born at Milford, Pike county, Pa., February 1, 1829, and was a descendant of Colonel Christopher Longstreet, of Sussex county, N. J., who represented Sussex county in the legislature of that state in 1785, 1786, 1787 and 1788. Colonel Longstreet removed from New Jersey to New Milford township, Susquehanna county, Pa., as early as 1803. The grave of his wife, who died in 1813, with its gray, moss-covered tombstone, is still to be seen in an old cemetery upon the hillside, a mile or two from New Milford village. He afterwards removed to Great Bend, and when the first bridge across the Susquehanna river was erected in 1844, Mr. Longstreet was appointed toll-gatherer and gate-keeper. He subsequently removed to Hamburg, Sussex county, N. J., where he spent the remainder of his days. William R. Longstreet, a native of New Jersey, was the son of Colonel Christopher Longstreet. His wife was Keturah Sayre. Lewis Longstreet, a native of Morris county, N. J., was the son of W. R. Longstreet. His wife was Elizabeth Roy Goble, of Sussex county, N. J. She was the daughter of Nathan and Azubah Price Goble, and granddaughter of Francis Price, of Frankford township, Sussex county, N. J. He was a man of much influence in his day. He was for years a justice of the peace, and solemnized most of the marriages of that early period. He maintained business relations, more or less extended, with most of the residents of the county, and established a reputation for integrity and kindness to those less abundantly supplied with worldly goods. On November 20, 1789, he was appointed one of the lay judges of Sussex county, and on November 26, 1794, he was re-appointed. (See page 952.)

S. P. Longstreet, son of Lewis Longstreet, read law with W. W. Ketcham, in this city, after completing his education at Wyoming Seminary. He practiced his profession in Wilkes-Barre until 1864, when he removed to Erie, Pa. He was interested in the coal business in Schuylkill county, Pa., and at Erie. He married, March 9, 1851, Laura Babcock, of Montrose, Pa., a daughter of Ezekiel Babcock and his wife, Lydia Gardner. They had no children, and she still survives him. Mr. Longstreet, at one time, was estimated to be worth two or three hundred thousand dollars, which he made in the coal business, but misfortune came and he became so involved that he was compelled to make an assignment. In early life he connected himself with the Methodist Episcopal church, and became a local preacher in that denomination. In February, 1876, after his failure at Erie, he went to Salt Lake City, where he was in charge of the Methodist Episcopal church for a period of eight months. He again entered upon the practice of his profession in that city, but in September, 1880, he was appointed pastor of the Broadway Methodist Episcopal church at Helena, Montana Territory. He died while occupying that position, April 5, 1881. It was the first death of a minister of the gospel that ever occurred in Helena. The late Francis Price Longstreet, of the Carbon county bar, was a brother of S. P. Longstreet.

LAZARUS DENISON REYNOLDS.

Lazarus Denison Reynolds was admitted to the bar of Luzerne county, Pa., August 4, 1856. He was a son of Chauncey A. Reynolds, a brother of Hon. William C. Reynolds. His mother was Mary, sister of Hon. Charles Denison. Lazarus D. Reynolds died, unmarried, July 25, 1858.

CHARLES TREADWAY BARNUM.

Charles Treadway Barnum was commissioned an associate judge of Luzerne county, Pa., November 12, 1856. He was the grandson of Lazarus Barnum, and the son of James Weed Barnum, who was born at Danbury, Connecticut, April 13, 1789. The wife of James W. Barnum, who was married at Kingston, Pa., January 5, 1812, the mother of C. T. Barnum, was Julia Treadway, who was born at Bridgeport, Connecticut, April 15, 1787. She was the daughter of John Treadway, whose name is in the assessment list of Hanover township in 1799, as the owner of fifty acres of land, one horse, two oxen, and three cows. He was drowned with two others in April, 1800, while fishing in the Nanticoke pool. Charles T. Barnum was born at Kingston January 7, 1813. He was a practical printer. He commenced to learn his trade in the office of the *Northern Pennsylvanian*, at Dundaff, Pa., and finished his apprenticeship in this city. He subsequently worked at his trade in this city, at Jersey Shore, Mauch Chunk, and at other places. After a few years he went to Lennox, Massachusetts, and in company with George Waldron published the *Lennox Eagle*. After a few years he sold out his interest in the paper and returned to the Wyoming valley. From 1855 to 1863 he was clerk of the commissioners of Luzerne county. For some years prior to his death he resided on his farm at Harvey's Lake. Judge Barnum married, in September, 1842, Sarah A. Seybert, daughter of Bernard Seybert, of Salem township. She died November 11, 1882. C. T. Barnum died January 11, 1887. Three children survived Judge Barnum —B. F. Barnum, of this city; James B. Barnum, of Harvey's Lake; and Harriet B., wife of F. L. Faries, of Bellwood, Pa.

WILLIAM MERRIFIELD.

William Merrifield was commissioned an associate judge of Luzerne county, Pa., November 12, 1856. He was a son of Robert Merrifield, and was born at Pine Plains, Dutchess county, N. Y., April 22, 1806. (See page 853.) The wife of William Merrifield was Almira Swetland, daughter of Belding Swetland, and granddaughter of Luke Swetland. In the report of Major James Norris, of the Third New Hampshire Regiment, which accompanied

General Sullivan in his march against the Indians, we have the following, under date of September 5, 1779: "The Army March'd at 10 o'clock, preceeded 5 miles to and Indian town Call'd Candaia or Appletown [On the east side of Seneca Lake—about a half mile from the lake, on both sides of a small stream, on lot seventy-nine Romulus.] wheir is an old orchard of 60 trees and many other fruits. The town consists of 20 Houses Very Beautifully situated near the lake, in the town are three Sepulchres which are very Indian fine where I suppose that some of their Chiefs are Deposited at this town we found a man by the Name of Luke Sweatland who was taken by the Savages at Wyoming last Summer and was adopted into an Indian family in this town Where has lived or Rather stayd 12 months, he appeared quite overjoyed at Meeting some of his Acquaintance from Wyoming who are in our Army, he says that the Savages were very much stratened for food from April till the corn was fitt to Rost, that his being kept so short on't for Provisions Prevented his attempting to Desert altho' he had frequent opportunityes by being sent 20 miles to the salt Spring to make salt which spring he says afforded Salt for all of the Savages in this part of the Country, he says that the Indians were very much allarm'd and Dejected at being beat at Newtown they told him they had a Great many wounded which they sent of by Water we Destroyed Great quantities of Corn here."

EZRA BARTHOLOMEW CHASE.

Ezra Bartholomew Chase, who was admitted to the bar of Luzerne county, Pa., April 7, 1857, was a descendant of Daniel Chase, a Free Will Baptist preacher, a native of New Hampshire, where he was born November 7, 1770. In 1816 he removed to Jackson, Susquehanna county, Pa. His wife was Catharine Fillbrook. John Chase, son of Rev. Daniel Chase, was also a Baptist minister. He removed with his father to Pennsylvania. He was born October 19, 1794, and died at Windsor, N. Y., in 1840.

E. B. Chase, son of Rev. John Chase, was born December 25, 1827, at West Windsor, N. Y. He was educated at Harford academy, afterwards Harford university, Harford, Pa. He read law with F. B. Streeter, at Montrose, and was admitted to the Susquehanna county bar August 19, 1850. He was elected a member of the legislature in 1852, and reëlected in 1853, and in 1854 was speaker of the house. He was probably the youngest man ever elected to that position. About 1851 he, in connection with his cousin, Hon. S. B. Chase, purchased the *Montrose Democrat*, and it continued under the charge of one or both of these editors until 1856, when they sold the establishment. The latter year he purchased the *Lackawanna Herald*, at Scranton, which had been a Know-Nothing organ, and changed the political character of the paper by making it a Democratic paper. The name was changed to *Herald of the Union*. Declining health induced Mr. Chase to sell out after a short time. In 1857 Mr. Chase removed to Wilkes-Barre, where he practiced his profession until the time of his death, February 15, 1864. At that time he was district attorney of the county. He was the author of a work of four hundred and ninety-five pages, entitled "Teachings of Patriots and Statesmen, or the Founders of the Republic on Slavery." Philadelphia, 1860. J. W. Bradley, publisher. Mr. Chase married, October 20, 1852, Amelia C. Shafer. She was the daughter of Embley Shafer, born in Sussex county, N. J., in 1803, died in 1884. His wife was Urania Turrell, who was born in Connecticut in 1808. William Turrell, her father, was born in Connecticut in 1781; removed to Montrose in 1816, where he died in 1853. His wife, whom he married in 1807, in Connecticut, was Polly Sylvia Benedict, who died in Montrose in 1873. Three children survived Mr. Chase— Elizabeth S., wife of E. Nancura Hunt, Wyalusing, Pa.; Amelia C., wife of William P. Stalford, Wyalusing; and Embley Shafer Chase, who married Mina B. Meylert, of LaPorte, Pa.

GEORGE SANDERSON.

George Sanderson, who was admitted to the bar of Luzerne county, Pa., September 14, 1857, was a native of Boston, where he was born February 25, 1810. His father was one of the solid men of Boston, engaged largely in trade with the West Indies. Mr. Sanderson, when a young man, studied and graduated in the Boston Latin School, but he could not be content to stay in New England. As to so many of her sons, so to him came that intense longing for other scenes and faces. The new life of the further west attracted him, and he traveled in New York state as a Universalist minister, editing a religious paper of that denomination at either Geneva or Rochester. He settled in Towanda, Pa., in 1835, and was admitted to the Bradford county bar in 1840, while residing there. He was deputy attorney general of Bradford county for some years, and during the years 1851, 1852, and 1853 represented Bradford, Susquehanna, and Wyoming counties in the state senate. In the latter year Mr. Sanderson became acquainted with George W. Scranton, and a warm friendship sprang up between the two men. Mr. Sanderson was able to be of considerable assistance to Colonel Scranton in securing the passage of bills which placed the mining and manufacturing industries of Scranton, then in their infancy but which have since grown to such gigantic proportions, upon a firm and stable basis. Colonel Scranton urged him to come to Scranton, describing in glowing terms the future of the young settlement. Mr. Sanderson came first in 1854 and again in 1855. Apparently he too saw clearly what a busy place the valley was destined to become, for in April of that year he purchased the Hitchcock farm of two hundred and twenty acres for sixty-five thousand dollars, a large sum in those days, yet within a few weeks he sold an undivided half of it for as much as he gave for the whole. Then he opened what is now Washington avenue, cutting the road out through the woods and building a corduroy road across the swamp, and amid the pine stumps he built for himself in 1856 the handsome residence now occupied by Mr. James Blair, which has remained practically unchanged from that day to this. He laid out Sanderson Hill in lots, opened up streets, adopted a liberal and public spirited policy toward settlers upon his lots, donated ground for school and church purposes, and served the young borough in 1857 and again in 1864 as burgess. He practiced law, too, in those days, and in company with his brother-in-law, Burton Kingsbury, in 1855, he went into the banking business under the name of George Sanderson & Company. The firm continued in successful operation until 1873, when it became merged into the Lackawanna Valley bank. About 1864, desirous of retiring in some degree from business, and also desirous of securing for his children greater educational advantages than the young settlement afforded, he removed to Philadelphia and purchased a handsome residence at Germantown, still retaining his interests at Scranton, which place he frequently visited ; but it was impossible for so busy a man to long remain content with circean dreams of idleness. He accordingly organized the Tremont Coal Company, whose lands lay in Schuylkill county. His acquaintance with prominent capitalists and business men in Philadelphia was very extensive, and they deferred largely on his sound judgment on financial matters in this part of the state. He remained in Germantown some three years and then returned to Scranton. It was about this time that he ran for mayor against the late William M. Monies, who won the race, however. He purchased, about 1869 or 1870, the Whaling property at Green Ridge, and with the same liberal policy that had marked his course in regard to the lots on Sanderson Hill, he built a street car railroad to afford easy access from these lots to the city. He opened up streets, laid out lots, and by every means in his power has labored indefatigably to build up Green Ridge, until, owing to his exertions, it has become a neighborhood of delightful homes, a suburb of which any city may well be proud. He secured, almost single-handed, and in the face of great opposition, the act of 1873 for the opening of Washington avenue, now the finest driveway in Scranton. He was from the first a warm advocate of the new county project, to further which he contributed liberally always of his time and money. His life was a singularly clean and pure one—upright and conscientious in all its various phases. He was a member of the city council in 1876; he would accept no remuneration for his services as banker, and in the controversy which followed the funding of the city debt his character came out untarnished. While he was a man of apparently austere manners and somewhat brusque exterior, these were but the rough husks that held the sweet kernel within ; for he was a man of great tenderness of heart, to whom pain and suffering of all kinds brought only sadness and distress. Yet it was only dear and familiar intimates who realized his full value as a man, for after the death of his oldest daughter, whom he very tenderly loved, he became more and more self-contained and reticent. He died April 1, 1866. In 1835 Mr. Sanderson married Marion W. Kingsbury, a descendant of Joseph Kingsbury, of Enfield, Connecticut, whose son, Lemuel Kingsbury, was the father of Colonel Joseph Kingsbury, father of Mrs. Sanderson. Colonel Kingsbury was born at Enfield, May 19, 1774. His grandfather, Joseph Kingsbury, offered to send him to Yale college if he would prepare for the ministry, but the offer, tempting as it was, had too many conditions attached for the young man, who looked upon a minister, as most people did then, as a little less than a demagogue, and felt that he was not of that material of which gods were made, and the offer was declined. At the age of nineteen he left the friends of his youth, and with a horse, a small sum of money, and a compass, he turned his face towards the Susquehanna to find a home and employment. He arrived at Sheshequin in the spring of 1793, and on the very day he was nineteen years old. He engaged at once with General Simon Spalding as a surveyor, and began a career that culminated in his appointment as agent for the vast landed estates of Vincent LeRay de Chaumont, known as the LeRay lands, Count de Chastelleux, McEwen and Davidson, the Bank of North America, and others. From an early period to his death he was a member and generous contributor to the religious denomination of Universalists. He was for many years a colonel of militia and postmaster of the town. He died June 22, 1849. The wife of Colonel Joseph Kingsbury, whom he married February 1, 1797, was Ann Spalding, a daughter of General Simon Spalding, who was born at Plainfield, Connecticut, January 16, 1742. He emigrated to Wyoming about 1774, and settled in Standing Stone in 1775. He was in command of a company of troops during the revolutionary war, and was in General Sullivan's expedition in 1779, and as it passed through Sheshequin valley he was so favorably impressed with its appearance and location that he then resolved to make it his future place of residence. He was a captain in the revolutionary army and was made a general of militia after the war closed. He entered the army September 11, 1776, and remained in service during the whole war. He was at the battles of Germantown, Brandywine, and others. His wife was Ruth Shepherd, whom he married April 15, 1761. Mrs. Sanderson died at her residence in Scranton, June 23, 1886. She was a consistent member of the Episcopal church, as was also her husband, who was a vestryman in the church of the Good Shepherd, and donated the land upon which the church was built. Mr. and Mrs. Sanderson had a family of five children, of whom four are living—J. Gardner Sanderson, George Sanderson, who was admitted to the bar of Luzerne county November 19, 1870 (See page 936); Anna Sanderson, and Mrs. E. B. Sturges. (See page 925.)

JOHN BRISBIN.

John Brisbin was admitted to the bar of Luzerne county, Pa., in 1857. He was a native of Chenango county, N. Y., where he was born in 1818. He remained at home, working as a farmer's boy, enjoying only the usual advantages of a common school education, until he was fifteen years old, after which he attended an academy for two years, teaching a country school in the winter; then went to New York as a clerk in a wholesale grocery and provision store, where he remained for two years, married his wife there, and went to Tunkhannock, Pa., where he read law, teaching school to pay his board. He was admitted to the bar of Wyoming county, Pa., in 1843. He continued in the practice of his profession there until 1855, when he received the appointment of counsel and general land agent of the Delaware, Lackawanna and Western Railroad Company, and removed to Scranton, where he opened a law office. He served in that capacity for two years, when he was appointed general superintendent, which position he occupied until 1863, when he was chosen president of the company, and continued in that capacity for about five years; he then resigned, and was appointed counsel and general adviser, which position he occupied until the time of his death, which occurred at Newark, N. J., where he then resided, February 3, 1880. In 1850, upon the death of Chester Butler, he was elected to fill the vacancy in congress for this district, and served in that capacity until March 4, 1851. Mr. Brisbin left no children. After making ample provision for his wife, he left a large estate to numerous charities.

GEORGE DOUGHERTY HAUGHAWOUT.

George Dougherty Haughawout, son of Peter Haughawout, was admitted to the bar of Luzerne county, Pa., January 18, 1858. He was a native of Rush township, Northumberland county, Pa., where he was born March 16, 1827. He was educated at the Danville, Pa., academy, and the university at Lewisburg, Pa. He read law with John C. Neville, at Pottsville, and was admitted to the Schuylkill county bar in 1854, and practiced in Schuylkill county until his removal to Scranton in 1857. He subsequently returned to Schuylkill county and practiced in Ashland until his death, which occurred August 8, 1886. He married, in 1885, Kate Leisenring, a daughter of Jacob and Mary Leisening, of Bear Gap, Northumberland county, Pa.

WILLIAM H. PRATT.

William H. Pratt was admitted to the bar of Luzerne county, Pa., January 4, 1859. His residence was in Dunmore, Pa. At the commencement of the late civil war he entered the service and lost an arm. His wife was Catharine, daughter of John Sherman.

ISAAC McCORD CAKE.

Isaac McCord Cake, who was admitted to the bar of Luzerne county, Pa., January 4, 1859, was a native of Northumberland, Pa., where he was born January 6, 1817. His paternal grandfather, John Cake, was a native of Berks county, Pa. His wife was Susan Kirk, a native of Perkiomen Cross Roads, Chester county, Pa. John Cake, son of John Cake, and father of Isaac M. Cake, was born in Berks county January 1, 1789. He was brought to Northumberland in the same year, where he resided until his death, June 20, 1864. He was a justice of the peace there for twenty-five years. His wife, whom he married February 22, 1811, at Northumberland, was Sarah McCord, who was born at Easton, Pa., July 8, 1789. She was the daughter of Joseph McCord, a native of Stuartstown, Tyrone county, Ireland, whose wife was Sarah Jane Green, a native of Cornwall, England. They were married in Dublin, and were members of a Methodist colony that settled on the Lehigh river, in this state. Isaac M. Cake read law with Charles W. Hegins, at Sunbury, Pa., and was admitted to practice in the courts of Northumberland county in 1844. During President Polk's administration he was revenue agent and custom house inspector at Philadelphia. During the late civil war he was captain of Company I, Ninety-sixth Regiment Pennsylvania Volunteers. He was a man of more than ordinary intelligence, well read, of sedentary habits, and a confirmed bachelor. While practicing his profession in this county he resided at Scranton. He died at Northumberland July 2, 1888.

JOSEPH WRIGHT.

Joseph Wright was admitted to the bar of Luzerne county, Pa., January 2, 1860. He was born in this city June 18, 1839, and was the son of Hendrick B. Wright. (See page 2.) His mother was Mary Ann Bradley Robinson, a daughter of John

W. Robinson. (See page 1184.) Joseph Wright practiced his profession in this city until April 23, 1861, when he was appointed adjutant of the Eighth Regiment Pennsylvania Volunteers, in the three months' service. He was mustered out with his regiment, July 29, 1861. On September 13, 1861, he was appointed captain of Company D, Seventieth Regiment, Pennsylvania Volunteers. He served in that capacity until his death, which occurred May 18, 1862, at the home of H. R. Coggshall, in Germantown, Pa., of typhoid fever contracted in camp before Yorktown, Va. He was buried in this city with military honors, May 20, 1862. Mr. Wright was an unmarried man.

JOHN PERRY CRAIG.

John Perry Craig was admitted to the bar of Luzerne county, Pa., January 3, 1860. His grandfather, John Craig, was a native of the north of Ireland, and at an early age emigrated to this country and settled in Columbia county, Pa. His son, John Craig, was a native of Columbia county. His wife was Mary Engle, a daughter of Silas Engle, a native of Germantown, Pa. John P. Craig, son of John Craig, was a native of Briar Creek township, Columbia county, Pa., where he was born February 18, 1829. He was educated in the public schools of his native township, at the academy at Berwick, Pa., and a law school at Poughkeepsie, N. Y., and read law with M. E. Jackson, at Berwick. He was first admitted to the bar at North Bend, Indiana, then at Pottsville, Pa., and finally settled in Shickshinny, in this county. He was an unmarried man. He died February 21, 1862.

ARTHUR HAMILTON.

Arthur Hamilton, who was admitted to the bar of Luzerne county, Pa., February 20, 1860, was a native of Scotland. He came to this country about 1852, and was for some time engaged in the works of Dickson & Company, in Scranton, as a faithful and ingenious machinist. Leaving this occupation and becoming a citizen of the United States, he turned his attention to the study of the law. On October 26, 1861, he entered the army as captain of Company H, Seventy-sixth Regiment of Pennsylvania Volunteers. He was killed at the battle of Coosawhatchie, South Carolina, October 22, 1862. He was an unmarried man.

CHESTER BUTLER BRUNDAGE.

Chester Butler Brundage was admitted to the bar of Luzerne county, Pa., May 8, 1860. He was born in the village of Conyngham, in this county, September 4, 1838, and was the son of Moses S. Brundage and his wife, Jane Broadhead, and the brother of Asa R. Brundage, of the Luzerne bar. (See page 62.) He was educated at the Wyoming Seminary, Kingston, Pa., and Eastman's Business College, Poughkeepsie, New York. C. B. Brundage read law with his brother in this city, and after his admission practiced here and in Poughkeepsie. He married, January 3, 1861, Marie J. Mitchell, a daughter of Jethro Mitchell, of Poughkeepsie. They had one daughter, Gertrude M. Brundage, who is now the wife of John S. Streeper, of Pottstown, Pa. Mr. Brundage died January 27, 1871, in the city of New York.

CORYDON HIRAM WELLS.

Corydon Hiram Wells, who was admitted to the bar of Luzerne county, Pa., August 30, 1860, is a son of John W. Wells. (See page 978.) Mr. Wells was born in Dundaff, Pa., October 1, 1826. He was educated at Madison Academy, Waverly, Pa., and studied law with Hendrick B. Wright, in this city, but immediately located in Scranton, where he resided until his death, March 24, 1888. His wife was Mary G. Bass. Mr. and Mrs. Wells had a family of two children—Thomas F. Wells, formerly of the Luzerne bar, now of the Lackawanna county bar, and Jennie R., wife of Rev. W. I. Stearns, pastor of the Washburn street Presbyterian church, Scranton, Pa. The *Scranton Republican*, in speaking of the death of Mr. Wells, said: "C. H. Wells was one of the most upright and most thoroughly respected men in this city, having spent a large share of his life here. He was always active in business and invariably just in every transaction. No one had aught to say against Corydon H. Wells. He was a highly revered member of the Washburn street Presbyterian church, and that congregation has lost a stalwart supporter of its spiritual and temporal needs. Politically, he was a democrat, but not pronounced in his views on any governmental question, and hence his opinions were respected by men of every political complexion, because of the well-known honesty of purpose which he ever maintained therein. He sought no office, but the responsible position of assessor sought and found in him one who was acceptable to all his fellow citizens, and by his death the city loses an able, upright, and experienced official. The city, the church, his neighborhood, his acquaintances, and his friends will all sincerely unite with his relatives in mourning the death of Corydon H. Wells." George A. Wells, of this city, and John C. Wells, of Ashley, are brothers of C. H. Wells.

JOHN HOLMES KETCHAM.

John Holmes Ketcham, who was admitted to the bar of Luzerne county, Pa., August 20, 1861, was a native of Wilkes-Barre, Pa., where he was born March 24, 1830. He read law with A. T. McClintock, of this city. He was educated at Wyoming Seminary, Kingston, Pa., and was for many years a clerk in the prothonotary's office, in this city. He was a brother of the late Winthrop Welles Ketcham, of the Luzerne bar.

ALBERT CHAMBERLAIN.

Albert Chamberlain, who was admitted to the bar of Luzerne county, Pa., September 3, 1861, was a native of Bennington, Vermont, where he was born December 29, 1811. He was a grandson of Benjamin Chamberlain, a native of Rhode Island, who was a soldier in the revolutionary war, and for a period of three months was a prisoner on board a prison ship in the East river, near New York. He died in 1822. His occupation was a scythe maker. Lewis Chamberlain, son of Benjamin Chamberlain, was a native of Rhode Island, who removed to Vermont in 1800, and married there, in 1810, Nancy Palmer. In 1813, with his wife and son Albert, he removed to Choconut, Susquehanna county, Pa., where he died, March 20, 1871, aged eighty-seven years. During the presidency of Andrew Jackson he received a commission as postmaster, which office he held without intermission or reappointment until his death, a period of forty-two years. Albert Chamberlain, son of Lewis Chamberlain, was educated in the public schools of his neighborhood, and studied law with Bentley & Richards, at Montrose, Pa. He was admitted to the bar of Susquehanna county August 21, 1843. He was district attorney of Susquehanna county for six years, and was also for a number of years a justice of the peace at Montrose. From 1869 to 1873 he was the United States assessor of internal revenue for the twelfth congressional district of Pennsylvania, and during this period he removed to Scranton from Montrose. While a resident of Scranton he was a member of the school board of that city. Mr. Chamberlain married, in 1851, at Middletown, N. Y., Harriet Durbrow, daughter of Joseph Durbrow. One son, Edward F. Chamberlain, is the issue of this marriage. Mr. Chamberlain died in Scranton December 21, 1877. His widow and son survive him.

SANFORD GRANT.

Sanford Grant, who was commissioned an associate judge of Luzerne county, Pa., November 23, 1861, was a native of Vernon, Tolland county, Connecticut, where he was born in 1800. He resided in Scranton the greater part of his life, of which he was one of the original proprietors. (See page 526.) He conducted the store of Scranton, Grant & Company, and in 1841 removed his family there. In September, 1845, Joseph H. Scranton purchased the interest of Mr. Grant and he retired from the firm. Sanford Grant was the son of Augustus Grant, a native of Vernon, and his wife Asenath Fuller, a native of East Haddam, Connecticut. Sanford Grant married, in 1827, Anna King, daughter of Lemuel King. His wife dying, he married a second time, in 1837, Mary McKinney, a daughter of Justus McKinney, a native of Ellington, Connecticut, whose wife was Phila Fuller, a native of East Haddam. Mr. Grant died January 29, 1886. He left two sons to survive him—James C. Grant, now deceased, and Hezekiah K. Grant, who resides at Phillipsburg, Pa.

JOHN REICHARD.

John Reichard was commissioned an associate judge of the courts of Luzerne county, Pa., November 23, 1861. He was a native of Frankenthal, Bavaria, now Prussia, where he was born May 24, 1807, and was a son of George Reichard, who kept the Red Lion hotel on the public square in that place. Judge Reichard left his native place in 1833, to come to America. He lived for a time with George F. Bamberger, now of this city, but then of Lower Smithfield township, Northampton county, Pa., who had preceded him from his native town three years, and in 1834 he came to this city. After his arrival here he established himself as a brewer, and from a small beginning it grew under his immediate direction and that of his sons, Colonel George N. Reichard and Henry

C. Reichard, to be one of the principal business enterprises of this city. Judge Reichard was not, however, the pioneer in the brewery business in Wilkes-Barre. At an early day Thomas Ingham started a brewery on River street, below Union, which he carried on for several years. He was succeeded by Judge Reichard's cousin, Christian Reichard, who conducted the business until 1834, up to which time all the materials used had to be hauled in wagons from Philadelphia. Judge Reichard soon purchased the establishment from his relative, where, after reconstructing and enlarging the works very materially, he continued the business until 1874, when the buildings were torn down and the machinery removed to the more spacious quarters now occupied by Reichards and Company (consisting of George N. Reichard, Jennie Reichard and George Weaver), on Water street, beyond the county prison. Mr. Reichard married, in April, 1834, Wilhemina Schrader, a daughter of John Nicholas Schrader, who died in this city, October 3, 1874. Mrs. Reichard was also a native of Frankenthal.

She had a right to claim some identity with the early history of our valley, she being a relative of Captain Philip Schrader, who was a conspicuous figure in the early history of Pennsylvania, and who accompanied General Sullivan as captain-lieutenant of the German battalion, in his expedition against the Indians in 1779. The following commissions of Captain Schrader are in the possession of John Reichard, a son of Judge Reichard: One as captain-lieutenant in the German regiment, dated June 16, 1779; one as captain of a company of rangers, dated September 10, 1781; one as captain in the corps of infantry commanded by Major James Moore, dated September 25, 1783; and one as one of the justices of the peace for Northampton county, dated April 1, 1806. The Wyoming Jaegers was one of the earliest and for many years most prominent of German organizations in this city. It came into being in 1843, and at its first meeting John Reichard was chosen captain. This position he held for several years. He was also the first president of the Concordia society, an honorary member of the Saengerbund, as well as being prominently connected with other social organizations. In 1853 and 1854 Judge Reichard was postmaster of the borough of Wilkes-

Barre. In 1867 he was appointed by President Johnson consul to Ravenna, Italy. For more than half a century Captain Reichard, as he was familiarly called, had been an active and leading business man in Wilkes-Barre, during which time his honesty and integrity as a man had never been doubted or brought in question. During the later years of his life Judge Reichard spent much of his time in the land of his nativity. He died on shipboard on returning to this country, August 19, 1884, his final voyage being his twenty-sixth trip across the Atlantic. He left to survive him the following children—Colonel George Nicholas Reichard, married to Grizzy Gilchrist, daughter of P. Mc. Gilchrist; Henry Colt Reichard, married to Jenny Griffin, daughter of Elias Griffin; John Reichard, married to Eliza C. Parrish, daughter of Gould P. Parrish (see page 593); Charles Wolf Reichard, married to Carrie E. Harrington, daughter of David C. Harrington (see page 874); Albertina L. Reichard, wife of the late J. H. Swoyer; Catharine F. Reichard, wife of C. H. Leonard. Helena, wife of the late M. A. Holmes. She became the second wife of J. H. Swoyer. Julia Reichard, another daughter, married Colonel E. A. Hancock, of Philadelphia. She is now deceased, leaving one son, James Hancock, a graduate of Princeton College of the class of 1888.

IRA D. RICHARDS.

Ira D. Richards was admitted to the bar of Luzerne county, Pa., November 26, 1861. He was born in 1826, and was a member of the Tioga county bar, and when admitted here he removed to Carbondale, where he resided up to the time of his death. From 1865 to 1869 he was district attorney of the recorder's court of Carbondale. In 1873 he was elected recorder, and on February 9, 1874, as he was entering the court house to discharge his duties, was taken with a severe hemorrhage which caused his death in about two hours. He was an able counsellor, a studious lawyer, and an upright judge. He left a widow but no children to survive him.

JOHN L. GORE.

John L. Gore was admitted to the Luzerne county, Pa., bar, January 22, 1862. He was the grandson of John Gore and his wife, Elizabeth Ross, and the son of John Gore and his wife, Ruth Searle. (See page 435.) His father was born in 1799, and died December 20, 1879. John L. Gore resided in Carbondale, Pa., and died there May 15, 1862. He was an unmarried man.

CANFIELD HARRISON.

Canfield Harrison, who was commissioned an associate judge of Luzerne county, Pa., July 3, 1862, was the grandson of Stephen Harrison, of Canaan, Connecticut, who moved with his wife and children to what is now Huntington township, this county, in April, 1778. After the battle and massacre he and his family returned to their former home in Connecticut, where they remained until 1789, when they returned to their former home in Huntington. His wife was Susanna Franklin, a sister of Colonel John Franklin. They had a son Jarius Harrison, whose wife was Huldah Fuller, who was the father of Canfield Harrison. He was born in Huntington in 1809. Mr. Harrison, in his early manhood, was a merchant, and in after years a hotel keeper. He resided in Carbondale for many years, and the Harrison house in that city derived its name from him. In 1861 he was mayor of the city of Carbondale. He married, in early life, Deborah Koons, a sister of Hon. John Koons. She was born in Monroe county May 7, 1811. They had no children. In the latter years of their life they resided in Bloomsburg, Pa., where they died; Mr. Harrison on February 28, 1880, and Mrs. Harrison September 2, 1887.

EDGAR LEROY MERRIMAN.

Edgar Leroy Merriman, who was admitted to the bar of Luzerne county, Pa., September 1, 1864, was a native of Franklin, Susquehanna county, Pa., where he was born January 7, 1844. His grandfather, Theophilus Merriman, was a native of Cheshire, New Haven county, Connecticut. He removed to Franklin township, Susquehanna county, Pa., in 1800. His wife was Susan Smith, a daughter of Captain Roswell Smith, also of Cheshire. The father of E. L. Merriman is Joseph L. Merriman (son of Theophilus Merriman), who was born in Franklin, September 1, 1817. His wife was Mercy Baker, a native of Greenfield township, Luzerne (now Lackawanna) county, where she was born February 14, 1816. Mr. Merriman was formerly a farmer, but has been engaged in the mercantile business for many years. During his early years Edgar was the brightest boy in the neighborhood. He was sent to a common school, where he received the first rudiments of his education. His fondness for study soon made him a good scholar, and he always stood at the head of his class. At twelve he was sent to the Montrose academy, and here again he applied himself diligently to his studies, and very soon pushed forward until he was among the foremost students. From Montrose he was sent to the Wyoming seminary, at Kingston, where he completed his education.

Expressing a desire to study law, his father managed, fortunately, to get him into the office of Hon. Charles Denison, who, at the time, was one of the most prominent lawyers in Luzerne county. Here he began his studies with a determination to succeed in the profession which he had chosen. Gifted with a natural love for the intricate details of the rather dry rudiments of the text-books, the ambitious student applied himself faithfully to his task. It was a proud day for him when he first entered court as a full fledged lawyer, and prouder yet when he was made aware of the flattering opinions entertained for him by the experienced and critical minds who applauded his efforts, and prophesied a brilliant future for him.

One thing which aided Mr. Merriman in his earlier career was the fact that he possessed a natural love for dignity, which led him to seek his associates among the older and more experienced members of the bar. He had an agreeable presence, and a bright, breezy way with him that won the regard of his legal friends, and all of them took a deep interest in his welfare, and were ever ready with their superior wisdom to enlighten him on any abstruse questions which puzzled him.

In 1865 Mr. Merriman, after practicing about a year, had gained many warm friends. The political conventions met that year, and his ambition led him to seek the nomination for assembly in his district. The young lawyer made every effort to obtain it, but his youth appeared to be the barrier which frustrated his desires. He did not get the nomination; but, nothing daunted, he applied himself more diligently to the labors of his profession, and gradually enlarged his sphere of work until his name became widely known and his practice more extended. Of course, he shared the benefits of being a pupil and associate of Mr. Denison, who aided him in every way possible.

In 1870 Mr. Merriman was elected district attorney on the democratic ticket over Alexander Farnham, Esq. His election to the position of district attorney, and the subsequent opportunities offered him to exhibit the rare abilities that he possessed, gave him greater notoriety, and brought him still more prominently before the public. At the conclusion of his term of office he went back to his professional labors, and was followed by a flattering patronage that brought to him fame and profit. In 1875 Mr. Merriman was made chairman of the democratic county committee, and on October 7, 1876, he was nominated by the democratic convention, assembled in Wilkes-Barre, as their candidate for congress. After his nomination he devoted nearly all of his time to the interests of his party, working night and day for that purpose. He had planned out an aggressive campaign, and if he had been spared his eloquent voice would have been heard throughout the length and breadth of Luzerne county in defense of those principles which he loved, and for which, it may be justly said, he sacrificed his young, hopeful, and honorable life.

Although Mr. Merriman was the very picture of health, those

who knew him best were aware that he was a great sufferer from internal disorders, arising from a diseased condition of the kidneys, heart, and liver, which were greatly aggravated under mental or physical excitement. The strain upon Mr. Merriman's nervous system after his nomination was calculated to inflame the maladies to which he was subject, and though frequently warned against undue excitement and overwork, he still persisted in going on with his labors, notwithstanding that none knew better than himself that he was liable to drop off at any moment. A few days before his death he complained to his friends concerning his condition, and though they advised him to retire a short time from the more exciting efforts of the campaign, he failed to act upon their suggestions until it was too late, and on Thursday evening, August 31, he went home to his family in great distress. He retired at once, and his physician was summoned, who, being acquainted with his disorders, applied the usual restoratives. On Friday he was much worse, and other physicians were called in consultation. They all felt that their patient's case was a hopeless one, but they labored hard to relieve him from the terrible agonies which he was enduring. Everything that skill and experience could suggest was brought into requisition, but Mr. Merriman's condition defied the united efforts put forth to restore him, and he continued to suffer and groan until early Sabbath morning, when death mercifully stepped in to relieve him of his agony.

Mr. Merriman was thoroughly conscious until a short time before his death. On Saturday morning Dr. Murphy informed him that there was no hope, that his death was simply a question of endurance. Mr. Merriman comprehended the awful significance of his physician's information, and replied that he knew he could not live; but it was reserved for him to say farewell to the wife and children whom he dearly loved, and to a few personal friends gathered around his dying bed. They watched his struggles as he neared the dark river, and their hearts were made sadder because of the brave spirit which was yielding itself up in the agonies of physical torture.

Upon the minds of his legal brethren the news of Mr. Merriman's death fell like a thunderbolt, and when they remembered

that his voice would be heard no more, that the breast which
heaved with generous impulses was stilled forever, that the bright
eye was dimmed, that the eloquent lips were mute and motion-
less, the light step palsied, and the great heart of their associate
locked in the cold and callous embrace of the dread destroyer,
they could utter nothing but sighs, and sink back into a dreamy
review of the past, and send out to their dead friend the incense
of generous recollections. On May 17, 1866, Mr. Merriman
married Ruth Lewis, the daughter of the late Sharp D. Lewis,
an old and respected resident of Wilkes-Barre. He died Sunday, September 3, 1876. Mr. and Mrs. Merriman had a family of
three children—Edgar Leroy Merriman, Lewis S. Merriman, and
Joseph Ross Merriman. Mrs. Merriman has since married Rev.
Charles S. M. Stewart, an Episcopalian minister of Whitestone,
N. Y.

CONRAD SAX STARK.

Conrad Sax Stark was admitted to the bar of Luzerne county,
Pa., November 30, 1864. He was the great-grandson of Aaron
Stark, who fell in the battle and massacre of Wyoming. His
grandfather was Daniel Stark, and his father was John D. Stark, of
Pittston township, in this county. (See pages 389 and 566.) C.
S. Stark was born in what is now Plains township, in this county,
April 12, 1836. He entered Wyoming seminary, at Kingston,
Pa., in 1854, and afterwards the New York Conference seminary.
He graduated from Union college, at Schenectady, N. Y., in the
class of 1860. Before, during, and after his college course he
taught school successively at Old Forge, Newton, Pittston, White
Haven, in the state of Maryland, and for a while was one of the
professors at Wyoming seminary. He studied law with W. G.
Ward, at Scranton, and commenced the practice of his profession
at Pittston. For fifteen years he had a large and increasing practice, enjoying in a remarkable degree and without abatement the
confidence and esteem of those who did business with him. He
established the People's Savings bank of Pittston. Largely under
his management as its president from the first, it was always a safe

and reliable institution. In the Methodist Episcopal church, of West Pittston, he was a charter member, trustee, and secretary of the board of trustees. He was also one of its Sabbath school teachers. He married, in early life, Georgia Mosier, a daughter of the late Daniel D. Mosier, of West Pittston. (See page 450.) C. S. Stark died at West Pittston March 26, 1880. He left to survive him his widow and three children—Edgar W. Stark, now a law student in the University of Pennsylvania; John Stark, and C. S. Stark.

PHILIP THOMAS MYERS.

Philip Thomas Myers, who was admitted to the bar of Luzerne county, Pa., January 6, 1865, was a native of Kingston, Pa., where he was born May 7, 1839. His father, Madison F. Myers, was a native of Frederick county, Maryland, in which state he was born and reared, and where he resided until the autumn of 1835. His mother was Harriet Myers, youngest daughter of Philip and Martha Bennett Myers, of Forty Fort. Martha Bennett, his maternal grandmother, was a daughter of Thomas Bennett, one of the original settlers of Wyoming, and one of the forty men who constructed the fort after which Forty Fort took its name. P. T. Myers was educated at Wyoming seminary, Kingston, and studied law in this city with Stanley Woodward. He practiced very little on account of ill health, the result of an accidental shot. Before this accident he was a young man of prominence and ability, and bid fair for a long life of usefulness. He died, February 13, 1878, at Kingston. His sister married the late Hon. A. J. Weaver, of Iowa. He was an unmarried man.

WILLIAM F. CASE.

William F. Case was admitted to the bar of Luzerne county, Pa., February 20, 1865. He had an office in Shickshinny, in this county. His widow subsequently married Luther M. Chase, of this city.

ISAAC JOSEPH POST.

Isaac Joseph Post, who was admitted to the bar of Luzerne county, Pa., April 30, 1866, was a descendant of Richard Post, whose name first appears on the records of Southampton, Long Island, New York, in May 1643, when a home lot was granted to him by the proprietors. In 1681 he is recorded as giving land to his son John, and in 1687 he gave land to his son Joseph. In 1688 he gave his homestead in Littleworth to his son-in-law, Benjamin Foster, and his daughter Martha, the wife of Benjamin Foster, and the last two were to provide for the wants of himself and his wife so long as they lived. He died about 1689. His wife's name was Dorothy. He had a son John, who died in 1687. He had a son Captain John, born in 1674. Captain John Post died March 3, 1741. He had a son Isaac, born 1712, and died May 8, 1785. He had a son Isaac, who died about 1788. He had a son Isaac, born August 12, 1784, at Southampton. He came to Montrose, Pa., with his stepfather, Captain Bartlet Hinds, an officer of the revolution, originally from Boston, who came into what is now Montrose in 1800, as an owner and agent of lands for ex-Governor Huntington, of Connecticut, under the title of that state. During the first years after the arrival of the first family of settlers in Montrose, Isaac Post was the mill boy, and often went down to the mouth of the Wyalusing on horseback after flour and provisions. He was also the cowboy and hunter; was depended upon mostly for venison, was acknowledged to be the best woodsman—surest to keep the points of the compass and find his way home from the chase. He chopped some acres of forest in the upper part of his place before any of the family discovered it, and when it was discovered Captain Hinds supposed some squatter had been trespassing upon his premises. Young Post had done this by hiding his axe; then taking a gun, as if on a hunt, he would go to his chopping. As he often brought venison home at night no one suspected his business. He chopped down the first tree in Montrose; helped build the first log house, in 1800; built the first frame house in 1806; the first store and the first blacksmith shop; was the first postmaster in 1808. He also built the first turnpike, 1811-1814; ran the first stage; was the first treasurer of the county. He passed through military grades from ensign to major, and from 1811 to 1814 was brigade inspector, and as such had charge of the Danville expedition. He built the academy in 1818; the Baptist meeting house in 1829; was a member of the state legislature in 1828 and 1829, and associate judge of Susquehanna county from 1834 to 1843. He was baptized into the Bridgewater Baptist church in 1810. In 1814 he was challenged by a recruiting officer, Lieutenant Findley, to fight a duel. He did not signify his acceptance, but Findley, on being told he could shoot a rooster's head off with a pistol, backed down and asked pardon. He gave the county all of the public grounds and half of the lots as marked on the first town plot. There was not, during his life, a public improvement in which he did not have a prominent part as originator or promoter. He was a prominent republican (as the democrats were originally called), and in 1817 was a delegate from Susquehanna county to the convention at Harrisburg that nominated William Findley for governor. When in the legislature he secured the passage of an act making Susquehanna county a separate election district, when he knew this would defeat his reëlection. He married his stepsister, Susana Hinds. Her father, Bartlet Hinds, was born at Middleboro, Massachusetts, April 4, 1755. He was baptized into the Middleboro Baptist church when about sixteen years of age by his father, Elder Ebenezer Hinds, then its pastor, and was the first Baptist church member that came into the county. He had served as a soldier, as private and first lieutenant, and was brevetted captain in the revolutionary army. He was shot through the left lung at the taking of Burgoyne; was one of the "forlorn hope," claiming to having had command of the detachment at the storming of Stony Point, and first proclaimed "the fort is our own;" served to the end of the war, after being wounded, in castle duty. He had a diploma entitling him to membership in the society of the Cincinatti, formed by officers of the army at the close of the revolution. For at least a dozen years after Captain Hinds brought his family to Luzerne (now Susquehanna) county the place was known as the Hinds settlement. He was the first justice of the peace. His age, his experience, his native shrewdness and energy of character, and his piety withal fitted him for a pioneer and a prominent actor in all that pertained to the civil and religious interests of a new county. He was greatly valued as a counsellor and faithful adviser. He died October 11, 1822. Rev. Albert L. Post, a Baptist minister, was a son of Isaac Post. His wife was Eleanor Williams, a daughter of Joseph Williams, of Pierstown, Otsego county, N. Y., who located in Susquehanna county in 1809. Isaac J. Post was a son of Rev. A. L. Post. He was born at Montrose June 21, 1837, and graduated from Yale college in the class of 1860. He read law with William and W. H. Jessup, and was admitted to the Susquehanna county bar January 20, 1862. Soon after his admission he entered the army and remained in the service about a year. He then accepted a position under the solicitor of the treasury department at Washington. His salary was eighteen hundred dollars a year. He acted there in many intricate cases of litigation for the government, being often detailed to settle large disputed claims. He remained in that position until 1866. He then went to Scranton and became a member of the law firm of Hand (Alfred) & Post. He married, June 23, 1868, Eliza B. Todd, daughter of I. M. Todd, of the state of New York. Mr. Post died July 10, 1885. Two children survived him—Albert Todd Post and Charles Joseph Post. Mrs. Post resides at Montrose.

THOMAS COLLINS.

Thomas Collins was commissioned an associate judge of Luzerne county, Pa., November 9, 1866. He resided in Dunmore, and had a son, Francis D. Collins, a member of the Luzerne county bar. (See page 905.)

GEORGE PALMER STEELE.

George Palmer Steele, who was commissioned an associate judge of Luzerne county, Pa., November 9, 1866, was a grandson of Peter Steele, a native of New Buffalo, Perry county, Pa.

He removed to Northumberland, then to Hanover, in this county, prior to 1790. He lived on the river road below the red tavern, and died there in 1823. He had a son, Joseph Steele, born in Perry county in 1773, who came to Hanover with his father's family. His wife was Sarah Ransom. (See page 384.) George P. Steele was born in Hanover in 1801. He was a son of Joseph Steele. He was sheriff of Luzerne county from 1841 to 1844, and represented this county in the senate of Pennsylvania from 1856 to 1859. His first wife was Susan B. Crisman, a daughter of Abram Crisman, a son of Frederick Crisman, who came to Hanover as early as 1788 and built the red tavern. She died in 1847. They had two children—one, a daughter, became the first wife of F. J. Leavenworth, and the second, a son, Harrison Steele. They are both deceased. George P. Steele married, for his second wife, Mrs. Lydia Doak (nee Eldridge.) She was the daughter of Robert Eldridge, a native of New London, Connecticut. George Palmer Steele, of Pittston, is the sole surviving issue of this marriage. Mr. Steele, during his life time, was principally engaged in hotel keeping. He erected the Luzerne house, at the corner of the public square in this city, which was known for years as Steele's hotel. He sold the same to Ziba Bennett, when the name was changed to the Luzerne house. Mr. Steele died in 1870.

GEORGE THOMAS SMITH.

George Thomas Smith, who was admitted to the bar of Luzerne county, Pa., April 3, 1867, was a son of the late Thomas Smith, of Waverly, Pa. (See page 871.) He was born at Waverly, in 1844, and was educated at Madison academy and the Harvard law school, Cambridge, Mass. Mr. Smith, at the age of nineteen, took a position in one of the government departments at Washington, D. C., which he held some three years, leaving it to enter Harvard law school. He also held a commission in the signal corps of the army, from which he was honorably discharged. He read law in this city with A. T. McClintock, and practiced here until his death, September 4, 1871. He married, in 1867, Louise Palmer, a daughter of the late Gideon W. Palmer, of Glenburn, Pa. (See page 194.) She still survives him. Mr. and Mrs. Smith had a family of two children—Edith Smith and George Palmer Smith. George T. Smith was a brother of Andrew J. Smith, of the Luzerne bar.

JOSEPH H. CAMPBELL.

Joseph H. Campbell, who was admitted to the bar of Luzerne county, Pa., November 12, 1867, was a son of Robert Campbell and his wife Catharine Mettler, a daughter of William Mettler. J. H. Campbell was a native of Rush township, Northumberland county, Pa., where he was born July 8, 1829. He was educated in the common schools of his neighborhood and at Lewisburg university. He also engaged in teaching in his young manhood. He married, October 22, 1855, Mary Reed, a daughter of Jacob Reed and his wife, Maria Jones, a daughter of John Jones and Margaret Rockefeller, his wife. They were natives of New Jersey. Three children were born to Mr. and Mrs. Campbell—Howard H. Campbell, a member of the Lackawanna county bar; Mary Gertrude Campbell, and George B. Campbell. Mr. Campbell read law with Judge Jordan, of Northumberland county, and Judge Cooper, of Montour county, and was admitted to the Montour county bar, at Danville, Pa., September 20, 1858. In 1861 he was elected district attorney of Montour county for a term of three years, and in 1864 was reëlected for a similar term. Shortly after the expiration of the latter term he removed to Scranton, where he practiced until his death, August 7, 1888.

ROWLAND METCALF KIDDER.

Rowland Metcalf Kidder was admitted to the bar of Luzerne county, Pa., April 27, 1868. He was the son of Lyman Church Kidder, who was the son of Luther Kidder and Phebe Kidder, his wife. (See page 1175.) L. C. Kidder was born in Waterford, Vermont, April 18, 1802. He died December 10, 1850, in Janesville, Wisconsin. He followed the occupation of a surveyor. He was a member of Company I, First Regiment Pennsylvania Volunteers, commanded by Captain E. L. Dana, in the Mexican war. He married, March 27, 1825, Mary Dana, born June 16, 1808, in Wilkes-Barre, who died March 17, 1861. She was the daughter of Anderson and Mary (Stevens) Dana. Hon. Luther Kidder, who was a member of the bar of Luzerne county, was a brother of Lyman Church Kidder. Rowland Metcalf Kidder, son of Lyman Church Kidder and Mary Kidder, his wife, was born July 3, 1842, in Wilkes-Barre. At the age of eighteen years he enlisted in the Sixth Regiment of Pennsylvania Cavalry at the breaking out of the war; was detailed for service as an orderly at army headquarters, and occupied that position during the period of General Hooker's command of the army of the Potomac; was near General Hooker when the latter was wounded at the battle of Chancellorsville. His own horse was killed by a shot at about the same time the general was struck. He was present and behaved with marked coolness and courage in most of the battles in which the army of the Potomac was engaged, and also in the different raids, scouts and skirmishes in which his regiment participated. He was wounded at the battle of Gettysburg, but soon recovered so as to rejoin his regiment, and at the battle of Spottsylvania, in June, 1864, was taken prisoner and confined at Andersonville until the close of the war. After returning home he studied law with his brother, Clarence Porter Kidder, in Wilkes-Barre. He removed to Colorado in July, 1868. He became deputy United States surveyor for the territory of New Mexico, and surveyed a large portion of the territory, located many mines, laid out several towns, and did considerable railroad work. He died (unmarried) at Silver City December 25, 1874.

ISAAC SMITH OSTERHOUT.

Isaac Smith Osterhout was commissioned, February 9, 1870, by Governor Geary, an associate judge of Luzerne county, Pa., to fill a vacancy caused by the death of George Palmer Steele. The Osterhouts, as their name indicates, came originally from Holland. They settled first in Connecticut, whence they removed to Dover, Dutchess county, N. Y. Jeremiah Osterhout, grandfather of Isaac S. Osterhout, removed from Dover in 1778 and settled at or near Tunkhannock, where he assisted in organizing the township of Putnam, one of the seventeen townships set apart to claimants under the Connecticut title. Isaac Osterhout, son of Jeremiah Osterhout, and the father of Isaac S. Osterhout, subsequently settled at a point now known as Lagrange, Wyoming county, Pa., where he engaged in merchandise and lumbering, and for some years kept a house for the accommodation of strangers and travelers. He married, at Old Forge, Susanna Smith, a daughter of William Hooker Smith. (See page 219.) The forge was originally built by Mr. Smith, but his son-in-law, Colonel Napthali Hurlbut, ran it at this time. I. S. Osterhout's mother was born in a house which formerly stood at the corner of Northampton and Franklin streets, on the lot owned and occupied by him at the time of his death, and now owned by G. W. Guthrie, M. D. The house Isaac S. Osterhout built and occupied at Lagrange is said to have been the first frame house erected between Pittston and Athens. This house is yet standing. Here I. S. Osterhout was born, October 26, 1806. In 1810 his father moved some three miles up the river, in 1818 to Black Walnut, and in 1822 to the Provost farm, six miles above Tunkhannock, where he died June 27, 1824. He had, prior to his death, a share in the Hunt's ferry shad fishery. About 1820 I. S. Osterhout took a load of shad, salted in barrels, to Salina, N. Y., to exchange them for salt. Mr. Kinney accompanying him took a load of whetstones. The trip was made in sleighs and occupied two weeks. The shad found a ready sale, but the whetstones were disposed of with much difficulty and at a sacrifice. When I. S. Osterhout was twelve years of age he was sent to school at the Kingston academy. In 1823 he came to Wilkes-Barre and engaged as clerk with Denison, McCoy & Davenport, who had a store on River street, where the Wyoming valley house now stands. He remained with them about a year, when he returned to Tunkhannock and engaged with Beach Tuttle, who was then in business there. In 1824 he went to Elmira, N. Y., and remained there until 1830, clerking for Tuttle & Covell. He then came to Kingston and clerked for Gaylord & Reynolds, and remained with them nearly a year. In the latter part of the last named year he came to Wilkes-Barre and entered into partnership in the mercantile business with his cousin, Whitney Smith. This partnership continued until 1834, when it was dissolved, and the business thereafter was continued by Mr. Osterhout alone. As an evidence of enhancement of values in Wilkes-Barre, it may be remarked that the premises occupied, now owned by H. Lowenstein, embraced thirty feet on Main street and fifty feet on the public square, with suitable space in the rear, and the rent was but thirty dollars a year. In 1837 Mr. Osterhout purchased of Rev. George Lane, for the sum of three thousand dollars, the valuable property still owned by the estate, comprising a frontage of one hundred feet on the northwest side of the public square, on which there was then a house and two stores. Mr. Osterhout continued in the mercantile business until 1859. He had, after years of toil and industry skillfully directed, acquired an ample competency. He held the offices of secretary and treasurer of the Hollenback cemetery at the time of his death, and most of the time from its organization in 1854. He was also at the time of his death secretary and treasurer of the Wilkes-Barre water company, and had been from its inception. He was also at the time of his death, and had been for thirty years, the secretary and treasurer of the Wyoming Athenaeum. On January 29, 1840, Mr. Osterhout married Elizabeth C. Lee, only daughter of Hon. Thomas Lee, of Port Elizabeth, Cumberland county, N. J., who was a prominent and highly respected citizen of that place, and represented the district in the congress of the United States. I. S. Osterhout died in Wilkes-Barre April 12, 1882, and his wife April 28, 1887. They left no children. His munificent bequest to the city for the founding and support of a free library, and his large donations for christian and charitable objects, entitle him to be ranked and remembered as its leading and most liberal benefactor. The accumulations of a long life of industry and economy were devoted by him to the highest welfare—the moral and intellectual culture of the citizens of the town in which most of that life was passed and in which those accumulations were made. His estate, which was bequeathed to the founding of the library, amounted to about four hundred thousand dollars. We herewith give the provisions of the will for the maintenance and management of said library:

"And I hereby give, bequeath, and devise all the rest and residue of my estate, real, personal, and mixed, to Hubbard B. Payne, of Kingston, Luzerne county, Pennsylvania, Lewis C. Paine, Edward P. Darling, Edmund L. Dana (since deceased, vacancy filled by the election of Charles M. Conyngham), Harrison Wright (since deceased, vacancy filled by the election of Andrew F. Derr), Andrew H. McClintock, and Sheldon Reynolds, all of the city of Wilkes-Barre, in said county, and the survivors or survivor of them, and their heirs and the heirs of the survivor of them, IN TRUST, nevertheless, to be held, appropriated, and used to and for the use and purpose of founding, establishing, and perpetuating in the said city of Wilkes-Barre a free library—the said residuary estate to be held and managed by my executors, hereinafter named, for five years from the time of my death, to accumulate, and the income of my said residuary estate for said five years to be added to said residuary estate, and the whole to be then used for and devoted to the establishing and maintaining in said city a free library, as aforesaid, to be called "THE OSTERHOUT FREE LIBRARY," and the whole residuary estate aforesaid, with the accumulations thereof, to be then conveyed and passed over by the said trustees, or their survivors and successors, to an incorporation, to be procured by the said trustees, or their survivors and successors, and named "THE OSTERHOUT FREE LIBRARY," of which the said seven trustees, or, in case of the death of any of them, the survivors, and such person or persons as shall be named by the survivors in the place of any of said trustees that may be deceased at the time of such incorporation being obtained, and the rector of St. Stephen's church, of Wilkes-Barre, and the pastor of the First Presbyterian church, of Wilkes-Barre, and their respective successors, shall be the directors, making a board of nine directors, the said rector and pastor and their respective successors to be *ex officio* members of said board, and in case of death, resignation, or removal beyond the county of Luzerne of any of the first mentioned seven directors, the remaining directors of said board shall fill all such vacancies as may from time to time occur, the said board to elect one of their number president, and one of their number secretary and treasurer for such term as may be fixed by the by-laws adopted by said board, and such other officers and employees as the said board shall find necessary and provide for under the by-laws that may from time to time be adopted. And in case there is any difficulty or delay in procuring, within five years from the time of my death, an act of incorporation such as I have recommended to be obtained, I hereby direct, authorize, and empower my said seven trustees, or the survivors of them, and such person or persons as such survivors may appoint to fill any vacancies from death, resignation, or removal from the county of Luzerne (which appointments I hereby authorize and empower a majority of my said trustees to make), to establish such free library, to be called "THE OSTERHOUT FREE LIBRARY," on such foundation and under such rules and regulations for the government thereof as they may adopt, to use and appropriate such portion of my said residuary estate and the accumulations thereof as they may consider judicious and proper in the erection and furnishing of a proper and suitable building for the said library, and the future requirements thereof, upon any lot owned by me in said city of Wilkes-Barre which they may select, or for the purchase of a suitable lot for such building in such location as they may consider best adapted for such building, at their discretion, and to use and appropriate such other portion of my said residuary estate and the accumulations thereof as they may decide upon to the purchase and procurement of books, maps, charts, and such other articles and things suitable for such library as they may deem proper and appropriate for a library, and to reserve, invest, and manage such other and remaining portion of my said residuary estate and the accumulations thereof to constitute a permanent fund, the income of which to be used and applied to the purpose of extending and increasing such library and defraying the necessary expenses of employing a librarian, and such other officers as may be found necessary, and of lighting, heating, and keeping open said library. And I hereby fully authorize and empower my said trustees and their successors to take such action in regard to the establishing and maintaining such library as they may judge fit and best, having in view the growth, preservation, permanency, and general usefulness of such library.

"And in case an act of incorporation is obtained for the aforesaid free library, I recommend an insertion of a provision that the directors named therein, as herein designated, shall from time to time fill all vacancies that may arise in their board by death, resignation, or removal from the county of Luzerne, by an election by the remainder of said board of suitable person or persons to fill all such vacancies as may from time to time occur in said board, and that in case of failure to fill any vacancies for three months, the president judge of the court of common pleas for Luzerne county shall appoint a suitable person or persons to fill such vacancies, until such proper election be held to fill such vacancies; my will and desire being that this trust shall not fail, and that the proper courts of said county shall have full power and authority to direct in regard to the proper application of this trust, so that my residuary estate and the accumulations thereof shall be used for and applied to the purpose to which it is hereby devoted, and my will is and I hereby direct that my said trustees, or their successors, or in case an incorporation is obtained, the directors thereof, may and shall, as soon after the expiration of five years from my death as they conveniently can, erect a suitable building for such free library in such location within the city of Wilkes-Barre as a majority may select, and of such size, style, and arrangement as a majority may decide upon, and on such lot as such majority select from lots owned by me, or may purchase and have conveyed to the corporation, if an incorporation shall have been obtained, or if not, to the proper then existing trustees, and when such suitable building is completed may and shall purchase and procure and place therein proper and suitable books and reading matter, for the establishment of a useful and desirable free library, under rules and regulations to be adopted for the government thereof, reserving, however, such portion of my residuary estate hereby devised, so that the income thereof shall be amply sufficient to secure the services of a permanent and suitable librarian, janitor, and such other officers as may be found necessary to keep such free library open and properly arranged, seated, warmed, and lighted for the free use of all persons seeking access thereto, under the rules and regulations adopted for the government thereof, and to increase the said library by the purchase and addition from time to time of such suitable books and reading matter as will render said free library most useful and improving to those that may resort thereto and avail themselves of the benefits thereof.

"And my will is and I further direct that in the erection and arrangement of the building hereby authorized, the same shall be so constructed that in addition to the space required for the accommodation of said free library and the increase thereof as hereinbefore provided for, a portion of said building shall be devoted to the use and accommodation of the Wyoming Historical and Geological society, without charge for rent, heat, or light of the rooms that may be devoted to and used for the purposes of said society; my said trustees, and their successors, or the directors of said free library, to designate the portion of said building to be used by said society, and to have the general control and supervision of said building. * * * *

"And I further authorize my aforesaid trustees and the survivors of them, and the successors of any vacancies, or the directors of the corporation, if such be obtained, at their discretion, to organize and establish a course of free lectures on some scientific or literary subject, or some other useful and improving subject calculated to interest and improve those who may attend thereon, not, however, to expend upon such course of lectures in any one year a sum exceeding two thousand dollars, and only when the income reserved for the increase of the library will bear the expenditure for such course without detriment to or interfering with the proper use and increase of the library, which I declare to be the main purpose to which I desire to devote my said residuary estate.

"And I further authorize my aforesaid trustees, and the survivors of them, and the successors of any vacancies, or the directors as aforesaid, to accept any gift, bequest, or devise of books, money, or property for the use of said free library, and to furnish shelves to be occupied by the books given or purchased with the proceeds of any such gift, bequest, or devise, and when the books donated or purchased are sufficient to fill an alcove or considerable space, to designate and mark such alcove or space with the name of the donor. In case of gifts of books, however, those in legal charge of said library shall determine whether the books offered as a gift are of such character as may be poper and suitable, and if in their judgment such books, or any of them, are not of such character, they shall reject the same; and all moneys and property bequeathed or devised to said library shall be expended by and be entirely under the control of those legally in charge of said library, to be by them devoted to the best interests thereof."

JABEZ ALSOVER.

Jabez Alsover, who was admitted to the bar of Luzerne county, Pa., May 3, 1870, was a native of Easton, Pa., where he was born September 26, 1843. He studied law in Mauch Chunk, Pa., with Daniel Kalbfus, and soon after his admission to the Carbon county bar removed to Hazleton, in this county, where he resided up to the time of his death. During the late civil war he served in the three months' service under Captain Horn, and afterwards enlisted for three years, and was discharged from the Frederick City (Maryland) hospital after a service of two years. At the time of his death, December 2, 1878, he was one of the attorneys of the Lehigh Valley Railroad Company, and also of several coal companies, and in addition had a large private practice. He married, in Mauch Chunk, in 1865, Hannah Dodson.

BENJAMIN FRANKLIN PFOUTS.

Benjamin Franklin Pfouts was commissioned an associate judge of Luzerne county, Pa., November 9, 1870. He is a descendant of John Pfoutz, who was the first settler, in 1755, in what is now Pfoutz's valley, Perry county, Pa. He was the first considerable land owner, hence had the honor of giving his name to the valley. Leonard Pfouts, son of John Pfoutz, was born at Berry's Falls, Perry county, Pa., January 18, 1774. The wife of Leonard Pfouts was Nancy Covenhoven (pronounced Cronover), a daughter of Robert Covenhoven. He was born, of Dutch parents, in Monmouth county, N. J., December 7, 1755. He was much employed during his youth as a hunter and axeman to the surveyors of land in the valleys tributary to the north and west branches of the Susquehanna. The familiarity thus acquired with all the paths of that vast wilderness rendered his services eminently useful as a scout and guide to the military parties of the revolution, which commenced about the time of his arrival at manhood. It is unnecessary to say that the graduate of such a school was fearless and intrepid, that he was skilled in the wiles of Indian warfare, and that he possessed an iron constitution. With these qualifications, at the call of his country in 1776 he joined the campaigns under General Washington. He was at the battles of Trenton and Princeton. His younger brother had also enlisted, but his father took his place, and the general, with his characteristic kindness, permitted the boy to return and protect his mother. In the spring of 1777 Robert returned to his home on the West Branch, where his services were more needed by the defenceless frontier than on the sea coast. Mr. Covenhoven was one of those men who were always put forward when danger and hard work were to be encountered, but forgotten when honors and emoluments were to be distributed. Nevertheless, he cheerfully sought the post of danger, and never shrank from duty, although it might be in an humble station. Few men passed through more hairbreadth escapes, few encountered more personal perils in deadly encounters with savages than Mr. Covenhoven. He was very useful to General Sullivan as a spy and a guide up the North Branch in 1779 to the Indian country. It is said that he was in the unfortunate company commanded by Lieutenant Boyd, and was one among the few that escaped the dreadful massacre. When the din of battle ceased and peace was restored to the land, Covenhoven came and settled permanently on the West Branch. He resided there until declining age admonished him to relinquish the pursuits of the agriculturist and seek a more quiet and sedate life. For a part of the time he resided with Colonel George Crane, near Jersey Shore, Pa., and the other part in the family of Leonard Pfouts, another son-in-law, near Northumberland, Pa, where he died October 29, 1849. He lies buried in the graveyard at Northumberland.

B. F. Pfouts, son of Leonard and Nancy Pfouts, was born at Jersey Shore, Pa., April 12, 1809. He was educated at Rev. John Hayes Grier's private school in his native place. Prior to his removal to this county he was deputy sheriff in Northumberland county. During the years 1857, 1858 and 1859 he was one of the commissioners of Luzerne county. Judge Pfouts died in Hanover January 6, 1874. He married, February 5, 1841, Mary Frances Sively. She is the daughter of George Sively, a native of Easton, Pa., where he was born April 30, 1789. He died in Hanover township, in this county, February 5, 1854. He was the son of George Sively, M. D., who came to this country from Germany when a young man. His wife was Jane Baldwin, whom he married in Philadelphia. He was a surgeon in the French army. He died near Easton December 12, 1812. The mother of Mrs. Pfouts was Frances Stewart, a daughter of Lieutenant Lazarus Stewart, jr. He was born in Lancaster county, Pa.; married Dorcas Hopkins; came to Hanover with his cousin, Captain Lazarus Stewart, about 1770; was lieutenant of the Hanover company; was in the battle and massacre of Wyoming, and was killed there July 3, 1778. He was the son of Alexander Stewart, who was the son of Lazarus Stewart, the emigrant. Judge Pfouts left to survive him one son—George Sively Pfouts, who was born in Hanover March 5, 1842. His first wife was Emma Quick, a daughter of Thomas Quick. She died February 23, 1873. He has since married Fanny A. Eckrote, a daughter of Peter A. Eckrote.

DENNIS ALEXANDER McQUILLAN.

Dennis Alexander McQuillan, who was admitted to the bar of Luzerne county, Pa., June 21, 1871, was a native of Wilkes-Barre, where he was born September 25, 1846. His father, Dennis McQuillan, for some years a school director of this city, was born in Cork, Ireland. His mother, Elizabeth McQuillan (*nee* McDonald) was born in county Louth, Ireland. D. A. McQuillan was educated in the public schools of this city, Dana's academy, and Yale college, graduating from the latter institution in the class of 1869. He read law with Stanley Woodward, and practiced in this city until 1872, when he removed to Portland, Conn., where he practiced his profession until his death, September 4, 1886. He married, August 27, 1879, Kate McKinley, a daughter of Archibald McKinley, a native of county Antrim, Ireland. Her mother, Eliza McKinley (*nee* Anderson) was born in the same place. Mr. and Mrs. McQuillan have had three children, Charles McQuillan being the only one who survives.

WESLEY S. WILMARTH.

Wesley S. Wilmarth, who was admitted to the bar of Luzerne county, Pa., October 16, 1871, was a native of Harford, Susquehanna county, Pa., where he was born October 7, 1834. He worked as a boy and man on his father's farm, and subsequently entered the law office of W. H. Jessup, at Montrose, with a view of fitting himslf for the legal profession. When the late civil war broke out he was about one of the first to enter the service. At the close of the war he returned to Montrose, and subsequently came to Scranton in 1870, when he entered the law office of Hand & Post, and there completed his studies. He died in Scranton May 8, 1875, leaving a widow to survive him.

WILLIAM VANDERBELT MYERS.

William Vanderbelt Myers, who was admitted to the bar of Luzerne county, Pa., February 13, 1872, was a son of the late Thomas Myers (see page 650) and Elizabeth C. Myers (*nee* Vanderbelt), his wife. He was born in Kingston May 31, 1850. He was educated at Saunders Institute, Philadelphia, and read law in this city with T. H. B. Lewis. He died September 24, 1874. He was an unmarried man.

JAMES BRYSON.

James Bryson, who was admitted to the bar of Luzerne county, Pa., March 21, 1872, was a native of Minersville, Pa. He read law in Columbia county, and was admitted to the bar there in December, 1869. He was district attorney of Columbia county while residing there. He was a son of John and Catharine (Gorrell) Bryson, natives of Ireland, who, coming to this country, were married in Philadelphia, from whence they removed to Minersville. The mother died at Harrison, Schuylkill county, Pa., but the father is still living and resides in Philadelphia. Mr. Bryson practiced law in Hazleton for a number of years, and in 1879 was the candidate for district attorney of Luzerne county on the labor ticket, but was defeated by Alfred Darte, the candidate of the republican party. He died at Philipsburg, Pa., in 1887. Hon. William Bryson, of Centralia, Pa., was his brother.

IVAN THOMAS RUTH.

Ivan Thomas Ruth was admitted to the bar of Luzerne county, Pa., October 28, 1872. He was a native of Forestville, Bucks county, Pa., where he was born June 18, 1847. He was the son of Jesse Ruth, a native of Montgomery county, Pa., where he was born in 1810. I. T. Ruth was educated in his native county and at Millersville, Pa., normal school, from which he graduated in 1866. He read law with George Lear, at Doylestown, Pa., where he was first admitted to practice. While following his profession in this county he resided at Scranton. He subsequently removed to Delmar, Iowa, where he died November 19, 1878. He was an unmarried man.

EUGENE W. SIMRELL.

Eugene W. Simrell was admitted to the bar of Luzerne county, Pa., June 4, 1874. His great-grandfather, William Simrell, emigrated with his family from Ireland and settled in Rhode Island. His grandfather, Nathaniel Simrell, son of William Simrell, was born in Rhode Island; married Lydia Wall; moved from Rhode Island and settled in Scott township, Luzerne (now Lackawanna) county, about the year 1800. Warren W. Simrell, son of Nathaniel Simrell and father of E. W. Simrell, was born in Scott township, and married Frances C. Decker, daughter of Stephen and Louisa (Giddings) Decker. E. W. Simrell was born in Scott township October 3, 1851. He received his education in the common schools of Scott township, Gardner's commercial school,

Scranton, Wyoming seminary, and at the Bloomsburg and Mansfield normal schools. In 1873 he entered the Albany, N. Y., law school, from which institution he graduated in 1874 with the degree of LL. B. He opened a law office in Scranton the same year. In 1875 he was appointed by the United States Circuit Court a commissioner for the western district of Pennsylvania, which position he held up to 1880. In 1879 he was elected district attorney of Lackawanna county. He was a married man.

HARRISON WRIGHT.

[The following biographical sketch of Harrison Wright was read before the Wyoming Historical and Geological Society May 8, 1885, by George B. Kulp, Esq., Historiographer. We insert it entire.]

> "Yea, hope and despondency, pleasure and pain,
> We mingle together in sunshine and rain;
> And the smiles and the tears, the songs and the dirge,
> Still follow each other like surge upon surge."

At the last regular meeting of this organization Harrison Wright sat with us, to all outward appearances in the full bloom of perfect health. His unselfishly ambitious love for the pursuits coming within the scope of this organization, making it impossible for us, during years past, to think of the organization without thinking of him as its most ardent friend and principal sustainer, was apparent in almost everything done at that meeting and noted in the minutes of its proceedings which have just been read to us. He was then as hopeful and enthusiastic as he was active and energetic. In every project the society looked to him, often for leadership, always for generous and important assistance. His natural talent for historical research, perfected by most careful cultivation, was in demand to elucidate the numerous subjects, in the examination and exposition of which this society zealously aims to be a careful student and intelligent teacher. We were with him then, and depending upon him then, as we had been with him and dependent upon him a hundred times before, and as we fondly hoped and expected to be with him and to depend upon him hundreds of times again. Yet in less that a fortnight he had been summoned to that other world, of which the highest knowledge attainable in this leaves us in darkness penetrable only by the light of the lamp of resignation and faith. It is generally understood that the illness which resulted in his death was caused by the insidious draughts of raw, damp air that found their way into the museum of this society at a time when he was engaged in gathering some details for a report upon its status, which report was his last official communication to us. If anything could, this fact would add to the gratefulness in which we hold his memory as one whose devotion to our society's interests was without a selfish thought, whose services rendered in its behalf were beyond computation in value and who was truly one of the chief pillars of its strength.

Harrison Wright was born in this city July 15, 1850, and was, therefore, at the time of his death, February 20, 1885, not quite thirty-five years of age. That he was enabled in so short a lifetime to accomplish so much, seems at first glance as surprising as it is that a man so full of usefulness and promise should have been called away, when there are so many others the world could much better have spared. That he inherited at least a part of his peculiar enthusiasm and fitness for the work in which he engaged is a conclusion which must force itself upon even those who have least faith in such inheritance, after they shall have informed themselves somewhat of the ancestry from which he sprung. That ancestry identifies the blood which flowed in his veins with that of the moving spirits in the earliest history of our city, county and state; in the primary and progressive developments of the vast mineral resources of this particular section of our great commonwealth; in the grandest unfolding of the sciences and arts in this country, and in various important scientific and patriotic undertakings in other countries. There is nothing particularly original in the manner of the presentation of the interesting facts which, in the performance of my duty as the historiographer of this society, I here follow—the work of compiling them having been well advanced by Harrison Wright himself in his lifetime.

Harrison Wright was the descendant in the sixth generation of John Wright, one of the first settlers of Burlington county,

New Jersey, and who was the first settler at Wrightstown, in that county, being in fact the founder of the village or little town of that name. He came from England in 1681 with William Penn's colony of Quaker immigrants. He held a commission of justice of the peace and captain of the militia under the royal seal of Charles II. A diary kept by this pioneer is still in the possession of the family. Among other things therein recorded it appears that he "subscribed and paid £3 towards building the brick meeting-house." This building is still standing, after a lapse of two hundred years, and was probably the first meeting-house erected in that state. It appears also that he "made the first barrel of cider in the state of New Jersey." The circumstances attending the jubilee over this "first barrel of cider" I must insert. In was an event in the history of the new country. "He invited all his neighbors to partake; they very willingly attended. Duke Fort was appointed tapster, and a merrier assemblage never took place in the neighborhood of Penny Hill, for so Wrightstown was then called." Among the curiosities contained in this old diary I add the following: "The soil is very productive and the earth yields very bountifully, but then, the farmer has poor encouragement, considering that those terrible pests, the wild geese and wild turkeys, destroy almost entirely one's crops." The wife of John Wright was Abigail Crispin, daughter of Silas Crispin, the elder. After the grant of Pennsylvania to William Penn, Silas Crispin was appointed surveyor general, and sailed with William Crispin, his father, John Beryar and Christopher Allen, who were appointed commissioners to go to Pennsylvania with power to purchase lands of the Indians and to select a site for and lay out a great city; but, dying on the voyage, Captain Thomas Holmes was appointed his successor, April 18, 1682. He was a native of Waterford, Ireland, and is said to have served in the fleet under Admiral Penn in the West Indies when a young man. He sailed from the Downs, April 23, accompanied by two sons and two daughters, Silas Crispin, the son of his predecessor in office, and John, the eldest son of James Claypole. Thomas Holmes made his home in Philadelphia, and owned land in Bristol township, Bucks county, Pa., but it is not known that he ever lived there. His daughter Hester married Silas Crispin, who came to America with him. These were the parents of Mrs. Wright. The mother of Silas Crispin, the elder, was a sister of Margaret Jasper, the mother of William Penn, which made him the first cousin of the founder. Samuel Wright, son of John Wright, was born at Wrightstown in 1719 and died in 1781. His wife was Elizabeth Haines, daughter of Caleb Haines, of Evesham. Caleb Wright, son of Samuel Wright, was born at Wrightstown, January 14, 1754. He married Catharine, daughter of John Gardner, in 1779, and removed with his family to the "Susquehanna country" in 1795. He purchased and settled upon a farm in Union township, Luzerne county, Pa., two miles above Shickshinny, where he remained till 1811 and then returned to New Jersey. Mr. and Mrs. Wright lived to a good old age after their removal to New Jersey, and their remains are interred at the Friends' burial-ground at East Branch, Upper Freehold, Monmouth county, N. J. Joseph Wright, son of Caleb Wright, was but a boy of ten years when his father removed from Wrightstown to the Susquehanna country. Previous to the return of his father to New Jersey he had married, and established a small retail store in Plymouth, and he alone of the family remained in our county. He was a resident of the town of Plymouth for more than half a century, and during that long period was intimately connected with its municipal government and was one of its representative men. He was the second person in the mercantile business in Old Plymouth. He, however, continued but a short time in this occupation, afterwards devoting his attention to the interests of his farm. His ancestors for two hundred years had belonged to the Society of Friends; he steadily adhered to the faith of this religious order of people to the hour of his death. Notwithstanding he had been expelled from the society, because he had married outside of the church limits and in direct violation of its discipline, he ever considered himself as one of the order, however, and bound by its formulas and creed. It is, however, somewhat difficult to reconcile his professed religious obligations in view of his conduct in entering the service in the war of 1812. We find him in Captain Halleck's company of Pennsylvania militia on the march for the defense of Baltimore. Patriotism had triumphed over sectarian fealty, the tri-colored cockade usurped the broad-brim. The regiment, however, never saw active service. Mr. Wright married, June 15, 1807, Ellen Hendrick, widow of Moses Wadhams, deceased. She was the daughter of John Hendrick, who was a descendant in the fourth generation of Daniel Hendrick (who was of Haverhill in 1645, and had been of Hampton in 1639) and Dorothy Pike, daughter of John Pike, of Newbury, in 1635. Joseph Wright had three sons. Hendrick Bradley Wright, his eldest, was a very prominent lawyer at the Luzerne bar. He represented Luzerne county in the lower house of the state legislature in the years 1841, 1842, 1843, and the latter year was speaker of that body. In 1844 he was president of the democratic national convention which nominated James K. Polk for the presidency. In 1852, 1853, 1861, 1862, 1863, 1876, 1877, 1878 and 1879, he represented Luzerne county in the national congress. He was the author of "A Practical Treatise on Labor," and "Historical Sketches of Plymouth," his native town. He died in Wilkes-Barre September 2, 1881. Caleb Earl Wright, the second son of Joseph Wright, is still living and resides at Doylestown, Pa. He is also a prominent lawyer. He was president of the first borough council of Doylestown, district attorney of Bucks county, and while a resident of Luzerne county held the office of collector of internal revenue under President Johnson, and was a member of the Pennsylvania constitutional convention of 1874. He is also an ordained minister of the Methodist Episcopal church, and is the author of a novel under the title of "Wyoming," from the press of Harper Brothers, and a romance under the title of "Marcus Blair," published by J. B. Lippincott & Co. The third and youngest son of Joseph Wright was Harrison Wright, the father of the subject of our sketch. He was born at Plymouth January 24, 1815. Perhaps no better estimate of his character can be given than that found in the proceedings of a meeting of the bar of this county held immediately after his death. At this meeting the late John N. Conyngham was president, E. L. Dana secretary, and Warren J. Woodward chairman of the committee on resolutions, which reported as follows: "We are summoned to this meeting under circumstances of most painful interest. We are met to render our professional tribute to the memory of Harrison Wright. Death within a few years past has made sad havoc in our ranks. Recently, and at brief intervals, we have been required to record the successive loss of Chester Butler, Luther Kidder and Horatio W. Nicholson. They were stricken down in the very prime of their usefulness and in the very summer of their years. The grasp of the common destiny of us all was unrelentingly and unrelaxingly fastened upon them in the midst of the strongest ties to life—in the enjoyment of high social and professional position—of the public confidence and regard—of the reputation that results from high office and great wealth. But in no instance has the blow fallen so severely upon us as it has fallen now. Mr. Wright has been constantly among us—with the exception of a few months passed in the legislature during the year 1855, he had devoted himself during almost twenty years to the practice of the law. Almost every man who is gathered here, from the very day of his admission into the profession, has been habituated to his presence in our courts. We have all been under obligations to him for assistance and advice, most readily and most gratefully rendered. We have felt deep obligations to him for the kindly spirit which has characterized the intercourse of the members of the bar, and which in a great measure was created by his counsel and example. It is due to his reputation, as well as to ourselves, that regret for his early death and respect for his memory and sympathy for his surviving family should be expressed by the members of that profession which he loved and honored and illustrated and adorned throughout his life. Mr. Wright was a thorough lawyer; deeply imbued with the profound principles which form the fountains of our legal system, he kept himself constantly familiar with the current exposition of those principles by the court. His acquaintance with the details and forms of business was most accurate and minute. In his whole heavy and long-continued practice he was, in every case, untiring, indubitable and indefatigable. In the preparation and trial of causes he was laborious, wary, methodical, accurate and prompt. And he was a most accomplished advocate. In all the long history of our old court house its walls have resounded to no eloquence more attractive or more effective than his. An entire generation of the people of our whole county must pass away before the memory of his fine person, his impressive manners and his prompt tones shall be forgotten. In the varied and growing business interests of the community the premature death of Mr. Wright will be severely felt. Born and bred in the Wyoming valley, his sympathies and his heart were here. To promote the prosperity of the county of Luzerne his time and his purse were always given. In the very best and most enlarged sense of the phrase, he was a man o public spirit. In the improvements made and progress around us the mark of his hand and intellect is everywhere visible. To the erection of our churches; to the schemes for the development of our mineral resources; to the organization of our gas company; to the measures requisite to secure the completion of the North Branch canal; to the efforts to extend to this county the general mining law, productive as this has been of such wonderful results; to the establishment of our law library; to every feasible scheme for the advancement of the material interests of our community, his influence and liberality have been ungrudgingly and effectively extended. He was a peculiarly unselfish man. And he threw into every effort for the public good, as he threw into every professional struggle in which his sympathies were aroused, all the astonishing vigor, energy and enthusiasm of his character, regardless of individual results for himself. It was a peculiarity of Mr. Wright's position that he numbered among the members of the profession an unusually large proportion of personal friends. His relations with many members of the bar were of the most intimate and confidential kind. With almost all of them these relations were marked by uniform courtesy and cordiality. He was a true, faithful, reliable and active friend, and no considerations of personal interest or personal ease ever induced him to abandon the man whom he had promised to serve or who held a claim for his service. In every relation of life Mr. Wright had upright and single aims. He was a resolute man. He pursued boldly and unflinchingly the path of duty open before him. And with his extraordinary abilities, his attractive and impressive manners, his clear, quick, sound judgment, the unbounded confidence of the community in his honor, integrity and faith, his steadiness of nerve and his strength of purpose, he wielded an influence upon systems and events around him almost without parallel or example. For reasons thus hastily and imperfectly sketched, we do

"*Resolve*, That we have learned the fact of the death of Harrison Wright, Esq., on August 25, 1856, with feelings of deep and abiding regret. His loss will be felt as an individual grief by each one of us, connected as we have been with him in relations of intimate social and professional intercourse, but we bow in submission to that Power that 'doeth all things well.' That we most cordially recognize the varied claims which Mr. Wright in his lifetime established upon our esteem, respect and gratitude; for his courtesy and kindness of heart; for his strict honor and manliness of character; for his great abilities, his learning and his eloquence; for his abiding love of his profession; for his laborious performance of every duty of an active and useful life, and for his unselfish devotion to the public good, we will cherish his memory while our own lives shall last."

Thus was the character of Mr. Wright portrayed by those who had the most intimate relations with him and who knew him best. [Harrison Wright left the following children to survive him: Harrison Wright, the subject of this sketch; Josephine Wright, who intermarried with Arthur W. Hillman; Augusta McClintock Wright, now deceased; Jessie L. Wright, now deceased, intermarried with W. J. Harvey, who left to survive her one son, Robert R. Harvey; Sarah H. Wright, who intermarried with G. W. Guthrie, M. D.; and Jacob Ridgway Wright.]

The wife of Harrison Wright, sr., and the mother of the subject of our sketch, was Emily Cist, daughter of Jacob Cist, and a descendant of Charles Cist, who was the son of a well-to-do German merchant, who had been attracted to St. Petersburg, Russia, at the beginning of the eighteenth century by the liberal inducements offered to foreigners by Peter the Great, and who there met and married Anna Maria Thomassen. Their second child, Charles Cist, was born in St. Petersburg, on August 15, 1738, and was baptized on the 21st of the same month in the Evangelical Lutheran church of St. Peter, in that city. At a very early age he showed such a fondness for and application to his studies that his father gave him every advantage which the schools of St. Petersburg at that period afforded, and already on April 23, 1755, at the age of sixteen, we find him matriculated as *studiosus medicinae* at the University of Halle, on the Saale, one of the leading universities of Germany. Owing to the incompleteness of the records of the medical faculty of the university at that time, it is impossible to state now how long he remained there or whether or not he took a degree, though it is likely he did take the latter, as he was later a practicing physician in St. Petersburg and had there a large apothecary and drug business. The liberal policy adopted by the far-seeing Peter towards professional and scientific men, as well as to the foreign merchants located in Russia, insured protection to Charles Cist in the early days of Catharine; and the income of his business enabled him to amass considerable property and to collect the finest cabinet of minerals in the city of St. Petersburg, and one whose rarities the highest dignitary of the church thought worthy of a Sunday visit to examine. But when his success was at its highest a change came. Filled with liberal ideas too far advanced to be tolerated in despotic Russia, he joined with others in a proposed revolution, which, being discovered by the authorities, was suppressed, his property confiscated, and he, in 1767, an exile at Omsk, in Siberia, from whence he escaped and fled, a political refugee, to the hospitable shores of America, arriving in Philadelphia, in the ship Crawford, on October 25, 1773. Directly after his arrival he met Henry Miller, who was at that time publishing a German paper in Philadelphia, entitled *Pennsylvanischer Staatsbote*, and who, desiring some competent person to translate articles from English exchanges into German for the *Staatsbote*, offered the position to Charles Cist until he should become acquainted in Philadelphia and acquire enough money to start in his regular business. The offer was accepted, and the printing business pleased him so well that he remained for two years with Miller, and in December, 1775, entered into copartnership with Melchior Styner, who had been Miller's foreman, and they established a printing office of their own. At the beginning of our revolutionary troubles this firm published a newspaper in the German language, but not receiving the necessary support and encouragement it was discontinued in April, 1776. Many pamphlets on the critical questions of those disturbed times were issued from the press of Styner & Cist, among others Thomas Paine's "American Crisis." During the war Styner and Cist were both enrolled as members of the Third Battalion of Pennsylvania militia, and on June 20, 1777, Charles Cist took the voluntary oath of allegiance and fidelity. Upon returning to Philadelphia after the evacuation of the British, the firm continued the printing business, and in the year 1779, besides publishing "Regulations for the Order and Discipline of the Troops of the United States" and a number of other pamphlets, they again commenced the publication of a German newspaper. In 1781 the copartnership, after existing for nearly six years—years most eventful in the history of this country—was by consent dissolved. Henry Miller, instead of discouraging the formation of this firm, seems to have aided and assisted in every way; and in after years when Cist had gained a competency and Styner was still struggling along, Henry Miller died and left the fortune, or a large part of it, which he had accumulated during a busy life, to Styner. In 1784 Charles Cist, together with Seddon, John O'Connor, and others, started an English newspaper entitled *The American Herald and General Advertiser*, but for want of encouragement it was discontinued; and at a meeting of the proprietors, held July 3, 1784, it was resolved that the publication of the paper should cease and the subscription money be refunded to the subscribers. On October 1, 1789, Charles Cist, together with Seddon, William Spottswood, James Trenchard, and the well-known Matthew Carey, started the *Columbian Magazine*, a monthly miscellany. Within the year 1789 Trenchard became the sole proprietor, and the subsequent numbers were published by him alone. Mr. Cist published between the years 1781-1805 a large number of religious, political and educational works, in at least four languages, among which, in German, in the year 1783, was "Wahrheit und guter Rath an die Einwohner Deutschlands, besonders in Hessen," and in 1789, "Der Amerikanische Stadt und Land Kalender;" and continued in the threefold capacity of printer, publisher and bookseller until his death in 1805. In this latter year he published, among other works, a reprint of Rev. Andrew Fuller's "The Gospel its own Witness." Mr. Cist was a member of the German Society of Pennsylvania; in 1782 was a member of the school committee, and in 1795 secretary of the association. He was also the secretary of the —— —— Fire Insurance Company

of Philadelphia, and announces in May, 1793, that this company
had procured an apparatus to save people from burning houses;
it consisted of an elevated basket. Under the administration of
the elder Adams he received the contract for printing official
documents. In the year 1800 he went to Washington and arranged at great expense a printing office and book bindery, purchased real estate, built several houses, and believed he had a
good, remunerative position, but it was not long after the victory
of the democratic party in 1801 that he lost his privileges and
returned to Philadelphia poorer than when he left. In writing to
his son Jacob in regard to his losses in Washington, under date
of February 7, 1803, he says: "Misfortunes follow one upon another and bear the more severely upon me at my time of life
when I, in a manner, must begin the world anew. But I trust in
Providence, and the conscience of the rectitude of my actions
supports me under the complicated evils that the loss of my place
has brought upon me. Heaven forgive my enemies; they have
done me more harm than they intended." In a back room of his
printing office he had arranged a small laboratory to which it
was his delight to withdraw, when business permitted, to experiment with chemicals. Here he discovered and patented colors
for dyeing from the quercitron bark; he manufactured on a small
scale cakes of water-color paints, and prepared, by grinding,
paints for oil painters. It was here, too, that he tested the "black
stone" discovered on the Lehigh by Philip Ginter and taken to
Philadelphia by Colonel Weiss, and which he pronounced to be
anthracite coal. He was one of the founders and largest stockholders of the "Lehigh Coal Mine Company," which was founded
in 1792. He died of apoplexy while on a visit to his brother-in-
law, Colonel Weiss, at Fort Allen, on December 1, 1805, and lies
buried in the Moravian burial-ground at Bethlehem. He was
sanguine in his disposition, punctual and of most rigid integrity
in his business relations, courtly in his manners, and yet of most
modest demeanor, which recommended him to all classes with
whom he came in contact. He was unassuming and unpreten-
tious, and yet his university education and his knowledge of the
literature of several languages rendered him welcome among the
savants of the then metropolis of the new world. The purity and

simplicity of his character was at all times a source of admiration with those who knew him, and when his trials and losses came he had the sympathy of every one. Even some of those who were the cause of them afterwards repented of the action which they had taken and tried to retrieve it by kindness to his son while he was in Washington. A brother and two sisters residing in Russia survived him, all of whom were married, and their descendants are to-day scattered throughout the length and breadth of Russia. He married, June 7, 1781, Mary, daughter of John Jacob and Rebecca Weiss, who was born in Philadelphia June 22, 1762, and had eight children, all of who were living at the time of his death.

The father of Mrs. Charles Cist, John Jacob Weiss, was born in the village of Wahlheim, near Bietigheim, in the kingdom of Wurtemberg, Germany, on July 20, 1721. His parents were John Jacob and Mary Elizabeth Weiss. He was confirmed in the Lutheran church of his native village in 1736, and in 1740 emigrated to America, landing in Philadelphia in September of that year. On October 24, 1746, he married Rebecca Cox, of Swedish descent. She was born November 23, 1725, in Passayunk township, now in Philadelphia, and reared in the Lutheran religion. Her father, Peter Cox, who died in January, 1751, aged sixty-three years, was the grandson of Peter Lawson Koch, who came from Sweden in 1641 with the third Swedish colony, and settled upon the Delaware. On January 8, 1749, when the United Brethren were favored with a particularly blessed day, the occasion being a visit of Brother John (Bishop Spangenberg) and others, John Jacob Weiss and his wife Rebecca were received into the Brethren's association and admitted to the holy communion. In the month of June, 1750, he purchased a hundred acres of land in Long valley, in the present county of Monroe, partly on Head's creek. He took the oath of allegiance to George II April 12, 1750, before Chief Justice Allen, and to the United States July 2, 1778. Mr. Weiss was a surgeon, and had his place of business for many years on Second street, Philadelphia. He died September 22, 1788, and was buried next day in the Moravian burial ground, in Philadelphia. His wife, Rebecca, died July 3, 1808. The old Moravian record says: "She was a communicant of our church and a simple, genuine follower of the Lord." Mr. and Mrs. Weiss had eleven children, of whom Mary, the tenth child, became the wife of Charles Cist. She was born in Philadelphia June 22, 1762, and was baptized the 25th of the same month by Rev. George Neisser.

It may not be out of place in this sketch of our late associate to portray the character of Colonel Jacob Weiss, the brother of Mary Cist. He was born in Philadelphia September 1, 1750, and after the commencement of hostilities between the mother country and the colonies he entered the continental service in the first company of Philadelphia Volunteers, commanded by Captain Cadwalader, and after having performed a tour of duty, he was, at the earnest recommendation of General Mifflin, then acting quartermaster general, to whom he had served an apprenticeship in the mercantile line, and who knew him to be a trusty and proficient accountant, appointed a deputy quartermaster general under him, and subsequently under General Greene, in which station he remained until General Greene took command of the southern army, October 30, 1780; the admirable arrangement of the quartermaster general's department and the able management of General Greene, enabled the army to move with facility and dispatch. The means possessed by the commissary's department were inadequate to supply the army's wants and frequently caused great distress, and often rendered its condition deplorable. The financial embarrassment which followed upon the rapid depreciation of the continental money was a greater bane to the cause of the patriots and a more insidious enemy than the powerful foe which confronted them. Prices rose as money sunk in value. The commissaries found it extremely difficult to purchase supplies for the army, for the people refused to exchange their articles for the almost worthless paper. At the close of the year 1779 thirty dollars in paper was only equal in purchasing value to one of specie. After the defeat of the American army in the battle of Brandywine, September 11, 1777, the road to Philadelphia was open to the enemy. There was great consternation among the people when they heard of the approach of the British army. Mrs. Weiss frequently spoke of the excitement that followed; every one tried to get away; fabulous prices were paid for all kinds of conveyances. Her husband was with the army, and she was left to her own resources. She was fortunate in procuring a conveyance, and taking with her the wearing apparel of the family and a few household articles, started with her family for Bristol. Upon her arrival there she found the hotel used as a hospital for the wounded soldiers. The sight of these greatly distressed her, as she said it was the most sickening sight she ever beheld. In the following month Colonel Weiss sent his family to Easton. During those perilous times he was almost constantly attached to and followed the various and often sudden movements of the main army, which proved a very harassing and arduous service. By the advice of General Greene, who, in his farewell letter to him, highly and affectionately commended him for the faithful performance of the various duties imposed upon him, he accepted the appointment of assistant deputy quartermaster general, at Easton, for the county of Northampton, in the fall of 1780, in which capacity he served until the close of the war. In June, 1780, Colonel Weiss moved his family from Easton to Nazareth. After closing up the business of his department in 1783, he retired from the public service, and purchased a tract of land on the Lehigh river, north of the Blue mountain, including the broad flats, upon which is located the town of Weissport, Lehigh county, Pa. This was the site selected by the Moravian missionaries in 1754 for their mission, when the land on the Mahoning became impoverished. Here they erected dwellings for their Indian converts and built a new chapel. To this wild and secluded spot he brought his family in the spring of 1786. The inhabitants were few and simple in their habits, unburdened by the restraints and conventionalities of modern life. Nor had they need of many of the things we now consider necessary to our health and comfort. An umbrella was considered a great novelty, and Mrs. Weiss at first attracted some attention by carrying one on a rainy day. The Colonel's residence was built near the site upon which Fort Allen (named in honor of Chief Justice Allen) formerly stood. "It was in the beginning of the month of January, 1756," writes Dr. Franklin, "when we set out upon this business of building forts. The Indians had burned Gnadenhütten, a village settled by the Moravians, and massacred the inhabitants; but the place was thought a good situation for one of the forts. Our first work was to bury more effectually the dead we found there. The next morning our fort was planned and marked out, the circumference measuring four hundred and fifty-five feet, which would require as many palisades to be made, one with another, of a foot in diameter each. Each piece made three palisades of eighteen feet long, pointed at one end. When they were set up, our carpenters built a platform of boards all around within, about six feet high, for the men to stand on when they fired through the loop-holes. We had one swivel-gun, which we mounted on one of the angles and fired it as soon as fixed, to let the Indians know, if any were within hearing, that we had such pieces, and thus our fort (if that name may be given to so miserable a stockade) was finished within a week, though it rained so hard every other day that the men could not well work." Within the enclosure around the Colonel's house was the well, which was dug inside the fort by Franklin's direction, and long remained as a memorial of the old Indian war, and also testified to what "Poor Richard" knew about digging wells. It continued to furnish an abundant supply of pure water until it was destroyed by the devastating flood, which swept through the valley of the Lehigh in 1862. The bell of the old Moravian chapel was found near this well by one of the workmen while digging a post-hole. Under the energetic management of Colonel Weiss the flats around his dwelling and the adjacent hills were rapidly cleared up and cultivated, while the surrounding forests furnished an abundant supply of lumber for his mills. To protect the soil from floods a fringe of trees was left along the bank of the river, and the Lombardy poplar was planted along the roads and around his dwelling to furnish shade. While thus engaged in transforming the wild glens of the Lehigh into fertile fields and changing these savage haunts into the peaceful abodes of civilized life, he probably realized that "peace as well as war has its victories." About this time he was also engaged in business with Judge Hollenback, trading under the firm name of Weiss & Hollenback. This partnership commenced as early as 1785 and continued as late as 1788. In the year 1791 an event occurred, in itself apparently trifling, but fraught with momentous results to the future interests of this section of country. This was the discovery of coal in the Lehigh district. The story of its discovery is doubtless familiar to many. Nevertheless, as Colonel Weiss was prominently connected with its discovery and first introduction to the public, a brief reference to the same may not be amiss. A hunter of the name of Philip Ginter had taken up his residence in that district of country. He built himself a rough cabin and supported his family by hunting in the dense and primitive forests, abounding in game. On the occasion to which we are now referring, Ginter had spent the whole day in the woods without meeting with the least success. As the shades of evening gathered around he found himself on the summit of Sharp mountain, several miles distant from home; night was rapidly approaching, and a storm of rain was advancing, which caused him to quicken his pace. As he bent his course homeward through the woods he stumbled over the root of a tree which had recently fallen. Among the black dirt turned up by the roots he discovered pieces of black stone. He had heard persons speak of stone-coal as existing in these mountains, and concluding that this might be a portion of that stone-coal, of which he had heard, he took a specimen with him to his cabin, and the next day carried it to Colonel Jacob Weiss. The Colonel, who was alive to the subject, took the specimen with him to Philadelphia and submitted it to the inspection of John Nicholson and Michael Hillegas, and also to Charles Cist, before referred to, the brother-in-law of Colonel Weiss, who ascertained its nature and qualities, and told the Colonel to pay Ginter for his discovery upon his pointing out the place where he found the coal. This was readily done by acceding to Ginter's proposal of getting, through the regular forms of the land office, the title for a small tract of land on which there was a mill-site, and which he supposed had never been taken up, and of which he was unhappily deprived by the claim of a prior survey. Messrs. Hillegas, Cist, Weiss, Henry, and some others soon after formed themselves into what was called the Lehigh Coal Mine Company, but without a charter of incorporation, and took up about ten thousand acres of till then unlocated land, which included the opening at Summit hill, and embracing about five-sixths of the

coal lands of the Lehigh Coal and Navigation Company. The
coal mine company proceeded to open the mines; they found
coal in abundance, but like the man who caught the elephant,
they hardly knew what to do with it. Between the coal mine
and the distant market lay a vast expanse of wild and rugged
mountains and valleys. The Lehigh river, in the season of low
water, in its then unimproved state, almost defied the floating of
a canoe over its rocky bed. There was an abundance of wood
at low prices and no demand for stone coal. A rough road,
however, was constructed from the mines to the Lehigh, about
nine miles in length. After many fruitless attempts to get coal
to market by this road and the Lehigh river, the Lehigh Coal
Mine Company became tired of the experiment and suffered
their property to lie idle for many years. But Colonel Weiss,
notwithstanding the inauspicious outlook, determined that the
coal should at least be introduced to the acquaintance of the
public. He filled his saddle-bags from time to time and rode
around among the blacksmiths in the lower counties, earnestly
soliciting them to try it. A few accepted the proffered supplies
and used it with partial success. The rest threw it aside as soon
as the Colonel was out of sight, quietly remarking that they
thought he must be getting crazy. William Henry, then engaged
in manufacturing muskets under a contract from Governor Mifflin, employed a blacksmith residing in Nazareth, and prevailed
upon him to try to make use of this coal, but after three or four
days' trial, altering his fireplace frequently, but all to no purpose,
became impatient and in a passion threw all the coal he had in
his shop into the street, telling Mr. Henry that everybody was
laughing at him for being such a fool as to try to make stones
burn, and that they said Mr. Henry was a bigger fool to bring
those stones to Nazareth. The coal mine company, desiring to
render their property available, granted very favorable leases to
several parties successively, only to have them abandoned in turn
when the difficulties and losses of the enterprise became manifest. The project was allowed to rest until the Lehigh Coal and
Navigation Company, by building dams and sluices and otherwise improving the navigation of the Lehigh, and constructing
a good road between the mine and river, succeeded in sending

coal to the Philadelphia market in sufficient quantities and at prices which at length attracted the attention of the public. In the year 1820 three hundred and sixty-five tons of coal were sent to market. This quantity of coal completely stocked the market and was with difficulty disposed of. Colonel Weiss, having had the misfortune to be deprived of his eyesight for about twenty years before his death, and later becoming extremely deaf, which misfortune he bore with exemplary resignation, did not enjoy seeing and being fully apprised of the fruits of his labor and ardent desires. He was a man of liberal education, strong minded, remarkable memory, and generous disposition, esteemed and respected by all who knew him. He died at Weissport January 9, 1839. Nearly three score years have passed away since he was compelled, by reason of advancing age and failing eyesight, to relinquish the active duties of life. How marvelous the results which have since taken place in the growth of that enterprise of which he was the pioneer!

Jacob Cist, eldest son of Charles and Mary Cist, was born in Philadelphia, on March 13, 1782. On September 5, 1794, when only a little over twelve years of age, his father sent him to the Moravian boarding school, at Nazareth, in Northampton county, Pa., where he remained three years, leaving on June 10, 1797, after completing the established course of study at that time required, which, besides a thorough study of all the ordinary English branches, included a knowledge of Greek, Latin, German, and French. His love for and talent of easily acquiring languages he seems to have inherited from his father, who was an accomplished and enthusiastic linguist, and the knowledge derived from a three years' course under competent teachers was the groundwork upon which he perfected himself in after years. Here, too, under the old French drawing-master, M. A. Benade, he acquired a considerable knowledge of drawing and painting. He was particularly happy in catching a likeness. On his return to Philadelphia, in 1797, he assisted his father in the printing office, devoting his spare hours to study, and in the year 1800, when his father purchased property in Washington city and erected a printing office there, he went to that place to take charge of the office. Upon his father's relinquishing the business in Washington he determined to locate there, and applying for a clerkship secured one in the postoffice department, which he retained from the fall of 1800 until he removed to Wilkes-Barre, Pennsylvania, in the year 1808. So well satisfied were Mr. Granger and his successors with the capabilities of Mr. Cist that upon his arrival in this city he was appointed postmaster, which office he retained until his death in 1825, thus having been for a quarter of a century in the employ of the postoffice department. His father, writing to him in 1802, says: "As it is to your good conduct in the federal city that I chiefly ascribe the confidence the postmaster general places in you and the kindness he shows in procuring you an advantageous post, I cannot refrain of recommending you the same conduct in your future stages of life as the surest means of forwarding yourself in the world with credit and reputation." His spare time in Washington he appears to have devoted principally to painting and literature. He has left a good picture of Mr. Jefferson and an admirable copy of Gilbert Stuart's portrait of Mrs. Madison, which she permitted him to paint, and a number of miniatures. Being obliged to mix his own paints, and not finding a mill to suit, he invented one and patented it in the year 1803.

He was a contributor to *The Literary Magazine* as early as 1804, and to Charles Miner's paper in Wilkes-Barre. Mr. Miner writes, under date of November 28, 1806: "I am charmed with your piece on 'Morning.' It possesses all the life, spirit, and variety of that charming season;" and December 26, 1806: "Your 'Noon' is in type. If you are but a young courtier at the shrine of the muses, you have been unusually fortunate in obtaining their approbation;" and February 19, 1807: "Your last letter containing your 'Night' was very welcome. The description is truly natural and elegant, and its only fault was its shortness. I hope you will often favor me with your poetic effusions or prosaic lucubrations;" and at other times he writes: "Your four pieces on 'Morning,' 'Noon,' 'Evening,' and 'Night' have been warmly commended by a literary friend in Philadelphia." Again: "From the friendship shown you by the muses, I suspect you visit their ladyships more than just 'a vacant hour now and then.' So great a portion of their favor as they have bestowed on you, I should not suppose was to be obtained but by a close and constant courtship. I thank you for the communication and shall always be happy to have my paper improved by the production of your fancy. Your address to your candle is excellent and shall appear next week."

He contributed to the *Port Folio* from 1808 to 1816. The publishers, writing to him in 1809, say: "We have to acknowledge many interesting and valuable communications from you. We rank you among our most valuable correspondents and will hope for a continuance of your favors." His communications to this magazine were many and varied; at one time it was poetry, at another the description of some new machine, sometimes over the letters "J. C.," and others over the letter "C." Many of the old settlers will still remember his sketches with pen and pencil of "Solomon's Falls" and "Buttermilk Falls." In the May number, 1809, is a drawing and description by him of Mr. Birde's "Columbian Spinster;" in the March number, 1811, a drawing and description of "Eve's Cotton Gin," and in the October number, 1812, an "Ode on Hope."

Jacob Cist was married on August 25, 1807, by the Rev. Ard Hoyt, to Sarah Hollenback, daughter of Judge Matthias Hollenback, of Wilkes-Barre, Pa., whom Charles Miner at that time described as "a charming little girl, apparently about sixteen years old, the natural rose on her cheek heightened by exercise, and a sweet smile playing about her lips." On her mother's side she was descended from old New England stock. Mrs. Hollenback's father, Peleg Burritt, Jr., was a grandson of Ensign Stephen Burritt, who, according to Hinman, was "a famous Indian fighter," and commissary general to the army in King Phillip's war, and his father, William Burritt, the first of the name in this country, was an original settler in Stratford, Connecticut, prior to 1650. Her mother, whose maiden name was Deborah Beardslee, was the granddaughter of Ebenezer Booth, the son of Richard Booth, by his wife Elizabeth (Hawley,) who was living in Stratford in the year 1640. Her father's grandfather was a landholder in Pennsylvania as early as 1729.

After his marriage he returned to Washington and remained there until the spring of 1808, when he removed to Wilkes-

Barre and entered into partnership with his father-in-law, under the firm name of Hollenback & Cist, which existed a number of years. For three years Mr. and Mrs. Cist lived at Mill Creek, but in the fall of 1811 they moved into their new house on Bank street, now River street, in this city. At an early day Jacob Cist's attention was attracted towards the uses of anthracite coal. He was a boy of ten years when his father experimented on the Lehigh coal and might possibly have seen him at work. He must often have heard his father conversing with Colonel Weiss, both in Philadelphia and Bethlehem, on the feasability of opening their mines and making a market for the Lehigh coal long before he was old enough to appreciate the importance of the undertaking or the disadvantages under which these pioneers in the coal trade labored in persuading people of the practicability of using stone-coal as a fuel, though in after years, by observation and study, he saw its importance and he learned by a practical experience the labor and disappointments attendant on its introduction to use. As early as the year 1805 he conceived the idea of manufacturing a mineral black for printers' ink, leather lacquer, blacking, etc., from the Lehigh coal, and the results of his experiments were secured to him by patent in the year 1808. In regard to his discovery Chief Justice Gibson wrote the following letter to Thomas Cooper, who published it in the *Emporium of Arts and Sciences*, Vol. II, new series, page 477:

"WILKES-BARRE, Feb. 23d, 1814.

"DEAR SIR—I send you a likeness of one of your friends. There is nothing remarkable in it, except that it is done with the stone-coal of this place instead of India ink. It is prepared for use by rubbing a bit of it on a fine hard stone in gum water, just thick enough to hold the particles in suspension. It is then laid on in the usual way with a camel hair pencil. By a comparison with a drawing in India ink you will, I doubt not, give the preference to the coal, as it will be found free from a brownish cast, always perceivable in the former. The harshness observable in the enclosed drawing arises from the extreme badness of the pencil I was obliged to use and not from the quality of the ink, (which is susceptible of the greatest softness). The coal is found to be superior to lamp or ivory black for paint, printers' ink, and blacking leather. It also makes the best writing ink for records that has yet been discovered. The color is deeper, and is not in the least effected by the oxy-muriatic acid or any other chemical agent, and must remain unaltered by time. The application of coal to these purposes was discovered by Jacob Cist, of this place. He has obtained a patent.

Very sincerely, your friend,
JOHN B. GIBSON.

Thomas Cooper, Esq."

To this letter Judge Cooper added the following note:
"The only objection to the preceding account of the uses to which stone-coal may be put, is, whatever mucilaginous substance be used to fix it on the paper, water can wash it away.

"But that it will afford a coloring matter, unattackable by any acid and unalterable by any time, cannot be doubted.

"The discovery is of importance.   T. C."

This patent was considered to be worth upwards of five thousand dollars, but a number of law-suits, arising from a constant infringement of it by manufacturers, so annoyed Mr. Cist that he was glad to dispose of it for a less sum. It is said that after the destruction of the patent office records by fire, some one else took out a patent for the same idea and is now working under it. After Mr. Cist had removed to Wilkes-Barre he made a study of the adjacent coal-fields, especially at the mines of the Smith Brothers, at Plymouth, and the old Lord Butler opening. He determined upon entering into the mining of coal as a business as soon as he should feel satisfied that the right time had come to introduce it in the cities in large enough quantities to make the adventure a profitable one. That time came in the year 1813, when the British squadron held both the Delaware and Chesapeake bays in a state of blockade. In the spring of that year he undertook to introduce it in Baltimore and Philadelphia. The former project proved a failure, but in the summer and fall he sent several wagon loads to Binney & Ronaldson, in Philadelphia, and their success appeared to encourage the mining of anthracite upon a larger basis, so that in December of that year

Jacob Cist, Charles Miner, and John Robinson secured a lease from the old Lehigh coal mine company of their property on the Lehigh river, near Mauch Chunk. Mr. Miner, in writing in the year 1833 to Samuel I. Packer on the formation of this co-partnership, says: "Jacob Cist, of Wilkes-Barre, my intimate and much lamented friend, had derived from his father a few shares of the Lehigh coal company's stock. Sitting by a glowing anthracite fire one evening in his parlor, conversation turned to the Lehigh coal, and we resolved to make an examination of the mines at Mauch Chunk and the Lehigh river to satisfy ourselves whether it would be practicable to convey coal from thence by the stream to Philadelphia. Mr. Robinson, a mutual friend, active as a man of business, united with us in the enterprise. Towards the close of 1813, we visited Mauch Chunk, examined the mines, made all the enquiries suggested by prudence respecting the navigation of the Lehigh, and made up our minds to hazard the experiment, if a sufficiently liberal arrangement could be made with the company." The following extract from the same letter is sufficient to give the reader an idea of what was accomplished: "On Tuesday, the 9th of August (1814), I being absent and there being a freshet in the river, Mr. Cist started off my first ark, sixty-five feet long, fourteen feet wide, with twenty-four tons of coal. Sunday, fourteenth, arrived at the city at eight A. M. The coal cost us about fourteen dollars a ton in the city. But while we pushed forward our labors at the mine (hauling coal, building arks, etc.,) we had the greater difficulty to overcome of inducing the public to use our coal when brought to their doors, much as it was needed. We published handbills in English and German, stating the mode of burning the coal, either in grates, smiths' fires, or in stoves. Numerous certificates were obtained and printed from blacksmiths and others, who had successfully used the anthracite. Mr. Cist formed a model of a coal stove and got a number of them cast. Together we went to several houses in the city and prevailed upon the masters to allow us to kindle fires of anthracite in their grates, erected to burn Liverpool coal. We attended at blacksmiths' shops, and persuaded some to alter the *tue-iron*, so that they might burn the Lehigh coal; and we were sometimes obliged to bribe the journeymen to try the experiment fairly, so averse were they to learning the use of a new sort of fuel, so different from what they had been accustomed to. Great as were our united exertions (and Mr. Cist, if they were meritorious, deserves the chief commendation), necessity accomplished more for us than our labors. Charcoal advanced in price and was difficult to be got. Manufacturers were forced to try the experiment of using the anthracite, and every day's experience convinced them, and those who witnessed the fires, of the great value of this coal. We sent down a considerable number of arks, three out of four of which stove and sunk by the way. Heavy, however, as was the loss, it was lessened by the sale, at moderate prices, of the cargoes as they lay along the shores or in the bed of the Lehigh, to the smiths of Allentown, Bethlehem, and the country around, who drew them away when the water became low. We were just learning that our arks were far too large and the loads too heavy for the stream, and were making preparations to build coal boats to carry eight or ten tons each, that would be connected together when they arrived at Easton. Much had been taught us by experience, but at a heavy cost, by the operations of 1814–15. Peace came and found us in the midst of our enterprise. Philadelphia was now opened to foreign commerce, and the coasting trade resumed. Liverpool and Richmond coal came in abundantly, and the hard-kindling anthracite fell to a price far below the cost of shipment. I need hardly add, the business was abandoned, leaving several hundred tons of coal at the pit's mouth, and the most costly part of the work done to take out some thousands of tons more. Our disappointment and losses were met with the spirit of youth and enterprise. We turned our attention to other branches of industry, but on looking back on the ruins of our (not unworthy) exertions, I have not ceased to hope and believe that the Lehigh navigation and coal company, when prosperity begins to reward them for their most valuable labors, would tender to us a fair compensation at least for the work done and expenditures made, which contributed directly to their advantage."

This adventure was so disastrous to the finances of Mr. Cist that he did not again engage in the practical mining of coal, though his mind was never idle in devising plans for the opening

of our coal-fields, and for a cheap and rapid mode of getting the
coal to market, and his pen was ever busy advocating both to the
general public. Although much had been said and written on
anthracite coal prior to 1821, Mr. Cist himself having published
a pamphlet on the subject in 1815, yet in that year the first exhaustive and scientific article on the subject was prepared by Mr.
Cist, being two letters, one to Professor Silliman and the other
to M. A. Brongniart. These, with extracts from Mr. Cist's pamphlet of 1815, were published in the *American Journal of Science*,
Vol. IV, and created no little excitement and discussion at the
time. In this article he gives the mode and cost of mining the
coal and the getting it to market. He gives three carefully taken
sections of the strata at "Smith's bed," "Bowman's mine," and at
"Blackman's bed." He attached a map showing that the coal
formation "extends in a S. S. westerly direction, from its commencement at the upper part of Lackawanna river, near the
Wayne county line, down the course of that river to its junction
with the Susquehanna; thence along the Susquehanna, keeping
chiefly the east side, leaving this river about eighteen miles below
this place (Wilkes-Barre) it passes in a southward course to the
head-waters of the Schuylkill river, etc., and from thence, after
its crossing three main branches, becomes lost, a small seam of it
only appearing at Peter's mountain, a few miles above Harrisburg." He then gives a list of the minerals found in this belt,
together with the dip of the coal and superincumbent strata. He
gives a list of rocks of which the gravel in the river's bed consists. Then follows a long description of the vegetable impressions. He gives the specific gravity of the coal exactly as it is
accepted to-day, and is the first to call attention to the fact that
the true fracture of the pure coal is conchoidal, and when appearing angular, lamellar, and cubical it is due to impurities. Altogether the article is an exceedingly interesting one.

James Pierce, in an article in *Hazard's Register*, in 1828, Vol.
I. page three hundred and fourteen, says: "The valley of Wyoming and its valuable beds and veins of coal have been correctly
described in No. I, Vol. IV, of the *Journal of Science*, by Mr.
Cist, an able naturalist, whose recent death is lamented by all
acquainted with his merit."

The correspondence here begun with Monsieur Brongniart continued until Mr. Cist's death. He sent a number of new species of fossil plants to Paris to M. Brongniart, who did him the courtesy to name them after him. In sending some specimens of the coal flora to Professor Silliman in 1825 Mr. Cist makes a strong point of urging the vegetable origin to the notice of the professor. His pen was at an early date busy in suggesting plans to get the coal to market. He was one of the first to lend his hearty coöperation to the internal improvement of the state. He took a lively interest in all the meetings held in the eastern part of the state, and was one of the committee of correspondence and afterwards a delegate from Luzerne, together with Nathan Beach, to the state convention, held at Harrisburg in August, 1825. At first he was a strong advocate of the canal system or a slack water navigation of the river. In writing to the *Baltimore American*, under date of December 5, 1822, he says: "From partial geological survey, the county of Luzerne possesses *coal, level free*, which, estimated at the low rate of twenty-five cents per ton in the mine, would amount to above one hundred millions of dollars, the value of which would be enhanced from twenty-five to thirty fold on its arrival at Baltimore or Philadelphia. In addition to the coal, level free, there is from ten to fifteen times that quantity accessible by the aid of steam engine, thus presenting an object alone sufficient to warrant the expense of rendering the river completely navigable, were the lumber, the wheat, pork, whiskey, iron, and the long list of other articles thrown totally out of view."

As early as 1814 he corresponded with Oliver Evans as to the practicability of using a steam engine and railroad at the mines on the Lehigh. In a letter to Evans, written December, 1814, he says: "I would thank you also for an estimate of the expense of your *steam wagon* for drawing out a number of low carts, say twenty to twenty-five, each containing one and one-half or two tons of coal, on a wooden railroad, with a descent of about one-third of an inch in a yard" (or forty-six feet to mile); to which Mr. Evans answers from Washington, January 3, 1815: "I would suppose that a descent of one-third inch to a yard could do without cogging the ways, which would save much expense. I had devised a cheap way of rising an ascent by means of a rope, as I apprehended no company could yet be formed in this country to lay iron and cogged railways for any distance. I therefore fixed on wooden ways, one for going, the other for coming back, as close to each other as will admit, and to cover the whole with a shed. This would, in the first making, cost little more than a Pennsylvania turnpike, and much less in ten years. I cannot state to you the expense of a carriage." Mr. Cist ran the levels from here to Mauch Chunk for one, and at the time of his death he was planning with a Mr. McCullough, of New Jersey, to organize a company to lay a railroad up the Lehigh to Wyoming valley. One of his daughters, when a little girl while at play in his study, remembers asking him "what he was so busy at." His answer was: "My child, I am building a railroad to pull things on over the mountain." Mr. McCullough, in writing to Mr. Hollenback shortly after Mr. Cist's death, intimates that in the death of Mr. Cist the railroad had met with its death, which was a fact.

In the year 1810 Jacob Cist, together with Jesse Fell, Matthias Hollenback, Thomas Dyer, Peleg Tracy, and others, founded the Luzerne County Agricultural Society, and he, with Dr. Robert H. Rose, was one of the first corresponding secretaries of the society. He did much towards the introduction of finer grades of fruit trees in our valley, joining with Washington Lee, Charles Streater, E. Covell, George Cahoon and many others of the old citizens of Wilkes-Barre and vicinity, who took pride and pleasure in their fruit gardens. He was accustomed every year to get for himself and friends quantities of the choicest fruit trees. He knew the value of the New York gypsum as a fertilizer and advocated its superiority in a paper read before the state agricultural society, January 12, 1813. This article was republished in the *Record of the Times*, at Wilkes-Barre, January 8, 1868. He was treasurer of the county of Luzerne for 1816, and treasurer of the Wilkes-Barre Bridge Company, 1816, 1817, 1818, of which he was one of the original stockholders and founders. He was one of the charter members of the old Susquehanna bank and its first cashier, appointed 1817, at a salary of $600. He drew the designs for the notes of the bridge company and of the bank. He geologized this whole section of country for miles up and down the river, finding, besides manganese and clays, a number of iron beds, in many instances purchasing the land outright, in others only leasing, and at the time of his death he owned large bodies of iron lands. As early as 1815 he entered into an arrangement with Samuel Messemer, of Northampton county, Pa., and John Vernet, of New London, Conn., to establish iron works on the site of the present town of Shickshinny. In the year 1822 he entered into a similar arrangement with D. C. Woodin, but I cannot learn that anything ever came of either. He early conceived the idea of preparing a work on American Entomology, and labored assiduously at this task until the year preceding his death, when it was so far completed that he contemplated publishing it, and sent his manuscript with several thousand drawings to a well-known English scientist for inspection; the letter acknowledging its receipt arrived in Wilkes-Barre after Mr. Cist's decease, but the manuscript and drawings have never been returned. They are now supposed to be in the collection of the East India Company, to whom the scientist left his collection at his death, some twenty years ago. He corresponded for a number of years with Prof. Say and Mr. Melsheimer, the later writing on entomology, under date October 6, 1818, speaking of the beauty and correctness of the drawings of insects by Mr. Cist, says: "Good and correct figures are undoubtedly well calculated to advance the knowledge of entomology. I am, therefore, the more solicitous that *you* would give to the world your promising labor on, and accompanied with descriptions, etc., of, the North American insects. Such a work would be very serviceable to the student of American insects." On the 15th of April, 1807, with Andrew and George Way, and others, he founded the Washington city glass works, drawing all the plans himself. On his settlement at Wilkes-Barre he tried for several years to found glass works and a pottery at that point, but failed, though he found within easy distance the clays, sand, manganese, etc., requisite to the successful carrying on of these enterprises. Jacob Cist did not know what it was to be idle; he was busy from sunrise until late in the night, either at science, music, poetry or painting, and during business hours at his business; he was a man ahead of his times, and an enigma to the good people of Wilkes-Barre, who pretty generally thought him an enthusiast, who was wasting his time on bugs and stones. Many people have lived to judge differently of him, and to appreciate his worth. He died on Friday, the 30th day of December, 1825, aged forty-three years. An obituary notice, published at the time, says: "In the death of Mr. Cist, society has lost one of its most valuable members, science one of its most ornamental and industrious cultivators, and the cause of public and internal improvements one of its most able and zealous supporters. Modest and unassuming in his manners, he sought no political preferment—was ambitious of no public distinction. But like a true lover of science, sought her in her quiet paths of peace. His researches into the geological structure and formation of our portion of the country, and particularly into the anthracite coal regions of Pennsylvania, have been extensive and indefatigable; and while they have contributed to enrich the cabinets of many scientific men, both in this country and in Europe, with mineralogical specimens, they have also been a means of calling the attention of our citizens to those vast mines of combustible treasures with which our mountains abound, and which we trust under Providence of giving employment to thousands of industrious men and prosperity and wealth to our county." The other local paper says: "In the death of Mr. Cist the community has sustained the loss of an able and industrious supporter of the cause of internal improvements. His indefatigable zeal in devising and perfecting plans for the improvement of our country by-roads and inland navigation, and by disseminating a knowledge of the extent, situation and value of our extensive regions of coal, have rendered him a public benefactor to our country. As a lover of the arts and sciences, his loss will be no less felt by those persons at home and abroad with whom he has been so extensively connected in their cultivation and support. Unambitious of public distinction, he has sought to render himself useful by devoting a considerable portion of his time and services for the common benefit of his fellow citizens, and by them will his loss long be regretted and his memory affectionately cherished." He left to survive him the following children: Mary Ann Cist, now deceased, intermarried with Nathaniel Rutter; Ellen E. Cist, now deceased, first married to Rev.

Robert Dunlap, D. D., and secondly to Nathaniel Rutter; Emily L. Cist, married to Harrison Wright; Augusta Cist, married to Andrew T. McClintock; and Sarah A. Cist, now deceased, intermarried with Peter T. Woodbury.

Matthias Hollenback, the father of Mrs. Jacob Cist, was the grandson of George Hollenback, a German settler, "who owned lands and paid quit-rents prior to 1734," in the township of Hanover, Philadelphia (now Montgomery) county, Pa. John Hollenback, a son of George Hollenback, was born about 1720, and probably emigrated with his father to this country when but a lad. The date of his arrival in this country is not known, but it was before the year 1729. In 1750 John Hollenback took up land in Lebanon township, Lancaster (now Lebanon) county, Pa., and in 1772 removed from that section of country to Martinsburg, Berkeley county, Va., where he died. The wife of John Hollenback was Eleanor Jones, of Welsh descent. Matthias Hollenback, the second son of John Hollenback, was born at Jonestown, Lancaster (now Lebanon) county, February 17, 1752. He came to Wyoming in 1769, in a company of forty young men from that part of the country. They were Stewarts, Espys and others, and they came with the intention of settling and becoming citizens under Connecticut laws, and aiding the Yankees in keeping possession of this section of our state. They became entitled to lands under a grant from the Susquehanna Land Company, which they acquired after they had been a short time in the valley. On their way to Wyoming the company encamped where Mauch Chunk is now situated, and after the coal interest had called into existence a thriving town there, Mr. Hollenback often humorously remarked that he ought to put in a claim to that place, for he was first in possession. The forty adventurers came into Wyoming through a notch of the mountains in what is now Hanover; and when the beautiful valley first broke upon their sight, young Hollenback, the youngest of the company, threw up his hat and exclaimed: "Hurrah, that's the place for me." He began business at Mill Creek, but soon removed to Wilkes-Barre; and having purchased a lot on what is now the west side of the Public Square, built a large frame house for a store and dwelling. He purchased his goods in Philadelphia, which were taken to Middletown in wagons and then transported by water to this and other places, where he had established stores. The first method of transportation was by Indian canoes; and he literally "paddled his own canoe" up the winding, rapid Susquehanna the whole distance, one hundred and fifty miles, many times, before he was able to procure a more capacious vessel and to employ men to manage it. Then he purchased a Durham boat, which he kept steadily employed. The present road leading through the swamp was but a little path. Mr. Hollenback in his business enterprises was prospered in a remarkable manner, and soon acquired distinction and was promoted to positions of public trust and responsibility. On October 17, 1775, he was commissioned as ensign in the "train-band in the 24th regiment in his Majesty's colony of Connecticut." On August 26, 1776, he was appointed by congress to serve as ensign in Captain Durkee's company of "minute men," a band raised for the protection of the people in the valley. These Wyoming companies were subsequently ordered to join General Washington's army. Mr. Hollenback was with the army in New Jersey in 1776 and 1777, and took part in several battles. He was in the battles of Millstone, Trenton, Princeton and Brandywine. That he was a man of more than ordinary courage and tact is evident from the fact that he was several times employed by Washington to visit the frontier settlements and outposts and report upon their condition. About the close of 1777, the settlement of Wyoming being menaced by the enemy, many of the men who were with the army came home, and among them was Mr. Hollenback. During the spring of 1778 fears were entertained for the safety of the frontier settlement of Wyoming, and as summer approached a sense of insecurity and alarm pervaded the community. Frequent scouting parties were sent out to ascertain the position of the enemy. On the 1st of July Mr. Hollenback, with a companion, was selected for the perilous duty. He proceeded sixteen miles up the river, where he came upon the fresh trail of the Indians and tories on their march to attack the settlement, and discovered also the bodies of several settlers who had been killed and scalped. Taking these bodies into his canoe, he immediately returned home and reported the presence of the enemy in great force. The inhabitants had already begun to assemble at Forty Fort, and were actively preparing for the defense of the valley. On the 3d of July, under the command of Colonels Butler and Denison, the little band marched forth to the memorable battle of Wyoming. Mr. Hollenback took a prominent part in this tragic action, acquitting himself with great gallantry and honor. He escaped the terrible slaughter which followed the defeat of the settlers, and after many thrilling adventures and hardships reached his home late in the night. From there he went directly to the fort situated on what is now the Public Square of this city. He announced his name at the gate, heard it repeated within. "Hollenback has come," was the joyful exclamation. "No, no," responded the familiar voice of Nathan Carey, "you'll never see Hollenback again; he was on the right wing; I am sure he is killed." The gate was opened, however, and Mr. Hollenback stepped in. It being dark, and there being no candles, Mr. Carey lit a pine knot to see if it was really Mr. Hollenback, and then, overwhelmed with joy, embraced him with a brother's affection. At four o'clock he set out on an Indian path to meet Spalding with his seventy men, for the purpose of getting them into the fort at Wilkes-Barre. He met them at Bear creek, but Captain Spalding declined the hazard. Mr. Hollenback, however, so far prevailed as to induce fifteen or twenty of the men to accompany him. On reaching the slope of the mountain near Prospect Rock, he discovered his own house on fire and savages in possession of the fort. Seeing all lost, he promptly directed his energies to the relief of the sufferers. He had procured from Spalding's commissary all the provisions he could pack on his horse, and following the fugitives, mostly women and children, he overtook them and led them through the wilderness. After a few weeks he returned to the valley and set about repairing his loss. His credit at Philadelphia being good, he obtained a few goods and began the world anew. He established his principal store at Wilkes-Barre, and branch stores at Tioga Point (now Athens), at Newtown (now Elmira), and at other places. He had partners in his various enterprises, several of whom in after years became prominent in the business world. In 1791 he was the business manager and purveyor for Pickering, while he was holding a treaty with the Indians at Newtown creek. He was made a justice of the peace after the establishment of the jurisdiction of Pennsylvania in Wyoming, and when the new constitution was formed, was appointed an associate judge of Luzerne county, in which capacity he served until the time of his death, February 18, 1829, the day after he was seventy-seven years of age. His first commission as lieutenant colonel is dated in 1787, another is dated in 1792, and still another is dated in 1793. The first of them was given by the executive council of Pennsylvania, and bears the autograph of Benjamin Franklin. He was a member of the board of trustees of the old Wilkes-Barre academy from 1807 to 1829, and was the first treasurer of Luzerne county. Colonel Hollenback always took great interest in religious affairs and the welfare of the church. He gave largely toward building the first church built in Wilkes-Barre, and was generally punctual in his attendance upon the services. His home was the home of ministers, and his hand always open to them. He was in many respects an extraordinary man, endowed with great capacity and courage, and with an indomitable will which overcame all obstacles. In all his business relations he was a pattern of punctuality, scrupulously faithful to public trusts and private confidence. His powers of endurance were very remarkable; he took all his journeys on horseback, and his business interests called him from Niagara to Philadelphia. Between Wyoming and the New York state line he owned immense tracts of wild land, which he often visited unattended, traveling for days and even weeks through the wilds of northern Pennsylvania, and being as much at home in the wilderness as in his counting-room. Judge Hollenback exerted much influence upon the progress and elevation of the country. He provided employment for many poor laborers; he furnished supplies to multitudes of new settlers; he took an active part in the early public improvements· he kept in circulation a large capital; and he was a living, almost ever-present example of industry and economy. Not Wyoming alone, but the whole country between Wilkes-Barre and Elmira, owes much of its early development and present prosperity to the business arrangements and the indomitable perseverance of Matthias Hollenback. Judge

Hollenback was employed by Robert Morris, the agent of Louis the Sixteenth, to provide a place of retreat for the royal household at some secluded spot on the Susquehanna. This was in 1793. He accordingly purchased twelve hundred acres of land lying in the present county of Bradford (then Luzerne), and embracing the locality where Frenchtown, in the township of Asylum, was subsequently built. The unfortunate monarch, however, never occupied this asylum in the wilds of Pennsylvania, albeit many of his subjects did. Louis Philippe, the late "King of the French," in 1795, came through "the Wind Gap" on horseback to Wilkes-Barre, and then made his way up to Frenchtown. [The children of Matthias Hollenback were Eleanor Jones Hollenback, now deceased, married to Charles F. Welles, father of Rev. H. H. Welles, of Kingston, John Welles Hollenback and Edward Welles of this city. He had other children also—Mary Ann Hollenback, married first to John Deshong, secondly to John Laning; Sarah Hollenback, married first to Jacob Cist, and secondly to Hon. Chester Butler; and Hon. George Matson Hollenback.]

The only son of Judge Hollenback, and the brother of Mrs. Jacob Cist, was George Matson Hollenback, who, inheriting a large fortune from his father, succeeded him in many of his business pursuits. In 1820 and 1821 he was treasurer of the county of Luzerne. In 1824 and 1825 he represented the same county in the legislature of the state. In 1842 he was appointed by Governor Porter one of the canal commissioners of the state, but his other business affairs allowed him to hold the commission but a short time. He was president of the Wyoming bank at the time of his decease, November 7, 1866, and had occupied that responsible position for more than thirty years, and for nearly a half century was connected with all the public affairs of the Wyoming valley.

Harrison Wright, the subject of our sketch, was the eldest son of Harrison Wright and Emily Cist. He early developed those mental traits which characterized his maturer manhood. Before he was fifteen years of age he had acquired a marked taste for history and the natural sciences, and he formed at that time an interesting cabinet of specimens and objects illustrative of his several pursuits. After a preparatory course of study at his home, he was, in 1867, matriculated as a student of philosophy at the university of Heidelberg, Germany. Upon the completion of four years of studious application in his chosen branches of learning, he was graduated in the spring of 1871, with the degrees of Master of Arts and Doctor of Philosophy. During his course at the university he became remarkably proficient in the German language and literature, and his natural aptitude for languages led him to the study of the French and Italian tongues, with both of which he became familiar. His especial study at Heidelberg was mineralogy; his excellence in his pursuit of this science induced his preceptor, the late Professor Blum—the leading mineralogist of his time—to select Mr. Wright as assistant professor of mineralogy; but a prolonged summer's absence from the university led to the appointment of another. Much of his time during vacation was spent in travel; he visited many of the capitals of Europe, and in seeking needed relaxation from the duties of the university, he acquired much practical knowledge of the customs and manners of the several countries. During the time he spent in Rome, he studied the archæology and explored many of the remains of the Ancient City. In this research he became associated with the members of the Archæological Society of Rome, who, in appreciation of his tastes and scholarly attainments, elected him a member of their society. He became also an honorary member of the Papal Club, a social organization of the officers of the Papal Guard.

He returned to America in the summer of 1871, and in the following autumn he entered as a student of law in the office of his uncle, Andrew T. McClintock, LL. D., of this city. After the prescribed course of study, during which he exhibited a marked aptitude for the dry precepts of the law, as for the more congenial researches in literature and science, he was admitted to the bar of Luzerne county, September 14, 1874, under circumstances which afforded ample assurance of his distinguished success in a profession to which his family had contributed several able members. But he, however, was attached to a vocation which offered distinction of a different kind, and soon abandoned the active practice of the law; but not until he had gained great credit and commendation for his able services as one of three auditors appointed by the court to make a special examination of the accounts of the county; a work which involved the minutest inquiry into its financial affairs for the preceding seven years, and the auditing of all the accounts in their multitudinous details; the practical results of which were the recovery of a large sum of money and the exposure and punishment of the parties guilty of the embezzlement. Mr. Wright was a democrat in politics, and like all his father's family, positive in his convictions. In a number of campaigns he accepted and intelligently and satisfactorily acquitted himself of the city contingent of the party. In this way he won the confidence and esteem of the members of his party, who repeatedly solicited him to accept political honors, but these offers, like the law, failed to lure him from the pursuits upon which his heart and ambition had long been set. He was once regularly nominated for a seat in the legislature, with such unanimity and cordiality as would almost certainly have insured his election, but, though willing to do service in the ranks whenever called upon, he peremptorily declined this proffered and well deserved reward. His leaning, in part inherited as I have already said, manifested in early youth and encouraged and intensified by his education, was towards literary and scientific pursuits. To these he gave much attention, even when studying and practicing law. He became a member of the Wyoming Historical and Geological Society, was immediately assigned a leading position in it, and found here a fruitful field for the employment of his varied talents. He took charge of and arranged its extensive mineralogical and other collections, adding to them from his own rich private stores and assiduously gathering valuable contributions from other sources. He prepared numerous papers of much value and interest on a diversity of subjects; he accumulated, by persistent research, many previously undiscovered facts in the history of the valley and of the coal-trade, until every material incident of each—so thorough was his study and so retentive his memory—was before him like the words upon a printed page, which enabled him at all times to answer with great clearness and accuracy all inquiries concerning either of these subjects. When the late Isaac S. Osterhout decided upon his munificent bequest

for the founding of a public library in Wilkes-Barre, Harrison
Wright was in the midst of these labors and had achieved the
reputation of being perhaps the best historical and scientific
authority in the community, and the testator's thoughts naturally turned to him as one fitted in all respects to take a leading
part in executing the trust, and he appointed him one of the
trustees. Had he lived he would have been of inestimable service in the preliminary arrangements for and securing the practical operation of the library in accordance with the generous
designs of its founder. All who knew Harrison Wright must
have been impressed with his unselfish and generous disposition,
his genial companionship, his thoughtful and kindly consideration in all his relationships, and his warm and true friendship, as
well as by his scholarly attainments, the wide scope of his mental
powers, and his extended and accurate learning in many and
diverse branches of human knowledge. His time, his talents,
and his means were but instruments toward the attainment of his
honorable ambition, the endeavor to let light in where darkness
had previously prevailed and open thoroughfares in the hitherto
trackless places in history and science. And in the every day
relations of life, there are many who could attest that his generosity was only bounded by his ability to give. His capacity for
labor—the exacting labor of the fields to which his inclinations
led him—was exceptionable. He did not deny himself reasonable recreation, but what he esteemed to be his duty was never
permitted to wait upon pleasures to which he was invited, and
the secrets of his success and of the results achieved in so short
a lifetime were his steadfastness of purpose and his continuity of
application. Where his strong sympathies led, his energies followed. When there was a new duty to be performed, he was
never too overburdened to undertake it, though other tasks in
various stages of progress were piled high before him. It is not
often that we can speak thus in praise of the achievements of one
so young as Harrison Wright was when he died, and yet abide
within the strict limits of the truth; but our friend was one among
a thousand. His sudden and generally unexpected departure
from among us has left a void in our ranks it will be difficult, if
not impossible, to fill. It is inexcusably ungrateful in the midst

of the Maker's many and munificent providences, to speak of any earthly loss as irreparable, but the loss of Harrison Wright to this society is as nearly irreparable as any loss could be.

MONTGOMERY JOSEPH FLANAGAN.

Montgomery Joseph Flanagan, who was admitted to the bar of Luzerne county, Pa., June 12, 1876, was a native of Pottsville, Pa., where he was born August 27, 1842. He read law with A. H. Winton, in Scranton, but practiced principally in this city. He was the son of William Flanagan and his wife Catharine Gannon, daughter of Timothy Gannon, who were natives of Ireland. He died February 1, 1880, at the residence of his mother in Plymouth, Pa. Mr. Flanagan was an unmarried man.

WILLIAM JOSEPH PHILBIN.

William Joseph Philbin, who was admitted to the bar of Luzerne county, Pa., November 22, 1876, was a native of Jenkins township, in this county, where he was born January 11, 1854. His father, Michael J. Philbin, was a native of county Mayo, Ireland, where he was born in 1819. He emigrated to this country in 1838 and settled in Washington, Dutchess county, N. Y. He removed to this county in 1844 and located at Port Griffith, in Jenkins township, where he engaged in the hotel business. His hotel was subsequently burned out. He then built a store and engaged in mercantile pursuits, which he continued until the spring of 1865. In 1859, during his residence at Port Griffith, he was elected captain of the Emmet Guards, Second Brigade, Ninth Division of Uniformed Militia of Pennsylvania. He was elected a justice of the peace in 1860. In 1864 he was elected prothonotary of Luzerne county for a term of three years, and was reëlected in 1867 for another term of three years. After the expiration of his second term as prothonotary, he became the proprietor of the Exchange hotel, in this city. Abandoning the hotel business, he was elected an alderman of the fifth ward of this city for a term of five years, and was serving his second term at the time of his death, November 5, 1879. He took a very active part in the incorporation of this city and was elected its first treasurer in 1871. He was also a member of the board of prison commissioners of Luzerne county. His daughter, Julia, became the wife of P. J. O'Hanlon, of the Luzerne county bar. William J. Philbin was an unmarried man and died in Brooklyn, N. Y., August 29, 1882.

FRIEND AARON WHITLOCK.

Friend Aaron Whitlock, who was admitted to the bar of Luzerne county, Pa., April 3, 1877, was a native of Exeter township, Luzerne county, Pa., where he was born December 30, 1850. His grandfather was Lewis Whitlock and his father was Enoch Whitlock. The Whitlocks were old settlers of Exeter township, and the name is to be found in the list of taxables in 1796. The mother of F. A. Whitlock was Mary Sickler, a daughter of John Sickler, of Exeter. Mr. Whitlock was educated in the public schools of his native township and in a select school in Illinois. He read law with W. G. Ward, in Scranton, and practiced in that city and Wamego, Kansas. While he resided in the latter place he was elected a justice of the peace. He married, in 1879, Eva Walter. Mr. Whitlock died November 24, 1880.

DANIEL STREBEIGH BENNET.

Daniel Strebeigh Bennet was admitted to the bar of Luzerne county, Pa., June 11, 1877. He was the son of the late George Bennet, of Montoursville, Pa., whose wife was Martha Strebeigh, a daughter of Daniel Strebeigh, of Montoursville. He was the son of Andrew Bennet and grandson of Thomas Bennet. (See page 630.) D. S. Bennet was born at Fairfield, near Williamsport, Pa., September 3, 1853. He was brought up on his father's farm, and received the advantages of such district and public schools as his neighborhood afforded, and afterwards was graduated with distinguished honors by the Pennsylvania state college in 1875. While there he took the prescribed three years' course in military tactics, thus fitting him for the position he was subsequently to occupy in the militia of the state. Soon after graduating he came to Wilkes-Barre and entered as a law student with E. P. & J. V. Darling. From a child he had a passion for a military life, and when only ten years old he participated in the battle of Gettysburg as a drummer boy attached to an independent company. Much of the credit is due him for the high standard which our local militia has reached. He was instrumental in organizing Company F of the Ninth Regiment, N. G. P., and was elected its captain July 14, 1870. On October 30 of the same year he was elected a major of the Ninth Regiment, and at the time of his death ranked as third major in the National Guard of Pennsylvania. In March, 1884, he was appointed quartermaster of the Third Brigade, on the staff of General J. K. Siegfried, with the rank of major. Major Bennet's industry and integrity soon won him an enviable place at the Luzerne bar, and even in the few years during which he had practiced he built up a legal business that would do credit to a much older man. He was a worker in the legal profession, as he was in everything which he undertook, and mastered every obstacle which presented itself. In June, 1883, he was elected a director of the Third school district, and was such at the time of his death. He discharged the duties of that trust with fidelity and marked satisfaction. In politics he was a republican, and one of the most active workers in the local organizations, notably the republican league of Wilkes-Barre. In August, 1884, he was nominated by acclamation for assembly from the First legislative district, comprising the city of Wilkes-Barre, and on the day following he was prostrated with the illness which caused his death. In 1880 Major Bennet was united in marriage to Mary Margaret Myers, daughter of Lawrence Myers, of this city. He died September 16, 1884. His widow, now Mrs. John P. Yeager, survived him. They left no children. During the summer of 1884 Major Bennet found that too close application to business had overtaxed his strength, and he participated in the state camp of the National Guard at Gettysburg, with the belief that the change of scene would fully restore him. On the contrary, it seems to have planted the seeds of that insidious disease, typhoid fever, which, before he was aware of it, had taken a firm and relentless hold of him. He returned to participate in the excitement of a political canvass, and no sooner was his object accomplished, and his nomination secured, than his bodily powers gave way and he took to his bed, his physician predicting a serious illness by reason of having deferred so long in seeking medical advice, and he died within a month.

WILLIAM ROBERTS KINGMAN.

William Roberts Kingman was admitted to the bar of Luzerne county, Pa., November 12, 1878. He was a native of Charleston, South Carolina, where he was born January 1, 1838. He belonged to an old and wealthy family and great care was taken with his education. He was sent to college early, and graduated from Columbia university with high honors when but twenty-two years of age. So greatly were his talents esteemed that immediately after leaving college he was offered the principalship of the high school at Charleston, a preparatory school of good standing. This position he held until soon after the breaking out of the late civil war. He was an ardent supporter of the southern cause, and enlisted as a private. He rose to the rank of captain of an artillery company, and for a time served on the staff of one of the Confederate generals. At the close of the war he returned to his position as principal of the Charleston high school, which he successfully conducted until 1870, when the school was broken up on account of a virulent outbreak of small-pox among the students. Shortly afterwards he visited

Wilkes-Barre, and while here was impressed with the field which this city afforded for a first-class preparatory school. After a few months, passed in adjusting his affairs in the south, he returned here in 1871 and opened his academy in the old Presbyterian school house. For three or four years the school flourished and turned out excellent scholars, and Mr. Kingman finally turned his attention to the preparation of pupils for college. During all this time, and in fact ever since he left college, he had studied more or less for the bar, his chosen profession being that of a lawyer. After the close of his school he continued his studies with redoubled ardor, in the office of E. P. Darling. Between the close of the school and his entering the profession of the law he occupied the position of bookkeeper at the First National bank. He was at one time one of the "seven years" auditors, to audit the accounts of the county officers. Mr. Kingman was a man of rare mental endowments. He had the true instinct of a Southern gentleman, and his politeness was proverbial. Mild and unassuming in his manner, he was little known outside of his own social circle, yet wherever known he was a favorite. He never married. He died in this city August 23, 1884. The mother of Mr. Kingman was Mary Roberts, who was a sister of the first wife of the late O. B. Hillard, of this city.

AARON JARED DIETRICK.

Aaron Jared Dietrick was admitted to the bar of Luzerne county, Pa., December 11, 1880. He came from German stock, his parents emigrating from Germany, and settling in Northampton county, Pa., removing afterwards to Columbia county, Pa. He was born, April 6, 1822, in Briarcreek township, Columbia county, and his early days were spent on the farm of his father, John Dietrick. Until quite a lad he could speak only the language of his parents, and his family still possess the bible of his boyhood days, printed in German. He became later a fine German scholar, and earned many a valuable retainer by this fact, and when he became a judge he more than once conducted a case entirely in German. He was apprenticed as a blacksmith when a lad, but did not complete this course of training, his talents inciting him towards one of the professions. After attending the district schools of his neighborhood, he became a pupil in Berwick academy, and afterwards in Wyoming seminary, at Kingston. After leaving these he entered as a law student with M. E. Jackson, of Berwick, supporting himself meanwhile by teaching school in the township where he was born. He was admitted to the bar, at Danville, August 14, 1847, after which he practiced law nine years in Laporte, Sullivan county, Pa. While there he held the office of deputy district attorney three terms, and served two terms as county treasurer. While residing in Sullivan county he received the nomination of his district for state senator, but was defeated in the election. In 1856 he removed to Williamsport, Pa., where he settled and engaged in the practice of the law. In January, 1864, he removed to Washington, D. C., and became interested in the settlement of claims before the different departments of the government. He resided in Washington about four years, when he returned to Williamsport, April 1, 1868, and resumed the practice of his profession. He also served as revenue commissioner for that judicial district. After the adoption of the Wallace law by the city of Williamsport, he was appointed city recorder by Governor Geary, on March 27, 1868, which office he held until 1875. Before the expiration of his term the new constitution was adopted, which retired him. At the ensuing election, June 4, 1876, Judge Dietrick was elected and commissioned to serve five years. It was here that he derived his title of judge, the office of city recorder being a tribunal of limited civil and criminal jurisdiction. At one time he was business manager of the Williamsport *Gazette and Bulletin*, and it was through his efforts mainly that the old *Gazette* and the *West Branch Bulletin* were consolidated, November 22, 1869. In 1880 he resigned his office of city recorder, and removed to this city.

Judge Dietrick was twice married, his first wife being Catharine E. Burke, daughter of William Burke, whom he met while teaching at Briarcreek. Three children suvive this union—Willard M. Dietrick, who was treasurer of the Williamsport school board, Ezra P. Dietrick, and Franklin Pierce Dietrick, the latter two being the Philadelphia shoe manufacturing firm of E. P. Dietrick & Company. Judge Dietrick was married a second time to Mary S. Kellog, of East Smithfield, Bradford county, Pa., who survived him, as do their two children—Edward H. Dietrick and Carrie M. Dietrick. Judge Dietrick was a consistent member of the Congregational church in Williamsport, and upon his coming to this city he united by letter with the First Presbyterian church. He was a man universally respected and revered, and as far as known had not an enemy. His gentleness of manner and evenness of disposition were his striking qualities, and he was never known to lose his temper even under the most trying circumstances. In his home he was a devoted husband and loving father, in the community he was a faithful citizen, in the church he was an unassuming but sincere member, in the legal profession he occupied an eminent position. He died in this city September 8, 1884. He had been ill about a year, his trouble dating with a business trip to Kansas in August, 1883, where he was interested in a mineral spring property. His health rapidly failed, and a change of scene—first to Atlantic City and then to Lake Carey—was powerless to check the ravages of his disease, which was a complication of bladder and kidney disorders. Throughout his illness he had been a most patient sufferer, and even when his malady was most excrutiating not a murmur escaped his lips, he calming the anxiety of his family by saying that it might be worse.

JOHN SEARLE COURTRIGHT.

John Searle Courtright was admitted to the bar of Luzerne county, Pa., January 11, 1876. He is a descendant of Benjamin Courtright, whose son, Cornelius Courtright, a native of Minnisink, N. J., near the Delaware Water Gap, was the first of the name in this county. He was born March 7, 1764, and was one of the prominent men of his day. He was one of the commissioners of Luzerne county in the years 1813, 1814 and 1815, 1830, 1831 and 1832. In 1816 he was a candidate for state senator in the district composed of Northumberland, Columbia, Union, Luzerne and Susquehanna counties, but was defeated by Charles Frazer. On January 1, 1806, he was appointed a justice of the peace. He held the office until 1840. In 1820, 1821 and 1823 he was a member of the legislature of Pennsylvania. He was a large landholder in this county, his first purchase being made December 30, 1789, from William Hooker Smith, and his second, September 19, 1791, from Timothy Pickering. He died at his home in Plains township, in this county, May 25, 1848. His wife, whom he married October 1, 1786, was Catharine Kennedy, a daughter of John Kennedy, a native of Dublin, Ireland. Benjamin Courtright, son of Cornelius Courtright, was born in now Plains township, March 19, 1789. He was a farmer the greater part of his life. He died at the residence of his son, J. Milton Courtright, in this city, January 22, 1867. His wife was Clarissa Williams, daughter of Thomas Williams. (See page 157). James Courtright, son of Benjamin Courtright, was born in Plains township, November 3, 1831. He is a resident of this city, and was treasurer of Luzerne county from December 22, 1873 to December 29, 1875. The wife of James Courtright is Ruth G., daughter of John Searle and his wife, Mary Stark, daughter of Henry Stark. (See pages 389, 566 and 1228). John Searle was the son of Constant Searle. (See page 1255). John S. Courtright, son of James Courtright, was born at Plainsville, Pa., July 21, 1855. He was educated in this city, and at Wyoming seminary, Kingston, Pa. He read law in this city with ex-Governor Henry M. Hoyt, and at Montrose, Pa., with D. W. Searle. After practicing a few years in this city he removed to Montrose, Pa., where he now resides. He married, in January, 1877, Ella V. Lathrop, of Montrose, Pa., a daughter of Azur Lathrop, son of Benjamin Lathrop. The latter was the son of Walter Lathrop, who removed from Connecticut to Luzerne (now Susquehanna) county, Pa., in 1803. Benjamin Lathrop was an associate judge of Susquehanna county from 1841 to 1846. His wife was a daughter of Asahel Avery, who removed

from New London county, Conn., to Susquehanna county in
1801. Mr. and Mrs. Courtright have one child—Sarah Lathrop
Courtright. Mr. Courtright comes, as will be seen, from a stock
not a few scions of which have made their mark in the communities in which they have severally resided. He has won for
himself, at the bar, a place that does credit both to himself and
to the distinguished gentlemen by whom his preliminary studies
were supervised.

JOHN RICHARD JONES.

John Richard Jones was admitted to the bar of Luzerne county,
Pa., June 8, 1880. He is the son of Edward Jones, who was born
near St. Donats, Wales, in 1814. He was educated at Cambridge
scientific school, and came to America in 1836 to avoid a sea
faring life for which his parents had intended him. He entered
the employ of the Delaware & Hudson Canal Company at Carbondale, Pa., as a miner, and was in a few years promoted to be
a mine boss, and in 1854 was placed in charge of the company's
mines in Archbald, Pa., where he remained until 1858, when he
became a partner in the successful coal firm of Eaton & Company, at
that place. In the fall of that year in company with two partners,
he commenced operations which led to the successful development of the coal fields of Olyphant, Pa., which were continued
until 1864, under the firm name of E. Jones & Company, and
then sold out their interest to the Delaware & Hudson Canal
Company. He was afterwards employed by the Erie Railway
Company in developing and perfecting their extensive collieries
near Carbondale, and is now actively connected with coal operations as a member of the firm of Jones, Simpson & Company, and
also as president of the Pierce Coal Company. In 1875 he was
elected a director of the Merchants' & Mechanics' bank, of Scranton. In 1876 he was the candidate of the republican party for
congress in the twelfth congressional district of Pennsylvania,
but was defeated by a majority of two hundred and eighty-six
votes in favor of his democratic competitor, William H. Stanton.
As a business man, he is prudent and sagacious. As a practical
geologist, he has few if any superiors in the mining regions. If

an unblemished reputation, a life spent in successfully developing the material resources of our country, and a well balanced mind are evidences by which it is safe to judge, it is not an exaggeration to call Edward Jones a successful man. He was burgess of the borough of Blakely in 1870 and 1871. He was also elected the first justice of the peace of the borough. He married, August 4, 1846, in New York, Mary E. Jones, a daughter of Richard Jones, a woolen manufacturer of Landilas, Montgomeryshire, Wales. John Richard Jones, son of Edward Jones, and Mary E. Jones, was born in the village of Archbald, Pa., on May 27, 1856. In 1858 his parents moved to Blakely, opposite the town of Olyphant, where he now resides. The subject of our sketch was educated in the common schools of Olyphant, and when seventeen years of age was sent away to boarding school. He was educated at Keystone academy at Factoryville and at the well-known Wyoming seminary. He remained about three years at these institutions, and then on September 28, 1876, entered Harvard Law School at Cambridge, Mass. On June 25, 1879, after pursuing a three years' thorough course in the common law, he graduated and received the degree of *Legibus Baccalaurei*, (LL. B.) He was admitted March 12, 1878, to practice law at the celebrated Middlesex bar, in the county of Middlesex, Mass. After passing a creditable examination by a board of examiners, composed of three of the most prominent members of that bar, September 23, 1879, he entered the law office of Alexander Farnham, Esq., at Wilkes-Barre, Pa., and remained there until June 8 following, when he was admitted upon motion of Andrew T. McClintock, Esq.— Mr. Farnham being absent from the city—to practice law in all the courts of Luzerne county. He practiced at our bar until October 8, 1880, when he entered the law office of R. W. Archbald, Esq., at Scranton, and was, on the same day, on motion of that gentleman, admitted to practice law in all the courts of Lackawanna county. He remained with Mr. Archbald until the latter was elected to the bench in 1884. Mr. Jones then removed his office from the Third National bank building into the Coal Exchange, where he is now engaged in the practice of his profession, which is large and extensive, his clients being from all parts of the county. He is counsel for many of the boroughs and school districts in that vicinity. Strict integrity and fidelity have characterized all his dealings with his clients, and he has the respect and esteem of everybody who knows him. He is a member of the Supreme Court of Pennsylvania, a member of the United States Circuit Court for the western district of Pennsylvania, and was recently admitted as a member of the Supreme Court of the United States, at Washington, D. C. In politics Mr. Jones is a republican. At present he is the chairman of the Republican Committee of the Fourth legislative district. He has represented his ward as delegate in nearly every republican county convention for the past five or six years, and has probably made more nominating speeches than any other person during those years; notably among them was the second to the nomination of R. W. Archbald, for additional law judge in the convention of July, 1884, in an effective speech which is still remembered by all who heard it; the nomination of Hon. Joseph A. Scranton for congress in the convention of August, 1885, and on the same day the nomination of Hon. J. B. Van Bergen for county treasurer. He was secretary of the convention of 1884, and was a member of the republican county committee for the same year, and did excellent service for his party. The republican electors of the Fourth legislative district (old Eighth district) have frequently unanimously chosen him to represent them in state conventions. He was a delegate to the state convention which met at Harrisburg, July 8, 1885, when Hon. Matthew Stanley Quay was nominated for state treasurer. This convention made him a member of the state committee for Lackawanna county. Again he represented his district in the state convenvention held at the same place June 30, 1886, and was made one of the vice-presidents of the same. In this convention he seconded the nomination of General E. S. Osborne for congressman-at-large in a strong and vigorous speech. Hon. Lazarus D. Shoemaker, of Wilkes-Barre, made the nominating speech. He was one of the three delegates from Lackawanna county that voted for Senator Davis, thus securing to him the nomination of lieutenant governor. Had the three delegates—Dale, Mitchell and Jones—voted against the senator, the nomination would have gone to Major Montooth, of Pittsburg, so close was the contest waged. In the state convention held August 17, 1887, he was a delegate and was appointed a member of the committee on permanent organization. He represented his district in the republican state convention held at Harrisburg, Pa., August 7, 1889, and was again appointed one of the vice-presidents of that body. He was first commissioned a notary public by Governor Henry M. Hoyt and has continued to hold that office for the past seven years. He is a member of the Blakely school board, having been reëlected for a second term, and has served as secretary of said board for three years. He is also a director of the poor of Blakely Poor District, and is secretary of that body. Thus it will be seen that he has the respect and confidence of the people. The committee of Veterans of the Grand Army of the Republic selected him to deliver the address of welcome at Olyphant on August 17, 1888, the occasion being the tenth annual reunion of the Five-County Veteran Association. In 1888 he was spoken of as an available candidate for district attorney of Lackawanna county, Pa. Had H. M. Edwards accepted the nomination of additional law judge of Lackawanna county, which was tendered him, Mr. Jones would have been nominated for district attorney. He married, December 4, 1884, Lizzie Eugenia Kenyon, a daughter of Rev. Jefferson B. Kenyon, a native of Pawling, N. Y. He removed to Blakely in 1832, and in 1836 married Rhoda H. Callender, a daughter of Samuel Callender, of Blakely. Mr. Kenyon was one of the earliest resident pastors of the Baptist church of Blakely, and retired from active service in 1871. He was an active member of the Blakely poor board and was the first burgess of that borough. Mr. and Mrs. Jones have a family of two children—Marshall Gray Jones and Helen Payne Jones.

GEORGE BAKER HILLMAN.

George Baker Hillman was born in this city May 21, 1867. He is the great-grandson of Joseph Hillman, whose son, H. B. Hillman was a native of Montgomery Square, Pa., where he spent his young manhood. At an early day he removed to

Mauch Chunk, Pa., where he was a partner in the mercantile business with Asa Packer, under the firm name of Packer & Hillman. Before the days of railroading in the Lehigh Valley, he ran packet boats between Mauch Chunk and Easton, and also between White Haven and Mauch Chunk. In 1842 he removed to this city and was one of the early coal operators in the Wyoming Valley. In 1847 he shipped ten thousand tons of coal from the old Blackman and Solomons Gap or Ross mines, to New York and Philadelphia on the Lehigh & Susquehanna Railroad. This was the first considerable amount of coal sent from this valley by that route. He for a time kept the old Eagle Hotel at the corner of Market and Franklin streets, where the Second National Bank now stands, but his principal business was that of a coal operator during his lifetime. In 1853 and 1854 he was burgess of the borough of Wilkes-Barre. In 1861 he was a member of the house of representatives, and was at one time a colonel in the militia, and he was known by young and old as Colonel Hillman. He died March 17, 1882. He married, May 4, 1831, Elizabeth Pryor, a daughter of John Pryor, a native of Mount Holly, N. J. His wife was Keziah Woodbury, a daughter of Richard Woodbury, of Mount Holly, and from whom the village of Woodbury, N. J. received its name. Mrs. Hillman is still living. H. B. Hillman, son of Colonel H. B. Hillman was born in Mauch Chunk, Pa., April 12, 1834. He has been engaged in the coal business the greater part of his manhood. In 1886 he lost his eldest son, Harry G. Hillman, twenty years of age, a bright and promising student of the Wilkes-Barre academy. As a memorial of this son the Harry Hillman academy owes its existence. We quote from its catalogue: "The admirable school building of the academy was erected by Mr. H. Baker Hillman, of this city. It is designed as a memorial of his eldest son, Harry Grant Hillman, a devoted pupil of the academy, whose untimely death was lamented by all who knew him. The lot and the building upon it are solely Mr. Hillman's gift. It is situated near the corner of West River and Terrace streets. The building, with a heavy foundation of stone, is of brick laid in red mortar. The cornices and sills are of cut stone ; the ornamentation is of terra-cotta. Externally it is of a handsome appearance,

and is highly creditable to the generosity which gave it, and to
the public appreciation which maintains it. The interior of the
building is planned from sketches made by the teachers, and is
therefore well adapted to its special uses. The first floor contains a large study room, with ample space for one hundred and
thirty-five single desks, two capacious cloak rooms, and a separate room in the rear for the primary department. On the second
floor are four large recitation rooms, an office, a reception room,
and a library room. The chapel and two large rooms for the
literary and scientific societies of the academy occupy the third
floor. Throughout the building there is plenty of air-space.
The ceilings are high; the hall-ways are wide; the rooms are
spacious. The building is heated and lighted throughout and
well furnished." H. B. Hillman is president of the board of
trustees of the Harry Hillman academy; a director of the
Peoples' Bank; secretary and director of the Vulcan Iron Works;
vice president and director of the Glen Summit Hotel Company,
and a director of the Electric Light Company. He is also a
vestryman in St. Stephen's Protestant Episcopal church. In 1871
and 1872 he was a councilman in this city. His wife, whom he
married February 19, 1862, is Josephine A. Hillman, daughter of
Joseph Hillman, of Nazareth, Pa., where he resided until he was
elected sheriff of Northampton county, Pa., when he removed to
Easton, Pa. George Baker Hillman, son of H. B. Hillman, was
educated in the public schools of this city and the Harry Hillman academy. He received his law education at the law department of the University of Pennsylvania, and was under the
instruction of Wayne McVeigh, of Philadelphia, and Dickson
(A. H.), and Atherton (T. H.), of this city. He was admitted to
the Luzerne county bar December 10, 1888. He is now in
Europe travelling with his father's family. It is too soon, perhaps, to make an entirely safe prediction as to Mr. Hillman's future
in his chosen profession. He appears, however, to have inherited,
in large part, the keen and prudent business instincts of his father,
and these, with the exceptional advantages he has had in the distinguished legal standing of the gentlemen who were his tutors,
constitute an equipment that should open up to him a successs-
ful and prosperous career.

GEORGE WASHINGTON MOON.

George Washington Moon was admitted to the bar of Luzerne county, Pa., December 10, 1888. He was educated in the public schools and high school, Easton, Pa., and Lafayette college, Easton, Pa., from which he graduated in the class of 1885, and read law with N. Taylor in this city. Mr. Moon was born in Scranton, Pa., July 4, 1860, and is the son of Silas R. Moon, a native of Scott township, Luzerne (now Lackawanna) county, Pa., who was the son of Henry Moon, a native of Dutchess county, N. Y. His mother is Mary E. Ward, a native of Scranton, and daughter of Conrad Ward, of that city. Mr. Moon has had the benefit of a good practical education as above shown, and is possessed of a patient energy that is invaluable in any walk of life, and especially in that of an attorney seeking to establish a practice. In the opportunities his professional career has thus far afforded (necessarily limited, because of the brief period that has elapsed since his admission), he has evinced an aptitude in analyzing a case and applying the features of the law that most closely fit it, that presage an ultimately paying and successful business.

WILLIAM JOHN TREMBATH.

William John Trembath was admitted to the Luzerne county bar December 10, 1888. He is the son of Thomas Trembath, a prominent hotel keeper of this city, a native of Penzance, Cornwall, England, who left his home at the age of nineteen, and was among the early adventurers to the gold fields of California and Australia. He came to this city in 1873, and has resided here since. His wife, the mother of W. J. Trembath, whom he married at Penzance, was Adelaide Love, of the same place. She was the daughter of Samuel Love, captain of a merchant vessel trading at Penzance. He was lost at sea. W. J. Trembath, son of Thomas Trembath, was born at Ballarat in the province of Victoria, Australia, December 16, 1859. At three years of age his father removed again to England, where he remained until William was six years of age, when he removed to this country. W. J. Trembath was educated in the public schools of this city, at Wyoming seminary, Kingston, Pa., and at Lafayette college, Easton Pa., graduating from the latter institution in the class of 1885. He read law with Nathaniel Taylor in this city. Among the quieter, hard-working younger members of the Luzerne bar, Mr. Trembath has already attracted no little attention. He is in no degree averse to, or afraid of the persistent and often wearisome labor that almost invariably is required in the building up of a legal practice, where high social influence or other adventitious aids are lacking, and herein displays a characteristic that almost always presages victory in the profession. He is a close student, has keen perceptions, is a ready reasoner and handles a case with much skill.

WILLIAM IRWIN HIBBS.

William Irwin Hibbs was admitted to the bar of Luzerne county, Pa., March 11, 1889. He is the son of Edward Montgomery Hibbs, a native of Bucks county, Pa., and grandson of John Hibbs, a native of the same county, who removed to Greenwood township, Juniata county, Pa., over fifty years since. The wife of E. M. Hibbs and mother of W. I. Hibbs, is Catharine Potter, daughter of John Potter, of Delaware township, Juniata county, Pa. W. I. Hibbs was born in Greenwood township, near Thompsontown, Pa., June 3, 1851. He was educated at the Millersville (Pa.) normal school and followed the occupation of a teacher for seventeen years. He read law with L. E. Atkinson, and was admitted to the bar of Juniata county, Pa., February 4, 1889. Mr. Hibbs' office is in Pittston, Pa. Nearly a score of years devoted to educational matters are not a bad groundwork for a legal career. The profession of school teaching is one in the pursuit of which there are many opportunities for acquiring knowledge that practice at the bar will develop profitable use for. It yields also a knowledge of human nature, which is not by any means the least useful accomplishment a lawyer can have. Mr. Hibbs has taken hold in the rapidly grown town to the north of us in a way that seems to promise the ultimate attainment by him of a first-class position in the line of practicing attorneys.

JAMES LINCOLN MORRIS.

James Lincoln Morris was admitted to the bar of Luzerne county, Pa., April 22, 1889. He is the son of Michael W. Morris, a native of Loughcurra, in the county of Galway, Ireland, where he was born March 1, 1830. The latter emigrated to this country in 1847, and located in Hawley, Pa. For six years he was engaged as clerk in a store and post office; for two years in the office of the Pennsylvania Coal Company, and for one year was in business for himself. In 1856 he removed to Pittston, where he has resided since. His principal business since he has resided in this county has been the mercantile and milling business. He is at present a member of the firm of Morris & Walsh, proprietors of the Keystone Roller Mills in this city. Mr. Morris has been a member of the school board of Pittston for fifteen years, and about all the school buildings that have been erected in that borough were erected during the time that Mr. Morris was on the board. He was treasurer of the Pittston school board for five years, and about the same length of time he was treasurer of the borough. He has been a director and treasurer of the Pittston Street Railway Company for fifteen years, and a director for eighteen years and one of the organizers of the Miners' Savings Bank, of Pittston. He is one of the most prominent Father Matthew men in the county, having taken the pledge from Father Matthew in 1842. He was for eighteen years treasurer of the Catholic Total Abstinence Union, of Pennsylvania. This office he resigned in June last. Mr. Morris was an original abolitionist, and on the organization of the republican party became one of its most active workers. In 1861 he was the candidate of the republican party for treasurer of Luzerne county. He was elected with the aid of the army vote, but that vote being declared unconstitutional, he was defeated by James Walsh, his democratic competitor. Mr. Morris was an ardent admirer of Horace Greely, and when he became a candidate for president, was active in the canvass, and upon his defeat became a democrat and has been active in its organization since. He married, June 11, 1857, Bridget E. Mulligan, a daughter of James Mulligan. He has a family of four children—James L., John W., Alice, wife of Eugene Mulligan, of this city, and Mary. James L. Morris, son of M. W. Morris, was born in Pittston, Pa., May 12, 1860. He was educated in the academy of the Immaculate Heart, at Pittston; in the public schools; and attended, for three years, the college of St. Hyancinthe, near Montreal, Quebec, Canada. He graduated from the Georgetown (D. C.) University in the class of 1882. He spent one year in the law department of Georgetown University and completed his law studies in the office of E. P. and J. V. Darling in this city. He has been a correspondent of the Scranton *Republican*, and of the *Union-Leader* of this city, and is at present one of the editors of the *Plainspeaker*, at Hazleton. He is also one of the court clerks. In 1888 he was secretary of the democratic county committee.

Mr. Morris is a young man of many excellent attainments. He has a wide acquaintance in all parts of the county, following upon his journalistic experience and his occupancy of the position of court clerk, and being of sunny disposition and genial manners, has made himself generally liked. His court clerkship necessarily gave him no little knowledge of the law and a familiarity with the methods of practice that must needs stand any observant and intelligent young man in good stead. His tastes incline him to continue giving part of his time to newspaper work, but his chances at the bar are among the best, if he shall see fit to give his attention chiefly to them.

THOMAS DARLING.

Thomas Darling, who was admitted to the bar of Luzerne county, Pa., April 22, 1889, is a son of the late E. P. Darling, of this city. (See page 88). The mother of Thomas Darling was Emily H. Rutter, a daughter of Nathaniel Rutter of this city. He was a native of Salisbury township, Lancaster county, Pa., where he was born in 1806. He came to this city in 1825, and has resided here since. He was first engaged as a clerk by Matthias Hollenback, and afterwards was a clerk for Ziba Bennett. He subsequently engaged in business with James D. Haff, as general merchants, under the firm name of Haff & Rutter, and when Judge David Scott became a partner, the firm was Haff, Rutter & Scott. In 1833 he went into business with George M. Hollenback, under the firm name of Hollenback & Rutter. This partnership continued until 1846, when Mr. Rutter went into business for himself, which he continued until 1888, when he retired. The grandfather of Nathaniel Rutter was George Rutter, a native of Germany. He came to this country and settled in Salisbury township, where Adam Rutter, the father of Nathaniel Rutter, was born. The mother of Mrs. Darling was Mary Ann Cist, a daughter of Jacob Cist. (See page 1353). Thomas Darling was born in Wilkes-Barre, Pa., May 29, 1863. He was educated in the public schools of this city, at the Wilkes-Barre academy, and Yale college, from which he graduated in the class of 1886. He read law with E. P. and J. V. Darling. A graduate of one of our leading universities, and the son and pupil of such eminent lawyers as his father and uncle, could not well help starting upon his professional career, if otherwise at all qualified, with success more than half won. The young man in this case has evidently fallen heir to not a few of the qualities that were the principal factors in the father's achievement of what was probably the most important practice (important in respect to the vast interests involved) enjoyed by any member of the Luzerne bar. He is only a beginner as yet, but his manner and bearing have made a good impression upon those of the older lawyers with whom he has been brought into contact in connection with his late father's and uncle's business, and these are generally agreed that he is destined to a leading place at the bar, if that object shall continue to be the goal of his ambition.

ADDITIONS, ALTERATIONS AND CORRECTIONS.

J. A. GORDON, p. 1. Mr. Gordon died at his residence in Plymouth, Pa., February 4, 1882.

H. B. WRIGHT, p. 2. Mr. Wright died at his residence in this city September 2, 1881.

E. W. STURDEVANT, p. 14. Mr. Sturdevant died at his residence in this city October 30, 1882.

E. L. DANA, p. 31. Judge Dana died at his residence in this city April 25, 1889.

STEUBEN JENKINS, p. 52. Mr. Jenkins was elected to the legislature of the state of Pennsylvania in 1882, and served in the regular session, and also in the extra session of 1883. He was appointed by Governor Pattison trustee for the State Hospital for the Insane at Danville for three years, and at the expiration of his term by Governor Beaver for an additional term of three years. He is the author of the following publications:

1878. Historical Address at the Wyoming Monument at the Centennial Commemorative Exercises, July 3, 1878, in pamphlet.
1879. Historical Address at the Centennial Celebration of the Battle of Newtown of August 29, 1779, etc. Published by the State of New York, in a large volume, page 451, etc.
1881. "A Celebration in ye Olden Time." Prepared by request of the Wyoming Historical and Geological Society, read at a meeting of that society and published in its proceedings.
1883. "The Pittston Fort." Prepared for and published by the same society.
1884. "Wyoming, Connecticut, Western Reserve." Published in the Historical Register, Harrisburg, by Dr. Wm. H. Egle, Vol. II, No. 1.
1888. "The Old Forty Fort Church"—Its history as a Presbyterian place of worship, etc., in pamphlet.
1889. Address at the Centennial Reunion of the Breese Family, at Horseheads, June 19, 1889. Published in *Chemung Valley Reporter*, June 20, 1889.

He is also author of the following biographies and genealogies of old Wyoming families, published in History of Luzerne, Lackawanna and Wyoming Counties: The Dana family, the Dorrance family, the Pettebone family, the Swetland family, the Slocum family, and some others in whole or in part. Also the Jenkins family of Rhode Island and Wyoming, published in the Historical Register of Rhode Island, and in pamphlet. He delivered an address before the Wyoming Historical and Geological Society, at the court house in the city of Wilkes-Barre, September 25, 1887, on the occasion of the celebration of the centennial of the formation of Luzerne county, which is to be published by that society with the other proceedings. "Mr. Jenkins the poet historian, has written much and well, but published little. Full of vigor, originality and dramatic power, his verses breathe the crispness of the morning air and the pungency of spring buds, and however defective we may find the finish of his work, we cannot but admit that their author possesses a well-stored mind and a high degree of poetic inspiration, which is always drawn from nature's great fountains. "Wyoming," a tale of the revolutionary war, "Manitou of Wyoming," and "The Concord Chase," his longest poems, contain many delightful descriptive passages. "The Forest of Life" is a collection of his shorter bits of verse, many of which evince a fair degree of lyric power."

GARRICK M. HARDING, p. 70. We were in error in stating that Judge Harding was born July 12, 1830. He was born July 12, 1827.

H. M. HOYT, p. 74. Ex-Governor Hoyt now resides in Philadelphia, Pa.

ALEXANDER FARNHAM, p. 84. See page 225 for Mr. Farnham's military record. After Mr. Ricketts' refusal to be mustered into the United States service, E. W. Finch was elected captain and Alexander Farnham first lieutenant. John D. Farnham, eldest son of Alexander Farnham, is now a senior in Yale University.

E. P. DARLING, p. 94. We were in error in stating that Colonel John Bull was the father of Rev. Levi Bull, D. D.; neither was his wife the daughter of Robert Smith. The wife of John Smith, the maternal grandfather of E. P. Darling, was Elizabeth Bull, daughter of Thomas Bull, of Chester county, Pa., who was born June 9, 1744, the son of William Bull, an early settler in that county. He received the meagre education afforded in his day, and learned the trade of a stonemason. Prior to the revolution he was the manager of Warwick furnace. When that struggle came he entered heartily into the contest, and assisted in organizing the Chester county Battalion of Associators of the "Flying Camp," commanded by Colonel William Montgomery, of which he was commissioned lieutenant colonel. He was taken prisoner at Fort Washington in November, 1776, and confined on the Jersey prison ship. After several months he was properly exchanged. He subsequently returned to his position as manager of Warwick furnace, where he remained several years. In 1780 he was appointed by the general assembly one of the commissioners for the removal of the county seat. He was elected a delegate to the Pennsylvania convention to ratify the federal constitution in 1787, and served as a member of the state constitutional convention of 1789–90. He was chosen a presidential elector in 1792, and from 1795 to 1801 represented Chester county in the legislature of the state. Prior to this he had purchased a fine tract of land on the head-waters of French creek, erecting thereon a grist and saw-mill, besides a large mansion, where he passed the evening of his days. Colonel Bull was one of the men of mark in Chester county, and prominent in public affairs for half a century. In business affairs he was enterprising, in social life generous and genial, and in his church a faithful officer. In recognition of his eminent services during the war for independence, congress, as well as his native state, granted him a handsome annuity. He died July 13, 1837. His first wife, and the mother of his children, was Ann, daughter of John and Ann Hunter, of Whiteland, Chester county. They had eight children. The wife of Rev. Levi Bull, D. D., was Ann, daughter of Cyrus Jacobs, a prominent iron merchant in Pennsylvania. E. P. Darling died October 19, 1889. The greater part of the members of the Luzerne bar met at the court house, in this city, on October 22. Hon. Garrick M. Harding called the meeting to order. Hon. Andrew T. McClintock was elected chairman, and Allen H. Dickson, Esq., secretary.

The following seven members of the bar were appointed a committee to draft resolutions of respect: Alexander Farnham, chairman, Hon. Charles E. Rice, Hon. D. L. Rhone, Hon. Garrick M. Harding, Hon. L. D. Shoemaker, George B. Kulp and George R. Bedford. The committee retired and after a short absence returned and Mr. Farnham read the following resolutions which were unanimously adopted:

"The members of the bar of Luzerne county are assembled to give expression to their deep sense of bereavement, occasioned by the death of their honored and beloved associate, Edward Payson Darling. Death is at all times a startling visitor, even when expected, but when he suddenly appears and strikes down from a community one of its foremost citizens, a shock is felt to its utmost bounds. That sense of loss which otherwise would be limited, takes on a public character and becomes universal. We are conscious of a great void where, just before, there had been an inspiring presence, and we feel that the light of a splendid example has gone out from us forever. There comes to the thought, the recollection of those qualities of mind and soul which marked him and which went to make up the excellence of his character as it stood revealed before his fellow men. We are possessed of a deep and earnest conviction that an irreparable loss has fallen to the community, and that the vacant place he left cannot well be filled during his generation. With what greater force do these suggestions affect us here assembled, when it occurs that a citizen, who has died thus honored and lamented, is one of our professional circle—a member of our own bar. Who, outside of the relationship of kindred and family, can so well testify concerning him as those, of similar vocation, who have had professional intercourse with him day by day, as the years have rolled by. * * * * From the very first, he ranked as one of the ablest of the younger members of the bar, and gave early promise of his subsequent brilliant professional career. His legal apprehensions were instinctive, and he was possessed of a quick, intuitive perception that enabled him to single out at once the essential point of a case and apply the principle of law which controlled it. He was, moreover, imbued with the learning of the law. He kept well abreast with the current of judicial decision. To a keen intelligence he united a broad and generous culture. His diction was of the purest and was conciseness itself. None could excel and but few equaled him in courtesy of demeanor. His whole bearing, and all that he said and did, indicated refinement of thought and action. Modest, gentle and unobtrusive, as he was, the superior qualities of his mind and nature were at once revealed and profoundly impressed those with whom he was brought into contact. At no time did he lose that sense of personal dignity which always commands involuntary respect. With these qualifications, no one stood better equipped for the duties of his profession. He gave, in addition, unremitting service to his patrons. But one result could ensue. He speedily rose to the highest rank, becoming one of the acknowledged leaders of our bar. His usefulness took even a wider range. He possessed the full confidence of the community, and his name was associated with most of its public enterprises. He was prominent in many of its financial institutions and in its organized charities and trusts. Not only do we mourn him as a leader fallen from among us, but also as a brother around whom our affections centered. The grace of his personal character—the charm of his personal qualities—his unfailing courtesy—the refined spirit which marked his demeanor—his generous nature and quick sympathies—all these made up a personality which was endearing, a personality whose example will abide with us, and whose memory will be green and unfading while we live. It is with these reflections that we have come to lay our tribute upon his bier; therefore, be it

Resolved, That the members of the bar of Luzerne county have learned with profound sorrow of the death of their fellow member, Edward P. Darling, Esquire.

Resolved, That in the death of Mr. Darling, not only has the community lost a foremost citizen, our profession a distinguished ornament, but each member of the bar feels a deep and abiding sense of personal bereavement.

Resolved, That we tender to the family of the deceased our heartfelt sympathies in the great sorrow which has fallen upon them.

Resolved, That a copy of these proceedings be presented the court at its next session and, with its permission, be placed upon the minutes thereof.

Resolved, That a copy of these resolutions be transmitted to the family of the deceased, and that they be printed in the newspapers of the county.

The resolutions were unanimously adopted, on motion of Mr. Brundage.

STANLEY WOODWARD, p. 97. John B. Woodward, son of Judge Woodward, is a member of the Luzerne county bar, and George S. Woodward, his other son, is in his second year at the medical department of the University of Pennsylvania. Both are graduates of Yale college.

AGIB RICKETTS, p. 105. Mr. Ricketts was born in Rohrsburg, Columbia county, Pa., October 12, 1834. We were in error in stating his birthplace as Orangeville, Pa.

CALVIN WADHAMS, p. 109. Mr. Wadhams died at his summer residence, Harvey's Lake, Pa., July 20, 1883.

E. H. CHASE, p. 125. Harold Taylor Chase a graduate of Harvard University is entered as a law student in his father's office.

ADDITIONS, ALTERATIONS AND CORRECTIONS.

ALFRED DARTE, p. 130. Captain Darte was elected district attorney of Luzerne county in November, 1888, over James L. Lenahan, by a majority of three hundred and ninety-nine votes.

HARRY HAKES, p. 134. Mr. Hakes is the grandson of George S. Hakes, instead of Lewis Hakes. See page 1198 for a corrected genealogy of the Hakes family. Mr. Hakes is the author of the genealogy of the Hakes family, a work of 220 pages, giving a history of the Hakes family in America.

GEORGE B. KULP, p. 148. Abraham Clemens, or Cleamans, father of Mrs. Jacob Kulp, was the grandson of Jacob Clemens, and son of Gerhart Clemens, who was born in 1680. He emigrated from the Palatinate on the Rhine in 1709. He purchased of David Powell in 1718 six hundred and ninety acres of land in what is now Lower Salford township, Montgomery county, Pa., on a branch of the Perkiomen creek, near the present village of Lederachsville. He built a mill there, known as Alderfer's, in 1726. This mill stood till 1823. He died in 1745. In 1718 he sold two hundred and fifty acres of his land to his son, Abraham Clemens, whose wife was Catharine Bachman. They had ten children, of whom Mary was the fifth. The old homestead is still in possession of some of his descendants. Abraham Clemens died in 1777. Abraham Kulp, the grandfather of George B. Kulp, was at one time a resident of Northampton (now Monroe) county, Pa. He resided on what is now known among the old settlers as Kulp's run, or, as some call it, Two-mile run, midway between Tobyhanna and Stoddartsville. Abraham Kulp removed from there in 1817, when Jacob Blakeslee, father of the present Jacob Blakeslee, moved into his house. The latter was born on the place and still resides there. Lyman Cobb Kulp, the only brother of George B. Kulp who grew to manhood, was at one time the publisher of the Rockport (Mo.) *Banner*. He was killed in the late civil war at the battle of Antietam. Rev. George H. Lorah, of Doylestown, Pa., a minister of the Methodist Episcopal Church, is a nephew of George B. Kulp, his mother, Amanda M. Lorah, being an elder sister of Mr. Kulp. The children of Mr. and Mrs. Kulp are John Stewart Kulp, M. D., now pursuing a post graduate course in the medical department of the University of Pennsylvania, Harry Eugene Kulp, and Mary Estelle Kulp. George B. Kulp is the president of the board of trustees of the Fourth M. E. church, of Wilkes-Barre. John Stewart, Esq., father-in-law of Mr. Kulp, was for fifteen years a director of the poor in the incorporated district composed of "Jenkins township, Pittston borough and Pittston township," composed of the boroughs of Pleasant Valley, Pittston and Hughestown, and the townships of Pittston, Jenkins, Lackawanna and Old Forge, and also for the same length of time, a director of "the poor of Providence," composed of the city of Scranton and the borough of Dunmore. He is president of that body. He is also one of the trustees of the Adams avenue M. E. church of Scranton.

GUSTAV HAHN, p. 162. The wife of Mr. Hahn died August 19, 1889. His son, Byron Gustav Hahn, is in the senior department of Lafayette college. He is also entered as a law student in the office of Henry A. Fuller.

E. S. OSBORNE, p. 164. In 1884 General Osborne was a candidate for congressman-at-large in the state of Pennsylvania. He had a majority in the state of 75,227. In 1886 he was also a candidate for congressman-at-large. He had a plurality of 47,615. In 1888 he was a candidate for congressman in the twelfth congressional district (Luzerne county) against John Lynch, democrat, and H. W. Evans, prohibitionist. He had a plurality of 1499 votes. John Ball Osborne, son of General Osborne, graduated from Yale college in the class of 1889. He is now a law student in his father's office. William Osborne, another son, is a cadet at the West Point military school.

D. L. RHONE, p. 170. In 1884 Judge Rhone was a candidate for reëlection as president judge of the Orphans' Court of Luzerne county. The republicans made no nomination against him, and he received the entire vote, 25,636. His daughter, Mary P., was married March 30, 1886, to Harry G. Marcy, of this city.

C. D. FOSTER, p. 184. In 1884 Mr. Foster was elected a member of the house of representatives of Pennsylvania from this city. He had a majority of 225 votes over J. S. Zirnhelt, his democratic competitor.

H. W. PALMER, p. 194. In 1889 Mr. Palmer was chairman of the Pennsylvania Constitutional Prohibition Committee. His eldest son, Bradley W. Palmer, is a graduate of Harvard University, in the class of 1888. He is a law student in his father's office.

D. L. O'NEILL, p. 235. Daniel L. O'Neill, Jr., and William A. O'Neill, sons of Hon. D. L. O'Neill, are entered as law students in their father's office.

E. K. MORSE, p. 245. Mr. Morse married, September 5, 1888, Margaret Isabel, daughter of Joseph B. Vannan, a native of Glasgow, Scotland, now a resident of Carbondale, Pa. He is superintendent of Van Bergen & Company's foundry and machine shops. A son, Kendall Morse, was born to Mr. Morse June 21, 1889.

R. J. BELL, p. 248. Mr. Bell died in this city May 26, 1889.

JAMES MAHON, p. 250. Mr. Mahon now resides in Scranton, Pa.

CHARLES L. LAMBERTON, p. 251. Mr. Lamberton now resides in the city of New York.

JOHN LYNCH, p. 282. In 1886 Mr. Lynch was a candidate for congress from the twelfth congressional election district of Pennsylvania. His competitors were J. A. Scranton, republican, and A. Knapp, M. D., prohibitionist. Mr. Lynch was elected by a plurality of 650 votes. In 1888 he was again a candidate, but was defeated by E. S. Osborne, republican.

ANDREW HUNLOCK, p. 307. We were in error in stating that Mr. Hunlock inherited a competency. This is not true. The wealth acquired by Mr. Hunlock is the result of his own efforts, aided largely by judicious investments.

BURTON DOWNING, p. 355. Mr. Downing married, November 2, 1886, Libbie H. Snyder, daughter of Alfred Snyder, of Scranton. Mr. Downing is now actively engaged in the practice of the law.

CHARLES E. RICE, p. 355. We were in error in stating that Moses Rice was born in 1797. It was the date of the birth of Thomas Arnold Rice, who was born in Eatonville, N. Y., and who died in 1880. We were also in error in relation to the Carr family. The grandfather of Eleazer Carr was Caleb Carr, who was born in East Greenwich, R. I. His son, Eleazer Carr, moved to Hancock, Berkshire county, Mass., shortly before the revolutionary war, and remained there until near 1800 (between 1790 and 1800), when, with his son Eleazer (the father of Vienna Carr), his wife and some other children, he removed to Salisbury, N. Y. About 1811 he sold his farm there and removed to Le Roy, Genessee county, N. Y. Charles E. Rice was the nominee of the republican party for law judge at the election in 1889. His competitors were Edwin Shortz, democrat, and Lewis D. Vail, of Philadelphia, prohibition. The vote was Rice, 12,197; Shortz, 11,062; Vail, 822. Mr. Rice succeeds himself as president judge of Luzerne county.

L. H. BENNETT, p. 413. We were in error in stating that Judge Hakes was a descendant of John Hakes. The fact is that John Hakes' name, while a resident of Lynn, Mass., was John Hawkes; after his removal to Windsor, where he resided for about twenty years, it was entered on the town records as John Hakes, with one exception, when it was spelled John Haykes, and when he removed to Deerfield, Mass., his name was again John Hawkes. At his death his estate was administered as John Hawkes. Judge Hakes was a descendant of Solomon Hakes. (See page 1198.)

W. H. MCCARTNEY, p. 427. In 1885 Mr. McCartney was the republican candidate for district attorney. He was defeated by James L. Lenahan, the vote standing—McCartney, 8604; Lenahan, 9191.

Q. A. GATES. Mr. Gates married, May, 7, 1885, Mary A. Clark, a daughter of the late Judson Clark, of Providence, who in his lifetime was one of the largest individual coal operators in the Lackawanna valley. Mrs. Gates died January 14, 1887, leaving to survive her one child, Elva Gates.

H. B. BEARDSLEE, p. 452. Mr. Beardslee died March 11, 1886, at Indian Orchard, Wayne county, Pennsylvania.

A. H. DICKSON, p. 458. Rev. John Casper Stœver, son of Dietrich Stœver, bürger and merchant of Frankenberg; name was entered on the ship's register with the addition of *sancro sanctæ theologiæ studiosus*. He spent his first year in America in the vicinity of Trappe, Montgomery county, Pa. In May, 1730, he settled on the upper waters of the Conestoga, near where New Holland, Pa., now stands. At this time he served as pastor of the Lutherans of Lancaster, Philadelphia and Berks counties. In September, 1732, Rev. John Christian Schultze arrived in Pennsylvania, and in 1733 he ordained Mr. Stœver at the Trappe, within a barn then used as a place of worship. The Augustus Lutheran church at Trappe was organized in 1732, and Rev. John C. Schultze was its pastor for a year, and from 1733 to 1742 Rev. John C. Stœver was its pastor. In the latter year Rev. Henry Melchoir Muhlenburg arrived in this country and became the pastor. How Mr. Muhlenburg became "the founder of the Lutheran Church in America" is beyond our comprehension, saying nothing of the Dutch Lutherans in New York and the Swedish Lutherans in Delaware and Pennsylvania. From 1728, the date of the arrival of Mr. Stœver in this country, his voice was heard preaching the gospel in all the German settlements in Pennsylvania. In 1733 he established "Die Evangelische Lutherische Gemeinde on der Kathores," where York, Pa., now stands. He regularly opened church records for the congregations he had organized at Mode Creek, New Holland, Lancaster, North Hill, Lebanon, and other places, and Father Stœver is justly entitled to be called the father of Lutheranism in Pennsylvania.

J. D. COONS, p. 468. Mr. Coons married, February 22, 1887, Ella Constine, a native of this city, and daughter of the late John Constine, a native of Duechersfeld, Bavaria, Germany. He was the son of Loeb Constine and his wife Babette (Mack) Constine. The mother of Mrs. Coons is Fanny Constine (nee Long), a daughter of the late Isaac Long, a native of Pretzfelt, Germany. Mr. and Mrs. Coons have a family of two children—John Constine Coons and Isador Coons.

L. B. LANDMESSER, p. 475. Mr. Landmesser was in 1889 the chairman of the republican county committee.

S. J. STRAUSS, p. 476. Mordecai Strauss, a brother of S. J. Strauss, now a third year's student in Johns Hopkins University, is entered as a law student in Gaius L. Halsey's office.

E. A. LYNCH, p. 488. Mr. Lynch married, October 7, 1888, Annie G. Lenahan, a daughter of Patrick Lenahan and his wife Elizabeth Lenahan (nee Duffy). (See page 558.)

O. J. HARVEY, p. 508. George Francis Nesbitt, a son of Abram Nesbitt, is a law student in the office of J. V. Darling.

H. C. MAGEE, p. 532. Mr. Magee died April 27, 1888, at Plymouth, Pa.

C. W. MCALARNEY, p. 533. Mr. McAlarney married, May 26, 1886, Clara Shonk, a daughter of John J. Shonk. (See page 543.) Mr. and Mrs. Shonk had one child, John Shonk McAlarney, who is now deceased.

ERNEST JACKSON, p. 538. Mr. Jackson was chairman of the democratic county committee in 1888.

GEORGE W. SHONK, p. 541. Mr. Shonk, during the year 1889-90, was chairman of the republican county convention. He is secretary and treasurer of the Cabin Creek Coal Company, of the Williams Coal Company of Kanawha, of the Kanawha Railroad Company, and of the Cabin Creek and Coal River Land Company. He is a director of the Wilkes-Barre Heat,

Additions, Alterations and Corrections.

Light and Motor Company, of the Kingston Electric Company, and of the Wilkes-Barre and Harvey's Lake Railroad Company. He is secretary and treasurer of the last named company. He is also a member of the coal firm of Haddock, Shonk & Company, and the Pocassat Coal Company, and is a life director in the Wyoming Seminary, in Kingston, Pa. Stanley Woodward Davenport, a student at law in the office of George W. Shonk, is the great-great-grandson of Thomas Davenport, the ancestor of the Davenport family in this county. His great-grandfather was Thomas Davenport, Jr. His grandfather was Oliver Davenport, and his father is Edwin Davenport. (See page 544). Mr. Davenport married, June 13, 1889, Mary Weir, daughter of Andrew Weir. (See page 423).

J. L. LENAHAN, p. 558. Mr. Lenahan was the democratic candidate for district attorney in 1888, but was defeated by Alfred Darte.

NATHAN BENNETT, p. 561. Mr. Bennett died June 1, 1889.

EDWIN SHORTZ, p. 564. Robert Packer Shortz, eldest son of Edwin Shortz, is a cadet at the West Point Military Academy. In 1889 Edwin Shortz was the candidate of the democratic party of Luzerne county for law judge. He was defeated by Charles E. Rice. In 1863 and 1864 he was county surveyor of Carbon county, Pa.

W. R. GIBBONS, p. 573. Mr. Gibbons married, July 17, 1888, Ella M. Smith, a native of Ashley, Pa., daughter of Michael Smith, a native of Ireland. The mother of Mrs. Gibbons, and wife of Michael Smith, is Bridget Masterson, daughter of Cornelius Masterson, a native of Trim, county of Meath, Ireland, who resided in Newark, N. J., at the time of his death. Mr. and Mrs. Gibbons have one child—William Michael Gibbons.

G. H. R. PLUMB, p. 603. Mr. Plumb married, February 2, 1887, Mary E. Van Buskirk, a native of Hamilton township, Monroe county, Pa. She is a daughter of Samuel W. Van Buskirk, son of Jesse Van Buskirk, whose wife was a Miss Burrett, and her father was a soldier of the revolutionary war. Mr. Plumb now resides in Minneapolis, Minn.

W. H. HINES, p. 610. Mr. Hines was elected to the senate of Pennsylvania in 1888. His plurality was 924. Rev. T. C. Edwards was his republican competitor, and D. C. Jeremy was the prohibitionist candidate.

JOSEPH MOORE, p. 617. Mr. Moore married, March 3, 1888, Bessie Athey, a native of Donaldson, Schuylkill county, Pa. She is the daughter of Michael Athey, a native of the county of Durham, England. His wife is Elizabeth Fotheringill, daughter of Joseph Fotheringill, also a native of the county of Durham.

C. F. BOHAN, p. 625. Charles Patrick Bohan, a brother of C. F. Bohan, is a student in the law department of Yale University.

ZIBA MATHERS, p. 626. Mr. Mathers died at his residence in Luzerne, Pa., March 12, 1888.

C. B. STAPLES, p. 658. Mr. Staples has removed to Stroudsburg, Pa.

P. A. O'BOYLE, p. 659. Mr. O'Boyle married, October 11, 1888, Rosalie T. Walsh, a native of Lee, Mass. She is the daughter of Dennis Walsh, a native of Dublin, Ireland, who emigrated to this country about 1850. The wife of Dennis Walsh was Maria Burke, daughter of Richard Burke, an architect in Dublin. He was a relative of Edmund Burke, the great statesman and orator.

P. C. KAUFFMAN, p. 680. Mr. Kauffman married, September 11, 1889, Katharine Barton, daughter of John Barton, of Hazleton. Mr. Kauffman now resides at Vancouver, Washington.

D. A. FELL, p. 687. Mr. Fell married, October 10, 1888, Frances Lawrence Bertels, daughter of Arnold Bertels, of this city. Mr. and Mrs. Fell have one child—Harold Bertels Fell.

J. B. WOODWARD, p. 690. Mr. Woodward married, June 6, 1888, Marian, daughter of T. S. Hillard. (See page 799.)

J. Q. CREVELING, p. 694. Mr. Creveling married, June 13, 1889, Annie M. Pressler, a native of Bloomsburg, Pa.

J. B. SHAVER, p. 696. Mr. Shaver died April 1, 1887, at his residence in Plymouth, Pa.

C. E. KECK, p. 700. Mr. Keck married, August 29, 1888, Eva May Hoover, daughter of F. R. Hoover, of White Haven, Pa. Her mother, the wife of F. R. Hoover, was Elizabeth Messinger, daughter of Daniel Messinger.

P. A. MEIXELL, p. 729. Mr. Meixell was married, April 18, 1888, to Ella Gertrude Wise, a native of Newburg, N. Y., and daughter of A. C. Wise, also a native of Newburg, and his wife, Alvira C. Peck, a native of Colerain, Mass., daughter of Samuel Peck, of Peckville, Pa.

W. A. WILCOX, p. 742. Mr. Wilcox now resides in Scranton, Pa.

HARRY HALSEY, p. 753. Mr. Halsey was married, September 3, 1888, to Helen Virginia Hartman, a native of Baltimore, Md., daughter of J. P. Hartman, also of Baltimore. Her mother, Virginia Horsely, is a daughter of Dr. Samuel Cabell Horsely, who was at one time a surgeon in the United States army.

E. F. McGovern, p. 773. Mr. McGovern married, April 18, 1888, Ellen E. Murphy, a native of Plains township, and daughter of Francis Murphy, a native of county Armagh, Ireland. They have one child—Mary Frances McGovern.

P. V. WEAVER, p. 788. Peter Weaver, father of P. V. Weaver, a native of North White Hall, Lehigh county, Pa., died at his home in Butler township September 12, 1889.

H. C. ADAMS, p. 807. Mr. Adams died in this city April 1, 1889.

ADDITIONS, ALTERATIONS AND CORRECTIONS. 1391

F. W. LARNED, p. 808. Mr. Larned married, December 15, 1888, Estella L. Neiier, a daughter of W. W. Neiier, a native of Hamburg, Pa. His grandfather was one of the pioneers of Schuylkill county, Pa., and at one time owned twenty-six hundred acres of coal land near Pottsville, which is known as Neiier's Hollow. W. W. Neiier removed to Wilkes-Barre in 1856. The wife of W. W. Neiier died November 16, 1889.

G. G. WALLER, p. 842. Mr. Waller died December 4, 1888, at Brooklyn, N. Y.

A. W. BANGS, p. 866. Tracy R. Bangs was the democratic nominee for attorney general in North Dakota in the election of 1889.

THOMAS M. ATHERTON, p. 867. Mr. Atherton was born April 12, 1829, in that part of Kingston township now known as Forty Fort. He was educated at Wyoming seminary, and read law with L. D. Shoemaker, in this city. He was postmaster at Huntsville from 1858 until he removed to the west in 1860. In the latter year he moved to Mitchell county, Iowa, and was appointed the first postmaster of West Mitchell, Iowa. In 1862 he was superintendent of the Mitchell county schools. He was postmaster of Osage, Iowa, under Presidents Grant, Hayes and Arthur, when he resigned, and President Arthur appointed Mr. Atherton's son, Frank G., as his successor. He established and edited the *Mitchell County Press* in 1865, and has conducted it successfully since. For the past two years his daughter, Mary W., has had charge of the local department. T. M. Atherton is the son of Anson Atherton, grandson of Elisha Atherton. The wife of Anson Atherton was Sarah Mitchell, daughter of Thomas Mitchell. T. M. Atherton married, May 9, 1850, Elizabeth T. Gilmore, daughter of Stephen M. Gilmore, who married, in 1816, Jane Doane, a native of Harrisburg. (See page 1195.) Mr. and Mrs. Atherton have a family of six children—Jennie S. Atherton, wife of Isaac Patterson; Anna Elizabeth Atherton, wife of Nathan Patterson; Frank G. Atherton, intermarried with Mollie H. Westler, daughter of the late Hon. Nathan G. Westler, of Nescopeck, who represented Luzerne county in the legislature of the state in 1869; Charles Snover Atherton, Mary W. Atherton, and Thomas M. Atherton.

JOHN B. MILLS, p. 905. Mr. Mills died October 22, 1889, at Riverside, Pa.

F. E. BURROWS, p. 936. Mr. Burrows was born October 6, 1842, in Pike township, Bradford county, Pa. He was educated at Fort Edward (N. Y.) Collegiate Institute and at Harvard Law School, from which he graduated in 1867. His great-grandfather, Daniel Burrows, was a native of Groton, Conn. He was a member of congress from 1821 to 1823, and was also collector of the port at Middletown, Conn. He received his appointment from President Jackson. He was also a minister of the Methodist Episcopal church. The grandfather of F. E. Burrows, Daniel Burrows, was a native of Hebron, Conn., as was also his father, Joshua Burrows. Mr. Burrows practiced his profession in this city, also in the city of New York.

WILLIAM LEE PAINE, p. 1003. This name should read William Lewis Paine.

J. W. MINER, p. 1246. Thomas Miner, the second son of Clement Miner, was born at Chow-Magna, in the county of Somerset, England, April 23, 1608. He emigrated to this country with John Winthrop in the ship Arabella in 1630, and settled at Salem in June of the same year. He went to Charlestown and back to Boston, and there married, April 26, 1633, Grace, daughter of Walter Palmer, of Rehoboth, Mass. He settled in Stonington, Conn., in 1653, and died there October 23, 1690. His wife Grace died the same year. His son Clement was born in 1640, and died November 8, 1700. In a letter written by Charles Miner, August 5, 1830, he says: "There is a vein of several feet in the Baltimore Bed which is pure and beautiful beyond description, and the mine recently opened by Messrs. R. Miner and Z. Bennett is remarkable for its purity and excellence so far as explored. The last mine I mention more particularly because Professor Silliman, in his interesting and, in the main, very correct notes on the Susquehanna and Lackawanna basin, speaks of this as only 5 or 6 feet deep. That is the depth to which coal has been taken out. The auger has been sunk 18 feet 4 inches into solid coal and is not yet at the bottom." Professor Silliman speaks of the "Bed of Messrs. Bennett & Miner, four miles east from Wilkes-Barre, and one and a half from the Susquehanna River." John Abbott, father of Stephen Abbott, built the first dwelling house in the present limits of the city of Wilkes-Barre. It was of logs, and located at the southwest corner of Main and Northampton streets. Asher Miner married, November 6, 1889, Hetty Lonsdale, daughter of Robert C. and Mrs. Shoemaker.

Wilkes-Barre, Pa., November 18, 1889.

LIST OF DECEASED PRESIDENT JUDGES, ADDITIONAL LAW JUDGES, ASSOCIATE JUDGES, NON-RESIDENT MEMBERS OF THE BAR, LIVING JUDGES AND RESIDENT LAWYERS OF LUZERNE COUNTY.

DECEASED PRESIDENT JUDGES.

NAMES.	PLACE OF BIRTH.	DATE OF BIRTH.	DATE OF COMMISSION	DATE OF DEATH.
Burnside, Thomas	Newton Stewart, Ireland.	July 28, 1782.	June 28, 1816.	March 25, 1851.
Chapman, Seth	Wrightstown, Pa.	January 23, 1771.	July 11, 1811.	
Conyngham, John N.	Philadelphia, Pa.	December 17, 1798.	April—1841.	February 23, 1871.
Cooper, Thomas	London, England.	October 22, 1759.	March 1, 1806.	May 11, 1840.
Gibson, John B.	Shearmans Valley, Pa.	November 8, 1780.	October 16, 1812.	May 3, 1853.
Jessup, William	Southampton, L. I.	June 21, 1797.	April 7, 1838.	September 11, 1868.
Rush, Jacob	Philadelphia, Pa.	———1746.	August 17, 1791.	January 5, 1820.
Scott, David	Blandford, Mass.	April 3, 1782.	July 7, 1818.	December 29, 1839.

DECEASED ADDITIONAL LAW JUDGE OF LUZERNE COUNTY.

Dana, E. L.	Wilkes-Barre, Pa.	January 29, 1817.	December 2, 1867.	April 25, 1889.

DECEASED ASSOCIATE JUDGES OF LUZERNE COUNTY.

Barnum, Charles T.	Kingston, Pa.	January 7, 1813.	November 12, 1856.	January 11, 1887.
Bennett, Ziba	Weston, Conn.	November 10, 1800.	February 21, 1842.	November 4, 1878.
Bradley, Abraham	Litchfield, Conn.	February 21, 1767.	August 17, 1791.	May 7, 1838.
Carpenter, Benjamin	Orange county, N. Y.		May 11, 1787.	
Collins, Thomas	Ireland.		November 9, 1866.	
Denison, Nathan	Connecticut.	January 25, 1741.	August 17, 1791.	January 25, 1809.
Fell, Jesse	Buckingham, Pa.	April 16, 1751.	February 5, 1798.	August 5, 1830.
Gore, Obadiah	Plainfield, Conn.	December 18, 1744.	May 11, 1787.	March 21, 1821.
Grant, Sanford	Vernon, Conn.	———1800.	November 23, 1861.	January 29, 1886.
Hancock, William	Wilkes-Barre, Pa.	December 18, 1799.	November 10, 1851.	January 7, 1859.
Harrison, Canfield	Huntington, Pa.	———1809.	July 3, 1862.	February 28, 1880.
Hollenback, Matthias	Jonestown, Pa.	February 17, 1752.	May 11, 1787.	February 18, 1829.
Hurlbut, Christopher	Groton, Conn.	———1757.	August 5, 1789.	April 21, 1831.
Kingsley, Nathan	Scotland, Conn.	January 23, 1743.	May 11, 1787.	———1822.
Kinney, Joseph	Plainfield, Conn.	———1755.	June 2, 1789.	———1841.
Koons, John	Stroudsburg, Pa.	August 23, 1795.	April 22, 1846.	February 13, 1878.
Merrifield, William	Pine Plains, N. Y.	April 22, 1806.	November 12, 1856.	June 4, 1877.
Murray, Noah	Litchfield, Conn.	———1736.	November 28, 1788.	May 11, 1811.
Myers, Lawrence	Germany.		July 7, 1790.	
Nesbitt, James	Connecticut.	June 12, 1718.	May 11, 1787.	July 2, 1792.
Osterhout, Isaac S.	Lagrange, Pa.	October 26, 1806.	February 6, 1870.	April 12, 1882.
Pettebone, Henry	Kingston, Pa.	October 5, 1802.	March 6, 1845.	May 5, 1851.
Pfouts, B. F.	Jersey Shore, Pa.	April 12, 1809.	November 9, 1870.	January 6, 1874.
Pickering, Timothy	Salem, Mass.	July 17, 1745.	October 12, 1786	January 29, 1819.
Reichard, John	Frankenthal, Prussia.	May 24, 1807.	November 23, 1861.	August 19, 1884
Reynolds, W. C.	Plymouth, Pa.	December, 1801.	March 15, 1841.	January 25, 1869.
Ross, W. S.	Wilkes-Barre, Pa.	August 11, 1802.	May 6, 1829.	July 11, 1868.
Shoemaker, C. D.	Kingston, Pa.	July 9, 1802.	August 21, 1830.	August 1, 1861.
Slocum, Joseph	Malden, R. I.	April 9, 1777.	April 28, 1851.	
Smith, William Hooker	New York.	———1724.	May 11, 1787.	July 17, 1815.
Steele, George P.	Luzerne county, Pa.	———1801.	November 9, 1866.	———1870.
Taylor, Edmund	Allyngford, England.	August 4, 1804.	January 15, 1850.	February 8, 1881.
Welles, Rosewell	Glastonbury, Conn.	August 20, 1761.	April 26, 1793.	March 19, 1830.

DECEASED MEMBERS OF THE BAR.

NAMES.	PLACE OF BIRTH.	DATE OF BIRTH.	ADMITTED.	DATE OF DEATH.
Adams, Henry Clay	Wilkes-Barre, Pa.	———1865.	May 19, 1888	April 1, 1889.
Allen, John I.			January 6, 1841.	
Alsover, Jabez	Easton, Pa.	September 26, 1843.	May 3, 1870.	December 2, 1878.
Beardslee, H. B.	Mount Pleasant, Pa.	April 15, 1821.	April 16, 1874.	March 11, 1886.
Beaumont, W. H.	Wilkes-Barre, Pa.	November 27, 1825.	April 8, 1851.	June 19, 1874.
Bedford, James S.	Waverly, Pa.	October 16, 1829.	January 10, 1854	December 2, 1865.
Bell, Rufus J.	Troy, N. Y.	September 9, 1829.	September 27, 1864.	May 26, 1889.
Bennet, Charles	Kingston, Pa.	February 28, 1819.	April 7, 1845.	August 6, 1866
Bennet, D S.	Fairfield, Pa.	September 3, 1853.	June 11, 1877.	September 16, 1884.
Bennett, Nathan	Wilkes-Barre, Pa.	July 7, 1852.	September 22, 1879.	June 1, 1889.
Bidlack, B. A.	Paris, N. Y.	September 8, 1804.	January 5, 1825.	February 6, 1849.
Blackman, Miner S.	Wilkes-Barre, Pa.	August 14, 1815.	January 2, 1843.	May 25, 1848.
Bowman, Caleb F.	Berwick, Pa.	February 21, 1822.	August 5, 1850.	January 25, 1874.

Deceased Members of the Bar.

NAMES.	PLACE OF BIRTH.	DATE OF BIRTH.	ADMITTED.	DATE OF DEATH.
Bowman, Ebenezer	Lexington, Mass.	July 3, 1757.	May 27, 1787.	March 1, 1829.
Bowman, James W.	Wilkes-Barre, Pa.	August 9, 1799.	August 8, 1820.	———1834.
Bowman, Samuel	Wilkes-Barre, Pa.	May 21, 1800.	August 8, 1821.	August 3, 1861.
Bradley, Abraham	Litchfield, Conn.	February 21, 1767.	September 2, 1788.	May 7, 1838.
Brisbin, John	Chenango county, N. Y.	———1818.	———1857.	February 3, 1880.
Brundage, C. B.	Conyngham, Pa.	September 4, 1838.	May 8, 1860.	January 27, 1871.
Bryson, James	Minersville, Pa.		March 21, 1872.	———1887.
Butler, Chester	Wilkes-Barre, Pa.	March 21, 1798.	August 8, 1820.	October 5, 1850.
Byington, T. L.	Johnsonburg, N. J.	March 15, 1831.	November 7, 1853.	June 16, 1888.
Byrne, Peter J.	Eniscorthy, Ireland.	———1799.	August 3, 1846.	June 30, 1875.
Cake, Isaac M.	Northumberland, Pa.	January 6, 1817.	January 4, 1859.	July 2, 1888.
Campbell, Joseph H.	Northumberland Co., Pa.	July 8, 1829.	November 12, 1867.	August 7, 1888.
Canavan, Martin	County Sligo, Ireland.	———1802.	August 10, 1852.	
Case, William F.			February 20, 1865.	
Catlin, Charles	Wilkes-Barre, Pa.	March 15, 1790.	March 28, 1814.	
Catlin, George	Wilkes-Barre, Pa.	July 26, 1796.	January 4, 1819.	December 23, 1872.
Catlin, Putnam	Litchfield, Conn.	April 5, 1764.	May 27, 1787.	———1842.
Chamberlain, Albert	Bennington, Vt.	December 29, 1811.	September 3, 1861.	December 21, 1877.
Chase, Ezra B.	West Windsor, N. Y.	December 25, 1827.	April 7, 1857.	February 15, 1864.
Collins, Oristus	Marlboro, Conn.	September 22, 1792.	April 8, 1819.	———1884.
Conyngham, John B.	Wilkes-Barre, Pa.	September 29, 1827.	August 6, 1849.	May 27, 1881.
Conyngham, John N.	Philadelphia, Pa.	December 17, 1798.	April 3, 1820.	February 23, 1871.
Covell, Edward M.	Wilkes-Barre, Pa.		January 2, 1843.	September 8, 1864.
Craig, John P.	Columbia Co., Pa.	February 18, 1829.	January 3, 1860.	February 21, 1862.
Crane, F. M.	Salisbury, Conn.	———1815.	April 4, 1838.	January 8, 1877.
Dana, E. L.	Wilkes-Barre, Pa.	January 29, 1817.	April 6, 1841.	April 25, 1889.
Dana, Milton	Eaton, Pa.	February 27, 1822.	November 6, 1846.	February 18, 1886.
Dana, Sylvester	Wilkes-Barre, Pa.	May 28, 1806.	November 7, 1828.	June 19, 1882
Darling, E. P.	Berks county, Pa.	November 10, 1831.	August 13, 1855.	October 19, 1889.
Darte, Alfred	Bolton, Conn.	July 14, 1810.	November 2, 1846.	August 13, 1883.
Denison, Charles	Kingston, Pa.	January 23, 1816.	August 13, 1840.	June 27, 1867.
Denison, George	Kingston, Pa.	February 22, 1790.	April 7, 1813.	August 20, 1832.
Dickinson, Israel			April 16, 1836.	
Dietrick, A. J.	Columbia Co., Pa.	April 6, 1822.	December 11, 1880.	September 8, 1884.
Drake, George C.	Wilkes-Barre, Pa.	May 25, 1806.	August 8, 1827.	June 27, 1878.
Dyer, Thomas	Windham, Conn.	———1771.	———1802.	September 21, 1861.
Evans, John		———1814.		
Flanagan, M. J.	Pottsville, Pa.	August 27, 1842.	June 12, 1876.	February 1, 1880.
Fuller, Amzi	Kent, Conn.	October 19, 1793.	January 11, 1822.	September 26, 1847.
Fuller, Henry M.	Bethany, Pa.	June 3, 1820.	January 3, 1842.	December 26, 1860.
Gordon, James A.	Corning, N. Y.	October 6, 1797.	August 7, 1822.	February 4, 1882.
Gore, John L.			January 22, 1862.	May 15, 1862.
Graham, Thomas		———1798.	———1800.	April 26, 1814.
Griffin, George	East Haddam, Conn.	January 14, 1778.	April 6, 1841.	May 6, 1860.
Hakes, Lyman	Harpersfield, N. Y.	March 23, 1816.	February 20, 1862.	December 8, 1873.
Hamilton, Arthur	Scotland.		November 4, 1847.	October 20, 1862.
Harvey, Elisha B.	Harveyville, Pa.	October 1, 1819.	January 18, 1858.	August 20, 1872.
Haughawout, George D.	Northumberland Co., Pa.	March 16, 1827.	April 3, 1833.	August 8, 1886.
Headley, Samuel F.	Litchfield, N. Y.	January 20, 1808.	August 3, 1847.	July 25, 1869.
Hill, E. S. M.	Carmel, N. Y.	December 20, 1822.	November 6, 1843.	———1874.
Hodgdon, Samuel	Philadelphia, Pa.	September 3, 1793.	April 4, 1842.	January 17, 1865.
Holliday, James			April 1, 1850.	———1874.
Jackson, Angelo	Erie, N. Y.		January 5, 1841.	July 23, 1879.
Jackson, M. E.	Herwick, Pa.	February 10, 1817.	April 6, 1831.	February,—1854.
Johnson, O. F.	Wilkes-Barre, Pa.	March 7, 1807.	January 14, 1823.	February 3, 1860.
Jones, Joel	Coventry, Conn.	October 26, 1795.	August 6, 1833.	June 1, 1883.
Jones, M. H.	Hebron, Conn.	September 11, 1811.	January 2, 1844.	
Jones, Nathaniel	Wilkes-Barre, Pa.	March 24, 1830.	August 20, 1861.	
Ketcham, J. H.	Wilkes-Barre, Pa.	June 29, 1820.	January 8, 1850.	December 6, 1879.
Ketcham, W. W.	Waterford, Vt.	November 19, 1808.	November 5, 1833.	September 30, 1884.
Kidder, Luther	Wilkes-Barre, Pa.	July 3, 1842.	April 27, 1868.	December 25, 1874.
Kidder, R. M.	Palmer, Mass.	July 6, 1790.	April 3, 1815.	July 13, 1861.
King, Henry	Charleston, S. C.	January 1, 1838.	November 12, 1878.	August 23, 1884.
Kingman, W. R.	Sherburne, N. Y.	July 28, 1811.	November 5, 1833.	October 8, 1887.
Lathrop, D. N.	Philadelphia, Pa.	August 19, 1819.	November 3, 1840.	August 11, 1847.
Le Clerc, E. E.	Harrisburg, Pa.	June 18, 1786.	April 25, 1806.	September 10, 1871.
Lee, Washington	Luzerne county, Pa.	May 8, 1821.	August 4, 1845.	March 26, 1883.
Lee, Washington	Wilkes-Barre, Pa.	March 2, 1829.	August 5, 1850.	September 22, 1861.
Lewis, A. C.	Delaware county, N. Y.	———1818.	August 4, 1840.	
Little, W. F.	Milford, Pa.	February 1, 1829.	August 6, 1855.	April 5, 1881.
Longstreet, S. P.	Perry Co., Pa.	February 6, 1848.	October 21, 1875.	April 27, 1888.
Magee, Henry C.	Wilkes-Barre. Pa.	———1812.	August 14, 1843.	May 27, 1852.
Mallery, E. G.	Middlebury, Conn.	April 17, 1784.	August 8, 1811.	July 6, 1866.
Mallery, Garrick	Wilkes-Barre, Pa.	———1812.	January 5, 1836.	———1838.
Mallery, P. B.	Luzerne, Pa.	October 25, 1858.	June 2, 1884.	March 12, 1888.
Mathers, Ziba	Hamilton county, N. Y.	June 12, 1804.	November 11, 1831.	January 4, 1873.
Maxwell, Volney L.	Jersey Shore, Pa.		January 23, 1826.	
McClintock, James	Wilkes-Barre, Pa.	September 25, 1846.	June 21, 1871.	September 4, 1886.
McQuillan, Dennis A.	Philadelphia, Pa.	———1779.	March 1, 1802.	———1815.
McShane, Francis	Philadelphia, Pa.	September 4, 1779.	August 3, 1816.	April 22, 1855.
Meredith, Thomas	Susquehanna Co., Pa.	January 7, 1844.	September 1, 1864.	September 3, 1876.
Merriman, Edgar L.	Yorkshire, England.	August 24, 1821.	August 3, 1847.	December 23, 1864.
Metcalf, Henry	Middletown, Pa.	January 13, 1820.	November 11, 1842.	June,—1877.
Miller, W. H.	Columbia county, Pa.	February 23, 1812.	April 13, 1839.	October 22, 1889.
Mills, John B.			October 31, 1816.	March 14, 1818.
Miner, Josiah H.	Doylestown, Pa.	January 29, 1825.	August 5, 1850.	February 5, 1859.
Miner, Joseph W.	Wilkes-Barre.	October 7, 1824.	April 7, 1846.	November 25, 1847.
Myers, John W.				

Non Resident Lawyers of Luzerne County.

NAMES.	PLACE OF BIRTH.	DATE OF BIRTH.	ADMITTED.	DATE OF DEATH.
Myers, Philip T.	Kingston, Pa.	May 7, 1839.	January 6, 1865.	February 13, 1878.
Myers, William V.	Kingston, Pa.	May 31, 1850.	February 13, 1872.	September 24, 1874.
Nicholson, G. B.	Salem, Pa.	May 31, 1826.	November 10, 1848.	February 12, 1873.
Nicholson, Horatio W.	Salem, Pa.	December 4, 1817.	April 6, 1841.	June 16, 1865.
Nicholson, Lyman R.	Salem, Pa.	April 12, 1832.	April 6, 1855.	July 13, 1863.
Overton, Edward	Clithers, England.	December 30, 1795.	August 5, 1818.	October 17, 1878.
Overton, Thomas B.	Manchester, England.	May 21, 1791.	December 31, 1813.	1819.
Paine, Thomas E.			April 7, 1830.	1843.
Palmer, Nathan	Plainfield, Conn.		1794.	
Parke, Benjamin			1825.	
Parker, Jonathan W.			August 8, 1836.	
Pearce, Cromwell	Wilkes-Barre, Pa.	July 1, 1823.	April 8, 1851.	June 16, 1872.
Peckham, A. K.	Bristol, R. I.	October 15, 1815.	August 1, 1842.	March 22, 1865.
Pettebone, Henry	Kingston, Pa.	October 5, 1802.	August 3, 1825.	May 5, 1851.
Philbin, W. J.	Luzerne county, Pa.	January 11, 1854.	November 22, 1876.	August 29, 1882.
Pike, Charles	Luzerne county, Pa.	February 1, 1830.	April 4, 1853.	September 12, 1882.
Post, Isaac J.	Montrose, Pa.	June 21, 1837.	April 30, 1866.	July 10, 1885.
Pratt, W. H.			January 4, 1859.	
Prentice, William			1799	October 6, 1806.
Randall, David R.	Richmond, N. H.	August 21, 1818.	November 4, 1847.	August 31, 1875.
Rankin, Daniel			August 7, 1850.	
Reynolds, L. D.	Plymouth, Pa.	July 1, 1833.	August 4, 1856.	July 25, 1858.
Richards, Ira D		1826.	November 26, 1861.	February 9, 1874.
Robinson, John T.	Wilkes-Barre, Pa.	December 30, 1814.	April 4, 1838.	August 28, 1848.
Ruth, Ivan T.	Forestville, Pa.	June 18, 1847.	October 28, 1872.	November 19, 1878.
Sanderson, George	Boston, Mass.	February 25, 1810.	September 14, 1857.	April 1, 1876.
Scott, David	Blandford, Mass.	April 3, 1782.	January 3, 1809.	December 29, 1839.
Scott, George	Wilkes-Barre, Pa.	June 30, 1829.	January 10, 1854.	September 26, 1861.
Shaver, James B.	Dallas, Pa.	January 24, 1859.	June 21, 1886.	April 1, 1887.
Sherrerd, Samuel	Philadelphia, Pa.	April 25, 1819.	April 4, 1853.	June 27, 1884.
Silkman, Charles H	Bedford, N. Y.	July 24, 1809.	January 1, 1838.	March 8, 1877.
Simrell, E. W.	Luzerne county, Pa.	October 3, 1851.	June 4, 1874.	
Slocum, J. J.	Wilkes-Barre, Pa.	January 27, 1815.	August 12, 1837.	February 27, 1860.
Smith, Cyrenus M.			August 6, 1839.	
Smith, George T.	Waverly, Pa.	1844.	April 3, 1867.	September 4, 1871.
Stark, Conrad S.	Luzerne county, Pa.	April 2, 1836.	November 30, 1864.	March 26, 1880.
Stewart, A. C.			August 8, 1812.	1817.
Stout, Asher Miner	Bethlehem, Pa.	September, 1822.	August 4, 1845.	April —, 1860.
Stout, Charles Miner			April 7, 1851.	
Struthers, James R.	Paisley, Scotland.	August 3, 1815.	August 6, 1844.	May 8, 1885.
Sturdevant, F. W.	Braintrim, Pa.	June 11, 1806.	April 3, 1832.	October 30, 1882.
Wadhams, Calvin	Plymouth, Pa.	December 14, 1833.	April 6, 1857.	July 20, 1883.
Wadhams, Noah	Wethersfield, Conn.	May 17, 1726.	1794.	May 22, 1806.
Waelder, Jacob	Weisenheim, Germany.	May 17, 1820.	August 4, 1845.	August 28, 1887
Waller, C. P.	Wilkes-Barre, Pa.	August 7, 1819.	August 7, 1843.	
Waller, George G.	Wilkes-Barre, Pa.	May 3, 1821.	April 7, 1846.	December 4, 1888.
Welles, Rosewell	Glastonbury, Conn.	August 20, 1761.	May 27, 1887	March 19, 1830.
Wells, C. H.	Dundaff, Pa.	October 1, 1826.	August 30, 1860.	March 24, 1888.
Wells, George H.			January 6, 1840.	
Wells, Henry Hill	Sussex county, Delaware.	February 18, 1797.	August 4, 1835.	
Whitlock, Friend A.	Luzerne county, Pa.	December 30, 1850.	April 3, 1877.	November 24, 1880.
Wilmarth, Wesley S.	Harford, Pa.	October 7, 1834.	October 16, 1871.	May 8, 1875.
Wilmot, David	Bethany, Pa.	January 20, 1814.	August 5, 1834.	March 16, 1868.
Wilson, Amzi	Pittston, Pa.	December 17, 1795.	November 7, 1840.	May 27, 1872
Winchester, S. S.	Baltimore, Maryland.	October, —1817.	November 6, 1843.	June 26, 1881.
Woodward, George W.	Bethany, Pa.	March 26, 1809.	August 3, 1830.	May 10, 1875.
Woodward, Warren J.	Bethany, Pa.	September 24, 1819.	August 1, 1842.	September 23, 1879.
Wright, Benjamin D.	Wilkes-Barre, Pa.	January 23, 1792.	April 7, 1820.	April 28, 1875
Wright, Harrison	Plymouth, Pa.	January 24, 1815.	November 6, 1838.	August 25, 1856.
Wright, Harrison	Wilkes-Barre, Pa.	July 15, 1850.	September 14, 1874.	February 20, 1885.
Wright, Hendrick B.	Plymouth, Pa.	April 24, 1808.	November 8, 1831.	September 2, 1881.
Wright, Joseph	Wilkes-Barre, Pa.	June 18, 1839.	January 2, 1860.	May 18, 1862.
Wurts, William	Montville, N. J.	November 25, 1809.	August 6, 1832.	July 15, 1858.
Wurtz, John J.	Longwood, N. J.	February 2, 1801.	August 2, 1831.	November 1, 1856.

List of Lawyers Now Residing Out of Luzerne County.

NAMES.	PLACE OF BIRTH.	DATE OF BIRTH.	ADMITTED.	RESIDENCE.
Alexander, J. M.	Cortland county, N. Y.		August 4, 1846.	Mount Dora, Florida.
Amerman, Lemuel	Danville, Pa.	October 29, 1846	December 24, 1875.	Scranton, Pa.
Archbald, R. W.	Carbondale, Pa.	September 10, 1848.	September 17, 1873.	Scranton, Pa.
Atherton, Thomas M.	Forty Fort, Pa.	April 12, 1829.	February 28, 1859.	Osage, Iowa.
Babb, E. B.	Pittston, Pa.	December, —1819.	April 5, 1843.	North Vernon, Indiana.
Bailey, A. M.	West Abington, Pa.	September 16, 1837.	February 25, 1862.	Orange City, Florida.
Bangs, A. W.	Bethany, Pa.	July 26, 1834.	August 31, 1858.	Grand Forks, Dakota.
Barnes, Frank V.	Athens, Pa.	June 14, 1848.	January 21, 1874.	Bismarck, Dakota.
Baumann, Anthony	Baden, Germany.	June 2, 1844.	May 12, 1880.	Scranton, Pa.
Bentley, George F.	Montrose, Pa.	April 4, 1850.	April 17, 1876.	New York.
Brace, Burrell	Wyoming, Pa.		August 20, 1863.	Keelersburg, Pa.
Breck, Charles du Pont	Wilmington, Delaware.	May 18, 1840.	August 8, 1861.	Scranton, Pa.
Bunnell, Lewis M.	Susquehanna Co., Pa.	December 8, 1835.	August 24, 1869.	Scranton, Pa.
Burnham, Horace B.	Spencertown, N. Y.	September 10, 1824.	August 12, 1844.	Richmond, Va.
Burns, Ira H.	Clifford, Pa.	July 19, 1842.	January 21, 1868.	Scranton, Pa.
Burr, James E.	Carbondale, Pa.	July 8, 1853.	May 20, 1877	Carbondale, Pa.
Burrows, Francis E.	Bradford Co., Pa.	October 6, 1842.	September 5, 1871.	Stevensville, Pa.

NON RESIDENT LAWYERS OF LUZERNE COUNTY.

NAMES.	PLACE OF BIRTH.	DATE OF BIRTH.	ADMITTED.	RESIDENCE.
Butler, George D.			November 9, 1869.	
Byrne, M. J.			December 5, 1866.	
Chase, A. A.	Luzerne county, Pa.	March 28, 1839.	August 20, 1862.	Scranton, Pa.
Cohen, George E.	Pittston, Pa.	July 24, 1862.	December 11, 1886.	Scranton, Pa.
Collins, Francis D.	Saugerties, N. Y.	March 5, 1844.	December 24, 1866.	Dunmore, Pa.
Collings, John B.	Wilkes-Barre, Pa.	December 17, 1846.	March 2, 1870.	Scranton, Pa.
Connelly, D. W.	Cochecton, N. Y.	April 24, 1847.	May 10, 1870.	Scranton, Pa.
Connelly, John F.	Scranton, Pa.	April 27, 1853.	June 4, 1874.	Scranton, Pa.
Cooley, D. C.	New York.		October 24, 1864.	St. Paul, Minn.
Coston, H. H.	Honesdale, Pa.	June 9, 1849.	October 4, 1875.	Scranton, Pa.
Courtright, John S.	Plainsville, Pa.	July 21, 1855.	January 11, 1876.	Montrose, Pa.
Dean, Arthur D.	Abington, Pa.	January 29, 1849.	January 4. 1875.	Scranton, Pa.
De Witt, George B.	Exeter, Pa.	October 1, 1845.	April 14, 1873.	Tunkhannock, Pa.
Dickinson, Wharton		September 9, 1849.	April 24, 1877.	
Dimmick, E. C.	Milford, Pa.	February 2, 1844.	September 17, 1875.	Scranton, Pa.
Durand, Silas H.	Herrick, Pa.	January 5, 1833.	November 20, 1860.	Southampton, Pa.
Edwards, Henry M.	Monmouthshire, Eng.	February 12, 1844.	October 18, 1871.	Scranton, Pa.
Ellis, Howard	Elkton, Md.	July 6, 1834.	August 15, 1864.	Ridgewood, N. J.
Espy, John	Luzerne county, Pa.	September 21, 1842.	April 20, 1868.	St. Paul, Minn.
Fitzsimmons, F. J.	Carbondale, Pa.	September 29, 1852.	March 19, 1878.	Scranton, Pa.
Foley, Thomas J.			April 14, 1873.	
Foster, Thomas L.	Bloomsburg, Pa.	August 30, 1823.	November 4, 1844.	Mauch Chunk, Pa.
Frisbie, Hanson Z.	Orwell, Pa.	June 8, 1819.	August 5, 1850.	Grantville, Kan.
Fuller, Frederick	Montrose, Pa.	March 13, 1837.	November 13, 1860.	Scranton, Pa.
Gabriel, C. V.	Plymouth, Pa.	January 1, 1859.	June 2, 1886.	New York.
Gearhart, W. H.	Northumberland Co., Pa.	December 8, 1839.	April 7, 1869.	Scranton, Pa.
Gorman, John A.	Hazleton, Pa.	September 7, 1854.	January 10, 1876.	Washington, D. C.
Gritman, Philo C.	Sherburne, N. Y.	October 29, 1828.	November 10, 1848.	Carbondale, Pa.
Gunster, F. W.	Lockweiler, Prussia.	September 15, 1845.	November 10, 1868.	Scranton, Pa.
Hand, Alfred	Honesdale, Pa.	March 26, 1835.	May 8, 1860.	Scranton, Pa.
Handley, John		January 7, 1835.	August 21, 1860.	Scranton, Pa.
Hannah, Daniel	Harford, Pa.	January 21, 1838.	February 21, 1867.	New Milford, Pa.
Hannah, H. M.	Harford, Pa.	September 13, 1842.	February 24, 1870.	Scranton, Pa.
Harding, Henry	Eaton, Pa.	November 4, 1848.	June 12, 1876.	Tunkhannock, Pa.
Harrington, D. C.	Jewett, N. Y.	December 8, 1834.	May 7, 1863.	Philadelphia, Pa.
Hawley, Charles L.	Montrose, Pa.	December 8, 1855.	June 13, 1877.	Scranton, Pa.
Heery, Michael	Longford Co., Ireland.		August 16, 1869.	Topeka, Kan.
Hill, John Nevin	Selinsgrove, Pa.	September 3, 1855.	December 13, 1878.	Sunbury, Pa.
Hitchcock, F. L.	Waterbury, Conn.	April 18, 1837.	May 16, 1860.	Scranton, Pa.
Horn, George S.	Scrantonia, Pa.	April 27, 1849.	April 3, 1872.	Scranton, Pa.
Hotchkiss, A. B.	Harford, Pa.	June 20, 1839.	August 18, 1862.	Los Angeles, Cal.
Hottenstein, A. S.	Montour county, Pa.	May 27, 1849.	September 12, 1871.	Milton, Pa.
Hoyt, A. G.	Kingston, Pa.	January 25, 1847.	March 2, 1870.	New York.
Hoyt, H. M.	Kingston, Pa.	June 8, 1830.	April 4, 1853.	Philadelphia, Pa.
Hoyt, H. M.	Kingston, Pa.	November 8, 1861.	September 7, 1883.	Spokane Falls, Wash.
Hull, Harry T.	Clifford, Pa.	May 24, 1847.	April 24, 1869.	Humboldt, Neb.
Hughes, Thomas R.	Bethesda, Wales.		January 9, 1878.	Scranton, Pa.
Jones, Harvey J.	Wilkes-Barre, Pa.	October 15, 1847.	June 8, 1872.	Gunnison, Col.
Jones, John R.	Archbald, Pa.	May 27, 1856.	September 23, 1879.	Olyphant, Pa.
Jones, Lewis	Exeter, Pa.	August 28, 1807.	August 5, 1834.	New York.
Jones, M. I.	Carbondale, Pa.	April 30, 1840	November 15, 1869.	Brooklyn, N. Y.
Jones, W. G.	Carbondale, Pa.	October,—1837.	April 10, 1861.	New York.
Kahler, O. C.	Bloomsburg, Pa.	February 20, 1825.	November 11, 1872.	Bloomsburg, Pa.
Kauffman, P. C.	Mechanicsburg, Pa.	August 13, 1857.	February 26, 1885.	Vancouver, Wash.
Kinsey, L. C.	Beach Haven, Pa.	June 30, 1844.	April 10, 1876.	Montgomery Station, Pa.
Knapp, H. A.	Barker, N. Y.	July 24, 1851.	February 23, 1875.	Scranton, Pa.
Lamb, Charles L.	Le Roy, Pa.	May 18, 1850.	September 21, 1874.	Minneapolis, Minn.
Lamberton, Charles E.	Carlisle, Pa.	January 4, 1829.	November 20, 1865.	New York.
Lathrop, Charles E.	Bloomingburg, N. Y.	March 5, 1827	January 12, 1857.	Carbondale, Pa.
Lathrop, Wilbur F.	Hillsdale, Mich.	April 13, 1849.	March 18, 1875.	Carbondale, Pa.
Lathrope, W. W.	Carbondale, Pa.	October 9, 1840.	August 8, 1864.	Scranton, Pa.
Leach, Harold	Scranton, Pa.	September 1, 1856.	September 28, 1877.	San Francisco, Cal.
Leisenring, J. S.	Selinsgrove, Pa.	April 2, 1847.	April 11, 1872.	Altoona, Pa.
Lewis, William	Philadelphia, Pa.	March 6, 1801.	January 5, 1825.	Brooklyn, Ill.
Linderman, R. H.	Philadelphia, Pa.	September,—1858	December 5, 1884.	Stroudsburg, Pa.
Little, Ephraim H.	New York.	March 23, 1823.	April 7, 1851.	Bloomsburg, Pa.
Loomis, F. E.	Harford, Pa.	February 7, 1834.	February 20, 1867.	Scranton, Pa.
Lusk, W. D.	Great Bend, Pa.	February 1, 1833.	September 28 1871.	Montrose, Pa.
Mahon, James	Carbondale, Pa.	March 17, 1837.	January 6, 1865.	Scranton, Pa.
Mahon, Peter A.	Pottsville, Pa.	—1849.	April 22, 1874.	Shamokin, Pa.
Mapledoram, F. C.	Monticello, N. Y		September 11, 1875.	Kansas City, Mo.
Maxwell, James L.	Northampton, N. Y.		November 4, 1844.	Danville, Pa.
McCoy, Edward I.	Huntingdon, Pa.	January 10, 1847.	April 10, 1876.	Tipton, Iowa.
McDivitt, S. P.	Alexandria, Pa.	August 5, 1848.	November 21, 1876.	Chicago, Ill.
McDormott, S. F.	Espy, Pa.	December 24, 1842.	April 4, 1867.	Coffeyville, Kan.
Merrifield, Edward	Wyoming, Pa.	July 30, 1832.	August 6, 1855	Scranton, Pa
Miner, William B.	Wilkes-Barre, Pa.	July 20, 1854.	January 11, 1881.	Lancaster, Wis.
Mitchell, Ira C.	Howard, Pa.	April 16, 1833.	August 7, 1862.	Dundaff, Pa.
Morse, E. K.	Wilkes-Barre, Pa.	March 16, 1843.	May 2, 1864.	Wellsburg, W. Va.
Murray, Thomas S.	New Hope, Pa.	February 2, 1819.	November 7, 1842.	Trenton, N. J.
Myers, George P.	Kingston, Pa.	February 5, 1826.	April 25, 1870.	Williamsport, Pa.
Myers, Philip	Kingston, Pa.	November 28, 1830.	August 8, 1855.	Chicago, Ill.
Nesbitt, Thomas			April 4, 1870.	
Nichols, F. H			December 12, 1881.	
O Flaherty, John			September 6, 1875.	
O'Hanlon, P. J.			June 4, 1874.	Denver, Col.
Orr, George M.	Dallas, Pa.	June 13, 1856.	June 6, 1887.	Kane, Pa.
Orr, Nathaniel M.	Dallas, Pa.	December 12, 1851.	September 23, 1875.	Kane, Pa.

LIVING JUDGES OF LUZERNE COUNTY.

NAMES.	PLACE OF BIRTH.	DATE OF BIRTH.	ADMITTED.	RESIDENCE.
Paine, William Lewis	Brooklyn, N. Y.	March 23, 1851.	April 6, 1874.	New York.
Painter, E. H.	Freeport, Pa.	February 22, 1843.	February 24, 1869.	Turbotville, Pa.
Parsons, Lewis E.	Lisle, N. Y.	April,—1817.	August 6, 1839.	Talladega, Ala.
Patrick, H. N.	Wilkes-Barre, Pa.	September 26, 1853.	September 3, 1878.	Scranton, Pa.
Patton, Henry D.	Fayette county, Pa.	July 28, 1845.	January 5, 1887.	Lancaster, Pa.
Peckham, D. L.			August 4, 1851.	Mill City, Pa.
Perkins, George	Susquehanna county, Pa.	May 8, 1820.	April 1, 1850.	Fond du Lac, Wis.
Peters, W. A.			November 20, 1882.	Seattle, Wash.
Phoenix, C. M.	Wyoming county, Pa.	August 28, 1854.	November 27, 1880.	
Pitcher, Charles R.	Waterloo, N. Y.	April 21, 1850.	February 23, 1873.	Scranton, Pa
Plumb, G. H. R.	Honesdale, Pa.	June 12, 1854.	January 18, 1881.	Minneapolis, Minn.
Price, Samuel B.	Branchville, N. J.	April 29, 1847.	April 23, 1873.	Scranton, Pa.
Pursel, B. F.			February 20, 1860.	Kansas City, Mo.
Ranck, John McG.	Union county, Pa.	April 19, 1831.	February 26, 1868.	Light Street, Pa.
Rank, D. N.	Union county, Pa.	February 16, 1835.	February 19, 1872.	Limestoneville, Pa.
Regan, J. D.	Canaan, Pa.	May 4, 1835.	August 19, 1867	Scranton, Pa.
Regan, Michael	Canaan, Pa.	——1836.	November 12, 1866.	
Rhodes, John B.			August 31, 1864.	Kansas.
Rhodes, Joseph C.	Mifflinburg, Pa.	October 2, 1818.	April 8, 1844.	Houtzdale, Pa.
Rhone, Samuel M.	Luzerne county, Pa.	September 25, 1851.	November 20, 1876.	Montgomery Station, Pa.
Robinson, William C.	Norwich, Conn.	July 26, 1834.	November 9, 1863.	New Haven, Conn.
Royce, C. E. K.	Lebanon Springs, N. Y.	January 13, 1817.	January 23, 1860.	San Francisco, Cal.
Sanderson, George	Towanda, Pa.	August 22, 1847.	November 19, 1870.	Scranton, Pa.
Scanlan, John J.	Inver, Ireland.	October 24, 1845.	September 20, 1873.	Patterson, N. J.
Smith, Andrew J.	Waverly, Pa.	December 15, 1837.	January 2, 1860.	Waverly, Pa.
Smith, Cornelius	County Cavan, Ireland.	October 25, 1838.	August 16, 1869.	Scranton, Pa.
Snyder, Jacob B.	Luzerne county, Pa.	July 7, 1824.	August 24, 1861.	Scranton, Pa.
Spratt, O. W.	Towanda, Pa.	April 22, 1841.	October 30, 1867.	Philadelphia, Pa.
Squier, George H.	Nicholson, Pa.	October 8, 1836.	September 16, 1872.	Carbondale, Pa.
Stanton, William H.	New York.	July,—1843.	November 10, 1868.	Scranton, Pa.
Staples, Charles B.	Stroudsburg, Pa.	November 24, 1853.	June 11, 1884.	Stroudsburg, Pa.
Stephens, Marlin B.	Dilltown, Pa.	May 10, 1860.	May 16, 1887.	Johnstown, Pa.
Stewart, Franklin	Wilkes-Barre, Pa.	November 14, 1822.	August 3, 1847.	Berwick, Pa.
Stiles, Milton	Hobbie, Pa.	February 3, 1849.	September 22, 1874.	Conway Springs, Kan.
Stoutenburg, J. E.	Chester, N. J.	December 14, 1845.	November 24, 1869.	Passaic, N. J.
Sturges, E. B.	Greenfield Hill, Conn.	February 15, 1845.	August 19, 1869.	Scranton, Pa.
Thorp, Moses M.	Canaan, Pa.	March 6, 1848.	April 11, 1873.	Waymart, Pa.
Todd, Charles W.	Sterling, Pa.	July 22, 1832.	April 14, 1860.	Carley Brook, Pa.
Torrey, James H.	Delhi, N. Y.	June 16, 1851.	November 20, 1876.	Scranton, Pa.
Ulman, J. E.	Rehrersburg, Pa.	January 25, 1828.	August 29, 1865.	
Unger, David			November 16, 1871.	Danville, Pa.
Van Fleet, Charles G.	Luzerne county, Pa.	June 3, 1847.	November 10, 1868.	Troy, Pa.
Vickery, L. D.			December 23, 1869.	Scranton, Pa.
Wadhams, S. F.	Plymouth, Pa.	May 21, 1854	May 28, 1877.	Duluth, Minn.
Ward, W. G.	Dover Plains, N. Y.	October 7, 1823.	November 10, 1851.	Scranton, Pa.
Ward, Z. M.	Tunkhannock, Pa.	February 17, 1837.	August 17, 1863.	Patterson, N. J.
Weitzel, Paul R.	Sunbury, Pa.	September 13, 1832.	August 17, 1858	Scranton, Pa.
Wells, T. F.	Dundaff, Pa.	September 17, 1853.	October 4, 1875.	Scranton, Pa.
Welles, C. H.	Dundaff, Pa.	April 16, 1845.	March 2, 1867.	Scranton, Pa.
Weltur, Joshua L.	Avoca, Pa.	February 23, 1848.	June 6, 1885	Scranton, Pa.
Wheeler, O. H.	Galway, N. Y.	August 20, 1818.	August 3, 1841.	Montana.
Wilcox, W. A.	Olean, N. Y.	July 25, 1857.	June 18, 1883.	Williamsport, Pa.
Willard, E. N.	Madison, Conn.	April 2, 1835.	November 17, 1857.	Scranton, Pa.
Wilson, Henry	Susquehanna county, Pa.	October 7, 1834.	August 19, 1859.	Honesdale, Pa.
Wilson, Milo J.	Factoryville, Pa.	January 31, 1838.	April 9, 1868.	Scranton, Pa.
Winton, A. H.	Scranton, Pa.	November 17, 1838.	August 22, 1860.	Scranton, Pa.
Woodward, George A.	Wilkes-Barre, Pa.	February 14, 1835.	August 26, 1859.	Washington, D C.
Wright, Caleb E.	Plymouth, Pa.	February 4, 1810.	August 9, 1833.	Doylestown, Pa.

LIVING JUDGES OF LUZERNE COUNTY.

PRESIDENT JUDGES.

NAMES.	PLACE OF BIRTH.	DATE OF BIRTH.	DATE OF COMMISSION	
Harding, Garrick M.	Exeter, Pa.	July 12, 1827.	July 12, 1870.	Resigned Jan. 1, 1880.
Rice, Charles E.	Fairfield, N. Y.	September 15, 1846.	January 5, 1880.	

PRESIDENT JUDGE OF THE ORPHANS' COURT.

Rhone, Daniel L.	Cambra, Pa.	January 19, 1838.	January 4, 1875	

ADDITIONAL LAW JUDGES.

Hoyt, Henry M.	Kingston, Pa.	June 8, 1830.	July 5, 1867.	Commission expired.
Handley, John		January 7, 1835.	January 4, 1875.	Commission expired.
Stanton, William H.	New York.	July—1843.	January 7, 1878.	Resigned Feb. 25, 1879
Woodward, Stanley	Wilkes-Barre, Pa.	August 29, 1833.	January 9, 1880.	

ASSOCIATE JUDGES.

Bristol, Silvester	Washington, N. Y.	July 12, 1813.	December 3, 1851.	Commission expired.
Morss, Daniel K.	Windham, N. Y.	January 27, 1821.	December 4, 1871.	Commission expired.

RESIDENT ATTORNEYS OF LUZERNE COUNTY.

NAMES.	PLACE OF BIRTH.	DATE OF BIRTH.	ADMITTED.
A. T. McClintock,	Northumberland, Pa.	February 2, 1810.	August 8, 1836.
Edward I. Turner,	Plymouth, Pa.	May 27, 1816.	November 5, 1839.
William P. Miner,	Wilkes-Barre, Pa.	September 8, 1816.	August 3, 1841.
L. D. Shoemaker,	Kingston, Pa.	November 5, 1819.	August 1, 1842.
Samuel McCarragher,	Princeton, N. J.	November 10, 1818.	November 7, 1842.
Wesley Johnson,	Wilkes-Barre, Pa.	December 20, 1819.	April—1846.
Steuben Jenkins,	Wyoming, Pa.	September 28, 1819.	August 3, 1847.
David S. Koon,	Dutchess county, N. Y.	September 9, 1818.	January 5, 1848.
F. J. Leavenworth,	Delaware City, Del.	January 24, 1827.	January 10, 1848.
George Loveland,	Kingston, Pa.	November 5, 1823.	August 19, 1848.
Asa R. Brundage,	Conyngham, Pa.	March 22, 1828.	April 2, 1849.
Francis L. Butler,	Wilkes-Barre, Pa.	September 15, 1827.	April 6, 1849.
C. I. A. Chapman,	Wilkes-Barre, Pa.	October 9, 1826.	January 8, 1850.
D. L. Patrick,	Farmers Mills, N. Y.	January 8, 1826.	August 5, 1850.
Garrick M. Harding,	Exeter, Pa.	July 12, 1827.	August 5, 1850.
Alexander Farnham,	Carbondale, Pa.	January 12, 1834.	January 13, 1855.
Stanley Woodward,	Wilkes-Barre, Pa.	August 29, 1833.	August 4, 1856.
Agib Ricketts,	Rohrsburg, Pa.	October 12, 1834.	January 6, 1857.
John Richards,	Woodstock, Vt.	August 16, 1830.	April 5, 1858.
Jerome G. Miller,	Luzerne county, Pa.	February 27, 1835.	April 24, 1858.
O. F. Nicholson,	Wayne county, Pa.	October 9, 1834.	April 24, 1858.
E. H. Chase,	Haverhill, Mass.	February 28, 1835.	January 4, 1859.
R. C. Shoemaker,	Forty Fort, Pa.	April 4, 1836.	April 4, 1859.
Alfred Darte,	Dundaff, Pa.	April 28, 1836.	May 12, 1859.
H. B. Plumb,	Luzerne county, Pa.	November 13, 1829.	November 21, 1859.
Harry Hakes,	Harpersfield, N. Y.	June 10, 1825.	January 25, 1860.
Geo. B. Kulp,	Reamstown, Pa.	February 11, 1839.	August 20, 1860.
T. H. B. Lewis,	Trucksville, Pa.	February 22, 1835.	August 22, 1860.
Gustav Hahn,	Stuttgart, Germany.	October 23, 1830.	February 18, 1861.
E. S. Osborne,	Bethany, Pa.	August 7, 1839.	February 26, 1861.
D. L. Rhone,	Cambra, Pa.	January 19, 1838.	April 1, 1861.
Charles D. Foster,	Luzerne county, Pa.	November 25, 1836.	April 23, 1861.
Henry W. Palmer,	Susquehanna county, Pa.	July 10, 1839.	August 24, 1861.
Charles M. Conyngham,	Wilkes-Barre, Pa.	July 6, 1840.	August 18, 1862.
George R. Bedford,	Waverly, Pa.	November 22, 1840.	November 10, 1862.
Hubbard B. Payne,	Kingston, Pa.	July 20, 1839.	August 20, 1863.
William M. Shoemaker,	Forty Fort, Pa.	June 20, 1840.	September 3, 1863.
D. L. O'Neill,	Port Deposit, Md.	December 10, 1835.	April 4, 1864.
Clarence P. Kidder,	Wilkes-Barre, Pa.	May 10, 1839.	April 4, 1864.
George Shoemaker,	Forty Fort, Pa.	June 28, 1844.	January 6, 1865.
John Lynch,	Providence, R. I.	November 1, 1843.	November 20, 1865.
Charles L. Bulkeley,	Wilkes-Barre, Pa.	January 15, 1843.	January 8, 1866.
Thomas J. Chase,	Luzerne county, Pa.	May 26, 1844.	November 12, 1866.
D. J. M. Loop,	Elmira, N. Y.	February 11, 1823.	December 1, 1866.
William S. McLean,	Summit Hill, Pa.	May 27, 1842.	August 19, 1867.
Andrew Hunlock,	Kingston, Pa.	May 1, 1839.	November 10, 1868.
D. M. Jones,	New York.	September 2, 1843.	February 27, 1869.
Elliott P. Kisner,	Hazleton, Pa.	August 1, 1845.	August 16, 1869.
Isaac P. Hand,	Berwick, Pa.	April 5, 1843.	November 15, 1869.
Edmund G. Butler,	Wilkes-Barre, Pa.	June 11, 1845.	November 17, 1869.
Burton Downing,	Luzerne county, Pa.	November 14, 1845.	November 19, 1869.
Charles E. Rice,	Fairfield, N. Y.	September 15, 1846.	February 21, 1870.
Benjamin F. Dorrance,	Forty Fort, Pa.	August 14, 1846.	August 20, 1870.
L. W. DeWitt,	Exeter, Pa.	December 3, 1845.	December 17, 1870.
George K. Powell,	Penn Yan, N. Y.	June 10, 1845.	June 12, 1871.
Sheldon Reynolds,	Kingston, Pa.	February 22, 1845.	October 16, 1871.
George S. Ferris,	Pittston, Pa.	April 28, 1849.	February 19, 1872.
E. G. Scott,	Wilkes-Barre, Pa.	June 15, 1836.	September 9, 1872.
Galus L. Halsey,	Nesquehoning, Pa.	July 12, 1845.	September 9, 1872.
Ernest Jackson,	Wilkes-Barre, Pa.	August 6, 1848.	September 9, 1872.
Lyman H. Bennett,	Harpersfield, N. Y.	February 20, 1845.	December 4, 1872.
Malcom E. Walker,	Waverly, Pa.	April 8, 1847.	January 6, 1873.
Michael Cannon,	Inniskeel, Ireland.	March 22, 1844.	January 25, 1873.
John A. Opp,	Muncy, Pa.	July 15, 1847.	February 24, 1873.
John T. L. Sahm,	Greencastle, Pa.	September 6, 1843.	April 23, 1873.
William H. McCartney,	Boston, Mass.	July 11, 1834.	September 12, 1873.
Barnet M. Espy,	Nanticoke, Pa.	May 16, 1846.	September 20, 1873.
William P. Ryman,	Dallas, Pa.	August 23, 1847.	September 20, 1873.
John T. Lenahan,	Port Griffith, Pa.	November 15, 1852.	October 27, 1873.
Francis M. Nichols,	Smithfield, Pa.	May 23, 1847.	October 28, 1873.
Emory Robinson,	Lenoxville, Pa.	July 6, 1849.	January 5, 1874.
Quincy A. Gates,	Wayne county, Pa.	December 19, 1847.	January 22, 1874.
Franklin C. Mosier,	Hughestown, Pa.	October 8, 1846.	February 26, 1874.
J. Vaughan Darling,	Reading, Pa.	July 24, 1844.	June 4, 1874.
Allan H. Dickson,	Utica, N. Y.	November 14, 1851.	September 14, 1874.
Joseph D. Coons,	Wilkes-Barre, Pa.	June 14, 1852.	September 14, 1874.
P. H. Campbell,	Scranton, Pa.	November 24, 1845.	September 14, 1874.
George H. Troutman,	Philadelphia, Pa.	January 18, 1842.	September 16, 1874.
Lewis B. Landmesser,	Ashley, Pa.	March 5, 1850.	April 5, 1875.
Seligman J. Strauss,	Wilkes-Barre, Pa.	August 19, 1852.	September 6, 1875.
G. Mortimer Lewis,	Merryall, Pa.	November 23, 1848.	September 6, 1875.

NAMES.	PLACE OF BIRTH.	DATE OF BIRTH.	ADMITTED.
George R. Wright,	Wilkes-Barre, Pa.	November 21, 1851.	September 6, 1875.
Edward A. Lynch,	Nesquehoning, Pa.	August 15, 1853.	September 11, 1875.
Charles H. Sturdevant,	Bellefonte, Pa.	May 18, 1848.	October 4, 1875.
Frank C. Sturges,	Greenfield Hill, Conn.	March 12, 1854.	October 18, 1875.
John B. Reynolds,	Wilkes-Barre, Pa.	August 5, 1850.	November 15, 1875.
A. H. McClintock,	Wilkes-Barre, Pa.	December 12, 1852.	January 20, 1876.
Charles W. McAlarney,	Mifflinburg, Pa.	December 20, 1847.	February 7, 1876.
John McGahren,	Ellicottville, N. Y.	March 8, 1852.	February 14, 1876.
Nathaniel Taylor,	Danville, Pa.	January 28, 1848.	April 5, 1876.
Thomas R. Martin,	Hagerstown, Md.	May 26, 1849.	April 10, 1876.
Oscar J. Harvey,	Wilkes-Barre, Pa.	September 2, 1851.	May 16, 1876.
Thomas H. Atherton,	Wyoming, Pa.	July 14, 1853.	September 29, 1876.
George W. Shonk,	Plymouth, Pa.	April 26, 1850.	September 29, 1876.
H. A. Fuller,	Wilkes-Barre, Pa.	January 15, 1855.	January 9, 1877.
Clarence W. Kline,	Jerseytown, Pa.	October 25, 1851.	January 10, 1877.
E. W. Sturdevant,	Wilkes-Barre, Pa.	November 12, 1854.	June 11, 1877.
Bernard McManus,	Beaver Meadow, Pa.	July 23, 1846.	November 19, 1877.
R. H. Wright,	Perry county, Pa.	December 4, 1841.	March 22, 1878.
P. V. Weaver,	Luzerne county, Pa.	March 11, 1855.	September 23, 1878.
A. F. Derr,	Klines Grove, Pa	May 29, 1853.	December 2, 1878.
James L. Lenahan,	Plymouth, Pa.	November 5, 1856.	January 28, 1879.
Frank W. Wheaton,	Binghamton, N. Y.	August 27, 1855.	September 2, 1879.
Emmett D. Nichols,	Ulster, Pa.	July 8, 1855.	September 16, 1879.
Edwin Shortz,	Mauch Chunk, Pa.	July 10, 1841.	March 29, 1880.
Jasper B. Stark,	Wilkes-Barre, Pa.	February 17, 1858.	April 26, 1880.
Martin F. Burke,	Pittston, Pa.	February 8, 1855.	May 10, 1880.
William J. Hughes,	Pittston, Pa.	December 30, 1857.	June 7, 1880.
Edward E. Hoyt,	Kingston, Pa.	January 22, 1859.	September 17, 1880.
Robert D. Evans,	Lewisburg, Pa.	August 17, 1856.	November 15, 1880.
William R. Gibbons,	Baltimore, Md.	September 18, 1857.	April 4, 1881.
William L. Raeder,	Gardner's Ferry, Pa.	November 27, 1654.	June 6, 1881.
George H. Butler,	Forty Fort, Pa.	September 2, 1857.	June 6, 1881.
W. H Hines,	Brooklyn, N. Y.	March 15, 1854.	June 6, 1881.
John D. Hayes,	Limerick, Ireland.	April 4, 1853.	June 11, 1881.
A E. Chapin,	New Columbus, Pa.	August 7, 1853.	October 19, 1881.
Henry W. Dunning,	Franklin, N. Y.	September 11, 1858.	June 5, 1882.
George H. Fisher,	Wilkes-Barre, Pa.	October 13, 1860.	June 5, 1882.
James N. Anderson,	Pittston, Pa.	January 7, 1856.	June 5, 1882.
William C. Price,	St. Clair, Pa.	March 2, 1858.	October 14, 1882.
Dennis O. Coughlin,	Luzerne county, Pa.	July 9, 1852.	November 20, 1882.
Joseph Moore,	Castle Eden, England.	July 3, 1851.	November 20, 1882.
John S. Harding,	Wilkes-Barre, Pa.	August 29, 1859.	November 21, 1882.
Cecil R. Banks,	Hollidaysburg, Pa	November 3, 1849.	January 10, 1883.
Cormac F. Bohan,	Pittston, Pa.	December 14, 1862.	March 15, 1884.
B. F. McAtee,	Clear Spring, Md.	December 28, 1843.	September 3, 1884.
Harry Halsey,	Philadelphia, Pa.	October 16, 1860.	November 28, 1884.
Tuthill R. Hillard,	Wilkes-Barre, Pa.	December 12, 1860.	June 6, 1885.
Samuel M. Parke,	Pittston, Pa.	May 4, 1859.	June 9, 1885.
Peter A. O'Boyle,	Killfine, Ireland.	November 10, 1861.	July 27, 1885.
Daniel A. Fell,	Wilkes-Barre, Pa.	November 23, 1858.	July 27, 1885.
John B. Woodward,	Wilkes-Barre, Pa.	April 3, 1861.	September 7, 1885.
Lord B. Hillard,	Wilkes-Barre, Pa.	December 5, 1861.	September 7, 1885.
Henry H. Welles,	Kingston, Pa.	January 21, 1861.	October 10, 1885.
Moses W. Wadhams,	Plymouth, Pa.	August 2, 1858.	October 10, 1885.
Anthony L. Williams,	Ebervale, Pa.	October 10, 1862.	October 12, 1885.
John M. Garman,	Thompsontown, Pa.	September 1, 1851.	January 29, 1886.
Liddon Flick,	Wilkes-Barre, Pa.	October 28, 1859.	June 2, 1886.
George D. Hedian,	Wilkes-Barre, Pa.	December 8, 1856.	June 4, 1886.
John Q. Creveling,	Columbia county, Pa.	June 6, 1861.	June 19, 1886.
Peter A. Meixell,	Luzerne county, Pa.	August 16, 1857.	September 20, 1886.
Charles E. Keck,	White Haven, Pa.	September 2, 1861.	October 18, 1886.
Anthony C. Campbell,	Wilkes-Barre, Pa.	June 7, 1862.	October 18, 1886
Thomas C. Umsted,	Faggs Manor, Pa.	October 10, 1862.	December 4, 1886.
James R. Scouton,	Elwell, Pa.	September 26, 1858.	January 6, 1887.
James M. Fritz,	Orangeville, Pa.	March 10, 1857.	January 29, 1887.
George P. Loomis,	Wilkes-Barre, Pa.	May 1, 1859.	January 31, 1887.
Edward F. McGovern,	Darlington, England.	September 10, 1860.	June 6, 1887.
George Urquhart,	Wilkes-Barre, Pa.	December 31, 1861.	June 27, 1887.
John F. Everhart,	Pittston, Pa.	June 18, 1859.	November 15, 1887.
Frank W. Larned,	Luzerne county, Pa.	May 30, 1859.	May 21, 1888.
Darryl L. Creveling,	Columbia county, Pa.	October 7, 1850.	June 18, 1888.
Alexander Ricketts,	Wilkes-Barre, Pa.	October 29, 1866.	September 28, 1888.
George B. Hillman,	Wilkes-Barre, Pa.	May 21, 1867.	December 10, 1888.
George W. Moon,	Scranton, Pa.	July 4, 1860.	December 10, 1888.
W. J. Trembath,	Ballarat, Australia.	December 16, 1859.	December 10, 1888.
William I. Hibbs,	Thompsontown, Pa.	June 3, 1851	March 11, 1889.
James L. Morris,	Pittston, Pa.	May 12, 1860.	April 22, 1889.
Thomas Darling,	Wilkes-Barre, Pa.	May 29, 1863.	April 22, 1889.

ERRATUM.

LIVING JUDGES OF LUZERNE COUNTY.

ADDITIONAL LAW JUDGE.

Hand, Alfred	Honesdale, Pa.	March 26, 1835.	March 4, 1879.	Commission expired.

NAMES.

Biographical sketches of the following named persons are contained in this volume:

	Page.
Alexander, John Marion	1231
Allen, John J.	1197
Alsover, Jabez	1319
Barnum, Charles Treadway	1285
Beaumont, William Henry	1274
Bedford, James Sutton	1283
Bennet, Daniel Strebeigh	1363
Bennet, Charles	1224
Bennett, Ziba	1202
Bidlack, Benjamin Alden	1134
Blackman, Miner S.	1215
Bowman, Caleb Franklin	1261
Bowman, Ebenezer	1050
Bowman, James Watson	1127
Bowman, Samuel	1127
Bradley, Abraham	1052
Brisbin, John	1292
Brundage, Chester Butler	1296
Bryson, James	1323
Burnside, Thomas	1098
Butler, Chester	1126
Byington, Theodore L.	1281
Byrne, Peter J.	1230
Cake, Isaac McCord	1294
Campbell, Joseph H.	1312
Canavan, Martin	1278
Carpenter, Benjamin	1047
Case, William F.	1307
Catlin, Charles	1096
Catlin, George	1103

Catlin, Putnam	1051
Chamberlain, Albert	1298
Chapman, Seth	1081
Chase, Ezra Bartholomew	1287
Collins, Oristus	1107
Collins, Thomas	1310
Conyngham, John Nesbit	1114
Conyngham, John Butler	1238
Cooper, Thomas	1076
Courtright, John Searle	1368
Covell, Edward M	1216
Craig, John Perry	1295
Crane, Frederick M	1184
Dana, Milton	1233
Dana, Sylvester	1142
Darling, Thomas	1379
Darte, Alfred	1232
Denison, Charles	1191
Denison, George	1087
Denison, Nathan	1057
Dickinson, Israel	1181
Dietrick, Aaron Jared	1366
Drake, George C	1141
Dyer, Thomas	1072
Evans, John	1075
Fell, Jesse	1061
Flanagan, Montgomery Joseph	1362
Fuller, Amzi	1130
Fuller, Henry Mills	1201
Gibson, John Bannister	1091
Gore, John L	1302
Gore, Obadiah	1047
Graham, Thomas	1061
Grant, Sanford	1299
Griffin, George	1063

Hakes, Lyman 1198
Hamilton, Arthur 1295
Hancock, William 1277
Harrison, Canfield 1302
Harvey, Elisha Boanerges 1235
Haughawout, George Dougherty 1293
Headley, Samuel Freeman 1170
Hibbs, William Irwin 1377
Hill, Elliott Smith Miller 1234
Hillman, George Baker 1373
Hodgdon, Samuel 1221
Holliday, James 1208
Hollenback, Matthias 1046
Hurlbut, Christopher 1056

Jackson, Angelo 1246
Jackson, Morrison Elijah 1195
Jessup, William 1185
Johnson, Ovid Frazer 1165
Jones, Joel 1130
Jones, John Richard 1370
Jones, Matthew Hale 1174
Jones, Nathaniel 1223

Ketcham, John Holmes 1297
Ketcham, Winthrop Welles 1240
Kidder, Luther 1175
Kidder, Rowland Metcalf 1312
King, Henry 1096
Kingman, William Roberts 1365
Kingsley, Nathan 1048
Kinney, Joseph 1055
Koons, John 1229

Lathrop, Dwight Noble 1177
Le Clerc, Edward Emmelius 1194
Lee, Washington 1079
Lee, Washington 1225
Lewis, Arnold Colt 1260

Little, William E . . .	. 1191
Longstreet, Samuel Price .	. . 1284
Mallery, Edward Garrick	. . . 1218
Mallery, Garrick	 1083
Mallery, Pierce Butler	. . . 1181
Maxwell, Volney Lee	. 1168
Mc Clintock, James	 1141
McQuillan, Dennis Alexander	. . . 1322
McShane, Francis	. 1081
Meredith, Thomas . .	 1097
Merrifield, William	1286
Merriman, Edgar Leroy	. 1303
Metcalf, Henry	. . . 1234
Miller, William Henry	 1214
Miner, Joseph Wright . . .	 1246
Miner, Josiah H	. 1101
Moon, George Washington . . .	. . . 1376
Morris, James Lincoln	 1378
Murray, Noah	 1054
Myers, John William	. . . 1228
Myers, Lawrence	. . 1057
Myers, Philip Thomas	 1307
Myers, William Vanderbelt . . .	 1323
Nesbitt, James	 1047
Nicholson, George Byron	 1238
Nicholson, Horatio W	. 1197
Nicholson, Lyman Richardson . .	 1283
Osterhout, Isaac Smith	. . . 1313
Overton, Edward	. . . 1102
Overton, Thomas Bleasdale . .	 1095
Paine, Thomas Edward . .	. 1143
Palmer Nathan	 1060
Parke, Benjamin	. 1139
Parker, Jonathan W	. 1182
Pearce, Cromwell	. 1271

Peckham, Aaron Kingsley 1209
Pettebone, Henry 1138
Pfouts, Benjamin Franklin 1320
Philbin, William Joseph 1362
Pickering, Timothy 1044
Pike, Charles 1278
Post, Isaac Joseph 1308
Pratt, William H 1293
Prentice, William 1062

Randall, David Richardson 1235
Rankin, Daniel 1263
Reichard, John 1299
Reynolds, Lazarus Denison 1285
Reynolds, William Champion 1197
Richards, Ira D 1301
Robinson, John Trimble 1184
Ross, William Sterling 1143
Rush, Jacob 1058
Ruth, Ivan Thomas 1324

Sanderson, George 1288
Scott, David 1101
Scott, George 1283
Sherrerd, Samuel 1279
Shoemaker, Charles Denison 1165
Silkman, Charles Henry 1182
Simrell, Eugene W 1324
Slocum, Joseph 1277
Slocum, Jonathan Joseph 1182
Smith, Cyrenus M 1190
Smith, George Thomas 1311
Smith, William Hooker 1047
Stark, Conrad Sax 1306
Steele, George Palmer 1310
Stewart, Alphonso C 1086
Stout, Asher Miner 1226
Stout, Charles Miner 1270
Struthers, James Robb 1223

Names.	1405
Taylor, Edmund	1242
Trembath, William John	1376
Wadhams, Noah	1061
Waelder, Jacob	1227
Waller, Charles Phillips	1219
Welles, Rosewell	1050
Wells, Corydon Hiram	1296
Wells, George H	1190
Wells, Henry Hill	1180
Whitlock, Friend Aaron	1363
Wilmarth, Wesley S.	1322
Wilmot, David	1177
Wilson, Amzi	1195
Winchester, Stephen Severson	1220
Woodward, George Washington	1146
Woodward, Warren Jay	1210
Wright, Benjamin Drake	1125
Wright, Harrison	1190
Wright, Harrison	1325
Wright, Joseph	1294
Wurtz, John J.	1167
Wurts, William	1169

INDEX OF NAMES.

VOLUME I, PP. 1 TO 504.   VOLUME II, PP. 505 TO 1038.   VOLUME III, PP. 1039 TO END.

Aaron, 833.
Abbott, 157, 1251-55, 1392.
Abrams, 904.
Ace, 984.
Ackley, 689.
Adair, 681.
Adam, 1139.
Adams, 45, 241, 87, 306, 43, 408, 656,666, 807-8, 87, 970, 1046, 74, 77, 90, 1189, 1210, 1335, 90.
Addison, 608.
Adgate, 316.
Aeris, 972-73.
Aertz, 1138.
Agnew, 28, 210, 1122, 51, 63.
Airgood, 768.
Albright, 41, 523, 27, 679, 880, 944, 1030.
Albrighton, 277.
Alden, 303-7, 748, 969, 1136, 1273-74.
Alderfer, 1385.
Aldrich, 656.
Alexander, 20, 257-58, 562, 852, 95, 1067, 1167, 1231-32.
Alexander, Czar of Russia, 933.
Alexander III, 252.
Allen, 11, 286, 318, 818, 919, 73, 1186, 97, 1327, 36, 38.
Allison, 95, 588, 1097.
Allsworth, 870-71.
Allyn, 900, 35.
Alricks, 1165-67.
Alsis, see Halsey.
Alsover, 39, 498, 556, 1319-20.
Alvord, 925.
Amerman, 39, 979-80.
Ames, 825.
Amsbry, 617.
Anderson, 555, 712-13, 1322.
Andre, 103, 15, 1127, 72.
Andrew, 429.
Andrews, 578, 711.
Andries, 281.
Andross, 1166.
Andruss, 578.
Anne, Queen, 766.
Ansbacher, 480.
Ansell, 860.
Antony, Marc, 1242.
Apple, 1257.
Appleton, 378, 1046.
Archbald, 39, 526, 855, 83, 955, 1016-35, 71-72.
Argyll, Bishop of, 203.
Arkeson, 774.
Armstrong, 218, 58, 64, 525-26, 648, 952-53, 1173, 1263.
Arndt, 1119, 1180.
Arnold, 263, 356, 523, 668, 93, 811, 1062.
Arnot, 671.
Arthur, 318, 683, 977, 1391.
Asbury, 212, 466, 638, 95, 1090, 1262.

Aspinwall, 1004.
Atherholt, 1138.
Atherton, 1, 26, 39, 161, 295, 516-32, 607, 51, 725, 867, 1007, 14-15, 1259, 1375, 91.
Athey, 1389.
Atkinson, 670, 1377.
Atwater, 884, 1232
Atwood, 897.
Auge, 1098.
Augur, 841.
Augustus, 892.
Aurbach, 802.
Austin, 794, 1029, 36, 64.
Avery, 595, 628, 1040-41, 1369.
Ayres, 1195.

Babb, 834-35.
Babcock, 745, 1285.
Bachman, 149, 1385
Backus, 881, 1072, 1109.
Bacon, 1123.
Bagnall, 237.
Bailey, 26, 39, 165, 78, 377, 671, 896-97, 982.
Baker, 434, 93, 772, 867, 920, 1244-45, 1303.
Balcom, 85.
Balcomb, 1236.
Baldwin, 48, 465, 576, 79, 758, 934, 63, 1033-35, 41, 53, 1110, 41, 55, 1201, 1321.
Ball, 168-69, 848.
Ballou, 654-56.
Balcyl, 255.
Baltimore, Lord, 719
Bamberger, 1299.
Bancroft, 97, 728, 1071.
Bangs, 853, 66-67, 1391.
Banks, 268, 589, 713-19, 1261.
Banning, 471.
Barber, 314, 1038.
Barclay, 140, 542.
Bardley, 195.
Barge, 149.
Barker, 444.
Barkley, 803.
Barksdale, 428, 590.
Barnard, 888.
Barnes, 832, 913, 58-59, 1187, 1245.
Barnet, 858.
Barnett, 556.
Barneveldt John of, 279.
Barney, 929.
Barnum, 13, 789, 1244, 77, 85-86.
Barr, 297.
Barrett, 883, 1263.
Barrington, 791.
Barton, 1126, 1390.
Bass, 978, 1297.
Bassan, 989.
Bassford, 903.
Batchelor, 845.

Batchley, 862.
Bates, 416-19, 717, 1041.
Bauer, 788.
Baughman, 680.
Baumann, 1001-02.
Baumann, see Bowman.
Baur, 25, 162, 488, 825, 1227.
Baxter, 37.
Bayard, 1181.
Beach, 1041, 1350.
Bean, 144, 717.
Bear, 680.
Beardslee, 249, 452-53, 817, 1314, 87.
Beatty, 681.
Bentlys, 955-56.
Beaulieu, 173
Beaumont, 484, 886, 932-33, 1100, 41, 1274-77.
Beauregard, 268.
Beaver, 878, 918, 68, 1013, 1381.
Beckwith, 506, 1064.
Bedford, 15, 19, 25, 38, 208-26, 417, 66, 592, 725, 41, 78, 915, 33, 1047, 1151, 1283, 1383.
Beebe, 323.
Beech, 1089.
Beecher, 384, 835, 98, 1218.
Beers, 561.
Behee, 604.
Beilby, 434.
Beissel, 144.
Belcher, 868.
Belden, 622.
Belding, 905.
Belford, 566.
Bell, 25, 248-49, 338, 999, 1386.
Bellows, 427.
Benade, 1342.
Benedict, 425, 90-93, 827-29, 1065, 1288.
Bennet viii, 856, 1224-25, 1363-65.
Bennett, 39, 135, 411-15, 561-64, 635, 30-50, 976, 1086-87, 1183, 1202-08, 1307, 11, 80,,87, 89, 92.
Henscoter, 813.
Benson, 167, 1069.
Bentley, 40, 843, 907, 13, 82-83, 1174, 1266-67, 98.
Benton, 1276.
Bergen, 162.
Berry, 598.
Bertles, 26, 789, 97, 1392.
Bertram, 397, 1095.
Beryar, 1327.
Betts, 840, 914.
Bevan, 569.
Beza, 966.
Biddle, 294, 741, 55, 820, 902.
Bidlack, 19-20, 132, 306, 43, 53, 88, 630, 813, vii, 1134-38, 1245.
Bigelow, 810.
Bigler, 99, 266, 588, 1155.

Index of Names.

Billings, 1198-99.
Bingham, 1109.
Binn, 1074.
Binns, 294-95.
Binney, 823, 1346.
Birde, 1344.
Birdseye, 693.
Birge, 750.
Birney, 321.
Birtel, 918.
Biscoe, 810.
Bishop, 955, 1217.
Bispham, 685.
Black, 159, 275-76, 78, 532, 1159.
Black Hawk, 857, 1105.
Blackman, 132-33, 604, 931-32, 1215-16, 1349, 74.
Blackstone, 459.
Blackwood, 1016.
Blain, 264.
Blaine, 87, 259, 430, 93, 618.
Blair, 258, 543, 1289.
Blakeslee, 498, 969, 1385.
Blanchard, 67, 464, 772.
Blank, 705.
Blatchley, 862.
Bleasdale, 1102.
Bliss, 751, 876.
Blith, 876.
Blois, 840.
Blum, 1359.
Boadicea, 577.
Boardman, 579.
Boal, 1153.
Bodenheimer, 480.
Bogaart, 793.
Bogert, 154.
Boggs, 1272.
Bogue, 1163.
Bohan, 625-26, 1389.
Boice, 390.
Bolmar, 868, 938.
Bolton, 1195, 1220.
Bonaparte, 715, 1194.
Bond, 344, 687.
Boniface VIII. (Pope), 252.
Booth, 21, 762, 66, 1344.
Boquet, 263.
Borbidge, 856.
Bordwell, 585.
Borodell, 1087.
Bosee, 102.
Boskirk, 793.
Bosseut, 547.
Bostick, 1041.
Bostwick, 937.
Boswell, 316.
Bouck, 1023.
Bouscher, 857.
Bovie, 793.
Bowen, 654, 1072, 1174.
Bowers, 437-38, 856.
Bowie, 953.
Bowman, 25, 48, 125, 75, 215, 3,19, 94, 99, 496, 509, 695-96, 714, 1001-02, 43, 50-51, 61, 90, 1115, 17, 27-30, 1261-63.
Boyd, 647-48, 722, 866, 1171-73, 1321.
Boyer, 729, 68.
Boylston, 666.
Brace, 901.
Braddock, 517, 715, 845, 98, 1271.
Bradford, 971-72.
Bradley, 585, 870, 991, 1052-54, 61, 1228, 88.
Bradstreet, 791.
Bragg, 234.
Brahl, 918.
Brainard, 376, 585, 921.

Brakeley, 738-39.
Brakenbury, 808.
Brandt, 608.
Brassington, 1271.
Bratt, 793.
Breck, 890-96.
Breese, 55, 57, 1381.
Breneiser, 156.
Brett, 1194.
Brevost, 172.
Brewer, 268.
Brewster, 28, 119, 94, 368.
Bridgum, 491.
Briggs, 899.
Brinham, 677.
Brink, 181.
Brintnall, 227.
Brinsmade, 323.
Brisbane, 165, 76, 1239.
Brisbin, 34, 1220, 92-93.
Bristol, 25, 1035-36, 1132.
Brittain, 475.
Britton, 982.
Broadhead, 63, 1008-11, 1138, 1204, 96.
Brocket, 674.
Brockway, 506.
Brodrick, 594, 838.
Brongniart, 1349-50.
Bronson, 547.
Brooks, 292, 428, 727, 1209.
Brougham, 1092.
Brower, 934.
Brown, 26, 297, 338, 55, 418, 542, 85, 748, 812, 40, 48, 950, 82, 1000-01, 59, 1143, 1233, 62-63.
Browne, 728, 811, 1280.
Brownell, 744.
Brubaker, 144.
Bruce, 252-55, 774.
Brundage, 25, 30, 62-65, 225, 88-89, 1011, 14, 1296, 1384.
Bryan, 991-93.
Bryant, 811.
Bryden, 713.
Bryson, 131, 264-65, 441-47, 1323-24.
Buchanan, 42, 257, 62, 64, 67, 1112, 54-55.
Bucher, 268.
Buchnan, 148.
Buck, 53, 89, 115, 598-600, 704, 1041, 1256.
Buckalew, 34, 179, 97, 271, 509, 711, 1179, 91, 96.
Buckingham, 61, 84, 363 65, 1119.
Bucknell, 979.
Buehler, 998.
Buell, 234.
Buford, 34.
Bulford, 187.
Bulkeley, 25, 63-64, 285-90, 833, 43, 1081.
Bull, 94, 743, 1173-74, 1332-83.
Bullock, 1041.
Bunnell, 39, 927-28.
Burdett, 1221.
Burdick, 196.
Burg, 810.
Burge, 376.
Burgoyne, 442, 623, 1010, 35, 55, 1309.
Burke, 402, 568, 1067, 1110, 1367, 1390.
Burleigh, 724.
Burnham, 840-42.
Burns, 912-13, 1024, 32.
Burnside, 391, vii, 1078, 98-1102, 53.
Burr, 110, 761-66, 990-93.

Burre, 763-64.
Burrett, 1389.
Burritt, 664, 1344.
Burrough, 747.
Burrows, 418, 680, 936-37, 1391.
Bursley, 971.
Burtis, 210.
Burton, 253-54, 915, 1020.
Bush, 1176.
Butler, 13, 24, 32-33, 39, 102-3, 16-17, 32, 89, 91, 206, 15-18, 58, 64, 97, 326-51, 63, 85, 87-88, 427, 95, 506-07, 62, 78, 95, 99, 601, 6-9, 35, 40-41, 44, 68-69, 90, 710, 49-50, 800-1, 24, 29, 33-34, 46-48, 928, 1039-43, 50, 65, 67, 84, 88-89, 1115, 24, 26-27, 74, 84, 12, 8-19, 26, 50, 52, 93, 1330, 46, 56, 58.
Buzzard, 174, 1196.
Bye, 898.
Byington, 1281-2.
Byrne, 904, 1230-31, 78.
Byron, 1024, 69.

Cadel, 203.
Cadwalader, 988-89, 1097, 1337.
Caesar, 1242.
Caffrey, 282.
Cahoon, 20, 1261, 1351.
Cake, 1294.
Caldwell, 720, 1089, 1252.
Calkins, 1088.
Callahan, 798.
Callaghan, 900.
Callender, 848, 1373.
Callyhan, 900.
Calvin, 139.
Camden, 236.
Cameron, 99, 1154-55, 79, 97.
Camp, 676.
Campbell, 25, 39, 266, 68-9, 470-73, 608, 698-700, 955, 80, 96, 1004, 80, 1226, 1312.
Canavan, 1278.
Canajoharie, priest of, 189.
Canby, 542, 69, 841.
Canfield, 1168.
Cannon, 39, 421-22, 472, 1033, 1183.
Capron, 906.
Capwell, 915.
Carew, 352, 1109.
Carey, 66, 216, 595, 833, 1089, 1257, 1334, 56.
Cargell, 228.
Carlisle, 542.
Carman, 192.
Carmichael, 93-94.
Carothers, 264.
Carpenter, 208, 411, 920, 1042, 43, 47, 97, 1182, 91.
Carr, 135, 339, 56, 599, 621, 868, 1165, 77, 1387.
Carrigan, 268.
Carrington, 409.
Carroll, 663, 960.
Carson, 1079.
Carter, 576.
Carver, 419, 667-68, 1242.
Cary, 352-53, 90.
Case, 157, 268, 849, 1307.
Casey, 880.
Cass, 236, 586, 623, 1275.
Cassidy, 980.
Caster, 692.
Catlin, v, 111, 213-15, 345, v, 613, 756-57, 59, 1031, vii, 43, 51-52, 61, 96, 1103-7.
Catoonah, 828.

INDEX OF NAMES.

Caulkins, 316.
Chadwick, 119,
Chalfant, 268.
Chamberlain, 543, 914, 1298.
Chamberlin, 39.
Chambers, 1095, 1116,
Champlin, 772, 1139.
Champneys, 270.
Chandler, 1189, 1228.
Chapin, 656, 709-12, 1264.
Chapman, 65-68, 304-5, 68, 633, 821, 37, 75-77, 982, 1041, 81-83, 1160, 69, 1260.
Charlemagne, 547.
Charles I, 324, 1130.
Charles, II, 2, 52, 255, 57, 1010, 1130, 1247, 1327.
Charles IX, 546.
Charlton, 1247.
Chase, 39, 105-6, 121-22, 25-27, 65, 290-92, 874, 97, 99-901, 35, 42, 1160, 1237, 40, 87-88, 1307, 1384.
Chastellux (Marquis de), 524, 1291.
Chaumont (de), 1291.
Chauncey, 286, 1109.
Cheeny, 982.
Cheetham, 1067.
Cheney (de), 1070.
Cherry, 946.
Chesebrough, 747-48.
Chew, 819.
Chickering, 227.
Child, 1238.
Childs, 1227.
Chittenden, 869.
Chitwood, 286.
Choiscuil (de), 892.
Christ, 479.
Chrystal, 352, 789.
Church, 134, 277, 406-7, 737, 1176, 99, 1244.
Cist, 30, 66, 499-500, 1094, 1127, 1332-34, 36-37, 40, 42-54, 58, 80.
Clanning, 862.
Clapham, 517.
Clapp, 958.
Clark, 264, 66, 363, 65, 425, 53-54, 538, 610, 771, 872, 84, 954, 1109, 1387.
Clarke, 19, 264, 872, 1131, 64.
Clarkson, 1130.
Classen, 141.
Claverhouse, 255.
Clawson, 913.
Claxton, 398.
Clay, 664, 1012, 1113, 89.
Claypole, 1144, 1327.
Clayton, 1181.
Cleamans, 148; see Clemens.
Clemmer, 678.
Clemens, 1385.
Clemons, 856.
Clerq, 192.
Cleveland, 111, 515, 903.
Clift, 48.
Clinton, 279-80, 1023-24, 1105.
Clive, Lord, 895.
Clothier, 751.
Clubine, 835,.
Clymer, 270, 1097, 1102.
Coates, 891.
Cochran, 683, 982.
Cochrane, 877.
Coffin, 679.
Coffrin, 304.
Coggshail, 2, 1295.
Cohen, 801-02.
Coit, 316, 61.

Colbert, 1244.
Colden, 1067.
Cole, 509, 606, 798.
Coleman, 318, 1012.
Coles, 447.
Collings, 25, 86, 886-87, 931-34, 1138, 1277.
Collins, 3, 15, 31, 33, 63, 69, 71, 197, 394, 542, 829, 42-43, 905-6, 1004, vii, 1107-14, 1119, 1220, 1310.
Colt, 338, 495-96, 506, 609, 776, 1260-61, 76.
Colvin, 475.
Comly, 884.
Compton, 1003.
Comstock, 750, 1264, 1199.
Comyn, 253-54.
Cone, 130, 1232.
Conger, 993.
Conkling, 425.
Connell, 874, 78.
Connolly, 935-36, 59-60, 68, 1033.
Conrad, 300.
Constantine, 547.
Constine, 468, 1388.
Converse, 318, 20.
Conway, 796.
Conyngham, v, 3, 15, 24, 31, 38, 48, 72, 79, 100, 5-6, 21, 65, 203-7, 55, 337-38, 66, 94, v, 866, 922, 1006, vii, ix, 1114-25, 65, 68, 82, 84-85, 88, 1212, 31, 37-39, 64, 69, 1316, 29.
Cook, 355, 486, 756, 979, 1244.
Cooke, 1069.
Cool, 610.
Cooley, 25, 903.
Coons, 39, 468-70, 80, 1388.
Cooper, v, 333, 46-47, v, 792, 1029, 59, 76-78, 81, 83, 1196, 1312, 45-46.
Coover, 683-84.
Cope, 1115.
Corbin, 406.
Corcoran, 1278.
Corker, 444
Cornwallis, 171, 293, 1040, 45, 79, 1135.
Corsen, 1028.
Corss, 593.
Corwin, 885.
Coryell, 268, 1248.
Coston, 39, 978.
Cottrill, 1232.
Coughlin, 615-17, 86.
Coulter, 1155.
Courtright, 1368-70.
Covell, 657, 1216-18, 1315, 51,
Covenhoven, 1320-21.
Cowen 857.
Cowie, 736, 864.
Cowles, 117.
Cowley, 1201.
Cox, 350, 1158, 1336.
Coxe, 786, 1259.
Craig, 419, 564, 707, 1295.
Craighead, 258, 264.
Cramer, 927.
Crane, 723, 904, 27, 1109, 77, 84, 1321.
Crary, 845.
Craven, 1070.
Crawford, 264, 539, 798, 1065.
Creveling, 694-96, 714, 814-15, 1390.
Crisman, 844, 1311,
Crispin, 1327-28.
Crittenden, 1012.
Creigh, 258.

Creswell, 268.
Crockett, 149.
Cromwell, 238, 380, 460, 662, 718, 1058, 87, 1113, 30, 1271.
Cronover, see Covenhoven.
Crook, 841.
Cross, 868.
Croswell, 1144-45.
Crothers, 968.
Cruden, 967.
Cruger, 369-70.
Cruttenden, 757, 59.
Cuddy, 266.
Cullen, 1278.
Cullick, 661.
Cuningham, 203.
Cuningham, see Conyngham.
Cunynghame, 255.
Cunyngham, see Conyngham.
Cummins, 726.
Cuningame, 203.
Cuningame, see Conyngham.
Cunninghame, 866.
Cunninghame, see Conyngham.
Curran, 1110, 1125.
Curry, 761.
Curtin, 74, 99, 166, 319, 418, 897, 929, 1153, 57, 1210, 31.
Curtis, 354, 1183.
Cutter, 1182, 94.
Cutting, 1068.

Dachs, 479.
Dagsworthy, 1180.
Dain, 497.
Dale, 1372.
Dallas, 652.
Dalrymple, 400.
Dalton, 950.
Dana, 31-41, 61, 64, 66, 79, 87, 125, 36, 62, 206, 40-41, 44-47, 63, 99, 312, 68, 469, 509, 39, 844, 80, 97, 933, 1037-38, 41, 1142-3, 94, 1211, 29, 33-35, 64-66, 1313, 16, 22, 29, 81.
Dandelot, 174.
D'Arcy, 719.
Darley, 621.
Darling, 30, 38-39, 88-96, 100, 289, 350, 439, 55-56, 86, 99, 500, 14, 52, 63, 9, 57, 66, 75, 87, 713, 21, 66, 95, 99, 948, 90-91, 1008, 1119, 80, 1316, 64, 66, 79-80, 82-84, 88.
Darlington, 1168.
Darrah, 898.
Darte, 39, 130-32, 411-42, 1001, 1232-33, 1324, 87, 8).
Davenport, 105-6, 84, 364, 544-45, 47, 72, 697-98, 810, 1257, 1314, 89.
David, 252.
Davidson, 191, 262, 1291.
Davis, 15, 26, 48, 126, 256, 67, 349, 516, 41-42, 658, 857, 928, 64, 1012-13, 1178, 1374.
Daw, 1035-36.
Dawes, 149.
Dawson, 833.
Day, 585, 988, 1145.
Dayton, 134-35, 938, 1199.
Deal, 1160.
Dean, 39, 961-65, 871-72.
Dearborn, 1079.
DeBlacons, 173.
Deble, 413.
Deborgur, 803.
DeBreck, see Breck.
Decatur, 392, 895, 927.
Decker, 555, 927, 1324.

Index of Names. 1409

DeFerrars, 255.
DeForest, 1069-70.
DeHutter, 281.
DeJersey, 758.
DeKay, 791.
Deitrick, ix.
Delafield, 1066.
DeLamberton, 251-52.
Dela..ey, 823-24.
DeMontule, 173.
Denison, 1, 3, 8-9, 21, 47-48, 53, 55-56, 59, 61, 119, 60, 65, 75, 89, 208, 16-18, 28, 33, 83, 328-29, 31-32, 62-63, 87, 93-94, 461, iii, v, 509, 538, 99, 638, 40-42, 49, 745, 48, 834, 46-47, 1027, 39, 41, 43, 47, 57, 87-90, 1118-20, 38, 57, 77, 91-94, 1219, 26, 29, 40, 54-55, 77-78, 85, 1303, 14, 56.
Dennis, 414, 772.
Denning, 895.
Denny, 258.
Depew, 813.
DePui, 46, 450, 62.
DeRencourt, 976.
Deringer, 1158.
Derr, 234, 458, 736-42, 921, 1316.
Derr, see Dorr.
DeRuyter, 279.
Deshong, 1358.
DeTrieux, 1070.
Dewees, 149.
DeWitt, 39, 201, 78-81. 371. 433, 930.
D'Hinayossa, 1165.
Dick, 635, 37.
Dickensheld, 678-79.
Dickinson, 386, 908, 88-89, 1181.
Dicksey, 762.
Dickson, 39, 457-67, 542, 649, 51, 1067, 14-15, 1296, 1375, 83, 87.
Dietrick viii, 1196, 1366-68.
Dietterick, 949.
Dill, 572, 1196.
Dilley, 861-62.
Dimmick, 28, 580, 950, 70-76, 994.
Dimmock, 970-71.
Dimmuck, 971.
Dinshert, 458.
Dixon, 302, 90, 1273.
Dixson, 542.
Doak, 1311.
Doane, 1195-96, 1391.
Dobb, 955.
Dodd, 168, 457, 954.
Dodge, 474.
Dodson, 179-81, 643, 754, 1320.
Dolan, 553.
Dolph, 885.
Dom Pedro I, 1111.
Donaldson, 338.
Donovan, 441.
Doolittle, 385, 1226.
Dorr, 458, 736-38, 1061-65.
Dorr, see Derr.
Dorrance, 25, 39, 87, 360-70, 87, 97, 413, 63, 39, 593, 652, 785, 1381.
Dorsey, 718-19.
Doubleday, 929.
Douglas, 830.
Douglass, 267, 430.
Dow, 734.
Downing. 351-55, 1387.
Doyle, 688.
Drake, 594, 609, 772, 905, 1127, 41-42, 1216, 50.
Draper, 506, 1272.

Driesbach. 913.
Drinker, 526.
Drum, 354, 726-27.
Dubois, 379-80.
Dudley, 216, 18.
Duer, 894-95.
Duffield, 258.
Duffy, 558, 1388.
Dugan, 298.
Dull, 268.
Dumer, 763.
Dunbar, 745.
Duncan, 258-59, 64, 1092, 1118.
Dundaff, 1125.
Dunlap, 264, 903, 1354.
Dunlop, 1016.
Dunn, 610, 874.
Dunning, 671-75, 884.
Dupetit Thouars, 174.
DuPont, 891-94, 974-76.
Durand, 869.
Durbrow, 1298.
Durkee, 331, 53, 88, 412, 36, 64, 526, 30, 633, 41, 1355.
Durkin, 283, 441.
DuTrieux, 790.
Dutton, 246.
Dwight, 21-22, 368.
Dyer, 1, 15, 33, 380, 1072-75, 1250-51, 1351.

Eads, 1071.
Earl, 542.
Earle, 1164.
Easterline, 1015.
Easton, 377, 743.
Eaton, 184, 364, 598, 662, 730, 1083, 1131, 1370.
Ebaugh, 268.
Eberhard, 805.
Eberwein, 458.
Eckrote, 1322.
Edgar, 898.
Edinger, 944.
Edmunds, 318.
Edson, 1257.
Edward I, 109, 251-54.
Edward III, 402, 1246.
Edward VI, 350.
Edward the Confessor, 109, 87.
Edwards, 40, 219, 853, 933. 38-39, 1032, 62, 71, 1373, 89.
Egle, 170, ix, 1381.
Eggleston, 460.
Elder, 397, 600, 816.
Elderkin, 963.
Eldred, 393, 580.
Eldridge, 855, 1240, 1311.
Eliot, 322, 757, 1087.
Elizabeth (Queen), 188, 541, 714.
Ellicott, 521.
Elliot, 519, 721-22, 898.
Ellis, 25, 205, 747, 902-03, 1118.
Ellsworth, 866.
Elsegood, 542.
Elwell, 4, 419, 1063, 1145.
Ely, 1141, 1216.
Emerson, 1238.
Emley, 25, 797, 1012.
Emmett, 1067, 1110.
Emmons, 868.
Endicott, 404.
Engle, 910, 1295.
Enno, 413.
Eno, 413.
Erath, 25.
Eshelman, 557.

Esler, 473.
Espy, 39, 412, 31-38, 816, 44, 45, 916-17, 1079, 1354.
Essex, Earl of, 237.
Estabrook, 361.
Esther (Queen), 212, 640.
Evans, 64, 281, 309, 48-49, 571-72, 783, 88, 1059, 75, 1249, 1350, 86.
Everett, 165, 338, 591.
Everhart, 804-7.
Everhart, see Eberhart.
Ewer, 808.
Ewing, 95, 342, 412, 518, 718, 1280.

Faherty, 726.
Fahy, 574.
Fairbanks, 909.
Fairchild, 246, 1170.
Faragut, 193.
Faries, 1286.
Farnham, 26, 39, 84-88, 122, 211, 25, 365, 417, 362, 70, 653, 60, 93, 807, 933, 1304, 71, 82-83.
Fayerweather, 762.
Fearne, 135, 1074.
Fein, 738-40.
Fell, 20, 158, 296, 344-49, 542, 687 90, 825, 1061, 77, 94, 1143, 1258, 1351, 90.
Fellows, 175, 321, 711, 994, 1230.
Fenelon, 547.
Fenn, 246.
Fenstermacher. 729-30.
Fenwick, 661, 875.
Ferguson, 163, 697.
Ferris, 40, 384-90, 414, 698, 807, 923.
Fewsmith, 475.
Field, 1067.
Fillbrook, 1287.
Fillmore, 586.
Finch, 26, 42, 47, 1089, 1382.
Findlay, 295, 309, 93, 565, 602, 21, 715, 870, 1050, 1151, 1309.
Finley, 256.
Fish, 362.
Fisher, 192-93, 675-76, 819, 1079.
Fisk, 361.
Fitch, 306, 521-22, 913, 1041, 1109, 1274.
Fitzgerald, 385, 600.
FitzHarding, 187.
FitzJohn, 187.
Fitzpatrick, 830.
Fitzsimmons, 996.
Flagg, 398.
Flanagan, 1084, 1362.
Flanigan, 39.
Fleming, 19, 1101.
Fletcher, 1137.
Flett, 1282.
Flick, 692-94, 1088.
Flynt, 791.
Fogg, 396.
Foley, 550, 950, 70.
Follett, 963.
Foote, 750-51.
Forbes, 409, 1004, 1109, 73, 1271.
Ford, 366, 68, 413, 593.
Fordsman, 1041.
Forest (de) 1070.
Forester, 873.
Forman, 1069.
Forney, 267, 683, 1146.
Forrett, 404.
Forsman, 343, 600.
Fort, 1327.

Index of Names.

Foster, 26, 39, 78, 184-93, 268, 364, 98, 535-36, 79, 807, 33, 37-40, 953, 1046, 1308, 1386.
Fotheringill, 1389.
Foulke, 149.
Fowler, 427, 771.
Fox, 140, 269, 391, 1100.
Franklin, 77, 215-20, 428, 518, 616, 29, 40, 43, 702, 10, 821, 24, 46, 1041, 45, 59, 62-63, 1145, 1215, 1302, 38-39, 57.
Frarice, 576.
Frazer, 775, 1019, 1369.
Freas, 1262.
Frederick Augustus, 1009.
Freeze, 356, 803.
French, 761.
Freneau, 1144.
Fremont, 77, 1179.
Freskin, 203.
Freyer, 149.
Frisbie, 513, 849-51, 1143.
Fritz, 802-4.
Frost, 1027, 29.
Frothingham, 1027-30.
Fry, 191.
Frye, 894-95.
Fulkerson, 686.
Fuller, 5, 39, 56, 61, 71, 86, 98, 121, 201, 25, 306, 56-57, 512, 575-603, 24, 37, 773, 73, 832, 87-89, 985, 1088, 1130, 49, 1201, 53, 99, 1302, 34, 85.
Fullerton, 755.
Fulton, 91-92, 521-22, 967.
Funck, 142.
Funk, 141, 45.
Futhey, 719.

Gable, 345.
Gabriel, 1014.
Gage, 916, 1044, 1135.
Gager, 978.
Galbraith, 264, 397, 1094-95.
Gale, 687.
Galt, 518.
Gallup, 174-75.
Gamble, 19, 797.
Gamelson, 187.
Gannon, 1362.
Gardiner, 875-76, 1186, 1254.
Gardiners, 621.
Gardner, 55, 620, 28, 789, 919, 62, 1285, 1324, 28.
Garfield, 87, 430, 654, 939.
Garman, 666-70.
Garrahan, 1014.
Garretson, 513.
Garrison, 308, 724.
Gartner, 997.
Gates, 39, 442, 48-49, 832, 948, 1034, 1387.
Gay, 465, 889, 909, 1190.
Gaylord, 186, 513, 622, 779-81, 850, 1315.
Gearey, 641, 83, 717, 49.
Gearhart, 39, 418, 922-23.
Geary, 71, 167, 354, 549, 733, 829, 1195, 1241, 1313, 67.
Geck, 700, 94.
Geck, see Keck.
Geddes, 280.
George, 610.
George I, 1018, 94.
George II, 744, 1336.
George III, 110, 1088.
George (King), 597.
Gerard, 1067-68.

Gerpheide, 849.
Gerry, 1146.
Gettle, 543.
Getz, 268.
Gibbon, 93.
Gibbons, 573, 1389.
Gibson, 48, 264, 829, vii, 1077, 83, 91-95, 98, 1159, 1345-46.
Giddings, 190, 576-80, 874, 1324.
Giering, ix.
Gilbert, 119, 180, 548, 789.
Gilchrist, 406, 1301.
Gildersleeve, 26, 721-24, 1726.
Gilligan, 1121.
Gillingham, 542.
Gillis, 380.
Gilmore, 867, 1196, 1391.
Ginter, 1335, 40.
Girard, 409, 1133.
Glassell, 1218.
Gloster, v.
Glover, 884.
Goble, 1284.
Godfrey, 567, 707.
Godschalck, 142.
Goff, 409.
Goffe, 1108.
Goodenow, 415, 747.
Goodrich, 123, 368, 1109, 98, 1238, 83.
Goodwin, 585, 624, 29, 796, 1065.
Gordon vii, 1-2, 251-52, 66, 83, 543, 610, 703, 817, 1381.
Gore, 53, 216, 346, 435-37, 629, 42, 813, 96, 1041-43, 47, 1502.
Gorges, 618-19.
Gorham, 1088.
Gorman, 39, 498-99.
Gorrell, 1323.
Gorton, 1028.
Goss, 616.
Gotshalk, 148.
Gough, 1077.
Gould, 1104.
Gouldsborough, 984.
Govett, 92.
Gowen, 453.
Graff, 348-49, 937.
Graham, 392, 94, 667, 847, 1000, 61.
Grandin, 1169.
Granger, 1343.
Grant, 195, 406, 413, 30, 38, 526-27, 733, 1010, 1177, 1241, 99, 1391.
Grattan, 1110, 25.
Gray, 103, 689-90, 957.
Gray (Duke of Sussex), 577.
Greeley, 430.
Greely, 749, 1379.
Green, 66, 121, 543, 97, 775, 872, 1294.
Greene, 778, 809, 948, 1044, 1337-38.
Greenley, 475.
Greeno, 960.
Greenough, 398-401, 731.
Gregg, 78, 1079.
Gregory, 827, 1107.
Gridley, 116.
Grier, 94-95, 258, 537, 720-21, 1170, 1321.
Griffin v, 31, 61, 69, 121, 335, v, vii, 1063-72, 1110, 84, 1301.
Grinnell, 794.
Griswold, 364, 430, 877, 1064.
Gritman, 39, 848.
Grow, 81, 509, 1178.
Growendyke, 192.
Grube, 548.
Guadalupe, 1071.

Guion, 92.
Gunn, 627.
Gunster, 853, 900, 17-18, 39, 44, 65, 95, 1033.
Gunther, 221.
Gurdon, 890.
Gurley, 972.
Gustavus III, 892.
Gustin, 1089.
Guthrie, 176, 623, 1022, 1314, 32.

Haddock, 1389.
Hadsell, 621.
Haff, 1380.
Hagerty, 660.
Hahn, 25, 39, 162-64, 469-70, 1385.
Haight, 334, 68-69, 1184.
Haines, 1142, 68, 1328.
Hair, 1017.
Haite, 75.
Haite, see Hoyt.
Hakes, 39, 71, 134-38, 51, 91, 307, 54, 56, 410, 13-14, 1198-1201, 1385, 87.
Hale, 321, 68, 490, 1131, 53, 1217.
Hales, 914.
Haley, 820.
Hall, 120, 75, 399, 448, 585, 749, 61, 89, 1084-85, 1196.
Halleck, 1328.
Hallett, 306.
Hallock, 1014, 1282.
Hals, 402-03.
Halse, 403.
Halsey, 402-12, 593, 709, 53-55, 1388, 90.
Hambleton, 1041.
Hamill, 23.
Hamilton, 258, 61, 792, 895, 1016, 1167, 1280-81, 95-90.
Hamlin, 187.
Hammond, 645-48, 811, 908, 71.
Hampden, 1113.
Hampton, 1080.
Hancock, 397, 437, 59, 563-64, 66, 791, 977, 1094, 1160, 1277-78, 1301.
Hand, 38-39, 313-26, 514, 875-79, 906, 09, 1d, 78, 83, 1031-33, 1189-90, 1267, 1310, 23.
Handley, 225, 883, 925, 68, 1032, 1266-67.
Handy, 512.
Hanluan, 205.
Hanluan, see O'Hanlon.
Hannah, 39, 908, 31.
Hannum, 106.
Hanspach, 478.
Hardee, 578.
Harding, 26, 30, 50, 53, 70-74, 86, 101, 07, 81, 97, 210, 83, 93, 358, 371, 417, 536, 86, 610, 18-25, 40, 68-69, 730, 885, 942, 83-84, 1041, 1158, 1237, 64-68, 1382-83.
Hardingson, 187.
Harkness, 262-65.
Harner, 768.
Harper, 825, 915, 1235, 1329.
Harring, 457.
Harrington, 26, 242, 441, 794, 853, 74, 923, 1301.
Harris, 54-55, 90, 199, 556, 643, 1085, 92, 1160, 89, 1223.
Harrison, 68, 76, 547, 1302.
Hart, 794.
Harter, 730.
Hartley, 54.
Hartman, 1390.

INDEX OF NAMES.   1411

Hartranft, 28, 66, 102, 67, 463, 844, 943, 1366.
Hartzell, 609.
Harvey, viii, 26, 39, 433, 76, 505-16, 18, 850, 905, 17, 1015, 1245, 1332, 88.
Hasbrouck, 279.
Haskell, 975.
Haslibacher, 144.
Hastings, 874.
Hatch, 623, 860.
Haughawout, 874, 1293.
Haven, 509, 825.
Haviland, 900.
Hawkes, 1387.
Hawley, 117, 762, 940, 90, 93-94, 1064, 1344.
Hawse, see Halsey.
Hawthorne, 404.
Hayden viii, 368, 413, 550.
Hayes, 48, 102, 413, 30, 63, 571-75, ix, 1391.
Haykes, see Hakes.
Haynes, 55, 103, 16, 661, 1230.
Hazard, 743-44, 837, 1319.
Hazzard, 45.
Headley, 1073-74, 1199
Heartley, 1096.
Heaton, 804.
Heckel, 940.
Hedian, 725-29.
Heemstreet, 793.
Heermans, 321, 884-85, 965.
Heery, 924.
Heffron, 250.
Hegins, 1294.
Hehl, 175.
Heintzelman, 77.
Heister, 295.
Heitzman, 789.
Held, 1139.
Hemingway, 413, 559.
Henderson, 510, 756
Hendrick, 3, 761, 1329.
Hendricks, 144, 263, 76, 790.
Henriks, 149.
Henry, 455, 516-30, 1079, 1104, 1340-41.
Henry VI, 403, 577.
Henry VII, 252.
Henry VIII, 403, 505.
Hensel 313.
Hepburn, 24, 879.
Herrick, 593, 966.
Herring, 1233.
Hersh, 1261.
Hess, 160, 1230.
Hewett, 368, 1255.
Hewitt, 73, 327, 30-31, 43.
Hewson, 1028.
Hibbard, 437, 664.
Hibbs, 25, 1377-78.
Hice, 815.
Hick, 795.
Hicks, 344, 548, 74, 1068, 1210.
Hickman, 459.
Hickok, 913.
Hiester, 288.
Higbee, 318.
Higgins iii.
Higginson, 1044.
Hill, 35, 75-76, 291, 924, 97-1001, 1180, 83, 97, 1234.
Hillard, 25, 248, 798-801, 1366, 90.
Hillegas, 1340.
Hillhouse, 321.
Hillman, 693, 1004, 1259, 1332, 73-75.
Hindman, 931.

Hinds, 1308-09
Hines, 610-15, 757, 1389.
Hinman, 491, 757, 1344.
Hitchcock, 20, 40, 188, 879-83, 1289.
Hoadley, 674.
Hoagland, 191-92.
Hobbs, 396.
Hobson, 578.
Hocksey, 963-64.
Hodgdon, 1016, 1221-23.
Hodge, 993, 1221-22.
Hodkinson, 1096.
Hoes, 278.
Hoffman, 1066-67, 1116.
Hoite, 75.
Hoite, see Hoyt.
Holben, 977.
Holburton, 761-62, 66.
Hold, 1217.
Holding, 515.
Holland, 1012.
Hollenback, 122, 71, 216, 18-19, 333, 437, 500, 93, 609, 64, 1042-43, 46, 55, 77, 99, 1127, 1202, 16, 53, 1339, 41-45, 51, 54-58, 80.
Holliday, 1208-09.
Hollingshead, 972.
Hollister, 59, 123, 1077.
Holmes, 772, 1240, 1301, 27.
Holton, 368.
Holyoke, 842.
Honeyweil, 696.
Honor, 277, 695.
Hood, 995.
Hooker, 114, 17, 322, 85, 91, 859, 1002, 1313.
Hoover, 561, 1390.
Hopkins, 238, 70, 364, 86, 661-62, 94, 925, 1003, 1321.
Hopkinson, 822.
Hopper, 454, 74.
Horn, 39, 708, 852-53, 944, 1319.
Hornbeck, 228.
Horneil, 683.
Horsely, 1390.
Horton, 985.
Hosmer, 364.
Hosie, 690, 953-58.
Hopkins, 889
Hotchkiss, 898-99.
Hotten, 576.
Hottenstein, 937.
Houghton, 334.
Houpt, 19, 414.
Houston, 1133.
Hovey, 378, 1034.
Howard, 841, 50, 902.
Howarth, 569.
Howe, 88, 93, 405, 520, 1214.
Howell, 673-74.
Hower, 863.
Howland, 385, 1004, 88.
Huyt, 26-28, 30, 38, 40, 61, 74-84, 99, 101, 52, 97, 206, 49, 339, 61, 413, 30, 60, 65, 509, 39, 68, 607, 27-51, 750, 81, 85, 878, 934, 977, 1013-14, 34, 1213-14, 21, 64, 68, 1344, 69, 73, 82.
Hubbard, 1195.
Hubbell, 623.
Hudson, 678.
Huet, 771.
Hughes, 268, 563-71, 616, 794, 995-96, vi.
Hulings, 1191.
Hull, 923, 78.
Hummell, 684.
Humphrey, 585, 850, 986.

Humphries, 67.
Hunlock, 26, 39, 301-08, 1386.
Hunt, 235, 368, 663, 1258, 88.
Hunter, 94, 555, 1363.
Huntington, 297, 861, 1064, 1108-09, 31, 42, 1247, 1308.
Huntting, 1186.
Hurd, 23.
Hurlburt, 853.
Hurlbut, 132, 292, 304, 604, 28-29, 1041, 56, 1245, 1314.
Hurlbutt, 849.
Hurley, 105, 949.
Huston, 22, 259, 63, 489, 551-52.
Hutchins, 1110.
Hutchinson, 542, 657, 743, 808, 912.
Hutchison, 268.
Hutton, 893.
Hyatt, 75, 828
Hyde, 208, 1064, 1109.

Ingersoll, 19, 110, 212, 1114, 61.
Ingham, 434, 83-86, 1257, 1300.
Inghram, 732-33.
Inman, 432, 539.
Innes, 1175.
Ireland, 1029.
Irenaeus, 314.
Irvin, 301.
Irvine, 264, 1173.
Irving, 350, 924.
Israell, 891.

Jackson, 36, 39, 300, 486, 538-40, 49, 644, 89, 841, 67, 86, 936, 61, 83, 1075, 1150, 89, 95-97, 1238, 46, 73, 75, 95, 98, 1367, 88, 91.
Jacob, 858.
Jacobs, 55, 58, 1383.
Jacoby, 807.
James, 192, 268, 995.
James I, 90, 237, 1010.
James II, 257, 1271.
James IV, 251.
Jameson, 301-07, 507, 836, 45, 1273
Janes, 772.
Jarrett, 149.
Jasper, 1328.
Jay, 437, 986.
Jeffers, 906.
Jefferson, 258, 408, 664, 781, 823, 998, 1046, 99, 1189, 1221, 1343.
Jenkins viii, 52-58, 193, 212, 16, 18, 68, 595, 622, 21, 753, 845, 963, 79, 83, ix, 1040-41, 1381-82.
Jenks, 541-43.
Jennings, 631, 33.
Jennison, 65.
Jeremy, 1389.
Jervis, 1024-25.
Jessup, 393, 674, 877-79, 82, 907, 83, vii, 1102, 22, 85-90, 1270, 1310, 23.
Jewett, 288, 339, 427, 842, 1064, 1111, 1219.
John, 187.
John the Baptist, 190.
John, King, 285, 1328.
John of Leyden, 139.
Johns, 898.
Johnson, viii, 24-25, 59, 126, 87-91, 272, 74, 300, 34, 44, 80-81, 468, 567, 79, 627, 81, 83, 763, 75-77, 824, 30, 976, 1012, ix, 14, 89, 93, 1119, 40-41, 65-67, 1204, 41, 1301, 29.
Johnston, 188.

Index of Names.

Jones 39, 66, 249, 308-10, 400, v, 511, 608, 64, 706-09, 56, 803, 15, 26-29, 66, 77, 90, 928-29, 48, 88, viii, 1130-34, 37, 42, 69, 74-75, 98, 1223, 40, 1312, 54, 70-73.
Jordan, 835, 1312.
Joseph, 892.
Judd, 509, 657, 1041.
Junkin, 77.
Justice, 342.
Jutan, 900.

Kahler, 949.
Kaine, 268.
Kalbfus, 1319.
Kantner, 814.
Karl IV, 805.
Karsdorp, 148.
Kassel, 142.
Kauffman, 680-86, 1390.
Kay, 473.
Kayingwaurto, 608.
Kearns, 167.
Keck, 700-09, 1390.
Keeler, 482.
Keenan, 1160.
Keene, 1223.
Keep, 243.
Keim, 19.
Keiser, 716.
Keith, 457.
Keller, 684.
Kelley, 498, 650.
Kellog, 757, 1368.
Kellogg, 623, 1211.
Kelly, 250, 650.
Kemmerer, 874.
Kemper, 1146.
Kendall, 247, 455.
Kennady, 722.
Kennedy, 542, 1226-27, 1369.
Kent, 459, 1068.
Kenyon, 1373.
Kenzle, 961.
Kerns, 237.
Keokuk, 1105.
Kesler, 220.
Ketcham, 26, 30, 64, 85, 135, 229, 70, v, 509, 67, 919, vii, 1157, 1240-42, 85, 97-98.
Keyder, 149.
Keyes, 1176.
Keys, 963-64.
Keyser, 144, 854.
Kidder, v, 33, 39, 51, 60, 71, 125, 240-45, 397, v, 559, 1121, 75-77, 98, 1204, 20, 83, 1312-13, 30.
Kilgore, 199.
Killbuck, 523.
Kilpatrick, 234, 378.
Kimberlin, 667.
Kimble, 452, 955, 1147.
King, 23, 706, 09, 920, 1096, 1275, 99.
Kingman, vii, 558, 629, 24, 766, 1365-66.
Kingsbury, 26, 317, 91, 881-82, 1289, 91.
Kingsley, 340-42, 1042-43, 48-49.
Kinney, 227, 475, 613, 1055-56, 1107, 1314.
Kinsey, 179, 795, 980-81.
Kipp, 923.
Kirby, 608.
Kirk, 344, 688, 1294.
Kirkbride, 542.
Kirkendall, 25, 513.
Kirkpatrick, 816, 1170, 75.

Kirkoff, 574.
Kirtland, 877, 1036.
Kishbauch, 949.
Kisner, 38, 96, 310-13, 549.
Klader, 181.
Klein, 549.
Kline, 39, 349-51, 74, 788, 961.
Klintob, 961.
Klotz, 547-48.
Knapp, 39, 594, 873, 912, 67-63, 1386.
Knauss, 560.
Knorr, 419.
Knowles, 1210.
Knox, 253, 750, 997.
Kobar, 683.
Koch, 1336.
Koester, 749.
Kolb, 138-49.
Kolb, see Kulp.
Koon, 39, 58-59, 1183.
Koons, 354, 560, 1171, 83, 1229-30, 1302.
Kotz, 1013.
Kramer, 1249.
Krouse, 547.
Kuhn, 58.
Kulp, 25, 38, 79, 105-06, 38-59, 76-78, 458, 626, 767, 833, 961, 1325, 83, 85.
Kunkle, 439.
Kuster, 144.
Kyle, 1095.

La Barre, 636.
Ladd, 665, 969.
Lafayette, 171, 367, 708, 879, 1010, 1138.
Lake, 175.
Lamb, 40, 448, 960-61, 87, 1081, 1228.
Lamberton, 25, 27-28, 251-82, 920. 1386.
Lambyrton, 252.
Lameroux, 545.
Lamertine, 718.
Landis, 144.
Landmesser, 39, 475-76, 738, 1368.
Landon, 270, 1041-42.
Lane, 508-09, 1245, 1315.
Lanehart, 729.
Langford, 611.
Laning, 20, 366, 1096, 1358.
Lape, 136.
La Perouse, 174.
La Porte, 170, 73, 503.
Larned, 808-14, 1391.
Larrabee, 849.
Larrish, 712.
Lathrop, 39, 246, 562, 841, 48, 57-62, 66, 68, 69, 90, 96, 97, 1109, 69, 77, 1369.
Lathrope, 26, 39, 58, 496, 901-02, 07, 50, 1007, 1169.
Latimer, 843.
Laud, 283, 778, 858.
Lauderbach, 685.
Lavoisier, 974.
Law, 26, 622.
Lawrence, 576, 686.
Lawton, 744.
Lazarus, 494, 609.
Lea, 129.
Leach, 479, 53, 994-95.
Leaming, 1052.
Lear, 1324.
Learned, 808-11.
Learned, see Larned.

Leavens, 811-12.
Leavenworth, 60, 1311.
LeClerc, 1182, 94.
Ledlie, 1128.
Ledyard, 1244.
Lee, 119, 166, 272, 428, 461-62, 511, 649, 74, 844, 63, 1004-07, 64, 79-80, 1208, 25-26, 1315, 51.
Leete, 1108.
Leffingwell, 1109.
Lehr, 865.
Leidig, 944.
Leidy, 806, 922.
Leighton, 440.
Leisenring, 839, 945-47, 1293.
Lemon, 269.
Lenahan, 131, 283, 440-42, 557-59, 774, 1385, 87-89.
Lengwicke, 1068.
Lenhart, 905.
Leonard, 243, 405-6, 1301.
Leopold, 892.
Lescher, 319.
Leslie, 429, 908, 31.
LeTellier, 547.
Levan, 410, 705-6.
Lewis, 25-26, 39, 43, 119, 60-61, 63, 246, 67-68, 371, 418, 39, 82-86, 535, 65, 85, 703, 10, 43, 72, 96, 817-24, 97, 1159, 1235, 45, 60-61, 1306, 23.
Lievens, 793.
Liggett, 44, 1007.
Lightfoot, 519.
Lincoln, 7, 9, 43, 48, 267-68, 469, 681, 83, 907, 1045, 1109, 79, 89, 1241, 74.
Linderman, 1008-13.
Lindner, 550.
Lindsley, 366-67, 593.
Line, 977.
Lines, 868.
Linn, 308, 572, 1153, 1282.
Lippincott, 309, 455, 825, 1329.
Little, 422, 98, 750-52, 851, 908, 15, 28, 38, 69, 1002, 1191, 1220.
Livey, 885.
Livingston, 1067.
Llewellyn, 554.
Lloyd, 149, 372.
Lock, 600
Locke, 37, 1110.
Lockhart, 1012.
Lockwood, 812.
Loftus, 447, 994.
Logan, 256, 372, 409, 942, 68-69.
Long, 25, 210, 468-69, 684, 1388.
Longfellow, 528.
Longley, 119.
Longstreet, 36, 690, 873, 1284-85.
Longstreth, 548, 586.
Lonsdale, 129, 1392.
Loomis, 26, 39, 413, 674, 771-73, 906-8, 31, 1141.
Loop, 292-98.
Lord, 116-17, 334, 61, 546, 907, 1036, 64.
Lorah, 1385.
Loring, 969.
Lossee, 411.
Lossing, 792.
Lothropp, 778, 837, 59-60, 902.
Lothropp, see Lathrop, Lathrope.
Louis XIV, 545-46.
Louis XVI, 172, 893, 1358.
Louis Phillippe, 173, 1358.
Lovat (Lord), 775.
Love, 1:82, 1376.
Loveland, 26, 39, 61-62, 84, 1198.

INDEX OF NAMES.

Lovell, 987.
Lowenstein, 1315.
Lowrie, 459, 720, 1159.
Lowry, 270, 74, 905.
Lucas, 756.
Lueder, 862.
Lukens, 519.
Lukins, 637.
Lumbert, 971.
Lunt, 380.
Lusk, 851, 937-38.
Luther, 139, 1008.
Lyman, 317, 321-23, 57, 906, 1110, 1218.
Lynch, 25, 282-85, 356, 441, 88, 553, 73, 610, 1013, 1386, 88.
Lynde, 111.
Lynn, 299, 562, 1282.
Lyon, 258.
Lyson, 109.
Lytle, 262, 64.

Macalester, 1160-61.
Macauley, 278, 444.
Macbeth, 203.
Macdonald, 90.
Macintosh, 1263.
Mack, 907, 1388.
Mackenzie, 1067.
Maclay, 1085.
Macmanus, 1153.
Maconaquah, 342.
MacVeagh, 84, 685.
Madill, 391.
Madison, 317, 1046, 1092, 1105, 46, 1275, 1343.
Maffet, 294-95, 1259.
Maffitt, 66, 531, 1260.
Maffit, 789, 1099.
Magee, 532-33, 817, 1388.
Maguire, 806.
Mahon, 250-51, 853, 924, 59, 1386.
Maintenon, (Madame de), 547.
Maiss, 479.
Malcolm, 203.
Mallalieu, 417.
Mallery, v, r, 15, 48, 98, 337-38, 393-94, v, 824, 972, vii, 1083-86, 90, 96, 99, 1111-12, 17-20, 37, 42, 49, 81, 1218-19, 61, 75.
Mangan, 573.
Mann, 629, 711.
Manning, 635-36.
Manville, 1210.
Mapledoram, 970.
Marble, 429.
Marcy, 320, 812, 1041, 1230, 1386.
Margaret of Anjou, 403, 577.
Marischal, 457.
Markham, 1281.
Markling, 458.
Marr, 1118.
Marshall, 25, 643, 757.
Martin, 10, 16, 39, 542, 56-57, 642, 823, 913.
Marvin, 186, 493.
Mary of Scotland, 194.
Mason, 662, 1088, 1217.
Masterson, 535, 1389
Mather, 149, 243.
Mathers, 626-27, 817, 138).
Matter, 716.
Mattes, 527.
Matthew, Father, 1378.
Matthews, 135, 970.
Maus, 973.
Maverick, 1228.
Maxwell, 24, 26-28, 86, 134, 604,

832-33, 36, 39, 902, 1017, 1168-69, 1279-80.
May, 1002.
Mayer, 1170.
Maynard, 268, 415.
Mayo, 1143.
McAlarney, 533-35, 696, 1388.
McAlister, 957.
McAllister, 1153.
McAloon, 421.
McAlpine, 776.
McAtee, 677-79.
McCall, 413, 511, 830.
McCalmount, 269.
McCanna, 625.
McCarrachen, 846.
McCarragher, 51.
McCartney, 39, 66, 73, 427-31, 539-40, 58, 855, 1227, 1387.
McCarty, 543.
McClellan, 8, 274-75, 400, 1162.
McClintock, 3. 23-30, 38, 40, 48, 86, 100, 17, 29, 97, 247, 89, 367, 456, 99-504, 776, 85, 689, 91, 1119, 27, 41, 91, 1223, 35, 39, 75, 82, 97, 1312, 16, 54, 59, 71, 83.
McCloskey, 904
McClure, 258, 70, 369, 608, 1001, 1162-64.
McCollum, 1189.
McComb, 1121.
McConnell, 268, 838.
McCoy, 471, 672, 981-82, 1314.
McCord, 1294.
McCormick, 553, 988.
McCranney, 407.
McCulloch, 1222.
McCullough, 947, 1351.
McDaniel, 548.
McDivitt, 39, 987-88.
McDonald, 239, 421, 72, 1322.
McDormott, 910.
McDowell, 46, 461-62, 649, 1215.
McEwen, 1291.
McFarland, 999-1001.
McGahren, 444, 535-36, 624, 730.
McGavin, 924.
McGee, 568.
McGinness, 940.
McGinty, 968, 825.
McGoldrick, 1174.
McGovern, 773-74, 1390
McGourty, 699.
McGroarty, 25, 440.
McHugh, vi.
McIntire, 532.
McIntyre, 423.
McIlvaine, 23.
McKarrachan, 641, 44, 816.
McKarrican, 1041.
McKean, 95, 208, 13, 60, 82, 821, 1060, 99, 1150, 72.
McKee, 457.
McKechan, 261.
McKechen, 257-58.
McKinley, 1322.
McKinney, 1074, 61, 1299
McKinstry, 811.
McKune, 941-43.
McLean, 28, 283, 98-301, 56, 514, 39, 73, 691, 976, 1012, 1037.
McLellan, 697, 1162.
McManus, 553-54.
McMillan, 451.
McMinn, 769.
McMurtrie, 455.
McNeish, 699.
McQuillan, 1322.
McShane, 1281.

McVannon. 667.
McVeagh, 460.
McVeigh, 1375.
Meade, 272
Mecklam, 941.
Meek, 836, 967.
Meixell, 729-30, 1390.
Melick, 738-40, 914.
Mellows, 165.
Melshimer, 1352.
Menno, 139-40.
Merakal, 851.
Mercer, 129.
Mercur, 25, 960.
Meredith, 13, 400, 817, 36, 967, 1097-98, 1151, 58-59, 80.
Merkel, 681.
Merriam, 842.
Merrifield, 853-56, 83, 1032, 1286-87
Merriman, 25, 86, 230, 920, 70, 1303-06.
Merryman, 126.
Merwyne, 641.
Messchert, 458.
Messemer, 1352.
Messenger, 165.
Messinger, 584, 1390.
Metcalf, 165, 416, 1234-35.
Mettler, 923, 1312.
Metzger, 517.
Meylert, 1223, 88.
Meylin, 144.
Michael, 537.
Mifflin, 259-60, 345, 564, 1053, 55, 1174, 1337, 41.
Miles, 152, 176-78, 451.
Miller, 26, 39, 100, 120-22, 44, 49, 75, 211, 68, 308, 54, 417, 433, 49, 54, 593-94, 699, 836, 911, 21, 49-50, 62, 1033-34, 1214-15, 34, 1333-34
Mills, 451, 583-86, 624, 905, 1391.
Miner, 1, 26, 42-44, 52, 66, 197, 295, 306, 35, 40, 41, 86, 464, 485, 506, 30-31, 96, 601, 29, 49, 60, 747, 833, 1007, 48, 53, 50, 1101, 20, 38, 41, 60, 1216, 26, 46-59, 1260, 75, 1343-44, 47, 92.
Minor, 1083, 88.
Minturn, 794.
Mitchell, 153, 268, 333, 554, 668, 91, 741, 69, 897-98, 921, 919, 1013, 1296, 1372, 91.
Moeser, 449.
Moeser, see Mosier
Moffit, 1041.
Mohler, 683.
Molick, 739-40.
Molick, see Melick.
Molines, 305.
Momauguin, 185.
Monaghan, 268, 515.
Monies, 1290.
Monroe, 317, 714.
Monson, 163.
Montague(La), 1079.
Montgomery, 204, 55, 79, 824, 1332.
Montooth, 1372.
Montross, 538.
Moon, 1376.
Moore, 204, 40, 78, 617-18, 1175, 1300, 89.
Mouland, 982.
Morville, 255.
Morey, 794.
Morey, see Mowry.
Morgan, 234, 309, 818, 938, 1179.
Morrill, 430, 683
Morris, 171, 517, 42, 820, 65, 930, 1102, 1249, 1358, 78-79.

Index of Names.

Morrison, 576.
Morse, 25, 55 225, 45-47, 1386.
Morss, 1036-38.
Morton, 409, 859.
Moseley, 1041.
Mosier, 39, 449-52, 1307.
Moss, 245-46, 449.
Mosser, 449.
Mott, 385, 580, 1008, 38.
Mountjoy, 237.
Mower, 910.
Mowry, 794.
Muhlenburg, 260, 1150, 1388.
Muirhead, 608.
Mulford, 314.
Mullens, 25.
Muller, 65.
Mulligan, 911, 1379.
Mullins, 305, 748, 1274.
Mumma, 681.
Munson, 163, 1217.
Murfee, 436, 812-13.
Murphy, 559, 642, 728, 812-13, 1305, 90.
Murray, 87, 97, 204, 53, 542, 722, 832-34, 1054-56, 94.
Musser, 206.
Myer, 790, 1085.
Myers, 25, 181, 629-31, 36, 39-40, 48-50, 726, 856-57, 935, 1057, 1136, 1221, 28-29, 1307, 23, 64-65.
Mygett, 909.

Nagle, 1105.
Naglee, 77.
Napier, 769.
Napoleon, 173, 539, 893-94.
Nash, 149, 184-86, 364, 968.
Natt, 22.
Neal, 63.
Neilson, 1069.
Neisser, 1337.
Nelson, 318, 338, 85, 466, 509, 69, 715, 1207, 40.
Nesbit, 1043.
Nesbitt, 40, 205, 16, 18, 507-08, 72, 934, 1042-43, 1338.
Nettleton, 657.
Neuer, 1391.
Neville, 1293.
Newberry, 368.
Newbold, 542.
Newbury, 583, 889, 1234.
Newman, 185.
Nichol, 866.
Nichols, 39, 245, 437, 42-45, 92, 536, 59-61, 618, 734, 1007, 10, 1043.
Nicholson, 25, 56, 61, 63, 69, 71, 123-24, 65, 71, 206, 33, 99, 417, 539, 872, 85, 901, 65, 1197-98, 1238, 83-84, 1330, 40.
Niebel, 1227.
Ninigrate, 662.
Nisbet, 457.
Niver, 926.
Nixon, 243.
Noailles, (de), 171.
Noble, 261, 384, 861, 1169, 77.
Norman, 721-22.
Norris, 94, 1173, 1286.
North, 268, 657, 911.
Northam, 751.
Norton, 749, 874.
Nott, 15, 367.
Noyes, 61, 747.

Oakes, 960.
Oakley, 164.
O'Boyle, 659-60, 1390.
O'Brien, 1279.
O'Callaghan, 900.
O'Collins, 1107.
O'Connor, 749, 1334.
Offa, 577.
O'Flaherty, 39, 969-70.
Ogden, 633-37, 962-63, 1067.
O'Hanlan, 356.
O'Hanlon, 39, 204-05, 959, 1363.
Ojidirk, 340.
Oldage, 164.
Olin, 1241.
Oliver, 731, 920.
Olmstead, 1034.
O'Mara, 924.
O'Neill, 25, 225, 233-40, 440, 72, 996, 1386.
Opp, 39, 422-23, 698.
Ord, 841.
Organ, 380.
Orr, 637, 976-77, 1015.
Orton, 15, 66, 98, 657, 1148-49.
Otto, 707, 1084.
Osborne, 38, 87, 164-69, 321, 413, 33, 568, 785, 883, 906, 17, 25, 984, 1126, 99, 1372, 86.
Osmond, 449.
Osterhout, 95, 222, 31, 594, 909, 50, 83, 1006, 1313-19, 1360.
Oswald, 684, 1190.
Otis, 55, 970-71.
Ousamequin, 352.
Overfield, 450-51.
Overton, 1095-96, 1102.
Owen, 1062, 1244.

Packer, 268, 400, 897-98, 935, 937, 1013, 1140, 79, 1347, 74.
Pagan, 1003.
Pagan, see Paine.
Page, 320, 598.
Paine, 26, 39, 207, 26-27, 96, 339, 461, 520-21, 62, 1003-07, 1143-46, 1316, 33, 92.
Painter, 39, 921, 1127.
Palgrave, 23.
Palmer, 26, 30, 38, 71, 79, 152, 194-203, 15, 354, 71, 444, 80, 512, 93, 699, 785, 1007, 15, 60-61, 1113, 1286, 98, 1312, 86, 92.
Pannebecker, 767.
Pannebocker, see Pennypacker.
Pardee, 310-11, 1258.
Park, 720.
Parke, 95, 531, 719-25, 63, 1139-40.
Parker, 119, 364, 425, 916, 1033, 1176-82.
Parks, 435, 1041.
Parrish, 26, 593-95, 602, 1125, 1301.
Parsons, 32, 115, 243-44, 446, 90, 513, 39, 52, 67, 609, 788, 92, 823, 29-31, 1015.
Partridge, 1180.
Pastorius, 372.
Patrick, 39, 68-69, 71, 210, 417, 538, 856, 996-97.
Patten, 268.
Patterson, 165, 290, 307, 562, 633, 715, 889, 987, 1391.
Pattison, 468, 980, 1381.
Patton, 730-35.
Paul, 1281.
Paulding, 265.
Pauling, 596.
Pawlings, 1143.

Payen, 1003.
Payen, see Paine.
Payn, 1003.
Payn, see Paine.
Payne, 11, 26, 30, 38, 101, 226-33, 475, 547, 67, 674, 728, 748, 812, 14, 930, 1003-07, 1143, 66, 1316.
Payne, see Paine.
Payson, 88, 882.
Peabody, 297.
Peale, 1105.
Pearce, 436, 587, 847, 1245, 71-74.
Peart, 180.
Pease, 1176.
Peck, 76, 208, 11, 46, 444, 495, 638, 50, 67, 755, 75, 879, 966-67, 94, 1063, 1196, 1244-45, 51, 1390.
Peckham, 852, 948, 1209-10.
Peeler, 1257.
Peironnet, 350.
Pell, 903.
Pendleton, 8, 746-48, 50.
Penn, 2, 91, 189, 344, 554, 701, 6, 835, 989, 1166, 1281, 1327-28.
Pennington, 1078.
Penny, 270, 73.
Pennypacker, 147, 372, 767.
Pepperill, 1133.
Pepys, 1020.
Perkins, 295, 334, 530-31, 849, 1110, 33.
Perry, 1110.
Perse, 610.
Peter the Great, 1332-33.
Peter the Hermit, 194.
Peterman, 1142.
Peters, 41, 205, 613, 1008.
Peterson, 700.
Petit, 1169.
Petriken, 268.
Pettebone, 20, 460-65, 617, 49, 871, 1138-39, 1381.
Petty, 626, 1180.
Pfouts, 25, 1320-22.
Phelps, 50, 290, 598, 757, 59, 99, 800, 1204, 07-08.
Philbin, 25, 959, 1362-63.
Phillip (King), 175, 227, 353, 1176, 1344.
Philips, 123, 1042.
Phillips, 290, 716, 24, 92, 899, 914, 1173.
Phinney, 504, 848.
Phoenix, 1002.
Piatt, 670, 726, 1220.
Pickens, 880.
Pickering, 215, 19, 93, 96, 1042-46, 53-55, 1223, 1356, 69.
Picket, 950.
Pier, 538.
Pierce, 228, 337, 495, 606-07, 21, 23, 27, 41-42, 44, 46, 957, 1040-41, 84, 1349, 70.
Pierrepont, 1108, 10.
Pierson, 55, 108, 542.
Piggins, 812.
Pike, vii; 25, 39, 652, 1278-79, 1329.
Pilmore, 716.
Pinney, 978.
Piollet, 268, 539.
Piper, 107, 816.
Pitcher, 965-67.
Pittinger, 514.
Pitt, 315, 1202-08.
Playford, 29.
Plaza (de la), 1071.
Pleasants, 412.
Plotz, 25, 242, 547-48.

INDEX OF NAMES. 1415

Plowman, 867.
Plum, 657.
Plumb, 132-34, 225, 323, 603-06, 28, 1389.
Plunkett, 205, 304, 639, 1125, 1215.
Poland, 318.
Polk, 5, 59, 99, 306, 716, 886, 1154-55, 1275-76, 94, 1329.
Pollock, 19, 354, 998, 1212.
Polly, 1215.
Pope, 1100.
Popham, 109.
Porter, 23-24, 191, 210, 490, 584, 716, 63, 825, 91, 986, 1004-15, 33, 99, 1151, 53, 64, 1224, 1231, 58.
Post, 39, 324, 909, 15, 38, 776, 938, 78, 1031-32, 1189, 1231, 1308-10, 23.
Posthelwait, 259.
Potosky, 174.
Potter, 290, 442, 582, 763, 1128, 1377.
Powell, 38, 371-84, 802, 1086, 1385.
Power, 923.
Pratt, 493-94, 840, 1293.
Prentice, 287, 843, 1063.
Prentis, 743.
Pressler, 1390.
Price, 39, 651-52, 799, 951-59, 1284.
Priddy, 677.
Priestley 1077.
Prince, 1143.
Pringle, 508.
Prior, 1000.
Pritchett, 374.
Proctor, 76.
Proud, 818.
Prudden, 364.
Pruner, 32, 1235.
Pryor, 1374.
Pursel, 25, 872.
Pursell, 874.
Purviance, 19, 266.
Pusey, 372, 889.
Puterbaugh, 25, 283.
Putnam, 415, 1181.
Pynchon, 763-64.
Pyne, 1000.

Quackenbos, 793.
Quarterman, 721.
Quay, 1372.
Quick, 1322.
Quincy, 791.
Quinn, 64.

Raeder, 25, 788-98, ix.
Rafferty, 905.
Rahn, 170.
Rahn, see Rhone.
Ramsay, 95.
Ramsey, 542.
Ranck, 39, 418, 913-14, 39-40.
Rand, 1028.
Randall, 25, 176, 268, 421, 681, 744-45, 885, 99, 1148, 83, 93, 1234-38.
Randolph, 408, 542, 1045, 1217.
Rank, 39, 939-43.
Rank. see Ranck.
Rankin, 25, 1183, 1263-64
Ransom, 331, 62, 85-89, 385, 432, 529-30, 79, 641, 98, 958, 1311.
Rathbone, 506.
Rawle, 1092, 1132.
Ray, 774.
Raymond, 164, 416, 990
Read, 19, 95, 1097, 1186.

Reagan, 24, 421.
Redfield, 758.
Red Jacket, 1105.
Reed, 820, 38, 911, 36, 1138, 1214, 82, 1312.
Rees, 520.
Reese, 716.
Reeve, 930, 1053-54, 65.
Reeves, 1104.
Regan, 25, 179, 904, 11.
Reichard, 25, 469-70, 789, 874, 1299-1301.
Reichel, 706.
Reigart, 458.
Reilly, 574.
Reiner, 149.
Rencourt (de), 976.
Reynolds, viii, 25, 34, 39, 210, 91, 365, 67, 495-98, 544, 717-18, 77-87, 99, 960, ix, 1197, 1285, 1315-16.
Rhodes, 835-36, 903, 1186.
Rhoads, 144, 519, 835.
Rhone, 79, 152, 65, 70-83, 356, 441, 72, 88, 643, 94, 96, 714, 897, 910, 81, 84-85, 1268, 1383, 86.
Rice, 38, 50, 87, 96, 135, 79, 228, 244-83, 99, 312, 55-59, 410, 13, 17, 44, 514, 31, 92, 603, 25, 920, 59, 1002, 1168, 99, 1267-68, 1383, 87, 89.
Richards, 100, 102-03, 114-19, 309, 338, 570, 608, 743, 938, 87, 1007, 1298, 1301.
Richardson, 316-25, 542, 89, 656, 749-50.
Richmond, 297.
Richter, 740.
Ricketts, 72-73, 101, 5-8, 22, 225-26, 31, 42, 47, 616, 70, 773, 83, 816-17, 965, 1037, 94, 1382, 84.
Rickety, 914.
Rider, 668.
Ridgway, 1177.
Riggs, 723, 1228.
Rinas, 544.
Ringler, 419.
Ritner, 244, 376, 93, 602, 1092, 1112, 50, 65.
Rittenhouse, 518-20, 22, 1173.
Robb, 936, 1142, 1224.
Robbins, 75, 97, 414, 542, 601.
Robert (King), 253.
Robert, J, 252.
Roberts, 11, 268, 77, 300, 649, 799, 803, 1366.
Robertson, 159, 451.
Robeson, 829, 1281.
Robins, 598.
Robinson, 13, 39, 43, 185, 335, 68, 446-47, 484, 671, 735, 900-01, 1184, 1294-95, 1347.
Rochefoucauld, 173.
Rockafellow, 95.
Rockefeller, 400, 1001, 1312.
Rockhill, 1281.
Rockwood, 709.
Rodgers, 656.
Roddy, 268.
Roe, 966.
Roeser, 516.
Rogers, 55, 770, 900, 1042, 1278.
Rohn, 1261.
Rollin, 518.
Ronaldson, 1346.
Rooper, 1051.
Roosevelt, 1068.
Roper, 1051.

Rose, 439, 593, 920, 94, 1351.
Ross, 20, 216, 93-96, 437, 62-63, 563-64, 680, 782, 819-21, 52, 67-67, 915, 35, 76, 1118, 43, 97, 1218, 50, 80, 1302, 74.
Rossiter, 747.
Rothermel, 565.
Rothrock, 426.
Rouderbush, 807.
Roumfort, 268.
Rounds, 1209.
Rowe, 1131.
Rowland, 55.
Roworth, 78.
Royal, 307.
Royce, 382, 920-21, 53, 8°
Royce, see Rice.
Rua (de la), 1126.
Rufus, (William), 402.
Ruggles, 133, 604-05.
Rupp, 681, 692.
Rush, 703, 89, 820, 1058-60, 78, 1..8.
Russel, 286, 409, 715.
Russell, 690, 850, 923.
Kust, 789.
Ruth, 1324.
Ruthven, 1022.
Rutledge, 904.
Rutter, 96, 772. 1353-54.
Ryman, 39, 438-39, 26, 6.5
Kynder[?], 140.
Ryswick, 862.

Sackett, 623.
Siddler, 718.
Sahm, 424-26.
Salisbury, 1189.
Saltonstall, 103, 16, 309, 75, 1330.
Sanderson, 39, 260, 878, 94, 926, 36, 1288-92.
Sands, 1068.
Santee, 610, 1257.
Satterlee, 216, 18.
Savage, 576, 869
Sawyer, 427.
Say, 1352.
Saye, 660.
Saylor, 467.
Sayre, 982-83, 1723.
Scanlan, 440.
Scates, 1177.
Schattenger, 150.
Schemmelfinnig, 78
Schenck, 941.
Schœpff, 521.
Schofield, 841.
Schooley, 697.
Schrader, 1300.
Schrage, 206.
Schropp, 523, 1270
Schultze, 1387-88.
Schumacher, 138, 767.
Schuyler, 423, 790, 92-93
Schwartz, 156, 937.
Scofield, 635, 40.
Scott, 33, 182, 221, 242, 390-402, 446, 60, 550, 77, 771, 1076, 95, 1101-02, 18, 60, 77, 85, 88, 1213, 75, 83, 1380.
Scouton, 735-36.
Scranton, 21, 167, 526-28, 854, 906, 35-36, 62, 1026, 1737, 89, 97, 1372, 86.
Scudder, 891.
Scull, 45.
Seaborn, 1186.
Sealy, 131.
Seamans, 250.

INDEX OF NAMES.

Searle, 429, 950, 1216, 54-57, 1302, 69.
Sears, 383.
Secord, 598, 601.
Secoy, see Secord.
Seddon, 1334.
Sedgwick, 428.
Seeley, 616, 985-86.
Seely, 662, 71.
Scelye, 732.
Seilheimer, 789.
Seldon, 506.
Sele, 660.
Selleck, 676.
Sellers, 19, 149-50, 519, 1151.
Selwyn, 429.
Sergeant, 820, 1092, 1151.
Sevigne (Madame de), 547.
Seward, 616, 1199.
Sewell, 791.
Seybert, 310-11, 851, 1286.
Seymour, 275, 1148.
Seys, 1258.
Seyster, 557.
Shafer, 696, 910, 1288.
Shaffer, 696-97.
Shaftesbury, 89.
Shakespeare, 195.
Shankle, 686.
Shannon, 268, 996.
Sharp, 833.
Sharpe, 839.
Sharpensteins, 1139.
Sharps, 1139.
Sharswood, 1122, 34, 57.
Shaver, 696-98, 817, 1390.
Shaver, see Shaffer.
Shay, 371.
Sheather, 877.
Shee, 1010
Sheffield, 339.
Sheldon, 323.
Shelly, 677-79.
Shennan, 509.
Shepherd, 1029, 1292.
Sheridan, 458.
Sherman, 76, 234, 412, 831, 49, 901, 40, 1041, 50, 1293.
Sherrerd, 224, 880, 909-10, 1279-81.
Sherwood, 762.
Shindel, 946-47.
Shipman, 498.
Shoemaker, 26, 38-39, 45-50, 100-01, 11, 13, 28-30, 44, 202, 33-35, 249-50, 391, 462, 75, 512, 638, 40, 49, 782, 1037, iii, 57, 89, 1130, 42, 65, 1207, 27, 40, 59, 1372, 83, 91-92.
Shonk, 39, 541-48, 610, 98, 1388-89.
Shortz, 564-66, 760, 961, 1387, 89.
Shreve, 904.
Shriner, 834.
Shugert, 1167.
Shultze, 128, 1186.
Shulze, 295, 311, 53.
Shuman, 660.
Shunk, 51, 503, 1100, 54, 1231.
Shupp, 388.
Sibert, see Seybert.
Sickler, 1363.
Sickles, 35.
Sieger, 679.
Siegfried, 1249, 1364.
Siewers, 66, 633.
Sigourney, 1110.
Silkman, 637, 1182-83, 1236, 63.
Sill, 47, 119, 638, 1088.
Silliman, 929, 1349-50, 92.
Sim, 1224.

Simcoe, 1045.
Simon, 517, 76.
Simons, 138, 288.
Simpson, 51, 816, 1021, 1370.
Simrell, 39, 1324-25.
Sipman, 767.[1]
Siroc, 473.
Sisson, 745, 965.
Sisty, 838.
Sitgreaves, 1051, 1130.
Sittser, 984.
Sively, 1321.
Skeel, 623.
Skiff, 484.
Skiles, 770.
Skinner, 14, 988.
Slade, 1084.
Slauson, 622.
Slawson, see Slosson.
Sleight, 280.
Slocom, 339.
Slocombe, 339.
Slocum, 59, 216, 21, 97, 338-44, 50-52, 462, 649, 844, 964, 1048-49, 1182, 94, 1206, 61, 77, 1381.
Slosson, 74, 622-24.
Sluman, 53, 593, 1040-41.
Sly, 1225.
Small, 614.
Smallwood, 383.
Smiles, 617.
Smith, 25-26, 89-95, 133, 169, 208, 11, 13, 19-22, 231, 417, 453, 515, 56, 59, 67, 74, 78, 95-96, 602, 23, 711, 21, 43, 50-51, 61, 63, 783-84, 95, 812, 17-18, 36, 47, 62, 69-72, 909, 24-25, 41, 72, 74, 1040-43, 47, 54, 59-60, 65, 1110, 60, 90, 1215, 77, 1303, 11-12, 14-15, 46, 49, 63, 82, 89.
Smythe, 153.
Snare, 143.
Snow, 1003.
Snowden, 222.
Snyder, 118, 208, 95, 392, 542, 663, 727, 926-27, 1083, 92, 99, 1150, 1387.
Socrates, 518.
Soller, 149, 458.
Soller, see Sellers.
Spalding, 54, 132, 218, 293, 388, 846, 1055-56, 1291, 1356.
Spangenberg, 373, 1336.
Sparhawk, 1133.
Spaulding, 331, 37, 640-41, 44, 1042.
Speakman, 1221.
Spencer, 1067.
Spinner, 749.
Spofford, 133.
Spoonly, 796.
Spottswood, 1334.
Sprague, 220, 1043, 64.
Spratt, 911-12.
Sprigg, 129.
Sprowl, 409.
Squier, 948, 1195.
Stacey, 718.
Stackhouse, 804.
St. Alban, 577.
Stafford, 1288.
Stamford, 306.
Standish, 305, 72, 1060, 87, 1281.
Stanford, 1274.
Stanislaus, 892.
Stanley, 915-16, 1218.
Stanton, 23, 48, 55, 105, 487, 613, 919, 55, 1266-67, 1370.
Staples, 498, 658-59, 1390.

Stark, 25, 39, 169, 229, 389-90, 451, 552, 566-68, 781, 897, 1007, 1228-29, 1306-07, 69.
Starr, 756-59, 611-13.
Statts, 790.
Staughton, 1065.
St. Clair, 362, 1091.
St. Cuthbert, 251.
Stearns, vii, 50, 213, 809, 923, 1297.
Steele, 25, 346, 85, 88, 923, 1310, 14.
Steere, 85.
Stein, 802.
Steinbach, 726.
Steinman, 993.
Stenger, 277.
Stephens, 371, 562, 744, 69-71, 958, 66.
Sternes, 809.
Sterling, 101, 295, 404, 50, 775, 1208-09.
Steuben, 54.
Stevens, 32, 174-75, 241-42, 338, 563, 607, 48, 80, 81, 83, 95-96, 1034, 1125, 51, 1313.
Stevenson, 747.
Stewart, 39, 56, 129, 205, 382, 430, 32, 67, 629, 34, 39, 41, 89, 816, 36, 44-47, 970, iii, 1079, 86-87, 1138, 1226, 73, 1306, 21-22, 54, 85.
Stickney, 45.
Stiles, 899, 961, 1196.
Stinson, 717.
Stirk, 557.
Stites, 528.
St. John, 61, 929.
Stocking, 114.
Stockton, 542.
Stoever, 458, 1387-88.
Stone, 22, 186, 286, 483, 539, 872, 962, 1052, 1193, 1220, 38.
Stoneman, 841.
Stoner, 415.
Storm, 493, 1013.
Story, 542.
Stout, 1226-27, 1270.
Stoutenburgh, 929-30.
Stover, 149.
Stowell, 1092.
St. Patrick, 237.
Strauss, 39, 476-82, 1388.
Straw, 727.
Strawn, 857.
Streater, 1139, 1351.
Strebeigh, 1363-64.
Streeper, 1296.
Streeter, 889, 1189, 1298.
Stroh, 626.
Strohm, 979.
Strong, 86, 117, 303, 67-69, 85, 413, 509, 1041, 84, 1110, 57-58.
Strope, 391.
Stroud, 626, 1115, 1256.
Struthers, 1223-24.
St. Simon, Duke of, 545.
Stuart, 156, 258, 491, 634, 1343.
Stubbs, 772.
Sturdevant, vii, 14-23, 39, 48, 61, 210, 353, 466, 88-90, 551-53, 62-64, 817, 976, 95, 1151, 1182, 1224, 1381, 1292.
Sturges, 39, 490-94, 558, 925-26, 87, 1292.
Sturgis, 490.
Stute, 252.
Stuyvesant, 491-92, 792, 1165.
Styner, 1333-34.
Sullivan, 54, 180, 221, 333, 87, 644, 919, 58, 77, 1079, 1173, 1287, 1291, 1300, 21.

Index of Names.

Suly, 1105.
Sumner, 77.
Summerfield, 444.
Sussex, Duke of, 577.
Sutliff, 711-12.
Sutton, 208, 11-21, 1052.
Swab, 961.
Swan, 298-99.
Swarts, 148.
Swartwout, 280.
Sweatland, 1287.
Sweet, 446.
Sweetser, 165.
Sweitzer, 149.
Swetland, 15, 210, 462, 64-66, 616-17, 781, 855, 1007, 1151, 1286, 1381.
Swift, 672, 748.
Swineford, 998.
Swinglins, 139.
Swope, 982.
Swoyer, 1301.
Syester, 677.
Sylvester, 856.
Syphers, 848.

Tabor, 1071.
Taft, 725.
Taggart, 754.
Tainter, 395.
Talcot, 792.
Talleyrand, 173.
Tallman, 1263.
Talon, 171, 173.
Taney, 489.
Tarryhill, 76.
Tattamy, 707-08.
Taylor, 20, 25, 39, 126, 537, 54, 86-87, 99, 772, 96--97, 818, 916, 1242-46, 74, 1376-77.
Teasdale, 206.
Tejada (de), 1071.
Tecumseh, 76.
Teeple, 949.
Teller, 930.
Templen, 806.
Ten Broeck, 791.
Terry, 368, 597, 99, 841, 47, 62, 81.
Terwilliger, 948.
Tha .sin, 584.
Tharp, 592-93.
Thayer, 936.
Theodolus, 547.
Thomas, 55, 76, 234, 653, 835-36, 73, 1035, 1174, 1226.
Thomassen, 1332.
Thompson, 318, 449-50, 658, 748, 1075, 1122, 61, 96, 1233.
Thomson, 95.
Thornton, 63, 193.
Thorntoun, 203.
Thorp, 280, 832, 949-50.
Thurston, 860.
Tiffany, 464.
Tilden, 273-76, 356, 959.
Tilghman, 823, 989, 1092.
Tillen, 515
Tobin, 904, 10-11.
Todd, 23, 873-74, 1310.
Tolan, 1224.
Tolles, 835.
Tomlinson, 858.
Tone (Wolf), 457.
Torrey, 39, 583, 985-87.
Totyl, 577.
Totyl, see Tuttle.
Toussaint, 64.
Tracey, 1109.
Tracy, 1052, 1160, 1351.

Trautman, 473.
Trautman, see Troutman.
Travers, 946.
Treadway, 676, 1286.
Treat, 869
Treffeisen, 476.
Tremain, 323.
Trembath, 1376-77.
Trenchard, 1334.
Trescott, 174, 710-11.
Trimble, 542, 1082.
Tripp, 340-41, 637, 962-65, 1041, 1183.
Tritle, 425.
Trott, 66, 98, 1160.
Trout, 268.
Troutman, 473-74, 685-86.
Trowbridge, 163.
Troxell, 25.
Truair, 318, 20.
Truax, 790, 1070.
Truax, see DeTricux.
Truckenmiller, 998.
Trucks, 697.
Trumbull, 287, 322, 436, 1041, 1184.
Trunkey, 200, 77, 878.
Tryp, 963.
Tryp, see Tripp.
Tubbs, 419, 694, 778.
Tuft, 409, 655-56.
Tupper, 969.
Turck, 1244.
Turgot, 893.
Turner, 31, 115, 206, 762.
Turney, 990.
Turrell, 482, 1288.
Tuthill, 799.
Tuttle, 461-62, 577, 637, 976, 1183, 1203, 1217-18, 1314-15
Twining, 542.
Tyler, 21, 68, 1092.
Tymperton, 710.
Tyng, 1116, 28, 76.

Ulf, 109.
Ulman, 39, 904.
Ulp, 676.
Ulsig or Ulsin, 577.
Unistat, 767-68
Umstead, 767-69, 1034.
Uncas, 662, 1111.
Underwood, 916.
Unger, 939.
Upham, 792.
Upson, 648, 1228.
Urquhart, 513-14, 797, 1015-16, 1223, 40.
Uteloch, 547.
Utley, 388-89.

Vail, 411, 1387.
Vallandigham, 6-9.
Van Arnam, 836.
Van Bebber, 138.
Van Bergen, 1372, 86.
Van Braght, 141-42.
Van Buren, 1068, 1178, 1275.
Van Buskirk, 1389.
Van Camp, 554-55.
Vau Campen, 20-21, 555.
Van de Meylyn, 584.
Vanderbelt, 935, 1323.
Vanderheyder, 793.
Van der Lipp, 598.
Vandersloot, 898.
Van Dyck, 792.

Van Dyke, 868.
Vane, 576, 1113.
Van Fleet, 907, 19-20.
Van Horn, 648-49.
Van Horne, 361.
Vanleer, 25.
Van Loon, 697, 1014.
Vannan, 1386.
Vannetta, 420.
Van Nort, 980.
Van Rensselaer, 369, 790.
Van Schaick, 793.
Van Schoick, 793.
Van Scoten, 813.
Van Scoten, see Benscoter.
Van Sintern, 141.
Van Valkenburg, 391.
Varner, 729.
Vaughan, 94, 518, 958.
Vaux, 268.
Vergennes (de), 893.
Vernet, 1352.
Vickery, 930.
Vidderow, see Wodrow.
Viele, 1068
Vinal, 665-66.
Vincent, 537, 1041.
Vinney (de), 516.
Vinton, 1129.
Virtue, 795.
Voke, 861.
VonLinderman, 1009.
Voos (de), 141.

Waage, 678.
Wadhams, vii, 26, 50, 109, 14, 215, 565, 613, 755-67, 990, 1061, 1329, 84.
Wadsworth, 166, 181, 66, 643.
Waelder, 469, 1227-28.
Wagner, 78.
Waite, 506, 15.
Wake, 830,
Wakefield, 890.
Wakely, 451.
Wakeman, 832.
Waldron, 1286.
Wales, 652, 1109.
Walker, 211, 415-21, 552.
Wall, 2, 453, 1324.
Wallace, 29, 252-55, 70, 76, 78, 593, 770, 1138, 1223, 1367.
Wallaze, 980.
Waller, 107, 11, 448, 756, 842-44. 1219-20, 1391.
Walley, 994.
Waln, 819.
Walsh, 1378, 90.
Walter, 1363.
Walters, 910.
Waltman, 985.
Walton, 626.
Walworth, 86, 1109.
Wampole, 150.
Ward, 39, 151, 451, 852-53, 79, 900, 18-19, 27, 44-45, 59, 1142, 87, 1306, 63, 76.
Warder, 395.
Warel (de), 796.
Warner, 1022.
Warren, 538, 810-11, 63, 915-16, 1234.
Washington, 54, 164, 205, 63, 304, 27, 408, 50, 520, 24, 67, 91, 600, 714, 22, 823, 24, 36, 73, 79, 958, 89, 98, 1012, 44-46, 91, 97, 1105, 09, 11, 35, 44, 79, 1252, 79, 1320, 55.

Index of Names

Waterbury, 622.
Watkins, 196.
Watrous, 911-12.
Watson, 144, 398, 542, 908, 1051.
Watt, 1076.
Watts, 1110, 18.
Way, 1052, 1352.
Wayne, 260, 737, 1172.
Weatherly, 1195.
Weaver, 788, 1300, 7, 90.
Webb, 7, 651-52, 841.
Webster, 202, 383, 462.
Weeks, 561, 842.
Weill, 1250.
Weiser, 189.
Weiss, 658, 839, 1335-42.
Weitzel, 39, 864-66, ix.
Welch, 1139.
Weld, 757.
Welding, 344.
Welker, 998.
Weller, 621.
Welles, 103, 19, 205, 15, 334, 500-03, 660-66, 908-10, 65, 95, 1043, 50, 61, 64, 84, 1117, 1358.
Welling, 728.
Welliver, 905.
Wells, 1, 116-17, 19, 394, 978-79, 86, 1067, 1180-81, 90, 1250, 96-97.
Welsh, 1013.
Welter, 686-87.
Wenceslas, 805.
Wendell, 790-94.
Wens, 144, 45.
Wentz, 674.
Wertz, 166.
Wesley, 209, 374, 1137.
Wessels, 790.
West 205, 517-18, 882, 88, 1167.
Westcott, 713, 992.
Westerhouse, 662.
Westler, 239, 1391.
Weston, 619, 986.
Westwood, 672.
Wetherby, 948.
Wetherell, 268.
Weytzel, see Weitzel.
Whaling, 1209, 90.
Whalley, 1108.
Wharton, 829, 1093, 1115, 32.
Whent, 916.
Wheaton, 654-58.
Wheeler, 765, 832, 89, 927, 1202.
Wheelock, 1109.
Wheelwright, 809.
Whipple, 710, 812, 915.
White, 66, 273, 404, 54, 518, 666, 73-74, 738, 71, 837, 53, 1000, 28, 46, 1115, 1246.
Whitefield, 374.
Whitemore, 656, 62.
White Eyes, 523.
Whitlock, 1176, 1363.
Whitney, 368, 538-39, 1142.
Whiton, 32, 243, 44.
Whittemore, 1028.
Whittlesey, 508, 44, 72, 623, 1041.

Whittlesly, 387.
Widderow, see Wodrow.
Wier, 423, 542, 1389.
Wigfall, 1133.
Wiggins, 541.
Wilcox, 742-53, 880, 1390.
Wilder, 242, 416.
Wildman, 541.
Wilem, 820.
Wilkins, 808.
Wilkinson, 722.
Willard, 39, 242, 382, 862-63, 89, 94, 920-21, 83, 86, 95.
Willet, 279.
Willets, 815.
William and Mary, 701.
William the Conqueror, 187, 541, 719, 96.
William the Silent, 279.
William III., 90, 1271.
Williams, 29, 156-59, 216, 18, 27, 68, 309, 451, 60, 564, 610, 53-54, 59, 713, 43, 59, 72, 94, 840, 971, 95, ili., 1184, 1253, 1310, 69.
Williamson, 25, 95, 1160, 1281.
Willing, 1102.
Willinson, 576.
Willis, 352.
Williston, 882.
Wilmarth, 1322-23.
Wilmot, vii., 1177-80.
Wilson, 39, 262, 344, 46, 428, 45, 59, 533, 687, 729, 68-69, 76, 821, 31, 44-45, 67-68, 914-16, 20, 48, 1078, 1105, 70-72, 95, 1242-45.
Wiswell, 306.
Winchell, 509.
Winchester, vii., 25, 27-28, 71, 77, 1220-21.
Windecker, 391.
Winslow, 380, 1085, 1110, 94.
Wintermoot, 328, 621.
Winters, 727.
Winthrop, 175, 316, 22, 24, 404, 583, 747, 62, 78, 808-09, 990, 1083, 1116, 1392.
Winton, 26, 39, 291, 417, 883-87, 1362.
Wires, 632.
Wirtz, 1167-68.
Wirtz, see Wurtz.
Wise, 1390.
Wishart, 252-53.
Wisner, 385, 828.
Witherell, 809.
Witherow, 720.
Witherow, see Wodrow.
Wodrow, 1016-23.
Wolcott, 1064.
Wolf, 5, 15, 128, 680, 871, 949, 1084, 1120, 40, 49-50, 86, 1262.
Wolfe, 279, 734, 75, 1186.
Wolsey, 853.
Wood, 66, 434-35, 37-38, 517, 733, 834, 917, 48.
Woodbridge, 55, 832, 1146.
Woodbury, 41, 1334, 74.

Woodhull, 368.
Woodin, 1352.
Woodring, 727.
Wodrow, 730, 865, 1016.
Woodruff, 656-57, 1067.
Woodward, v, 15, 19, 24-25, 31, 33, 38, 66, 71-74, 77, 81, 86, 97-104, 16, 18, 57, 62, 210, 24, 31, 42, 71, 75-76, 89, 338, 97-98, 400, 66, 68, 75, v, 565, 86, 690-91, 711, 781, 830, 856, 68-69, 905, 22, 35, 42, 72, vii, 1042, 78, 1112, 20, 22, 46-64, 69, 78, 83, 91, 1210-14, 34, 68, 1307, 22, 29, 84, 90.
Woolsey (Cardin l), 194.
Woolson, 1051.
Wooster, 482, 1069.
Worden, 977.
Worrall, 475, 795-98.
Worrell, 795-98.
Worthington, 833, 40, 1257.
Wortman, 610-11, 13.
Wray, 258-59.
Wright, vii-viii, 2-14, 20, 25, 38-39, 43, 56, 59, 63, 69, 71, 128, 53, 65, 78-79, 86, 230-31, 38, 42, 74, 311, 24, 35, 94, 441, 87-88, v, 509, 14, 44, 54-56, 68, 72, 87, 713, 31, 61, 87, 817, 24-26, 48, 55, 73, 99, 901, 16, 23, 35, 1014, 36, vi, vii, 46, 1109, 17, 25-26, 41, 84, 90, 1216, 41, 47, 49-51, 59, 1278-79, 94-95, 97, 1316, 25-62, 81.
Wurts, 1169.
Wurtz, 1167-69, 1200.
Wyckoff, 1084.
Wyer, 459.
Wyllys, 55.
Wyman, 808.
Wyngaart, 791.
Wynkoop, 549, 84.
Wynne, 980.
Wynton, 254.

Yardley, 542.
Yarrington, 496, 776.
Yates, 412.
Yeager, 1365.
Yeates, 205, 1060, 1125.
Yniestra, 1126.
Yocum, 144.
York, 596-602.
York, Archbishop of, 191.
Vorsten, 795.
Yost, 1257.
Young, 383, 678-79, 1277.

Zeigler, 25, 142.
Zirnhelt, 1386.
Zimmerman, 144.
Zinzendorf, 141, 47, 373-74.
Zollicoffer, 589.
Zuches (de la), 255.
Zug, 681, 84.

HISTORICAL INDEX.

Abington Baptist Association, founding of, 120.
Abington, settlement of, 121, 453-54, 872, 994.
Adams, John Q., poem by, 886-87.
Addresses by
Agnew, Chief Justice, 1163-64.
Buckalew, Charles R., 1191-92.
Cameron, Simon, 1192-93.
Denison, Charles, 8.
Fuller, Henry M., 589-91.
McClure, A. K., 1162-63.
Olin, W. H., D. D., 1241-42.
Randall, Samuel J., 1193.
Tremain, Lyman, 323.
Sturdevant, E. W., 16-19.
Woodward, George W., 1159, 1161-62.
Wright, H. B., 5-6.
Alden, Priscilla, 305.
Attorneys—
Deceased, 1393-95.
Non resident, 1395-97.
Resident, 1398-99.
Augur Screw, invention of, 520.
Avondale disaster, 759-60.

Bedford, Deborah, an early Methodist, 208-09.
Bennetts and Hammond, captivity of, 545-48.

BATTLES, ETC., MENTIONED.

Antietam, 100, 107, 22, 63, 201, 428, 71, 880, 942, 1030, 1233, 1385.
Black Hawk war, 857.
Bloreheath, 403.
Boston, siege of, 450.
Bottom's Bridge, 77.
Bound Brook, 386.
Boyne, 90, 154, 1271.
Braddock's expedition, 517, 715.
Brandywine, 264, 386, 708, 37, 879, 1010, 44, 97, 1172, 1280, 92, 1337, 55.
Buckshot war, 562.
Bull Run, 126, 428, 71, 510, 1010.
Bunker Hill, 102, 1051, 1139.
Campaign of 1758, 326.
Canada, Expedition against, 775, 1073.
Canada, surrendered to the British, 279.
Cape Breton, 1159.
Cedar Mountain, 471.
Cerro Gordo, 33, 549-50.
Chancellorsville, 34, 206, 91, 471, 880, 1313.
Chapultepec, 549-50, 1194.
Charles City X Roads, 428, 511.
Charleston, 79.
Chickamauga, 234.
Civil war, 324, 57, 400, 12, 22, 27, 33, 50, 355, 70, 656, 863, 89, 92),

46-47, 77, 1068, 85, 1113, 38, 89, 1223, 28, 31-35, 39, 61, 70, 93-94, 1319, 23, 85.
Colonial war, 914.
Cool Arbor, 428.
Coosawhatchie, 1296.
Creek war, 392.
Crimean war, 976.
Crown Point, 1072.
Culloden, 397.
Dorchester Heights, 1055.
Elk River, 234.
El Pinal Pass, 33.
Exeter, 1215.
Fair Oaks, 77.
Falls fight, 323.
Fisher's Hill, 428.
Fort Allen, 1338-39.
Fort DuQuesne, 1173.
Fort Durkee, 777.
Fort Fisher, 421.
Fort Gregg, 78.
Fort Griswold, 130.
Fort Johnson, 1239.
Fort Niagara, 608.
Fort Sumter, 268, 71.
Fort Ticonderoga, 135.
Fort Wagner, 78.
Franco-Prussian war, 1068.
Fredericksburg, 428, 71, 880.
France, war with, 1072.
French, Expedition against the, in, Canada, 773.
French and Indian war, 386, 431, 845, 1111, 1271.
French Revolution, 893, 974.
French war, 326, 36, 578, 607, 1133.
Gaines Mills, 427-28, 511.
Germantown, 386, 629, 754, 1044, 97, 1172, 1280, 92.
Gettysburg, 34, 100, 23, 65, 206, 26, 47, 64, 72, 428, 71, 929, 1284, 1313, 64.
Gulph Mills, 484.
Hastings, 796.
Hatcher's Run, 37.
Haymarket, 36.
Hessians, capture of at Yorktown, 1135.
Indian Hill, 54.
Indian war, 517, 707.
Irish Rebellion, 298.
Jalapa, 33.
King Phillip's war, 227, 353, 1176, 1344.
Lafayette, 234.
Lake Erie, 75.
Lake George, 608.
Lexington, 14, 1028, 34, 51.
Long Island, 93.
Malvern Hill, 427, 511.
Marengo, 539.
Marye's Heights, 428.
Mechanicsville, 427, 511.
Mexican war, 549, 852, 934, 89, 1010, 1194, 1227, 29, 51, 61, 70, 77, 1313.

Middleton, 234.
Millstone, 386, 1355.
Mine Run, 428, 471.
Monmouth, 164, 69, 814, 979, 89, 1280.
Mud Fort, 386.
Nanticoke (Indian battle), 1215.
Narragansett fight, 505, 810.
Naseby, 1087.
New Amsterdam, captured by English, 1165.
New Amsterdam, retaken by Dutch, 1166.
New Amsterdam, surrendered to Governor Andross, 1166.
New York, Evacuation of, 1091.
Nile, 174.
Ohio Indians, St. Clair Expedition against. 1091.
Paoli massacre, 1271.
Paxton Boys, murder of Indians by, 518.
Pennamite and Yankee war, 53, 213, 306, 437, 507, 607, 31, 49, 1040, 1135.
Peninsular war, 471.
Pequod war, 114, 628.
Perote Castle, capture of, 33.
Perryville, 915.
Petersburg, 428, 471.
Plattsburg, 58.
Plunkett's battle, 304, 639, 1215.
Plunkett, expedition of (1775), 639.
Pontiac war, 376.
Port Royal, 34, 766.
Princeton, 1097, 1280, 1320, 55.
Prusso-Austrian war, 1008.
Puebla, 33.
Queen Anne's war, 765.
Rappahannock Station, 428, 71.
Revolutionary war, 53, 55, 62, 85, 88, 93, 102, 15-16, 25, 30, 35, 47, 56, 208, 31, 311, 23, 35-36, 37, 53, 55, 63, 405-06, 42, 46, 52, 82, 520, 49, 63, 79, 85, 93, 96, 604, 08, 28-29, 55, 58, 65, 92, 710, 29, 37, 61, 814, 28, 42-43, 50, 64, 66, 73, 79, 90, 905, 14, 27, 52, 64, 76-77, 70, 97, 1009-10, 51, 53, 74, 84, 91, 1111, 27, 43, 47, 50, 68, 72-73, 92-93, 98, 1272, 74, 80, 91, 98, 1320, 82.
Richmond, 511.
Roanoke Island, 527.
Roses, War of the, 403, 577.
Rover, 234.
Salem Heights, 428.
Saunder's House, 428.
San Angelos, 549.
San Juan D'Ulloa, 33.
Saratoga, 1034-35, 55.
Scotch Valley massacre, 180.
Sepoy Campaign, 471.
Seven Days' Battle, 511.
Shelbyville, 234.
South Anne River, 428.
South Mountain, 163, 428, 71, 880.

Spottsylvania, 206, 428, 71, 1313.
Springfield, 1280.
St. Bartholomew, massacre of, 369.
Stone River, 474.
Stony Point, 1172, 1309.
Sullivan's expedition, 333.
Thirty Years' war, 869.
Trafalgar, 569.
Trevellion Station, Va., 131.
Trenton, 879, 1735, 1280, 1320, 55.
Valley Forge, 879, 927.
Venitian war, 618.
Vera Cruz, 33, 549-50, 1194.
Waterloo, 471.
War of 1812, 317, 90, 92, 549, 67, 738, 68, 815, 73, 1046, 97, 1146, 99, 1244, 72, 1328.
Weldon Raid, 37.
Weldon Railroad, 428, 71-72.
West Point, 427.
Whisky Insurrection, 496, 1128.
White Plains, 1172.
Wilderness, 36, 206, 428, 71.
Winchester, 428.
Wolf Tone Rebellion, 457.
Wyoming, Battle and Massacre, vi, 14, 46, 67, 70-71, 87, 102, 28, 32, 56, 86, 209, 13, 31, 41, 93, 95, 304, 06, 07, 28-31, 34, 36, 43, 53, 87-89, 91, 431-33, 35-36, 50, 52, 460-61, 64-65, 84, 95-96, lil, 506-07, 13, 28-29, 31, 44-61, 63, 67, 72, 99, 604, 07-08, 10, 16, 20, 23, 36-37, 40-42, 48, 52, 64, 68, 710, 73, 76-77, 813, 28, 36, 42, 44, 47, 57, 914, 32, 77, 1041, 88, 1119, 34-35, 47, 1215-16, 29, 52-56, 73, 13C2, 06, 80, 55-56.
Yorktown, 14, 927, 1044.

BOOKS, ETC., MENTIONED.

Albany, Genealogies of the First Settlers of, Pearson, 793.
America, Information concerning, Cooper, 1078.
American Crisis, Paine, 521, 1333.
American Statesmen, Young, 383.
Analecta, Wodrow, 1020.
Ancient History, Rollins, 518.
Annals of America, Holmes, 792.
Appleton's American Cyclopædia, 1046.
Appleton's Annual Encyclopædia, 378.
Argument in favor of the Bible, narration of Man's Creation, &c., 443.
Beacon Lights of History, Lord, 546.
Benedicts, Genealogy of the, in America, 490.
Bible, Its own Witness and Interpreter, 988.
Binn's Justice, 1074.
Book of Forms, Leisenring, 946.
Book Hunter, Burton, 1020.
Boston, History of, 74.
Bradford County, History of, 847.
Breath of Life, The, 215.
Breese Family, Address at Centennial Reunion of, Jenkins, 1381.
Bucks County, Pa., History of, Davis, 256, 541.
Bucks County, Pa., Legends of, Wright, 825.

Burke's Peerage, 204-05.
Celebration of ye Olden Time, Jenkins, 1381.
Centennial Address, Edsall, 1281.
Character of Christ, Rush, 1059.
Charges on Moral and Religious Subjects, Rush, 1059.
Charlestown Genealogies, Wyman, 808.
Chatauqua County, N. Y., History of, Young, 383.
Chester County, History of, Smith, 818.
Christian Baptism, 1059.
City's Danger and Defense, Logan, 942.
Clavis Rerum, Robinson, 901.
Coal Trade, History of in Luzerne and Lackawanna Counties, 44.
Columbia County, History of, Freeze, 803.
Commentaries upon the Intestate System, and the Powers and Jurisdiction of the Orphans' Court of Pennsylvania, Scott, 401.
Concord Chase, The, Jenkins, 1382.
Constitutional Liberty, Development of, in the English Colonies of America, Scott, 401.
Contingent Remainders, Fearne, 1074.
Dakota Nation, Calendar of the, Mallery, 1086.
Delaware county, Pa., History of, 795, 817.
Denison, Capt. George, A record of the descendants of, 47.
DeWitt, John, Grand Pensionary of Holland, History of the Administration of, 280.
Early Emigrant Ancestors, Our, Hotten, 576.
Early Methodism, Peck, 208, 11, 495, 638, 67, 755, 1089, 1244, 51.
Eight Years' Travel and Residence in Europe, 214.
Elementary Law, Robinson, 901.
Emporium of Arts and Sciences, Cooper, 1078, 1345.
English Cases, 903.
Fitch, Life of, 521-22.
Following the Drum, Viele, 1068.
Forest of Life, Jenkins, 1382.
Future Retribution, Examination of the doctrine of, 656.
Garfield, President, Life of, Burke, 654.
German Emigrants, Names of, Rupp, 692.
Gospel its Own Advocate, The, Griffin, 1066.
Gospel its Own Witness, The, Fuller, 1334.
Governor's Letters, Johnson, 1165.
Griffin, Rev. E. D., Memoirs of, Sprague, 1065.
Hakes Family, Hakes, 1385.
Harmony of the Gospels, Strong, 509.
Hazard's Register, 1340.
Hazleton Travellers, Miner, 157, 386, 530, 668, 1251.
Historical and Biographical Sketches, Pennypacker, 147, 372.
Honesdale, Pa., Memorial Sermon on the Abandonment of the former house of worship at, Dunning, 672.
Hood on Executors, 182.
Human Understanding, Locke, on the, 1110.
Indians, The former and present number of our, Mallery, 1086.
Indians of the Rocky Mountains and the Andes, Last Rambles among the, 215.
Institutes of Justinian, Cooper, 1078.
Kirwin Letters, Murray, 87, 722.
Labor, A Practical Treatise on, Wright, 10, 1329.
Lackawanna and Wyoming Counties, History of, 176.
Landed Gentry, 402.
Lecture Sermons, Ballou, 656.
License System Repugnant to Sound Constitutional Law, The, Nichols, 560.
Literary Remains, Griffin, 1069.
Lethe and Other Poems, Jones, 309.
Letters and other Writings, Rice, 357.
Lodge 61, F. and A. M., History of, Harvey, 514.
Lo - Lathope Family Memoir, Huntington, 861.
Lopez Ned, 607.
Luzerne County, Annals of, Pearce, 847.
Luzerne County, Brief of Title in the seventeen townships of. A syllabus of the controversy between Connecticut and Pennsylvania, Hoyt, 81, 361.
Manitou of Wyoming, Jenkins, 1382.
Marcus Blair, Wright, 825, 1329.
Martyr's Mirror, VanBraght, 141-47.
McCoy, Henry Porter, Sermon on the death of, Dunning, 672.
McKinney's Justice, 1074.
Mechanics' Liens, Law of, in Pennsylvania, Johnson, 1167.
Medical Jurisprudence, Cooper, 1078.
Mind, Watts on the, 1110.
Money and Legal Tender in the United States, Linderman, 1011.
Montgomery County, Pa., Biographical Notices of Prominent Citizens of, Auge, 1098.
National Economy, Young, 383.
New England Memorial, Morton, 859.
New York, Colonial History of, 608.
Next President, The, Jones, 309.
North American Indian Gallery, Catlin, 1106.
North American Indians—
Gestures, signs and signals among, collection of, Mallery, 1086.
Manners, Customs and Conditions of, Catlin, 214.
Pictographs of, Mallery, 1086.
Sign Language Among, Mallery, 1086.
Introduction to the Study of Sign Language Among, Mallery, 1086.
North American Portfolio, 214.
Norwich, History of, 316.

HISTORICAL INDEX.

Notes on Scripture, Jones, 1133.
Of the Covenant, 64.
On the Lackawanna, Wright, 825.
Our English Surnames, 195.
Palmer, Records, 194.
Parables, Notes on the, Ballou, 655.
Patriarchal Age, The, Jones, 1134.
Pennsylvania, Digest of the Laws of, Parke & Johnson, 1140.
Pennsylvania—
  History of, 170, 703.
  Land Titles in, 489.
  Manners of German Inhabitants of, Rush, 703.
Pequot War, History of, Gardiner, 876.
Philadelphia, Leaders of the Old Bar of, Binney, 823.
Philosophical Retrospect on the General Outline of Creation, &c., Bradley, 1053.
Pittston Fort, The, Jenkins, 1381.
Plumb Family, History, Biography and Genealogy of the, in America, 605.
Plutarch's Lives, 518.
Plymouth, Historical Sketches of, Wright, 10, 186, 544, 72, 824, 1014, 1329.
Political Economy, Lectures on the Elements of, Cooper, 1078.
Political Essays, Cooper, 1078.
Practice and Process in the Orphans' Courts of Penna., Rhone, 182.
Puritans, History of the, 63.
Puritan Settlers, Hinman, 757.
Rachael Craig, Wright, 825.
Ransom, Capt. Samuel, Genealogical Record of the Descendants of, &c., 389.
Recollections, Breck, 891.
Rees, Encyclopedia, 520.
Revolution, Field Book of the, Lossing, 792.
Sanctification, Skinner, 988.
School Dictionary, The (1829), Turner, 207.
Science of Government, Young, 383.
Scotland, History of the Sufferings of the Church of, Wodrow, 1017, 19, 21.
Select Sermons, Ballou, 656.
Shell Beds, Reynolds, 787.
Story of Joseph, Jones, 1134.
Sufferings of Christ, The, Griffin, 1066.1
Talcott's Genealogical Notes, 792.
Teachings of Patriots and Statesmen, Chase, 1288.
Theory and Practice of Teaching, 320.
Treatise on the Atonement, Ballou, 655.
Treatise on Patent Law, Robinson, 901.
Trial of a Saving Interest in Christ, Guthrie, 1022.
Trinity, The, in Redemption, 988.
United States, Regulations for the Order and Discipline of the Troops of, Styner & Cist, 1334.
West, Life of, 518.
Westwood, Rev. Henry C., D.D. Discourse on the Installation of as Pastor of the First Presbyterian Church of Honesdale, Pa.,

Dunning, 672-73.
Wharton's Digest, 1093.
Wilkes-Barre, City of, Reynolds, 787.
Wilkes-Barre, First Presbyterian Church of, Reynolds, 787.
Windham County, Conn., History of, 360,
Wyoming, Wright, 825, 1329.
Wyoming, History of, 43, 52, 67, 335, 40-41, 621, 29, 1056, 1260.
Wyoming, Its History, stirring incidents and romantic adventures, Peck, 650.
Wyoming, and its early settlers, Old Memories of, Gordon, 7.
Wyoming, Jenkins, 1381.
Wyoming Monument, Historical Address at, Jenkins, 1381.

Bethany, Pa., second house built in, 985.
Bridgehampton, purchase of, 673.
Buckshot War, 562.
Butler, Col. John, Memorial Tablet to, 607-08.
Butler, Col. Zebulon, Report of on Battle and Massacre of Wyoming, 330-32.
Carbondale disaster, 956.
Catlin, George, Indian painter, 214, 1103-07.
Charcoal Furnace erected at Shickshinny, 1170.
Civil War, early prisoners, 125-26.

COAL.

Avondale disaster, 739-60.
Baltimore Bed, 1392.
Blackman Bed, 1349.
Bowman's Mine, 1349.
Carbondale disaster, 956.
Discovered in Lehigh District, 1340.
Discovered at Wyoming, 52.
Early Mining, 66, 783-84, 1257, 1347-48.
First ark load of, shipped on the Lehigh, 1341, 47.
First burned in grates, 347-49, 783-84, 891, 97.
First used by blacksmiths, 346, 437.
Mined near Mauch Chunk, 66.
Mineral beds made from, 1345.
Shipped to Harrisburg and Columbia, 779.
Shipped to Columbia (1807), 783.
Smith's Bed, 783, 1349.
Cloth, made from nettles, 827.
Connecticut Legislature, Luzerne (or Westmoreland) county representatives in, 1040-41.
Connecticut and Pennsylvania Troubles, 484-85, 1145.
Connecticut—Susquehanna Land Co., 1273.
Connecticut, First Presbyterian Church in, 360.
Courts—
  Early, 1060-61.
  First held in Wilkes-Barre, 102.
  Mayor's, Carbondale, 1268-69.
  Mayor's, Scranton, 1269.
  Orphans', made separate, 1268,
Dana, E. L., Letter to, requesting

him to be a candidate for Judge, 38-40,
Dana, E. L., Reply to letter, 40.
Darling, E. P., death of, 1383-84.
Dodson, Abagail, Captivity of, 180-81.
Duel in Cumberland county, Pa., 259.
Durham Boats, 1243-44.
Dusnore, Who named after, 174.
Earthquake in Peru, 378-82.
Easthampton, L. I., Purchase of, 314, 673.
Fort Allen, 1339,
Forty Fort, Capitulation of, 189, 332.
Forty Fort, M. E. Church of, 466, 695.
Foster township, named after A. L. Foster, 839.
Friends, Society of, 2, 140.
France and the United States, Treaty between (1778), 520.
Germans, Pennsylvania, 371-72.
Germany, Tradesmen wandering in, 477-79.
Gilbert Family, Captivity of, 180.
Gildersleeve, W. C., Abolitionist, 723-24.
Gnadenhutten, Burned by Indians, 1338.
Hanover township, First settlement in, 303.
Hammond and Bennetts, Captivity of, 645-48.
Harding, Garrick M., Attempted impeachment of, 72-73, 107.
Harry Hillman Academy, established, 1374-75.
Hazleton, Early, 1257.
Herald of the Times, First newspaper established in the county, 1247.
Hillard, T. R., Trip around the world by, 799-800.
Honesdale, First house erected in, 985.
Hosie, John, Carbondale disaster, 956.
Hoyt Family Reunion, 76.
Hoyt, Capture of Col. Henry M., 79.
Hugenots, 545-47.
Hutchison Controversy, 743.
Ice Freshet (1784), 870.
Indians, Attack by, on Thaddeus Williams' house, 158.
Indians, Last men killed by, 305.
Iron ore discovered in Providence (now Scranton), 20-21.
Joanna Furnace, 89.
Judicial Districts of Pennsylvania
  Eighth, 1075, 1264.
  Eleventh, 1264-65, 67.
  Twenty-sixth, 1264.
  Forty-fifth, 1267.
  Forty-sixth, 1267.
Judges—
  Deceased—additional law, 1393.
  Deceased—associate, 1393.
  Deceased—president, 1393.
  Living—associates, 1397.
  Living—additional law, 1397, 99.
  Living—president, 1397.

HISTORICAL INDEX.

Kingston, First resident physician in, 539.
Kulp, Eli S., Resolutions on death of, 151.
Kulp, Jacob, Marriage certificate of, 148-49.

Lackawanna & Bloomsburg Railroad chartered, 781.
Lackawanna County, First Methodist class established in, 215.
Lackawanna Valley, First regular Presbyterian preaching in, 722.
Lehigh Coal & Navigation Co. R. R. built, 782.
Litchfield County—
  Judges of Probate (1772-75), 1045
  Justices of the Peace (1772-75), 1039, 41.
Lothropp, Rev. John, independent minister, 857-60.
Lutherans, Early, 458, 1387-88.
Luzerne County—
  Act of Assembly organizing, 1039-43.
  Bible Society, 1206, 76.
  Courts, 1057-58, 61, 75-76, 90-91, 1101-02, 85, 1264, 70.
  Courts organized, 1042-43.
  First county superintendent of schools in, 319.
  First election in, 215-17.
  First fulling mill in, 244.
  French colony in, 170-74, 1358.
  Formation of, 1039.

Madison Academy, 417.
McClintock, A. T., Letter to, requesting him to be a candidate for Judge, 25-26.
McClintock, A. T., Reply to the letter, 27-28.
Methodists, Early, 208-09, 12, 338-39, 755, 1089-90, 1136.
Mennonites, History of, 138-47.
Mills, Early, 211-13, 826.
Mine Road, 45.
Miner's Mill, 1250.
Mineral black made from Lehigh coal, 1345-46.
Montrose, First settlers in, 1308.
Moravians, 372-75.
Murray, Noah, First Universalist preacher in Luzerne county, 1055
Morss, Judge, Resolutions on retirement of, 1037.

Nantes, Edict of, 545.
New Columbus, Early settlement of, 1229.
New Haven, Founding of, 184-85, 364.
New London Academy, 95.
New London, burning of, 1062.
Newark Township, purchase of, 168.

NEWSPAPERS MENTIONED.

Albany Statesman, 8.
American Genealogical Review, 278.
American Herald and General Advertiser, 1334.
American Journal of Science, 1349.
American Law Times Reports, 903.
Anthracite Monitor, 10.
Atlantic Monthly, 455.
Baltimore American, 1350.
Banner America, 938.
Banner, Rockport, Mo., 1385.
Boston Advertiser, 8.
Boston Traveller, 8.
Bradford Settler, 390.
Bucks County Intelligencer, 42, 1248.
Carbon County Transit, 838.
Catasauqua Herald, 1261.
Catholic Mirror, 726.
Catskill Packet, 1144.
Charleston City Gazette, 1144.
Chemung Valley Reporter, 1381.
Chicago Herald, 309, 834.
Christian Herald, Cincinnati, 834.
Cincinnati Commercial Gazette, 309.
Cincinnati Daily Gazette, 834.
Columbia Democrat, 652.
Columbian Magazine, 1334.
Commercial Advertiser, New York, 8.
Daily Advertiser, Phila., 1144.
Democratic Standard and Know Nothing Expositor, 1197.
Democratic Wachter, 162, 468, 88, 1227.
Doylestown Correspondent, 42, 1248.
Doylestown Democrat, 1248.
Elmira Advertiser, 798.
Evening Star, Scranton, 886.
Federalist, 1077.
Free Mason's Monitor, 347.
Free Press, Detroit, 2.
Galva Union, 412.
Gazette and Bulletin, 1367.
Gazette and Commercial Intelligencer, 1247.
Grant County Herald, 1007.
Harrisburg Argus, 1140.
Harrisburg Patriot, 274, 78.
Harrisburg Telegraph, 534.
Herald, 830.
Herald and Presbyter, Cincinnati, 835.
Herald of the Times, 1247.
Herald of the Union, 1288.
Historical Register, 1381.
Historical Review, 702.
Independent Volunteer, 888.
Interior, 835.
Janesville (Wis.) Gazette, 927.
Journal of Commerce, 1067.
Keynote, 515.
Keystone, 1140.
Lackawanna Herald, 1288.
Lackawanna Jurist and Law Magazine, 996.
Lancaster Intelligencer, 342.
Law and Equity Reporter, 903.
Leader, 154, 455.
Legislative Record, 409.
Lehigh Pioneer & Mauch Chunk Courier, 838.
Lennox Eagle, 1286.
Lippincott's Magazine, 455.
Literary Magazine, 1343.
Luzerne County Federalist, 42, 1247-48.
Luzerne County Herald, 453, 55.
Luzerne Democrat, 638.
Luzerne Legal Observer, 1234.
Luzerne Legal Register, vii, 154, 394, 1117.
Luzerne Union, 102, 06, 28, 54, 249, 453-55, 592, 1220, 27.
Magazine of American History, 515.
Mauch Chunk Courier, 838-39.
Mercury, Charleston, 78.
Milton Economist, 937.
Mitchell County Press, 867, 1391.
Montrose Democrat, 1288.
Montrose Gazette, 888.
Montrose Republican, 907.
Mountain Echo, 419.
Mountaineer, Conyngham, 2.
New York Evening Post, 8.
New York Herald, 1067.
New York Observer, 314.
New York Tribune, 8, 309, 938.
New York Weekly Digest, 902.
New York World, 429.
North American Exchange and Review, 455.
Northern Democrat, 888.
Northern Eagle, 1137.
Northern Pennsylvanian, 1195, 1286.
North Star, Montrose, 849.
Occident, 834.
Olive Branch, 1248.
Owego Democrat, 369.
Pennsylvania Farmer and Common School Intelligencer, 1140.
Pennsylvania Correspondent, 1249
Pennsylvania Correspondent and Farmers' Advertiser, 1248.
Pennsylvania Gazette, 519.
Pennsylvania School Journal, 320.
Pennsylvania Magazine of History and Biography, 90.
Pennsylvanian, 1211, 13.
Pennsylvanischer Staatsbote, 1333
Philadelphia Press, 309, 681, 938, 1146.
Philadelphia Times, 884.
Pittston Free Press, 1261.
Pittston Gazette, 794, 98.
Plainspeaker, Hazleton, 1379
Port Folio, 1344.
Princeton Review, 988.
Real Estate Intelligencer, 795.
Record of the Times, 43-44, 776, 94, 1007, 1251, 60, 1351.
Reformer, 248.
Reporter (The), 903.
Republican Farmer, 466, 932, 1138-39.
Republican Farmer and Democratic Journal, 159.
Republican, Rockford, Ill., 907.
Scranton City Journal, 321.
Scranton Daily Times, 899, 919.
Scranton Register, 1234.
Scranton Republican, 1297, 1379.
Scranton Times, 899, 919, 95.
Scranton Law Times, 900.
Scranton Weekly Times, 900.
Spectator and Freeman's Journal, 724.
Springfield Republican, 8.
Star of Freedom, 1249.
Star, Washington, 993.
State Guard, Harrisburg, 682.
Susquehanna Democrat 294, 1260.
Susquehanna Register, 888, 1260.
Susquehanna County Republican, 888.
True Democrat (The), 1277.
Tunkhannock Republican, 321.
Union-Leader, 154, 455, 594, 1220, 1379.
Universalist Expositor, 655.

HISTORICAL INDEX. 1423

Universalist Magazine, 655.
Vermont Chronicle, 117.
Village Record, 42, 1249.
Volksfreund, 1002.
Wayne County Herald, 453-54, 882, 1197, 1211.
West Branch Bulletin, 1367.
Wilkes-Barre Advocate, 1260.
Wilkes-Barre Gazette, 43, 507, 1247.
Wyoming Democrat, 1220.
Wyoming Herald, 833, 1257.
Wyoming Republican, 1216, 37, 60.
Yale Literary Magazine, 99.
Yates County Chronicle, 380.

North Branch Canal, First boat launched in at Shickshinny, 1229
Old Forge, Early iron works at, (1789), 221.
One Hundred and Forty-third Regiment, Leave for Washington, 34.
One Hundred and Forty-third Regiment, Mustered out of service, 37.
Osterhout Free Library established, 1316-19.

Palmer, Derivation of name, 194-95
Paxtang Boys, 1079.
Paxton Rangers, 431, 518, 816, 44-45.
Pearl Family, Captured by Indians, 180.
Pennamite and Yankee troubles, 631, 37, 49, 963.
Pennsylvania Common Schools, 1203-04.
Pennsylvania, Meeting to sustain the laws of, 217-19.
Pennsylvania, Proclamation of, Governor forbidding settlement in, 1039.
Pennsylvania Troops, Third Regiment, P. M., 100; Forty-First Regiment, P. M., 100; Fifty-Second Regiment, P. V., 77; Three Hundred and Third Regiment, P. M., 225.
Peru, Earthquake (1868), 378-90.
Philadelphia, British standard hoisted in, 820.
Philadelphia and Wilmington, Purchase of land lying between, from Indians, 1166.
Physicians, First in Wyoming, 220
Pickering, Timothy, abducted, 293, 1045.
Plymouth, First minister in, 110.
Plymouth, First merchant in, 506.
Plunkett's Expedition, 639.

Pumpkin Freshet (1785), 830.
Punxsutawney, Town of, laid out, 542.
Puritan wall paper, 1027.

Quakers, arrival of in America, 2.
Quinipiac, Purchased from Indians, 185.

Redemptioners, 702-04.
Ricketts, A., Letter of to Town Council, 106.
Ross, General, sword presented to, 294.

Scotch-Irish emigration, Causes which led to, 90, 256-57.
Scranton, Early, 20-21, 340, 524-27, 853-54, 963, 1289-90, 1299.
Scranton, Riots in, 942-43.
Selma, Ala., Destruction of, 831.
Slavery, 16-19, 991-92, 1152-53.
Slocum, Francis, Indian Captive, 340-43, 1048-49.
Smith, Wm. Hooker, early Presbyterian, 222.
Southampton, Purchase of, 673.
Standish, Myles, 305.
Stewart, Lazarus, 845-47.
Strikes, 167, 942.
Susquehanna County, Early, 42, 887, 912, 1139-40, 1308.
Swamp Church, 736-37.
Swetland, Luke, Indian prisoner, 1287.

Taunton, Mass., Purchased from Indians, 505.
Trenton Decree, 1040.
Tyrone Rebellion, 235-38.

Vallandingham, C. L., Letter of, to the democracy of Ohio, 7.

Wadham, Manor of, 109.
Wallenpaupack, 1147-48.
Wayne county, First resident lawyer in, 580.
West, Benjamin, painter, 517-18.
Westmoreland—
  Area of, 1039.
  Court House and Jail of, 133.
  Proclamation forbidding settlement at, 1039.
  Town organized, 333-34, 1040.
  Troops raised in, for Continental Establishment, 1039.
  County, 334, 1039-41.
  Judges (1776), 1041.
  Judges of Probate (1772-75), 1041.
  Justices of the Peace (1778), 1041
  Lawyers in, 1041.

Sheriff, (1776), 1041.
Wilkes-Barre—
  Courts first held in, 102, 914.
  Early Germans in, 468.
  Fencibles, 514.
  First brewery in, 1300.
  First brick building in, 297, 338.
  First daily Paper in, 934.
  First dwelling house erected, 1392.
  First female seminary in, 66.
  First M. E. Church, 1205.
  First minister in, 188-90.
  First Sunday School in, 339, 93.
  First Weekly Paper in, 1247.
  Fort, 133, 157.
  Guard, 510.
  Home for Friendless Children, 1208.
  Memorial Church, founding of, 111-13
  Public schools of, 79, 152-53, 176-78, 197, 238, 40.
    Colored, 152-53.
  St. Stephen's P. E. Church, 1276.
  Telephone established in, 795, 981.
Wilmot Proviso, 1178,
Woodward, Stanley, Resolutions on retirement from fire department of Wilkes-Barre, 101-02.
Wyoming—
  Articles of capitulation at, 1088.
  Antillierists, 469, 510.
  " leave for Mexico, 33.
  Bank Infantry, 510.
  Battle and Massacre of, 132, 332-33, 28-30, 42, 62, 87-89, 528-29.
  Centennial, 57, 102, 777.
  Coal discovered at, 52.
  Engraving of, 621.
  First marriage in, 47, 1088.
  First Church built, 446.
  First birth in, 47.
  First settlement of, vi, 528.
  First student sent to Yale College, 241.
  Jaegers, 162, 469, 1300.
  Light Dragoons, 125.
  Matross, 75
  Meeting of proprietors and settlers, 52.
  Monument, Gift of land for, 909.
  Monument, laying of corner stone of, 133.
  Monument, inscription on, 1219.
  Resolution in regard to the declaration of independence, 53.
  Second settlement of, vi.
  Volunteers, 506.
  Wyoming Seminary founded 385, 1240.

www.ingramcontent.com/pod-product-compliance
Lightning Source LLC
Chambersburg PA
CBHW032012220426
43664CB00006B/220